Derby County – the turbulent '8[0s]

By Stuart Fors[yth]

<u>Volume 1 of 3: January 198[0]</u>

1.1 Pretext
1.2 – 1980
1.3 – 1981
1.4 – 1982
1.5 – January to summer 1983

For Zoe, Harry, Jade & Elijah

Chapter 1.1 – Pretext

Colin Addison, Derby County's newly appointed manager, arrived at the Baseball Ground to start work in July 1979. Handsome, tanned and well turned-out, Addison looked every inch the modern football boss. In his early dealings with the press, he spoke with passion and conviction, vowing to "restore the pride" and "bring back the glory days". Addison, born in Taunton, Somerset, was an ex York City, Nottingham Forest, Arsenal and Sheffield United forward, who had become player manager of Hereford United in October 1971, ending his playing career with 119 goals in 377 league appearances. He had won promotion from to Division Three in the club's first season of League football. He had left Hereford for a short spell in South African football as manager of Durban City, then returned to England as assistant at Notts County, before taking over the top job at Newport County. After turning around the fortunes of the South Wales club, First Division West Bromwich Albion came in for his services and he had done well as assistant to Ron Atkinson.

Addison's appointment, on a £25,000 per year deal, following the sudden resignation of his predecessor Tommy Docherty at the end of the 1978-79 season, was greeted with more than a few raised eyebrows. He was, after all, only an assistant in his previous job at West Bromwich Albion. Here he was taking the top job at Derby County, who had been Champions of England just four years previously, and FA Cup semi-finalists even more recently. The Rams paid West Brom £45,000 for the release of Addison from his contract at the Hawthorns.

A few days after Addison was appointed, the Sunday newspapers got to work on the beleaguered Rams, leaving the new manager in no doubt about the scale of his task. "The Derby manager's job is the toughest in soccer. It's rather like being left the national debt in a maiden aunt's will" (News of the World). "Addison has just become the manager of Derby County, a situation as desolate as a graveyard" (Sunday Express).

The new manager stepped into a club which was in a severe downward spiral. Docherty's team had narrowly avoided relegation from the First Division and the shrewd Scotsman had jumped ship just hours before he was to be pushed by the club's Directors, returning to his former club Queens Park Rangers, who had finished 1 place and 6 points below the Rams. After being initially welcomed by supporters, excited by a reputation forged at Manchester United and Aston Vila, the Doc (as he liked to be called) rapidly became a hate figure and fans had chanted and protested for his sacking during the second half of the 1978-79 season. It all seemed so far away from Docherty's assertion on the eve of the season "we are challenging for a place in Europe" – however, as far as his days at Derby County were concerned the Doc could talk the talk, but he could not walk the walk.

Addison brought with him as assistant the former Plymouth Argyle defender John Newman (at a cost of £10,000 in compensation to Grimsby Town). Frank Blunstone, Docherty's assistant, had wanted to stay at Derby but there was no place for him – eventually

Blunstone moved to Greece for a year in a coaching role before returning to Derbyshire to open a wine bar, Cary's, in Ashbourne (a joint venture with local businessman and future Derby County Director and owner Peter Gadsby). Newman was another with lower league pedigree but no experience at the top level of English football. A player at Birmingham City, Leicester City, Plymouth and Exeter City, Newman was appointed manager of Exeter following the departure of former Derby and England winger Frank Broome. After leaving Exeter, Newman guided Grimsby Town to promotion from the Fourth Division in 1978-79. The appointments were a gamble – Addison and Newman conceded as much during their press introductions. Ron Webster, the former Rams full back and, by the summer of 1979, a youth coach at the club, was fulsome in his praise "(Addison's) approach reminds me very much of what happened when Brian Clough arrived". Another invoking the spirit of Clough and Peter Taylor was club secretary Michael Dunford who said in September 1979 "there is no doubt that Derby fans have taken to the present management as they have no other since their predecessors Brian Clough and Peter Taylor. Dunford was appointed to his position just days after Addison was appointed manager.

Addison invoked the spirit of Sir Winston Churchill in his first programme notes (22nd August 1979) "we offer you no quick solutions, we make no promises (apart from) we shall work as we have never done before to put the club back to the top reaches of the First Division". Addison acknowledged that his first task was to give the club stability and credibility, and, in perhaps a sly dig at his predecessor Docherty and the players, "to improve the work rate and up the dedication". Addison stated his aim for the season "to avoid relegation…we can aim for nothing more in the first season" – it was not ambitious, and it was not achieved.

Cash was to be made available for Addison to bring in his own players "but not in abundant quantities, so we have to be selective". The new manager insisted that the squad quality was "superior to the results managed" and he ended his first column for supporters by insisting that "attitude can move mountains…since we came here John Newman and I have found the attitude of the Derby County players to be just right".

Addison and Newman had not worked together before. They knew each other as players but it had not been until Addison had been manager of Hereford United that the two had become friends – Newman was born in Hereford and his family lived in the area – they began to socialise and attend matches together, and Newman had become something of a confidante to Addison. Ron Atkinson came calling for Addison and took him to First Division West Bromwich Albion as assistant, and Newman took over at Grimsby Town and achieved quick success, taking the club up from Division Four in his second season in charge. Derby were not the first club to approach Colin Addison while he was assistant manager of West Brom – he had been offered the top jobs at both Cardiff City and Sunderland. Of the staff left behind after Docherty's hasty escape, Addison retained the services of chief Scout Gordon Clayton (albeit not for very long – Clayton was replaced by Alan Ashman in October

1979), as well as youth coach Ron Webster and reserve team coach Richie Norman. Gordon Guthrie, the long serving trainer / physio, also stayed at the club.

Despite the trauma of seeing their beloved Championship-winning team dismantled and their favourite players sold, Derby's supporters still had a First Division side to watch, and season ticket sales were perhaps better than could have been expected following Docherty's ruinous 2 years. Within a few weeks, however, it became clear that the club was living on borrowed time at the top level and Addison, Newman and the squad left behind by Docherty were not equipped to survive an 11th successive season with the Country's elite. Derby had eventually finished 1 place above relegation in the 1978-79 season, with 31 points from 42 games – they were comfortably safe as the bottom 3 clubs (Chelsea, Birmingham City and Queens Park Rangers) were all very poor, gathering just 67 points between them. It was to be only a temporary stay of execution.

As Docherty was leaving the Baseball Ground, the Police were moving in. A major investigation into financial and legal affairs at the club, allegedly concerning dealings with the North American Soccer League, was launched. Record books were seized, Directors and club staff questioned, and fingers pointed. Ultimately, no charges were brought but the whole affair left a bitter taste and showed the club in a very poor light. Stuart Webb, who would later return in a different role, left the Derby as the investigations continued. "Who blew the whistle?" was the question of the day.

The first programme of the new season, issued on 22nd August 1979, summed up the situation thus:

> "This evening sees the resumption of football on the Baseball Ground stage. Not only those with the best interests of Derby County Football Club at heart will breathe sighs of relief.
>
> "The various events of the close season which have kept the club name seemingly permanently in the news are well known, but we are obliged to draw attention to the more sensational reporting of our affairs which was both puerile and offensive.
>
> "The classic example was the front page "news" in a tabloid daily that police were probing allegations involving vice girls in football clubs, after "stumbling on the scandal when they began an enquiry at Derby County.
>
> "The police dismissed this yarn as "drivel, completely without foundation". That denial may have been missed by some, but not we hope, by our supporters"

Chairman George Hardy, the man who had unsuccessfully attempted to lure Brian Clough back to the Baseball Ground in 1977, was another casualty in the fall out from the Police investigation. He was succeeded in the Chair by Richard Moore, a chartered accountant who at the time was managing director of a Long Eaton knitwear firm. Behind the scenes wrangling, so often the curse of Derby County, was making an already difficult situation even worse. Mr Moore paid tribute to his predecessor, acknowledging that Hardy had held the chair "in the most difficult period the club had had for many years" and credited Hardy for "performing an arduous job with vigour". Addison could have done without it, and things started badly on the field – the rams failed to score in any of their first 4 league games.

It should be noted that not everybody was pleased to see the back of Tommy Docherty. Long-serving physiotherapist and trainer Gordon Guthrie, for example, described Docherty as "a great man, who has incredible knowledge of football…I for one will be sad to see him go", going on to acknowledge that whilst the Doc was usually thought of in the negative by Derby's supporters, a lot of the players he inherited were "over the top" in terms of age and the manager had little choice but to chop and change to bring a more youthful look to the squad. It was not a view that was widely agreed with, but Guthrie was in a unique position to judge, having served under more than 10 managers at the time of comment.

Moore and Hardy (who stayed on as a club director) were joined on the board by President Sam Longson O.B.E, vice chairman Bob Innes, vice president Bill Stevenson and directors Arthur Atkins and Bob Muholland (Longson's son-in-law).

Away from the Baseball Ground, there were rumblings of discontent from other shareholders. In the autumn of 1979 several of the smaller shareholders began discussions aimed at obtaining a bigger voice within the club, a collective voice – eventually the Derby County Shareholders Association was formed under the Chairmanship of local motor trader Dick Joel. The Association insisted that their intentions were to support the club – "we shall do everything in our power to help Derby County and try to make them a great club again" – indeed, the club board were kept informed of progress throughout the formation of the Association and Chairman Richard Moore gave it tacit support – "as long as it is intended to help the club neither I nor the board could possibly object". Along with Joel, other officers of the Association were Eddie Strachan (secretary), Ian Samways (treasurer), John Kirkland, Roy Crisp and Graham Barnes. Of Kirkland in particular, more later.

The Baseball Ground had undergone some alterations during the summer of 1979. £20,000 had been spent on a new stand roofs, and "general improvements" on toilet facilities had been carried out. Supporters felt that this was long overdue, many had complained about the facilities during the previous season. The biggest improvement was the notorious Baseball Ground pitch, which was renovated (again) in June 1979 and players complimented the improvement for the pre-season match with Dutch side Roda Kerkrade in the summer, compared to the awful state of the pitch in the spring of 1979. Groundsman Bob Smith commented "(the pitch) is in its best condition since the big dig up of 1975…we have a real chance this time of beating the problems, the real test will be deep winter". A family viewing area had been established in the Ley Stand "where families can watch the Rams as a unit – our primary aim is to attract, and hold (families) interest", said club secretary Michael Dunford. Supporters were less happy, however, with crowd segregation at the Baseball

Ground – terrace supporters complained that the Rams' vocal support in the Osmaston End terrace and on the Popular (Pop) side were split by visiting fans, who at the time were housed in one half of the Pop side, the Colombo Street section (in which 5,500 supporters could be officially be housed although on occasion it appeared many more than that found their way in). Supporters had campaigned to have this changed but the Police resisted, citing segregation outside the ground as the reason.

The rams came under fire during the 1979-80 season from visiting supporters for charging more for terrace places than their home counterparts were charged. Derby countered by blaming "printing and administrative expenses" to justify the £1.50 price for away fans compared to £1.30 for home fans. Where a large contingent of away fans was expected (particularly Nottingham Forest in November 1979, Liverpool in December 1979 and Manchester United in February 1980, the entire Colombo section of the Pop side was given over exclusively to away fans (rather than the usual policy of advising Derby supporters to avoid that area).

Another change for the 1979-80 season was the matchday publication, which was controversially changed from a newspaper "Ram Newspaper" to a magazine "Ram Magazine" after 8 seasons. The change had been brought about by economics and reliability issues – circulation had fallen from a peak of more than 70% of the gate in the newspaper's heyday in the early 1970's, down to just under 60% by the spring of 1979. Late deliveries of the paper had become a problem, and it was decided to engage Leicester firm Hemmings to produce a glossy matchday magazine in the summer of 1979. The switch to a matchday magazine, however, proved to be an error of judgement on behalf of the club and sales started badly (a little over 40% of the gate, and got worse). A vociferous campaign among supporters demanding the return of the Ram Newspaper eventually hammered the final nail in Ram Magazine's coffin and it was scrapped after 10 issues, the 10th and final magazine being issued for the home game against European Champions Nottingham Forest on 24th November 1979, of which more later. The Newspaper, priced at 25p when it returned at the start of December 1979, fared little better. At this time, just 11 other Football League clubs produced a Newspaper format matchday programme, the other 80 preferring a more traditional magazine style publication.

Some famous faces left the club before the start of the 1979-80 season. David Nish, the supremely elegant England International left back, was forced to quit football after succumbing to a serious knee injury. Nish gave up on his hopes of playing professionally again when he decided to take a Testimonial game at the Baseball Ground on December 3rd 1979, where Derby County Championship XI took on the current Rams side (after which he would no longer be allowed to play in England), having been unable to find an English club willing to take a chance on him, following his 3 knee operations – "I can run as well as ever and you don't lose your skills on the ball, but turning or changing direction quickly is a problem". Nish planned to go to the USA and play for Tulsa Roughnecks in the spring of

1980. Nish's abiding memory of six happy years at the Baseball Ground was the 1974-75 Championship side "a great squad to play among", especially the Easter Monday 1975 win at Burnley "when the team flowed like magic – though the previous Saturday's 5-0 home defeat of Luton when Roger Davies scored all 5 comes a pretty close second". Nish's troubles had started after scoring a goal against Sheffield United, when he injured his knee in the process – "after that I was never really the same again".

Peter Daniel was another who ended a long and distinguished Rams career in the spring of 1979. Crowd favourite Charlie George had been sold to Southampton (the board had blocked a proposed move to Nottingham Forest). Derby's fans were rapidly losing their heroes, and substandard replacements were not cutting the mustard.

There was some good news on the playing front. Roy McFarland agreed to sign a new 2-year contract after the departure of Tommy Docherty, having ended speculation linking him with a move away from the Baseball Ground. Another positive for Addison was that the side he inherited was relatively young – only McFarland, Bruce Rioch and John Duncan could be considered veterans by the summer of 1979. Docherty had sold almost all the players who had won the First Division title in 1974-75 which, whilst leaving the club with a far worse squad in terms of ability, had at least brought down the average age. There had been some bright performances by youngsters during that depressing 1978-79 season. Winger Paul Bartlett and forward Andy Clayton had impressed during brief spells with the first team, and Steve Spooner and John Clayton also looked promising. The club offered apprentice contracts during the summer of 1979 to 16-year olds David King (Derby Schools), Paul Halford (Notts Boys), Anthony Reid (South Notts Boys), Ian Dalziel (Durham County) and Colin Murphy (Notts County Youths).

Addison and Newman had been disappointed by the scouting and youth set up when they arrived at the Baseball Ground, describing it as "sub-standard" and believing there was not too much first team potential within the reserves and youth teams. They recruited the former West Bromwich Albion and Carlisle United manager Alan Ashman as Chief Scout, replacing Gordon Clayton, and then appointed former Lincoln City youth coach Geoff Worth to the role as Youth Development Officer (the first time such a role had been in existence at Derby). Clayton, the former Manchester United goalkeeper, moved to Turf Moor to take up a role as chief scout for Burnley.

Alan Ashman, after his appointment at the Baseball Ground, was scathing of the club's youth development policy such as it had been since the late 1960's – "it's ludicrous that only Steve Powell and David Langan from the present senior squad have come through from apprentice level". Ashman promised to scout "highways and byways for promising youngsters". In his early months at Derby, Ashman was engaged with plugging gaps in the senior squad, as injuries, lack of form and disciplinary problems plagued manager Colin Addison. Ashman engaged a network of 13 scouts from across England to help – whereas Tommy Docherty and Frank Blunstone had largely backed their own judgement in the signing of players, Addison and Newman were keen to share responsibility with professional scouts, under the guidance of Ashman. Ashman concentrated his efforts on North East England, Yorkshire, Nottinghamshire and Lincolnshire.

Ashman had an early success with his scouting for promising youngsters – in December 1979 the club signed 20-year-old striker Kevin Wilson from non-league Banbury, on Ashman's recommendation, for a fee of £20,000. Wilson went on to make well over 100 appearances for Derby's first team.

The first task of Youth Development Officer Geoff Worth was to stop the trend of local footballing talent drifting out of Derbyshire. The Sheffield clubs, Ipswich, Norwich, West Brom and, particularly, Nottingham Forest, were regularly engaging promising youngsters from Derbyshire schools who had been raised as Derby County fans. Much of the issues stemmed from local parents and schools retaining a great affinity with former manager Brian Clough, who was still revered in the Derby area and had done so much to ingratiate himself with the local community during his 6 years with the Rams. Local coaches and teachers would often "tip off" Clough and his partner Peter Taylor, when quality youngsters emerged.

Geoff Worth claimed, in February 1980, that "we have now ensured we know about every boy in this area who has any sort of potential". It was a step forward, but the process would take a long time to have any significant effect. Worth enlisted the support of Derbyshire FA official Ken Blood and local FA coach Duncan Bird – "their help is vital to us if we are to be well in the picture. From what I have seen there is a great deal of talent here in Derbyshire right down to under 13 levels". 21 youngsters were signed on schoolboy forms during Addison's first 6 months at Derby – however of these 21, only defender Graham Harbey went on to play first team football at Derby County. Worth's judgement also came into question with his declaration that the Rams had signed "the best young goalkeeping prospect in the Country" when the club, on Worth's recommendation, signed Robert Palmer, a native of Hull, on associated schoolboy forms. "Robert was wanted by everybody, but we got him because he and his parents were impressed by our set up…I am absolutely delighted".

Attendances at the Baseball Ground were low and falling. The club, in an increasing state of desperation, launched a "Hard-Core Supporter" voucher scheme in November 1979. This scheme presented by the club as a response to loyal supporters among the 16,000 or so "sensed the increasing possibilities of a return to better days….asking what return they would get for their loyalty if and when present day absentees jump back on the bandwagon". It was all sounding rather fanciful – the reality was that the Derby bandwagon, if there was one, was in reverse gear and attendances at the Baseball Ground were destined never to return to the heady levels of the early 1970's. Over in Norway, the thriving Derby County supporters club Norwegian branch, could not understand why so many had deserted their beloved Rams – secretary Einar Sand wrote in the autumn of 1979 "what are the Derby public thinking about? Gates are not good and we here in Norway who are Rams fans, and remember we have more than 100 members, are speechless about that".

Colin Addison, writing in February 1980, described the Rams hard core support as "up to the unique standard of Manchester United's, who stayed loyal throughout when the Reds went down in 1974 – so have ours, only we haven't as many as they have". It was an intriguing comment given that the Rams had not yet been relegated. The Rams' remaining 16-17,000 fans did indeed present a loyal and vocal home support, staying with Addison and the team for most of the 1979-80 relegation season and a good proportion of the following season. Most clubs were suffering from poor attendances in this era – on the day Derby drew 16,872 for home game against Crystal Palace (who themselves had brought less than 100 fans to the Baseball Ground), Norwich City (4th in the league) drew 16,467, Bolton Wanderers 13,963 and Stoke City 15,253 for their First Division fixtures.

Away support was also dwindling, with numbers down to the low hundreds following the Rams on their travels. Columnists and correspondents in the programme frequently complained about the poor away support and appealed for more fans to travel to watch the side. A combination of regular hooliganism, little or no segregation, and a poor Rams side who were usually well-beaten on their travels in this era, was blamed. "Bill X", a Pop sider and regular away follower, who penned a regular column in the matchday programme in the late 1970's, wrote "fans who travel are always likely to find trouble waiting for them at the other end". It was not an era in which to wear your club colours with pride on "enemy soil". The "Ramaway", which was a train put on specially to take Rams fans to away games in the early and mid-1970's, was cancelled towards the end of the Docherty era due to lack of interest – for some games less than 50 fans registered their interest. Replacing the Ramaway was a coach service, the "Rams Roadrider", which proved far more popular and enduring, and indeed still in existence nearly 40 years later. Some fans suggested that hooliganism was on the decline by the late 1970's – Rams supporter Barry Smith, who travelled home and away with the club, commented in November 1979 "An awful lot of yobboes who used to descend on football for their aggro-raising have got tired of the game. They are looking for their excitement elsewhere, and it's made football watching a darned sight more pleasant. Here at Derby we've lost a lot of the worst troublemakers, and it's one blessing that the lower gates have given us". Smith was certainly qualified to comment on troublemaking at football, having once been hospitalised and unable to work for over 4 months after being set on by hooligans after a game at Leeds United. Smith concluded "it's better up North than down South" – presumably Leeds were the exception.

When the Rams finally notched up their first win of the season, a 3-2 defeat of Arsenal, only 16,429 were there to see it. That win, on 8th September 1979, lifted Derby to 20th place in the First Division. Things had to change, and Addison's response was an autumn transfer spree – defender Steve Emery (Hereford United), former Rams forward Roger Davies (NASL), defender Keith Osgood and midfielder Barry Powell (both Coventry City), became the manager's first signings for Derby. Heading out of the club were Steve Wicks (back to Chelsea, the club Docherty had signed him from, and for the same fee), and Gordon Hill (who followed his former boss to QPR, having made it quite clear to Addison that he had no interest in remaining at the Derby).

By late October, the Rams were still in 20th position (out of 22) in the First Division. They had won just 2 games since the victory over Arsenal and had scored 11 goals, 4 of which had come in a 4-0 home crushing of Bolton Wanderers in which talented but injury-prone centre forward John Duncan and quick but erratic winger Paul Emson had both scored twice. Duncan led the goalscoring chart with 4 in 7 games, but he had also missed 5 games through injury and Derby had scored only 1 goal in those 5 matches. At the other end of the pitch, 19 goals had been conceded by a back four in which only full backs Dave Langan and Steve Buckley had been ever present. The departed Wicks had been replaced at centre back by Aiden McCaffrey (a Docherty signing from the previous autumn), and club legend Roy McFarland managed just 6 games before succumbing to injury and being replaced first by Dave Webb, and then by Osgood. Whichever combination Addison tried, the results remained depressingly similar.

David McKellar, a £2,500 signing from Scottish non-league side Ardrossan Winton Rovers, came into the side for the home game against West Bromwich Albion on 3rd November 1979. Goalkeeper McKellar had been playing reserve team football since Docherty had signed him for Derby in March 1978. The Rams' regular keeper John Middleton had played his final professional game in a 2-3 defeat at Stoke City the previous weekend, injury having ended his career at the age of just 23. McKellar's arrival into the side coincided with Derby's best run of form in the entire campaign – West Brom were beaten 2-1 (Gordon Hill scoring his last goal for Derby, followed by Steve Emery's first), and 7 days later the Rams recorded their first away win of the season with a 2-0 victory at Bristol City (Duncan's 5th of the season followed a rare strike from midfielder Vic Moreland). A fortnight after the win at Ashton Gate came one of the more famous games in Derby's history.

European Champions Nottingham Forest, managed by former Derby boss Brian Clough, came to town on Saturday 24th November. Forest were heavy odds-on favourites to crush Addison's Derby side, sitting 19th in the table. 27,729 were present to witness a stunning performance from the rams – goals from Duncan (2), Emery and Irishman Gerry Daly (returning from injury to inspire Derby's midfield) gave the rams a sensational 4-1 victory over the reds. Daly, by then, was one of the club's longest-serving players, having been signed by Docherty's predecessor Colin Murphy for £175,000 from Manchester United in March 1977. Derby's team for that famous victory over Nottingham Forest also included new signings Barry Powell, Keith Osgood, Roger Davies and Steve Emery. For once, injuries had not hamstrung Addison – although Roy McFarland was still out.

After such a positive November, fans could be forgiven for having a renewed sense of optimism. Derby had taken 6 points from a possible 8, scoring 8 goals and conceding just 3.

There were signs that Addison's new players were an improvement on the ones left behind by Docherty, and key men Daly and Duncan had returned to fitness. Optimism however, proved short lived. On 1st December Derby were beaten 2-0 at Brighton and Hove Albion and followed that miserable display by picking up just 2 points out of a possible 12 in the month of December.

Only 15,381 were at the Baseball Ground to witness a miserable goalless draw with Norwich City on December 8th (12,000 less than had seen Nottingham Forest beaten a fortnight before). Derby were no longer the attractive, attacking side that had wowed crowds during their 1974-75 League Championship winning season. The following 2 home games were dreadful – first Liverpool, 3 days before Christmas, then Coventry City, on Boxing Day, took the points back with them. The Liverpool game marked a final appearance in a Rams shirt for Bruce Rioch, who had given Addison more than his fair share of problems both on and off the field. Rioch was eventually sold to Seattle Sounders in March 1980, following a complete breakdown in communications with the manager, of which more later. Making his debut against Liverpool was Trevor Whymark, the former Ipswich Town and England International striker who joined on loan from Sparta Rotterdam. Whymark partnered Roger Davies in a toothless attacking display which caused no problems whatsoever to Liverpool's superb back four of Neal, Hanson, Thompson and Kennedy.

For the Boxing Day "must win" Baseball Ground clash with Coventry, Addison replaced Rioch and Emery with Jonathan Clark (a Welsh midfield player signed with considerable fanfare by Tommy Docherty) and Paul Emson. Clark scored, but it was in vain as goals from Tommy English and Bobby McDonald secured both points for the visitors. Trevor Whymark, having played just 1 and a half (promising-looking) games on loan, was sent back to Sparta Rotterdam having gone down with Glandular Fever.

The Rams bade farewell to the 1970's, their most glorious decade, on 29th December 1979 in front of 22,554 at Goodison Park, where Everton were held to a 1-1 draw. Roger Davies scored Derby's goal. The team on that day was: McKellar; Langan, Osgood, Webb, Buckley; Clark, Daly, Powell (B), Emson; Davies, Duncan. On the eve of the 1980's the Rams stood 21st in Division One – one place off the bottom of the First Division.

Chapter 1.2 - 1980

Derby County travelled to Leeds United for their First Division encounter at Elland Road on New Year's Day, 1980. During the prior decade, the clubs had become bitter rivals as first Brian Clough and Don Revie, and later Francis Lee and Norman Hunter, fought their battles on and off the pitch. But the glory years of the early 1970's were long gone, and where once Peter Lorimer, Billy Bremner, Johnny Giles and Allan Clarke had tussled with Charlie George, Archie Gemmill, Bruce Rioch and Kevin Hector, now there was Roy Greenwood, Paul Emson and Jonathan Clark for the Rams, and squad men like Wayne Entwhistle, Gary Hamson and Gwyn Thomas for Leeds. The managers too, not Clough, Revie or Mackay but Colin Addison and Jimmy Adamson – the attendance 24,271 not the 40,000 of 10 year's previously.

In front of **David McKellar** in goal, the Rams lined up with right back and relative long servant **Dave Langan**, an Irish international who had made his international debut in 1978 and went on to win 26 caps over the next decade. Langan had been spotted, and snapped up quickly by Derby's scouts in February 1977, while playing for Dublin club Cherry Orchard and had become one of Derby's most consistent and reliable performers under first Docherty and then his successor Addison. Langan would go on to make 155 senior appearances for the Rams, scoring 1 goal, before becoming Birmingham City's record signing at £350,000 after Derby's relegation from the First Division in May 1980, having handed in a transfer request in January 1980. Popular wherever he played, Langan also served Oxford United during their heyday in the mid-late 1980's – at both Birmingham and Oxford, the manager who signed him was future Rams boss Jim Smith.

Langan was often thought of as a quiet individual, but he could be strong-willed, such as when he spectacularly fell out with Colin Addison before an FA Cup tie at Bristol City, leading to a fine and disciplinary action from the manager. He also managed to upset his International manager, the former Leeds United midfielder Johnny Giles, who frequently refused to select Langan despite his replacements being clearly inferior. In March 1980 Giles told the Irish Times "I made it clear that even if Langan had to be called upon (for a game against Cyprus, when Ireland's first and second choice right backs were unavailable), he would occupy at best a place on the substitutes bench". Langan, denying rumours that he had hit Giles in an argument in 1978, said "in all my time with the Irish team he has never once spoken to me, not one word".

Angry and upset and being overlooked by his Country, Langan was nevertheless keen to prove Giles wrong and, after returning to the Rams side in the spring of 1980 produced some of his best football, often being regarded one of the best right backs in the First Division. Long after he had given up hope of regaining his cherished Irish national team place, he received an unexpected recall from new manager Jack Charlton and went on to be ever present in qualifying for Ireland's successful Euro 1988 campaign. Langan, who became registered disabled after his playing career, retains huge affection among Irish football fans, and his autobiography "running through walls" published in 2012 is a poignant and entertaining read.

At left back, Dave Langan's full back partner was another long serving and popular player, **Steve Buckley**. "Bucko", as he became known at Derby, possessed a big heart and a fine shot, which often blitzed into the middle tiers of the Osmaston and Normanton stands, and less often made the goal nets billow. Buckley, born in Eastwood in October 1953, started out as a semi-professional player for Borrowash Victoria, a Derby-based non-league side. He then moved a few miles down the A38 to Burton Albion – this was 1974 and Derby County were otherwise occupied winning League Championship titles and giving the cheque book a regular airing. Buckley would have signed for the rams for nothing, and could have, had circumstances been different. Instead he went to Luton Town and stayed there for 4 seasons until Derby County, and Tommy Docherty, decided to bring him back to the East Midlands in January 1978 – Buckley would finish on 366 appearances and 24 goals for the club, twice winning its Player of the Year award in the process, having served under 5 different managers at Derby.

Langan and Buckley were rarities at Derby County in the mid-late 1970's. Both survived Tommy Docherty's frantic stop-start in-out transfer frenzy between the autumn of 1977 and the summer of 1979. Both were popular with fans, who turned up to games without a clue of who they would be watching in a Derby shirt each weekend. Buckley's 366 appearances for the club puts him 18th in the club's all-time appearance chart (at the time of writing), he was one of the few who stayed on after the club almost went out of existence in the spring of 1984, and he was still a regular in the side that Arthur Cox put together when he had to rebuild the squad from the Third Division, in 1984-85. Langan might have still been there too, but the money being offered by First Division Birmingham City was too good for the relegated and financially stricken Rams to turn down in the summer of 1980. Addison had not wanted to lose Langan but was given no option - £350,000 in those days was a fortune, especially to a club on the brink of financial ruin.

For the Leeds United game, manager Addison again paired **Keith Osgood** and Dave Webb in central defence. Osgood, the former Tottenham Hotspur centre half, had been transferred from the North London club to Coventry City in January 1978, following their relegation from the First Division the previous summer. Unusually for a central defender, Osgood was a regular penalty taker and had scored 10 times from the spot for Spurs. At Coventry, who had paid £130,000 for his services, he had struggled to hold down a regular first team place and was happy to move to Derby County when Colin Addison made his approach for the then 24-year-old in October 1979. Eventually Osgood's Coventry team mate, midfielder, Barry Powell, became part of the same deal and both were signed by Derby on the same day. Despite never managing to fully establish himself as a regular at the Baseball Ground, the flamboyant and photogenic Osgood managed 69 games for the Rams and continued his impressive goals return with 10 goals and stayed beyond relegation at the end of the 1979-80 season, before heading back to London to join Leyton Orient in December 1981.

David Webb was a big name in football when Tommy Docherty signed for Derby him from Leicester City in December 1978. As a member of Chelsea's fine team in the late 1960's and early 1970's, Webb had been close to England International caps but found himself competing for a place in central defence in an era in which England could choose from the likes of Bobby Moore, Jack Charlton and Norman Hunter as well as Derby's Roy McFarland and Colin Todd. Born in East London on 9th April 1946, Webb was 24 when he rose to national prominence with a fine performance in Chelsea's FA Cup Final Replay victory over Leeds United – scoring the winning goal by heading in Ian Hutchinson's long throw in extra time. He also played in Chelsea's European Cup Winners Cup winning side in 1971, again in central defence although much of his Chelsea career was spent playing at right back. Webb joined Queens Park Rangers in July 1974 after making 230 appearances for the Stamford Bridge club – a series of financial and business issues marred his time at Loftus Road, but he stayed long enough to help QPR to a runners-up spot in the First Division in 1975-76. Another move, to Leicester City in September 1977, proved less than successful and by the time he joined Derby, in December 1978, Webb was clearly a declining force.

Webb was one of those players who had welcomed Colin Addison's arrival at the Baseball Ground, even going as far as to say "I've worked for a dozen bosses, and I rate this one as the best yet. He's just what the club wanted".

In and out of the side at Derby, firstly in Docherty's disastrous final season at the club, then in Addison's first season, Dave Webb made just 26 appearances for the club spread over 17 months, almost all of them at centre back rather than his preferred position of right back (where the steady, reliable Langan had the shirt), before leaving following relegation in May 1980. After joining Bournemouth, initially as a player, Webb was appointed manager in December 1980 and went on to forge a fairly successful career in management, mostly in the lower leagues. Retaining considerable business interests, he also had a spell as owner of Brentford football club in the mid 1990's.

In midfield, Addison's team for the New Year's Day 1980 clash at Elland Road was boosted by the return of **Steve Powell** after injury. Powell replaced his namesake Barry Powell in the starting 11 (Barry dropping to the bench). It was Steve Powell's first game since the 0-4 defeat at Southampton back in September 1979. Unlike Barry Powell, Steve was almost universally popular with the Derby fans and came from a family of Derby County players and supporters – his father Tommy Powell being a club stalwart of the 1950's. Steve Powell was never going to start his career anywhere other than the Baseball Ground and he signed schoolboy forms at Derby County for manager Brian Clough in 1971, while studying at Bemrose School in the City. In fact, Powell never played for any other club in England, his only dalliance away from Derby was a short spell on loan at Tulsa Roughnecks in the North American Soccer League in 1979 – "I love the States…but the standard of soccer disappointed me. It's no place for a professional who is dedicated to his career, but it did me fine for one summer" – Powell's main complaint about his spell in the NASL concerned the astroturf pitches, which certainly did not suit a player already becoming known as injury prone. Unlike his team mates Gerry Daly and Roger Davies, Powell felt it was a mistake to play football 12 months a year and vowed never to return to the NASL.

Injuries robbed Steve of much of his peak years, and he managed a total of 352 senior games over a period of 14 years, scoring 20 goals. He was also a victim of being so versatile – preferring to play as a defensive midfielder "where I have time and space to see what's happening in front of me", he was very often drafted in to cover injuries or suspensions in other positions and this led, in some quarters to the accusation of "jack of all trades, master of none".

Steve Powell made his Derby County debut aged just 16 years and 30 days, against Stoke City in a Texaco Cup tie at the Baseball Ground in October 1971. Already Captain of England Schoolboys, Powell showed remarkable maturity in that and the following game, but it was his performance in the final league fixture of 1971-72 that propelled him to stardom amongst rams' fans, as Liverpool were beaten 1-0 in the victory which gave Derby the Football League Championship Title for the first time. Powell played at right back in that game, and throughout his career he switched between defence and midfield and developed a fearsome reputation in the game. Unfortunately for Powell, who as a youngster had seemed certain to win full England caps, injuries soon caught up with him as first his back, then his pelvis and then knees, let him down badly. Powell always fought back manfully after injuries but, like Roy McFarland, his best days came at the start of his career. An injury-free Steve Powell, with a yard or two of extra pace, could have played 50 times for his Country – unfortunately the closest he got was a solitary appearance for England Under 23's against Scotland in 1974.75. Powell played under 7 different managers at Derby and stayed with the club until being released to take over as player coach of non-league side Shepshed Charterhouse at the end of the 1985-86 season.

Powell had been delighted to welcome Colin Addison and John Newman to the club – "with no disrespects to anybody, I must say that for the first time since the days of Cloughie and Peter Taylor there is a purpose and a direction", he said in September 1979, continuing "they are very close to the lads…they are interested in the players as people as well as players", finishing with the very far off the mark "by the time they are finished you can bet the club will be mighty near the top again at the very least".

Alongside Powell in midfield was **Jonathan Clark**, an interesting player who flattered to deceive on many occasions and never truly won-over the Rams supporters. Undeniably talented, Welshman Clark produced sparks of quality which, had he been able to consistently show, would have made him a much more valued and appreciated player. Born in Swansea on 12th November 1958, Clark had been a highly thought-of youth team player at Manchester United, before Tommy Docherty swooped to sign the youngster for Derby

County from his former club for £50,000 in September 1978. The deal prompted considerable complaint from Old Trafford, where the hierarchy complained that Docherty was poaching staff and players on behalf of his new club. Clark had made just one senior appearance for Manchester United, in November 1976, before his move to the rams. Making his Derby County debut at the end of September 1978, Clark would go on to make 56 appearances in the next 3 years before leaving for Preston North End at the end of the 1980-81 season. Despite an improvement in form after Addison and Newman replaced Docherty, including man of the match performances against Bristol City and Ipswich Town in the autumn of 1979 (indeed one supporter writing to the matchday programme in November 1979 described Clark as "a revelation – when he was signed by the previous manager we heard a great deal about (Clark's) skills but saw little of them. Indeed, it has taken a few weeks under Colin and John Newman for Clark to blossom, but he is really turning it on now" – despite this the Welshman continued to find himself in and out of the side. Clark never really made a name for himself and he was one of those who Derby supporters were not sad so see the back of, when he was released at the end of his contract.

Gerry Daly, the Irish international player, was a popular and talented member of the Derby side and lined up against Leeds United alongside Powell and Clark in midfield. Daly joined the rams in March 1977 from Manchester United, like Clark, but unlike Clark was already a much-admired player by the time Colin Murphy paid £175,000 to bring him to Derby County. A native of Dublin, Daly had been spotted playing for Bohemians in Ireland by the then Manchester United manager Tommy Docherty, who had paid the Irish club £20,000 for his services in 1973. Manchester United's supporters were enraged by the club's decision to sell him to Derby, although Daly himself had pushed for the move – he and Docherty had never got on, and the player was unhappy when Docherty was appointed manager of the rams just 6 months later.

Despite his poor personal relationship with the manager, including threats to hand in a transfer request in the summer of 1978 had the Rams prevented him from playing in North American soccer, and consequently missing the first few games of the English season, for a reputed £25,000 fee (Daly later claimed it was more like $10,000) Daly had performed well under Docherty and was one of the stars of the side which Colin Addison inherited in the summer of 1979. In 1977, Daly scored a famous goal against Manchester City at the Baseball Ground from the penalty spot, which had to be repainted due to deep and clinging mud. Throughout his early career, at both United and Derby, Daly's goal scoring record was excellent for a midfield player (23 in 111 appearances for United, and 31 in 112 at Derby). He was an outstanding penalty-taker, and highly adept at arriving late into the box to finish off attacking moves. It was a pity that Daly had not been with Derby County 5 years earlier than he was, as he would have been a valued asset to that fine side which won the Championship of England twice in 3 years.

Following another deal with the NASL (this time 2 summers with Boston Tea Men, who paid the Rams £50,000 for the player's services starting in 1979 – meaning he would again miss the first few matches of the 1979-80 season – "surely a small price to pay to keep Gerry happy at the Baseball Ground" said the club's programme in the spring of 1979) Daly stayed at Derby until the club were relegated in May 1980. Despite having a comparatively poor season in 1979-80, Daly was another, like Langan, who Colin Addison had wanted to keep but the club was neither willing nor able to offer a First Division level contract to the player and he signed a 4-year deal with Coventry City instead. Before he left, Daly fired a parting shot at the club – "why have I had a such a disappointing season?I simply lost my form and all the time I've been here we have been a struggling side. We have needed propping up at the back and I am an attacking midfield player. I am not at my best in a side going backwards, but my form has generally held up".

Lining up on the left wing for Derby at Leeds was **Paul Emson,** a talented yet erratic player and another who was in and out of the side and often flattered to deceive. Somewhat ungainly, with unfeasibly long legs, and possessing terrific pace, Emson could light up dismal games with an occasional burst down the wing – then provoke sighs of frustration in the crowd with an over-hit cross or a stumble at the crucial moment. Emson had been in and out of the side – very often made scapegoat for defeat after defeat, and when he did get a start often found himself a victim of crowd barracking – it could be a lonely place out on the touchline in front of the Pop side, when Derby were doing badly.

Emson had been spotted by Tommy Docherty's assistant Frank Blunstone while playing for non-league Brigg Town, he was clearly a big fish in a small pond and the rams moved swiftly to agree a £5000 fee to secure his services in September 1978 – at the time Emson was almost 20 and had been ignored by several League clubs who had sent scouts to watch him. Colin Addison, however, did not rate Emson as highly as his predecessor had and the young winger featured only sporadically, especially when England International Gordon Hill returned to full fitness in October 1979. He would go on to make 138 appearances for Derby, 21 of those as substitute, scoring 13 goals – and was never really considered a regular, despite staying at the club until the summer of 1983, when he moved to Grimsby Town. He continued to ply his trade in the lower leagues until the early 1990's.

On the right flank at Elland Road was **Roy Greenwood**. "Reggie", as he became known, was something of a figure of fun at the Baseball Ground and was never accepted by, or appreciated by, the supporters. A left winger by trade (although often pressed into service at centre forward or on the right at Derby), Greenwood suffered from being compared with his outstanding predecessors at Derby but was ill-equipped to step into the shoes of the likes of Kevin Hector, Alan Hinton or Charlie George. The club tried its best to bring supporters into line behind Greenwood – "there are crowd pleasing players, and there are players' players. One of the latter is Roy Greenwood, whose tremendous skill off the ball is admired by his Baseball Ground playing colleagues", according to the programme.

Greenwood, a regular, albeit unkind addition to many Derby County supporters "worst ever" teams, joined the Rams in January 1979 from Sunderland (for whom he had made 56 appearances and had been part of a promotion-winning side in 1975-76). He had made his name at Hull City, where he was a popular player and a prolific goal scorer (for a winger) with 24 goals in 126 games. His Derby career started badly and got worse, and he ended with 1 goal in 31 games before transferring to Swindon Town on 29th February 1980. Nobody was sorry to see him leave – Greenwood's stated aim when joining the rams was "to play in Europe with Derby", this, like Docherty's similar pronouncement in the summer of 1978, was to prove painfully wide of the mark.

Derby's centre forward on the first day of the 1980's was **Roger Davies**. Big, strong and lion-hearted, the popular Wolverhampton-born striker was in his second spell at the club. Standing 6'3" tall, Davies represented an imposing challenge to defenders and, as well as aerial ability, he was not short of skill on the ball either. After leaving school early, Davies plied his trade around the non-league scene in the midlands – starting at Bridgnorth Town in the Midland Football Combination, then onto Bedford Town and finally to Worcester City of the Southern League.

Derby County's scouts had spotted him playing for Worcester in 1971, then aged 20, and had moved quickly to agree a £12,000 fee early in the 1971-72 season. It was a lot of money for a non-league player, but it proved to be one of the masterstrokes of the Brian Clough / Peter Taylor managerial partnerships. Davies joined the Rams reserve squad and played a starring role in their 1971-72 Central League title victory, and at the start of the following season made a loan move to Preston North End, from where he was recalled after just 2 games.

Davies's Derby County debut came on 4th November 1972 in a 0-4 defeat away at Manchester City. Despite that result, the big centre forward retained his place in the side and was a regular in all competitions during the 1972-73 season. It was during that run in the side that he wrote himself into Derby folk-lore when he scored a hat-trick at White Hart Lane against Tottenham Hotspur as the rams fought back from 3-1 down to win the FA Cup replay 5-3 after extra time. In the March 1975 he achieved another notable feat when scoring all 5 goals in a 5-0 thrashing of Luton Town at the Baseball Ground.

As well as considerable goal scoring talent, Roger Davies could be somewhat hot-headed, and was sent off in one of Derby's biggest ever matches, the 2nd leg of the European Cup Semi Final against Juventus at the Baseball Ground in March 1973 (reacting to intense provocation from the Italian's defenders).

Davies was controversially transferred to Belgian League side Club Bruges in August 1976, having made 114 appearances and scored 31 goals. The rams received £135,000, and Davies went on to have a very successful year in Belgium, scoring 21 goals in just 34 games as Bruges won their domestic league title, being named Belgium's Player of the Year in the process. He returned to England in December 1977, this time with Leicester City, coincidentally making his debut with the Foxes against Derby County on 10th December 1977. After struggling with first injuries, then form at Leicester (making just 26 appearances in 14 months), Davies was signed by his former Rams team mate Alan Hinton, now manager of North American Soccer League club Tulsa Roughnecks. Another injury-plagued spell saw him restricted to 22 games in the USA (8 goals).

It was from Tulsa that Derby's manager Colin Addison swooped to sign Roger Davies for his second spell at the club, in the autumn of 1979. Davies's "second debut" for the Rams was on 22nd September 1979 in a 1-0 home win over Middlesbrough. At the time of the signing, Addison appealed to supporters to get behind the somewhat controversial signing of Davies – "(Davies) has had something of a love-hate relationship for the club, but right now there is nothing he would love better than to prove in a Derby jersey that he is still First Division class…if Roger can turn it on for us it will be a tremendous bonus. I ask his critics among us to give him both chance and encouragement" Due to the complex NASL rules in place at the time, Tulsa Roughnecks retained the rights to Davies's contract and Alan Hinton, by now manager of rivals Seattle Sounders, convinced his new club to obtain contractual rights for the player, should he wish to return to the USA.

Davies's ambition was to play again in the USA and particularly for his friend and former Derby County team mate Alan Hinton, and he played his 136th and final game for Derby on 23rd February 1980, in a 2-1 victory over Tottenham Hotspur, the club against whom he had made his name, some 7 years previously. With 34 goals in total, Davies, whilst never prolific, was a fairly reliable and regular scorer for the Rams. He moved to Seattle Sounders and in a 2-year spell scored 32 goals in just 65 games, being chosen as the NASL's most valuable player in 1980. He retained a strong connection with Derby County, working for the club for many years in various capacities including ambassador, hospitality and as radio commentator / summariser.

Substitute for the game at Leeds was **Barry Powell**, dropped following the 1-1 draw at Everton on 29th December 1979, and replaced in the Rams' midfield by Steve Powell, who had recovered from his most recent injury.

Barry Powell, another who, like Roy Greenwood, is a regular candidate for Derby supporters' "worst ever" teams, became one of Colin Addison's first signings when he joined from Coventry City in October 1979 (on the same day as his Coventry team mate Keith Osgood). He had been an England Under 23 International in 1974 while playing for Wolverhampton Wanderers, for whom he had appeared in the 1974 League Cup Final win over Manchester City at Wembley. An attacking midfield player, who had been very highly thought-of at both Wolves and Coventry, Powell had already made 228 appearances in the football league (34 goals) when Addison made his move – the player signing a 3-year deal at the Baseball Ground.

In a total of 86 appearances for Derby County, Barry Powell scored 7 goals and stayed with the club until his contract expired at the end of the 1981-82 season, at which time he moved to Hong Kong club Bulova. Powell's dismal form, and bad luck, at Derby was typified by results in his first 23 games for the club, of which just 4 were won, and included a run of 13 matches without a win between 1st December 1979 and 23rd February 1980. In later years, Barry Powell managed several clubs at non-league level and achieved success at Hednesford Town by winning the FA Trophy in 2004. In many ways, Powell typified the status of Derby County in those years around the turn of the decade – declining, living off past glories and surrounded by negativity – He was very much a player of his time, and had a torrid 3 years at the Baseball Ground.

The Rams went down 1-0 at Leeds on New Year's Day, a Tuesday, their 7th game without a win. 4 days later they travelled to Ashton Gate for an FA Cup 3rd Round tie and were beaten 6-2 by Bristol City. Addison made 2 changes for the cup tie – Barry Powell started in midfield, Steve Powell having been moved to centre back to replace Dave Webb, who had been injured at Leeds. Dave Langan, the right back, was replaced by Steve Emery, and Vic Moreland came in for the erratic Paul Emson, who had suffered a chastening afternoon at Elland Road.

Langan's relationship with Addison had hit rock bottom and there was a public fall-out with the manager in the days leading up to the Bristol City game, culminating in the full back handing in a transfer request after being fined and disciplined by the manager, having decided that Derby's relegation battle was doing nothing for his career prospects. There were others who felt the same and the Rams Newspaper of February 2nd, 1980 referred to "other players (who might follow Langan's lead" and also "some players may have little heart for the continued fight". The club defended Addison repeatedly via its official publication – "if the Rams go down it is the players who must be held mainly responsible" and "it should be noted that the vast majority of the contracts being worked were concluded not by Colin Addison, but by his predecessors", ending its editorial with the highly debateable "Colin Addison and John Newman have achieved a great deal in seven months, even though the league table doesn't yet reflect their hard work". In fact, the first rumblings of fan discontent with Addison's management had been stirred by the Langan affair – whilst supporters, in the main, had understood the manager's need to clamp down on disciplinary problems, many fans did not agree with Addison's subsequent refusal to pick the popular full back whilst a transfer was being sought. The club, acknowledging the sense of discontent, dispatched Supporters Club co-ordinator Ernie Hallam around the 17 branches – Hallam conceded that whilst "everyone is behind Colin Addison and John Newman, that's for sure...there seems to be a little criticism when it comes to some recent team selections...the omission of David Langan upset many club members as it was felt to hurt the team performance more than the player. Paul Emson (said the members) has wide support and most would always have him in the side". Supporters club membership, at 700 plus, remained well up on the same time the previous year (as anti-Docherty feeling mounted).

On behalf of younger supporters, Junior Rams Coordinator Steve Stone reported in February 1980 that "membership is knocking on the door of the record number achieved 3 years ago" and that "membership applications are still pouring in". It was evident, however, that the recent successes of local rivals Nottingham Forest, under the management of the still hugely popular Brian Clough, was having a serious effect on the football supporting trends of local youngsters – and Derby were the ones missing out most of all.

Steve Emery had been Hereford United's first apprentice professional, when Colin Addison was manager at Edgar Street. He had been at Hereford for 5 seasons when Addison decided to spend £100,000 to bring him to Derby County in September 1979. It was a huge fee by the standards of the day. Emery was a defender or midfielder and filled in at full back, wide midfield or defensive midfield during his near 4 years at the Baseball Ground but never established himself as a regular – making a total of 75 appearances for Derby before joining Newport County in 1983, then quickly moving back to Edgar Street from Newport and ended his career as one of Hereford's longest serving players, making 333 appearances for the Shropshire club.

Midfield player **Vic Moreland** was born in Belfast in 1957 and became a Northern Ireland international, making 6 appearances for his Country. Moreland's career is something of an unusual one – he started at Glentoran, spent a couple of seasons at Derby, but then made his name in the USA with 6 successful seasons in the NASL and 7 equally fruitful in the Major Indoor Soccer League (MISL), starring for, among others, Tulsa Roughnecks, Dallas Cowboys and Witchita Wings. His playing career, which started in 1973, did not end until 1996.

Moreland had made 159 appearances for Glentoran before they sent him on loan to Tulsa Roughnecks in the summer of 1978. He returned from the USA in 1978 and was promptly sold to Derby County for £90,000 in a joint deal with his Glentoran team mate Billy Caskey – the Rams had been tipped-off about the players by a Belfast scout and moved fast to secure the pair before other English scouts had the chance to see them in action for the Northern Irish club. Tommy Docherty was especially excited by the signing of Moreland, who he described as "First Division quality" and our player of the future".

In 2 seasons at Derby, Moreland had largely failed to live up to his billing, making 42 appearances before being sold (again in a joint deal with his friend and team mate Caskey), to Tulsa Roughnecks for $100,000, at the start of March 1980 as the Rams parlous financial situation started to become apparent. Moreland stayed in Tulsa after his playing career ended and ran a soccer academy in the City for many years.

Following the defeat at Leeds, and the awful FA Cup battering at Bristol City on January 5th, manager Addison made his move in the transfer market, swooping for Cambridge United striker **Alan Biley**. Biley was signed on January 10th, 1980 after the Rams had been tempted first in the summer of 1979 and then again in the Autumn – being put off by Biley's loss of form in September and October 1979. The flamboyant, stylish Biley had complied an excellent goalscoring record for Cambridge – 74 goals in 162 since his free transfer move to Abbey Stadium from Luton Town in 1975 and had scored 11 in 24 during the current season at the time Derby eventually made their move. Biley had been watched by a host of first division scouts including first Gordon Clayton, then Alan Ashman, for Derby – but, like Derby, most had moved their attention elsewhere after the striker with the striking resemblance to singer Rod Stewart had gone 14 games without finding the net. Immediately prior to his move to the Baseball Ground however, Biley had found serious form and had scored 9 in his previous 10. It was an exciting signing and Biley said a few weeks after his move "I like the First Division atmosphere…I don't intend to lose it now I've got it at last, not if I can help it". It was fighting talk and Biley was adamant "there's nothing wrong with this side that a bit of confidence wouldn't do wonders for….a win or two and we will climb…maybe halfway up to halfway".

Biley, who had stayed in club digs, shared with team mate Kevin Wilson, during the week for the first few months of his time at Derby, bought a house in Shelton Lock in April 1980, moving in with his girlfriend and his dog, which he named "Ram". He became a firm favourite for his performances on the field and was highly thought-off of it as well, as a regular attender and contributor to Derby County's supporters club functions (including one round trip from his family home in Cambridge to Matlock Bath on a Sunday evening, to present prizes at a South Peak supporters club branch – "what a lad!, he didn't even charge expenses" said branch Chairman Bill Brownson.

Local and national media did not share Biley's confidence. Following an reasonable display in a 2-1 home defeat (a 3rd successive defeat at the Baseball Ground) to Crystal Palace on 12th January 1980 (in which Biley made his debut and Keith Osgood struck a superb 30 yard goal for the Rams) – the Rams were unlucky when Palace had taken the lead in the first half when a Terry Fenwick shot deflected awkwardly off Steve Powell, deceiving goalkeeper David McKellar in the process - Sunday Times reporter James Wilson said "Derby, of course, could still escape the drop but on yesterday's form it seems an improbability. They show all the indications of a team destined for the drop" and went to on say, more controversially "In view of recent happenings at the Baseball Ground on and off the field I doubt if it will really be much of a loss if they do go down". Neil Hallam, writing in the Derby Trader, wrote "There is still, with 17 games remaining, time for a revival. But is there the skill and the spirit to bring one about? Those who believe there is must know something most of the supporters don't. Resignation, it seems, is now widespread". The Rams had battled bravely against Palace, but the lack of quality was evident – errors at the back and chances wasted in attack cost them dearly once again.

Following a 2-0 defeat at Arsenal on January 19th, Derby Evening Telegraph's columnist penned "The gloom deepens. There was nothing at Highbury on Saturday to give even the most optimistic supporter a glimmer of hope" – Addison struck back in the Rams newspaper "it is lack of confidence which has brought us only two points from the last 18, and not one win since we thrashed Forest (on November 24th 1979)..we have our weaknesses which have been accentuated by injuries, illnesses and other troubles....but I totally disagree that we have no players of first division calibre". The display against Arsenal was so poor that even the partisan Rams Newspaper was moved to call it "a depressing display which deserved nothing more than (it) received". The Rams had held on for an hour at Highbury, but that was exactly what it was – hanging on – before David Webb conceded a needless penalty, and the Gunners cruised home by a 2-goal margin, which flattered Derby.

On 2nd February 1980 Derby lost 3-1 at home to Manchester United in front of a bumper crowd of 27,783, boosted by some 7,000 United fans who filled the Colombo section of the Pop Side. Barry Powell scored Derby's consolation goal. For the first time since serious hooliganism marred the Rams game against the Red Devils at the Baseball Ground in 1976, when rival fans fought each other on the pitch, United's supporters had not been able to buy tickets (legally) for matches at Derby. The Rams regular "terrace correspondent" Bill X welcomed them back "they are an institution, they are good for football, we couldn't do without them", going on to take a swipe at "people in the seats who tend to quit first...you only had to look at the half empty Ley Stand this season to realise the truth – the people who stay loyal are we Rams fans who stand up".

After the Manchester United game, Derby stood 21st out of 22 in the First Division with 16 points from 25 games (6 wins and 4 draws - at the time it was still 2 points for a win). Only Bolton Wanderers (11 points) stood between the Rams and the very bottom of the league. The situation was becoming very bleak although West Brom (20 points), Stoke City (19) and Bristol City (18) had not managed to open any significant gap above Derby.

On the bench for the Manchester United game was central defender **Aiden McCaffrey**, who returned to the first team squad for the first time since being replaced by David Webb in the side for the game against Nottingham Forest on 24th November (which was the last time Derby had won a game).

McCaffrey, born in Jarrow in 1957, was Captain of the England youth side in his early days at first club Newcastle United. Turning professional in 1974, he made his debut in the First Division as an 18-year-old and went on to make 59 appearances for Newcastle before Derby manager Tommy Docherty came in for him before the start of the 1978-79 season and a fee of £60,000 was agreed. In 2 seasons at the Baseball Ground, McCaffrey failed to establish himself and he was sold in the summer of 1980 following relegation to the Second Division – Bristol Rovers paying £70,000 for his services – eventually making 37 appearances for the Rams, scoring 4 goals. McCaffrey, however, was not without his supporters during his short stay at Derby. W.Hooley, writing in the Ram Newspaper in February 1980 complained "it's worthy of note that since Aiden McCaffrey was dropped, Derby's fortunes have steadily got worse". Not everyone shared Mr Hooley's opinion – McCaffrey was another player signed to cover the frequent absences through injury of club captain Roy McFarland, and another who failed to live up to that difficult task –

McFarland, meanwhile, had begun yet another comeback attempt, playing for the reserves against Bolton Wanderers reserves at the Baseball Ground on January 26th, 1980 (a game which also featured ostracised full back David Langan) – his first match since being injured in a League Cup tie at Middlesbrough back in September 1979. After nearly 6 years battling a succession of injuries, started when he snapped an Achilles tendon playing for England at Wembley in 1974, McFarland's latest comeback was greeted cautiously by Rams supporters – how they needed their skipper back fully fit, leading their side in what was becoming an increasingly desperate 1979-80 season. The club were keen to manage expectations – "a half-paced Roy Mac would still be as good a central defender as most" (the Ram, 2nd February 1980).

McFarland appeared again the following Tuesday in a friendly at Luton Town and was reported to be "not far away" from being ready for a return to the first team. The friendly had been hastily arranged following Derby's exit from the FA Cup, meaning there was no first team fixture scheduled for the weekend of 26th January. Addison's side drew 0-0 at Kenilworth Road and as well as McFarland, the manager included David Langan and Steve Carter in a largely full-strength side.

Manager Addison attempted to strengthen his side again at the end of January 1980, when he had a £50,000 bid accepted by Burnley for their 29-year-old striker Paul Fletcher, whom Derby had hoped to pair with Alan Biley in attack. Fletcher was known to be very strong in the air and it was felt that this would an ideal attribute in support of Biley. Discussions, however, broke down when the player did not like the idea of a short-term contract, preferring not to uproot his family from their Lancashire home for what could have been only a few months of First Division football. According to Addison "at the moment we don't have a great deal of money…and third and fourth division clubs are asking (huge sums) for untried youngsters". Fletcher went on have to a fine career in the business side of football, starting with Colne Dynamoes then going on to serve first Huddersfield Town, then Bolton Wanderers and then Burnley as Chief Executive in later years and co-wrote the novel "Saturday Bloody Saturday" with politician Alastair Campbell. The Rams search for a partner for Biley continued and was soon to reach a conclusion.

Off the field, the club was struggling. Support was down to 16 – 17,000 and there was nothing happening on the pitch to encourage lost supporters to return. Michael Dunford, the club secretary, remained bullish despite this, saying in February 1980 "off the field Derby County have never been as ambitious, as forward-looking, as they are now". The Rams had indeed been leaders in many commercial ventures over the previous decade – most notably when, in 1976, Swedish motor company SAAB had agreed to sponsor the club's shirts on what was to be a very big money deal, only to be thwarted by a Football League rule banning advertising from playing shirts. As early as 1972, the Rams had been pioneers when their European Cup Tie at the Baseball Ground against Zeljeznicar Sarajevo became the first ever game in Britain to be financed by sponsors. The Rams training ground,

Raynesway, was one of the first to incorporate a multi-use sports hall and gymnasium, to be used by the local community as well as the football club.

Dunford announced on 2nd February 1980 that the development of the Baseball Ground area, including spaces beyond the Normanton Stand and Shaftsbury Crescent to provide more and better car parking, had been agreed with the City Council and was "three years away at most". Facilities in and around the Baseball Ground were cramped and old fashioned, sorely in need of an upgrade. In addition to this, the secretary confirmed that the following season (1980-81) "it was almost certain" that, executive boxes would be installed at the back of the Ley Stand – in an attempt to engage local industry and commerce and increase income. The Rams were relatively late adopters of the executive box concept – more than half of their fellow First Division clubs already had them at their stadiums.

Dunford's final comment, in the Spring of 1980, that executive boxes would not be introduced at the expense of standing spectators "for it is on the terraces where Derby County earns the bulk of their support. And it is the regular standing supporter to whom we aim most of the improvements we plan for the eighties", was to prove far wide of the mark.

A week after losing to Manchester United, the Rams went to Middlesbrough and were easily beaten 3-0. The manager had bowed to public pressure (or resolved his differences, as the official line went) and recalled transfer listed Dave Langan at right back, but more significantly club Captain **Roy McFarland** returned to the side.

The word legend is overused, especially in football, but when it comes to Roy McFarland and Derby County, it is certainly warranted. Famously woken and dragged from his bed by Brian Clough, to sign for the Rams on 25th August 1967 – McFarland, a masterly, graceful centre back, went on to make 442 appearances for the club, scoring 44 goals. At the time of signing, the 18-year-old had played just 35 games for Tranmere Rovers – it was a masterstroke by Clough and Peter Taylor, perhaps the greatest of all their signings. McFarland, graceful, quick, elegant and superb on the ball possessed a devilish will to win and became a fan favourite as the Rams climbed from the bottom end of Division Two to Champions of the Football League and European Cup semi-finalists. Along the way, he picked up 28 England caps – it would have been more like 100 had McFarland's later career not been dogged by injury.

McFarland had been linked with moves away from the Baseball Ground in the 1978-79 season, being linked especially with a move to Coventry City, but had quashed such speculation by signing a 2-year contract in the summer of 1979. He had been planning to leave Derby "until the boss and John Newman arrived last summer. They convinced me with their enthusiasm. I decided there was a big future for the Rams and I still do" – the deal was not without controversy; McFarland's fitness had been a serious issue for 5 years and he had not managed anything like a full season since 1973-74. The fans still loved him though –

but in the spring of 1979 he was no longer the player to drag the Rams through a successful First Division relegation scrap.

McFarland eventually left the club when that final contract expired in May 1981, moving to Bradford City in a Player-Manager capacity – he was an instant success, leading Bradford to promotion from Division Four and playing 40 games in the process during the 1981-82 season, before returning to the Baseball Ground under controversial circumstances as Assistant Manager to Peter Taylor in the Autumn of 1982, bringing his assistant Mick Jones with him. The Rams were heavily fined for their alleged "tapping up" of McFarland and Jones.

Born in Liverpool in 1948, McFarland only ever played professionally for Tranmere, Derby County and Bradford and spent most of it at Derby – as player, assistant manager, assistant and most recently Club Director (plenty more of that later). He remains a revered and respected figure at the club and is arguably Derby's greatest ever defender.

At Middlesbrough, Addison had gone with a very defensive-looking line up including, in addition to Langan and McFarland, Osgood, Webb, McCaffrey and Buckley (6 defenders) – with Daly and Barry Powell in the middle of midfield and Davies partnering Biley in attack. McFarland was sent off (for 2 bookable offences) and McCaffrey went off injured. It proved to be the low point of this most disappointing of all seasons, the Rams barely troubling Middlesbrough's goal throughout the entire 90 minutes at Ayresome Park.

Derby finally halted their run of 6 successive defeats on 16th February at the Baseball Ground, against Southampton, in front of 16,535. The match was drawn 2-2, Derby's goals scored by Barry Powell and Roger Davies. This game was notable for the debut of young **Steve Cherry** in goal, replacing McKellar who had suffered a particularly chastening afternoon at Middlesbrough the previous Saturday. McKellar's form was often unpredictable – he could be a superb shot stopper but appeared to suffer with confidence and could be error-prone. He was not a favourite with Rams fans – many of whom had grown accustomed to the steady and reliable Colin Boulton in the early and mid-1970's, and found it hard to understand why Derby had been unable to find a reliable performer between the sticks since Boulton had lost his place in the side some 4 years previously – his successors, Graham Moseley, John Middleton and now McKellar, did not come close to matching Boulton's consistency. Of McKellar, typical letters to the Ram newspaper of the day, such as Pop Side season ticket holder K.R.T's "A national reporter said that If the Rams had a first-class goalkeeper, they would have some ten points more by now….I and most Rams fans I know agree wholeheartedly".

Steve Cherry, Nottingham born, was 19 years old when he made his Football League debut and had joined Derby County as an apprentice in the summer of 1975, when the Rams were still reigning Football League Champions. Cherry, a boyhood Nottingham Forest fan, had wanted to join Forest but they showed no interest, nor did Notts County. He had long been touted as a hot prospect but was not considered ready for first team football in the 1978-79 season despite the Rams troubles in the goalkeeper position but was awarded a professional contract by Tommy Docherty in 1978. Colin Addison, with only David McKellar on the books for the 1979-80 season, trusted Cherry enough to make him back up to the Scotsman – and gave him his League debut at the Baseball Ground in February 1980.

Cherry was spotted by a freelance scout called Jim Kirk while still at school and playing local football in the South Notts League, Kirk recommended the youngster to Derby's scouts Ernie Roberts and Bert Johnson, who recommended offering schoolboy terms. He became frustrated in the 1980-81 season after the Rams signed Yakka Banovic and Cherry found himself back in the "A" team – and he was allowed to go out on loan to Fourth Division Port Vale for a spell in November 1980.

He had a very long career in professional football and was still playing in the Football League as late as 1998-99, having featured for no less than 14 clubs before finishing his career at non-league Belper Town in the mid 2000's. He made a total of 77 appearances at Derby County between February 1980 and August 1984, when he was sold to Walsall for £25,000 following Derby's relegation to the Third Division, new manager Arthur Cox preferring his new signing Eric Steele as first choice keeper.

Always popular with Derby supporters, Cherry was voted player of the year in 1982-83 and was very unfortunate to be remembered for one terrible error in an FA Cup Quarter Final replay against Plymouth Argyle in 1984 (when he allowed a corner to go directly into the net) – fans had soon forgotten that it was Cherry's heroics in the initial tie at Home Park which had enable the Rams to achieve a replay. Cherry won player of the year awards at both Plymouth (1988) and Notts County (1992) and it was at Notts County where he stayed the longest, making 266 appearances for the club between 1988 and 1995.

A week after the draw with Middlesbrough, the Rams picked up their first win in 3 months, in front of an improved attendance of 21,183, when Tottenham Hotspur were beaten 2-1 at the Baseball Ground. Cherry retained his place in goal and McFarland returned from suspension to partner McCaffrey and Dave Webb in the centre of defence. Buckley and Langan were employed as attacking full backs and in midfield were Emery and Barry Powell. Roger Davies and Alan Biley continued in attack. The Rams goals were scored by Biley and McCaffrey. After the win against Spurs, Derby moved on to 19 points and while they were still 21st in the League, the gaps above them were closing.

On March 1st, 1980, at Villa Park, Derby were unlucky to lose 1-0, Allan Evans scoring the goal for Aston Villa. The Rams fielded debutant striker **David Swindlehurst**, on loan from Crystal Palace, for the first time – partnering Alan Biley in attack, Swindlehurst provided much needed power and aerial ability in a much more dangerous-looking Derby side. The Rams had wanted to sign the Palace striker on a permanent basis but did not have the cash to complete such a deal and had to instead settle for a loan with the intention to make the arrangement permanent, when cash became available.

David Swindlehurst had made 237 appearances for Crystal Palace, scoring 73 goals, when Colin Addison moved to sign him for Derby County at the end of February 1980 – Addison had failed in his attempt to bring in Paul Fletcher from Burnley and Swindlehurst had been his second choice. Joining initially on loan for 2 months, Swindlehurst became an instant hit with Rams fans and Derby's board eventually found the resources necessary to make the deal permanent in April 1980, breaking the club's transfer record to pay £410,000 for the powerful centre forward.

Swindlehurst's whole-hearted displays quickly won over Derby supporters and his partnership with Alan Biley breathed life into the 1979-80 season when the duo came close to firing the club to unlikely survival in the First Division, from the position of almost certain relegation in the winter of that season. He had been at Palace since a schoolboy and had become a huge favourite at Selhurst Park, and was, at 25 years old, still at his peak when he arrived at the Baseball Ground on 3-year contract.

After 125 games for Derby, and 32 goals, and with his contract close to expiring, the Rams were forced to sell Swindlehurst to West Ham United for a cut price £160,000 in March 1983. At the time of Swindlehurst's sale, he could perhaps have been realistically valued at £500,000 but by then Derby County were in such a desperate financial state that they had to accept West Ham's bid – the alternative was to lose the player on a free transfer when his contract expired a month later. The Rams could not afford to offer the Edgware born striker a new deal.

After leaving Derby, Swindlehurst played for West Ham and Sunderland, followed by a short stay in Cyprus where he made 13 appearances for Anorthosis Famagusta, then came back to the UK to finish his career at Wimbledon, Colchester and Peterborough United. He was capped once at England B level, and once at England Under 21 level. He went on to manage several non-league clubs in the South East, most recently at Whyteleafe in 2006.

Leaving the Baseball Ground in March 1980, as Swindlehurst arrived, were midfielders Vic Moreland and Bruce Rioch. Both went to the USA to play in the North American Soccer League, Moreland to Tulsa Roughnecks (along with his friend, reserve team striker Billy Caskey) and Rioch to team up with ex Rams winger Alan Hinton at Seattle Sounders. It had been a miserable second spell at Derby for Rioch, who had been sent off twice in 1977-78 and had fallen out with both Tommy Docherty and Colin Addison – the final straw for Addison had been a public display of petulance by Rioch before the FA Cup tie against Bristol City at Ashton Gate in January 1980, where the manager openly had his authority questioned – Rioch was suspended from the club and as soon as the opportunity arose to move him out, he was gone (Dave Langan had been part of the same incident, but he had subsequently made his peace with Addison). Unlike Rioch, Moreland had made no real impact at Derby, having arrived with something of a fanfare from then manager Tommy Docherty – he suffered from comparisons with the truly great midfielders who had gone before him, and never showed the consistent level of performance (or ability) which was necessary to play in the First Division.

Derby County's connections with the North American Soccer League (NASL) were substantial and had allegedly formed part of the investigation into corruption which had beset the club in the summer of 1979. Along with Moreland and Rioch, no fewer than 27 other players with Rams connections had played or coached with teams in the original NASL, which ran from 1968 to 1984, and sanctioned both outdoor and indoor soccer on a professional level in the USA. The NASL reached its peak popularity in 1979-80 with some of the greatest footballers of all time, including Pele, Johan Cruyff and George Best taking part, but even then, attracted very small live audiences (an average of 14,440 per game in its most popular season). As the US economy began to enter recession, the money ran out and the vast sums of money being spent on foreign players could not be sustained (clubs, such as Altanta Chiefs, for example, were losing $7 million per year) – competition, in the form of Major Indoor Soccer League (MISL) hammered the final nail into the coffin of the NASL, in 1984.

Following their battling but ultimately fruitless trip to Villa Park, the Rams returned to the Baseball Ground for a home game with Stoke City on Saturday 8th March. In fact, they faced 3 vital, and distinctly winnable games in a row – after meeting Stoke, they were due to face bottom of the table Bolton Wanderers (away) and fellow strugglers Bristol City (home). These 3 games, said Addison, would define the season – should the Rams manage to pick up maximum points, they would be well placed to avoid the drop. In fact, they managed 4 points out of the 6 available.

For the game against Stoke, the Rams were able to field their most experienced players, McFarland and Steve Powell, and reverted to a regulation back 4 with Keith Osgood partnering McFarland. Biley and Swindlehurst caused The Potters' defence all sorts of problems but Derby were held to an exciting 2-2 draw (goals from Biley and Osgood). An encouraging attendance of 22,695, boosted by a good contingent from Stoke, suggested there were signs of renewed interest from the local public.

The Rams travelled to Burnden Park for the game at Bolton Wanderers on 14th March. Bottom of the table Wanderers already looked doomed, and for Derby it was quite simply a "must win" game. It was a dull game, but the Rams turned out 2-1 winners as first Biley, then Swindlehurst (his first goal for the club), took Derby on to 22 points and a step closer to their nearest rivals in the First Division table (Manchester City and Everton). Manager Addison had the rare luxury of being able to name an unchanged side for the Bolton game. Derby's away support at Bolton was noticeably improved, the mood was improving – the Rams had booked up 10 Roadrider coaches for the trip to Burnden Park, compared to a couple of months earlier when they had struggled to fill a single coach for some of the longer away trips.

Back at the Baseball Ground for the last of the three vital "relegation battles", the Rams faced Bristol City on March 22nd, 1980. Manager Addison made 1 change, bringing in Barry Powell for the unfortunate Jonathan Clark. The crowd was down from the previous 2 home games, but 17,020 was not bad considering less than 100 away fans had travelled.

The Bristol City game was football entertainment at its best. Both teams attacked with abandon and the result 3-3 reflected the excitement of the match. The Rams looked dead and buried at 2-0 down after just 26 minutes, then Alan Biley scored a hat trick within 9 minutes either side of half time (a poachers effort as the ball fell loose following a corner late in the first half, a fine second after latching on the Barry Powell's excellent through ball and outpacing the defence, and finally a to turn the game on its head a penalty cooled converted in front of the Osmaston End). Unfortunately, a poor defensive mix up just 4 minutes after Biley's penalty cost the Rams both points. On the day, Derby had been both explosive in attack and shaky in defence – but it had been fine entertainment and Derby suddenly, almost from nowhere, looked a side capable of picking up points in the First Division.

The Rams continued their improvement with a 1-1 draw away at Bobby Robson's high-flying Ipswich Town on March 29th, where Gerry Daly returned from injury after missing the previous 6 games, replacing Steve Emery in midfield. It was a great point for the Rams but should have been 2, they dominated the game at Portman Road and led until the final 6 minutes of the game, missing 2 penalties (Barry Powell and Daly's efforts were both saved) - Town's goalkeeper Paul Cooper putting in an astonishing display (including one save from an Osgood free kick which was later described as "save of the season") to deny the Rams more goals than the one they got, a Dave Swindlehurst header from Daly's corner. Derby had played more like a side in contention for a European place than one battling against relegation. At the back, Osgood and Roy McFarland had begun to look like a promising partnership. Osgood, who had been somewhat error-prone in the early days after signing for Derby in the Autumn of 1979, was clearly benefitting from McFarland's calm and classy presence – "it's not just because Roy is such a great player", he said, "he uses his vast experience to help the players around him...on the pitch he is continually talking, advising how best to tackle situations. There is no doubt he is one of the reasons I have hit better form in recent weeks". Also helping was Osgood's move from Warwick to a new home in Allestree – a move encouraged and assisted by Colin Addison and John Newman – "I have never been part of a squad more dedicated to their club than the present squad...in the long term that is certain to mean there is a big future for Derby County. And I most certainly want to be part of it".

Notable for the game at Ipswich was a very encouraging travelling support, some 1500, who roared the Rams on for the full 90 minutes – the contrast with the less than 100 who had travelled to recent away games at Middlesbrough and Arsenal just a few weeks previously, was quite remarkable. Supporters clubs had reported interest "at a level akin to the League

Championship days" and local private coach operators were swamped with enquiries. After the Ipswich game, the Rams had 24 points and were above Bristol City (23) and Bolton Wanderers (20). Everton and Manchester City (both 28) were the only realistic targets if Derby were to escape relegation.

Every game was now vital. Leeds United were the next visitors to the Baseball Ground, on Saturday April 5th. In the Ram Newspaper, manager Addison appealed to supporters "give us the tools and John Newman and I will finish the job", as they urged season ticket holders to renew their tickets for the 1980-81 season and thus provide essential finances to enable the club to strengthen the team. Addison's first task was to find the cash needed to sign Dave Swindlehurst on a permanent basis – his loan was due to expire on 20th April, meaning he would miss the potentially crucial final home game of the season against Manchester City - "I desperately hope the cash can be found. We need Swindles, and he wants us".

Off the pitch, the Rams announced details of the 16 executive boxes - "at 20 feet by nine, probably the biggest on any League ground in the Country" – which were to replace the back 5 rows of the Ley Stand. Initial take-up was encouraging, The Rams held a function in the Sportsman's Club at the Baseball Ground on 2nd April 1980 at which interest was declared for all 16 boxes, with two- and three-year initial leases being discussed. The level of interest was such that the Rams were able to construct the boxes at zero cost, financed by leasers. Club Director Bill Stevenson said at the time "we have visited similar facilities at several First Division clubs and we think we are in a position to offer something as good as any in the Country...the boxes can attract the type of (client) who will not only use football as a platform for the promotion of their products...they're in a position to inject into the club more money". Derby County, despite their obvious financial problems, continued to think big and indeed act big.

Against Leeds United, the Rams' stunning revival in both form and results continued. In front of a very encouraging 22,745, Derby ran out comfortable 2-0 winners against the mid-table Yorkshire side. Goals from Paul Emson (a rare header) followed by a fine chipped finish from Barry Powell put Derby 2 up inside 20 minutes as the Baseball Ground atmosphere reached a crescendo not heard since the win over Nottingham Forest back in November 1979. However, the game was marred by a series of aggressive and damaging fouls by Leeds players, with Derby suffering injuries to key midfielders Steve Powell and Gerry Daly, with Barry Powell also taking a serious knock later in the game. It was yet another blow to both Steve Powell and Daly – Powell was 6 games into his latest comeback and Daly just 2. Perhaps the players were not fully fit, but the robust approach of Leeds certainly did not help. The Derby Evening Telegraph summed it up nicely – "if the Rams were forced to contain Leeds after the interval, at least part of the reason was the steadily diminishing number of fit players on their side". Times were changing – Karen Hallam, a season ticket holder from Riddings, became Derby's first ever female mascot when she led the Rams out against Leeds.

Derby, on 26 points, now faced 2 very difficult-looking away games in 2 days over the Easter period, with visits to mid table Coventry City on Easter Monday, and then league leaders Liverpool the following evening. Of the forthcoming trips, Rams Newspaper terrace correspondent Bill X wrote "I trust the growing contingent of Rams fans will be there to cheer the lads on…at Bolton and Ipswich you were really great". Whilst Coventry was described as "not the awkward place it used to be for visiting fans", caution was advised to Rams fans travelling to Anfield – "the Anfield Road End is a fairly safe bet…I say fairly safe…some Liverpool supporters may also be in that part of the ground" – ending his column by warning "the great danger at Anfield is from pickpockets, so please do not take any more cash with you than you really need"

At Highfield Road, Derby fought for their First Division survival and deserved a point, unluckily going down 2-1 with a depleted side containing McCaffrey and Emery in midfield in place of the injured Steve Powell and Daly. By this time the back 4 was settled and Langan (making his 150th competitive appearance for Derby), Osgood, McFarland and Buckley lined up for the 7th successive game. In attack, Biley and Swindlehurst were establishing an exciting partnership (also their 7th game in a row as a strike pair). Emson had hit form and was into a long run in the side on the left wing. Unfortunately, the midfield had been thrown into a state of turmoil by injuries, forcing manager Addison to chop and change. Aiden McCaffrey had equalised Ian Wallace's opener, with a ferocious shot, but despite having several good chances to take the lead, the Rams had eventually gone down to a winner from winger Steve Hunt.

After Highfield Road, the trip to Liverpool was daunting to say the least. Derby, by now, were looking like relegation certainties, results having gone against them elsewhere, and Liverpool, especially at Anfield, were close to invincible around this time. Yet another midfield player was injured, this time Barry Powell, so Addison drafted in Jonathan Clark to partner McCaffrey in central midfield. So severe was the injury crisis, that the manager was forced to select reserve team striker **Kevin Wilson** as substitute.

Wilson had been signed on the recommendation of Chief Scout Alan Ashman in December 1979, the Rams paying £20,000 to non-league Banbury for the 18-year-old striker. When he first came to Derby, he was housed in digs in Normanton, shared with Alan Biley – John Newman, the Rams Assistant Manager saying at the time "Alan is a sort of confident, ebullient and yet very nice character who will bring it out in Kevin…young Wilson is a natural and he is going to be some player if he works hard at it…he has the natural goal itch of a born striker…Colin and I are excited by his possibilities". Biley said of his housemate "watch out for the lad, he eats and sleeps football"

One year before his First Division debut in a game at Anfield against Liverpool, Wilson had worked as a food sales representative, selling peas amongst other things. Dave Swindlehurst, like Biley and encouraging and positive influence on the youngster, said "he is discovering that scoring can be as easy as shelling peas". Wilson, at the time, was knocking them in regularly for the Rams' reserves, scoring 6 before his First team debut. He had joined Banbury United as a part time professional in September 1978 and had suffered a setback when Sheffield United rejected him following a trial.

Sheffield United's loss was Derby's gain as Wilson went on to play 122 first team games (plus 19 appearances as substitute) for Derby, scoring 41 goals and serving 4 different managers, before being sold to Ipswich Town in January 1985 as Arthur Cox was forced to wheel and deal to mould the squad he wanted – at the time of his sale, Wilson was considered one of Derby's prized assets and the deal caused a considerable stir amongst Rams fans.

After a very successful spell at Ipswich (49 goals in 119 appearances, Wilson went to Chelsea for £335,000 in 1987 and became a big favourite at Stamford Bridge (55 goals in 155 games), before leaving for Notts County. Along the way, he picked up 42 caps for Northern Ireland. He went into management at Northampton Town and then at several non-League clubs including Bedford Town, Kettering Town, Ilkeston and most recently at Nuneaton Town (in 2016).

Kevin Wilson was a fine player for Derby, performing well personally usually in poor sides, but he is often most fondly remembered as the player who was sacrificed to bring in much needed cash to fund the signings of Gary Micklewhite, Geraint Williams and Trevor Christie – as the Rams rebuilt their squad during the 1984-85 season.

Derby were outclassed at Anfield in front of nearly 41,000 and went down 3-0, the closest they came to scoring was a disallowed effort by Swindlehurst. Kevin Wilson replaced Paul Emson in the second half, for his professional debut. The defeat made relegation almost inevitable and it was sad that, no sooner had things begun to look up at the Baseball Ground, everything was about to come crashing down.

One thing which had been a success was the club's decision to scrap its short-lived experiment with a magazine style matchday programme. The return of Ram Newspaper was widely welcomed by Derby fans (although not by collectors, the Rams missing out on the British Programme Collectors award because "it is not as easy to store….(Derby) would have won the most improved programme award had they not reverted back to Newspaper format". For the club, it was a straightforward decision – the paper sold twice as many copies as the magazine had. The magazine had lost money (£5,000, had the club persisted with it for a full season) but the paper made a profit – and as finances were by now in dire straits, every penny was needed. The club had already decided, by the winter of 1980, that the Newspaper format would continue for the following season. In the event, the Ram Newspaper made a net profit of £6,626 for the season 1979-80, compared to £6,321 the season before.

Derby's club shop, the Ramtique, had also received a facelift, relocating a few yards down Osmaston Road in the City Centre (from number 55 to number 39, and was rebranded the "New Look Ramtique" for an official re-opening on 10th April 1980, Rams manager Colin Addison was engaged to perform the official opening duties and supporters could pick up bargains such as a souvenir pen (8p), a Derby County tie (£3.25) and a Rams Sweat Shirt (in six colours - £7.99). The first 50 customers also received a free Derby County Lampshade (normal price £1.99). In the event, manager Colin Addison and players Alan Biley, Dave Swindlehurst and Steve Powell spent 90 minutes signing autographs as excited kids and parents filled the new look shop on its opening day.

Derby's seventh annual awards night was to be held at Romeo's & Juliet's, on Colyer Street in the City. A date had been set for Wednesday April 22nd, 1980, 3 days before the Rams were due to play their final home game of the season, against Manchester City. Entertainment, including cabaret act Barley, plus award presentations including Player of the Year and Miss Derby County 1980 ("contestants must be over 16 and must enclose with their entry a full-length photograph, entrants will be judged from the picture") were promised. Tickets were offered to all spectators priced £2.00. The awards night was very well attended, in fact more tickets were sold than for any such event since the 1975 League Championship year – the big winners were Steve Buckley (Player of the Year, as voted for by 6,738 fans – ahead of runner-up Alan Biley and third placed Dave Langan), Mrs Denise Gregory of Ilkeston (Supporter of the Year) and 20 year old Elaine Bacon of Youlgrave (Miss Derby County). The Evening's biggest cheer, however, was reserved for manager Colin Addison's announcement that David Swindlehurst was to be signed on a permanent basis.

The big issue in English football in the spring of 1980 involved sponsorship and advertising. At the time, both BBC and ITV categorically refused to allow any advertising on football shirts for any game being broadcast by either channel. This had been a bone of contention for England's leading clubs since the mid 1970's when Derby County themselves had led a campaign to have the ban ended (having made an agreement with motor manufacturer SAAB which they hoped would include shirt advertising). At an extraordinary general meeting of the football league clubs in March 1980, it was unanimously agreed to call again for the ending of the shirt advertising ban. At the time, every football league club in England received £25,000 per year from the broadcasters, in return for the agreement to abide by BBC and ITV rules, including the shirt advertising ban. The clubs became increasingly hostile, some suggesting that they could stop games being broadcast on TV if the BBC and ITV rules were not changed.

The issue of players' wages was also becoming more and more of a talking point. The Professional Footballers' Association was pressing for a change in contract terms for its members, rejected by clubs as "players have already won freedoms unthinkable even a handful of years ago, and they now take out of the game as much (if not more) than the game can stand….the tail is wagging the dog". Jimmy Hill, previously a vociferous supporter of football players' rights, and by now a Director of Coventry City, had changed sides and made his feelings quite clear – "clubs must not only run their own affairs, but they must remain employers who negotiate with their employees. There can be no mandate for the players to become the administrators. Their job is to play".

Despite Derby's increasingly desperate struggle against relegation, the partnership in attack of Alan Biley and Dave Swindlehurst had proved to be a fine combination, and it was to Colin Addison's credit that he had signed and paired them. Biley had started slowly (no goals in his first 5 games) but had then exploded into life with 6 in the next 5, including a hat trick against Bristol City at the Baseball Ground. He was in no doubt of the reason for his startling improvement – "I owe it all to Dave. The difference he has made since he came into the side is quite startling". Swindlehurst returned the compliment – "Alan is a fine little player, a tremendous worker, and a forager...I enjoy twinning in with him, we complement each other and it's great to be hunting as a pair".

Biley was scoring most of the goals, but Assistant Manager John Newman was in no doubt that "Swindles" (as the big striker became known) would soon be weighing-in as well – "Dave is a natural striker of the ball and he knows where the goal is. He is the man we have been looking for since Colin and I came here. The pair of them complement each other and could make a big name for themselves as a pair". Club Captain Roy McFarland added "these two have blended perfectly...Dave is an excellent target man and Alan is going to the right places to feed off him"

Biley began drawing comparisons with Derby County's great goal-scorer of the late 1960's and early 1970's, Kevin Hector. At just 23 years of age, Biley had scored 80 career goals from 175 games, and had already played in all 4 divisions of the football league. He also appeared to be resilient, having missed only 3 of a possible 134 games in his previous 3 seasons. He liked to play alongside bigger men, doing particularly well alongside big George Reilly at Cambridge United before linking up with Swindlehurst at Derby.

As Swindlehurst and Biley established themselves as first choice strikers, Roger Davies was released from his contract in March 1980 and moved to the USA to team up with former Derby winger Alan Hinton at Seattle Sounders. Davies's return had not proved the success Addison had hoped for and he had managed just 5 goals in his second spell with the Rams, albeit struggling manfully at times in a poor side which, over the winter of 1979-80 lacked both technical ability and confidence. Fans were appreciative of his efforts, regardless of poor returns – Chris Smith of Ripley, corresponding to the Ram Newspaper in April 1980 writing "he came back to help when we were in a difficult position...and gave 100% in every match he played...he deserves a presentation or something to commemorate his work for us...had he stayed he would have scooped Player of the Year for effort and true sportsmanship". Colin Bladon of Ashby-de-la-Zouch added "thanks Roger Davies for all the hope and enthusiasm he has given us during the last few months...he never let his head hang low. He always kept fighting".

Derby, by now virtually certain to be relegated, returned to the Baseball Ground for a home game against Brighton & Hove Albion on 12th April. The Rams had announced that season ticket prices would be frozen for the following season (albeit most likely to be to watch Second Division football). Chairman Richard Moore announced, even before relegation was mathematically certain "we are sure that under Colin Addison and John Newman we can spring right back". Addison himself said "unless a miracle happens it's going to be second division football for us next season. That need not be a disaster, not if you stay with us". Moore announced that match day prices would be increased from £1.30 to £1.50 for all terrace places except the visitors' enclosure, which would be £2.00. Seating prices for 1980-81 would range from £2.20 (Normanton Stand) to £5 (Paddock). Seats in the B Stand and Ley Stand Centre were to remain at £3.50.

The "Hard Core Supporters" scheme, in which vouchers were collected to prove attendance, was to reward those who had collected all 11 vouchers with a free seat for the final home game of the season, against Manchester City. Indeed, the mood amongst Derby supporters was astonishingly positive given the Rams' now almost certain relegation – hopes were very high for the following season and many expected the club to bounce straight back up. This mood was only heightened as Brighton were easily beaten 3-0 in front of a promising attendance of 17,257 - the visitors bringing less than 100 fans from the South Coast.

Derby ran Brighton ragged and could easily have won 6 or 7 nil, the change from only a few weeks previously was quite incredible and Addison's comments of the week before the game "I feel sick at some of the teams finishing above us in the First Division" was quite appropriate for the Seagulls. Alan Biley opened the scoring from the penalty spot, beating Brighton's former Rams goalkeeper Graham Moseley in front of the Osmaston stand, and the striker added a second when he fired in from close range following good work from Aiden McCaffrey, who headed substitute Paul Emson's cross back across goal and into the path of Biley. The goal of the game was scored by Keith Osgood, who cracked a 35-yard rocket into the bottom corner of Moseley's net. The Brighton game marked a first start for young striker Kevin Wilson, who came in to the team following a promising appearance as substitute at Liverpool – Emson dropping to the bench but soon being brought on after Swindlehurst picked up a knock.

A week later the Rams travelled to the City Ground, Nottingham to face local rivals Nottingham Forest. Derby had put in a superb performance in the reverse fixture earlier in the season, beating the Reds 4-1, and with Derby in good form, hopes were high that the already relegated Rams could pull off another shock. Kevin Wilson retained his starting place and Steve Powell returned from injury in place of Steve Emery, to partner McCaffrey in central midfield. Steve Buckley, the left back, played his 100th league game for the Rams (at the time, he had never missed a single game since joining the club from Luton Town – all but 6 of his games for Derby were in tandem with Dave Langan at right back). David McKellar, in goal, made what turned out to be his final appearance for Derby. This time Derby were unable to pull off what would have been a shock victory but fought hard, eventually going down 1-0 to the reigning Champions of Europe, who were clearly the better side on the day and had chances to score more than 1 – Forest's goal coming just before half time, a stunning strike after a free kick had been tapped sideways to Scottish International left back Frank Gray, who's 30 yard shot left McKellar with no chance, the Rams defensive wall having broken up allowing Gray all the space he needed.

Defeat at the City Ground, which had all but mathematically consigned Derby to the Second Division, was followed by the final home game of the 1979-80 season, on 26th April 1980. The crowds continued to turn up in good numbers – this time 22,572 (albeit boosted by the usual large following from Manchester). City, who, like Derby, had also had a poor season and only narrowly avoided relegation themselves, were no match for the Rams on the day – Derby running out 3-1 winners with another Biley penalty, followed by Swindlehurst and then an own goal making the marks for the Rams. Gerry Daly returned from injury to replace Jonathan Clark, and Barry Powell also came in to the midfield, with McCaffrey dropping back into defence to replace the injured Keith Osgood.

Addison had led his players out 5 minutes before kicking off against Manchester City, to the kind of reception one would expect for a side challenging for the Championship, rather than one which was all but certainly about to be relegated. The Rams support was once again quite sensational as the Osmaston End and Pop Side terraces roared on their team.

The board had also provided quite astonishing support to Addison – they had, in the week prior to the Manchester City game, sanctioned a club record £410,000 fee to be paid to make Dave Swindlehurst's loan into a permanent deal. The club regarded Swindlehurst as vital to their plan to get the Rams back into the First Division at the first time of asking – it was a very risky strategy and the club's finances were being extended to their absolute limits. The Ram Newspaper of 26th April made the situation clear – "(The Board of Directors) have had to stretch the club's financial resources to near breaking point", going on to explain how transfers worked around that time, and especially how the Swindlehurst deal had been achieved – "Buying on hire-purchase faces the club with further heavy payment obligations, in addition to a hefty bank overdraft which must be cleared before late summer". Chairman Richard Moore, having sanctioned the Swindlehurst deal, justified his decision thus: "without the players the manager needs we could find ourselves at best standing still. And that's not good enough, so the board has been positive", going on to appeal to the supporters to back the club with early season ticket purchases – "the more advance sales Derby County can effect in the close season the more cash there is available for team building". The club was "hard up to the hilt", conceded the Chairman "but come what may we'll get the team Colin needs". It was a quite remarkable vote of confidence for a manager who had all but taken his side to relegation in his first season in charge.

The club asked supporters to commit for 2 years, to improve cash flow and "to ensure they get the same price for 1981-82 as 1980-81…I am asking every supporter who can afford it to take out one of the new two year season tickets" (said Moore) The final word was left to the Chairman – "we are most certainly taking risks, but for the sake of the team we want, we simply must". These actions, and these words, were to hang like a millstone around Derby County's neck for the next 4 years.

The reality though, was the clubs relegated from the First Division lost on average around 25% of their season ticket holders for the start of the next season. Derby hoped to buck that trend and some ultra-optimists even forecast that they would increase their season ticket holder numbers for what they hoped would be a promotion campaign.

When considering the financial collapse which was just around the corner at Derby County, a review of the era of Tommy Docherty, Addison, George Hardy and Moore is essential. The club teetered on the edge of ruin in the winter of 1983, but, as some of the statements made around 1980 clearly demonstrate, the seeds of destruction had been sown in preceding years. The club was living well beyond its means by the 1979-80 season and instead of reigning in the spending, Richard Moore and his board gambled on spending more – speculate to accumulate – the only thing they accumulated, however, was more and ultimately ruinous debt. In November 1980, Moore announced at the Annual General Meeting that the club was running a deficit of £800,000, and that interest charges alone for the coming year would be a £180,000 – the numbers were frightening. By the time of that AGM, the bank had refused to extend the club's overdraft (as it probably should have done much earlier). The club, whilst remaining, to the outside World at least, confident, was in a state of crisis – the board of Directors had no answers, Derby County was a ship heading for the rocks, and nobody knew how to steer to safety.

Docherty is often blamed in contemporary discussions on the subject, but, in his defence, he was under pressure to rebuild an ageing team, and quickly – that said, some of the deals sanctioned by Docherty were catastrophic – examples being winger Leighton James being swapped for Don Masson, both being valued at £175,000 at the time, which sounds ok until one considers that James had cost Derby £300,000, and Masson ended up going to Notts County in exchange for Steve Carter, who arrived on a free transfer. Docherty's exchange deal involving Rams midfielder Archie Gemmill and Nottingham Forest's goalkeeper John Middleton is another example often cited (albeit somewhat unfairly – Gemmill had pushed for a transfer and the club were left with no choice but to let him go).

Colin Addison's deals, overall, proved equally disastrous for the Rams. Barry Powell, for whom Derby paid £350,000 (which was widely considered a ridiculously high fee at the time), eventually left on a free transfer when the club could no longer afford his £25,000 annual salary. Keith Osgood, who cost the Rams £145,000, ended up leaving for just £10,000, following the tragic death of his wife. The Rams were also very unlucky, for example when the fine striker John Duncan (a big money Docherty signing), had his career ended by injury – a situation soon to be repeated with defender Alan Ramage.

Richard Moore, the Chairman, an accountant by trade, backed Addison and John Newman to such an extent that they were effectively given an open cheque book, and more often than not the managerial duo (as inexperienced in the First Division as Moore was in football) made poor decisions, spending fees that the club could ill-afford on players who were not good enough for that level of the game. In Moore's defence, he was not even in the Country when Barry Powell and Osgood were signed – he was away running his business – in line with most Chairman of that era, Moore was combining his duties with the football club with his duties running his own Companies.

Eventually, Moore would concede that the direction the club was taking was not the correct one – but by the time common sense prevailed, it was already too late. It was not until the well into the 1980-81 season that the Chairman conceded that the Rams would have little chance of recouping their huge outlay on most of the players but would have to sell anyway. It was an astonishing about-turn, considering that a bid of £650,000 from Tottenham Hotspur for Alan Biley had been turned down immediately after relegation in the summer of 1980 – the club would have doubled their money on Biley had the bid been accepted, in the event the gamble backfired and Biley was sold for less than half of that amount a year later. It should be added in the interests of balance that Sam Longson, the club's President, claimed that Tottenham's bid for Biley was never brought to the attention of the Board.

It is pertinent to note that player purchases around this time were conducted somewhat differently to how they are dealt with now, some 40 years later – back in the late 1970's and early 1980's it was common practice to buy players on what was effectively a hire-purchase agreement – a sum, very often £50,000, was paid up front and the balance of the transfer fee would then be settled over the duration of the player's contract. As Tony Francis put it in his superb "There was some football too…", "make a bad buy now, and your successors would reap the whirlwind" – in Derby's case this is exactly what happened.

Addison remained confident, at least in public. "we are now close to completing the squad which can get us back to the top again. A couple of buys, a bit of wheeling and dealing this summer and we can go into next season with real hope. Our heads are very high after the performances of the last few weeks". On Biley and Swindlehurst he said "I would have bet my bottom dollar that they would have made a big impact on the top flight had they had the chance next season. They should undoubtedly wreak some havoc in Division Two". The last word, though, should be left to Assistant Manager John Newman, who wrote in the season's final Ram Newspaper "I'll bet my bottom dollar the next decade is going to be as exciting as the last fashioned by Brian Clough and Peter Taylor" – he may well have been right, it was indeed exciting, usually for the wrong reasons however.

Michael Dunford, the secretary, added "this is a message to the fans, the wasted years are gone. The club is alive and bubbling…this season has brought us back from the dead and the board is backing (Addison's) judgement to the hilt". Dunford said that the club had seriously considered starting a fund for donations "scores of people asked us to do this", but on balance it was felt more appropriate to ask increased commitment with 2-year season tickets, and for supporters to buy lottery tickets (the club at the time ran 3 different lottery schemes).

Addison had indeed inspired a significant revival, of that there could be no doubt. If the season had started on February 23rd, for example, Derby would have finished half way up the First Division table. The significance of that day was it marked Roy McFarland's return to the side, and Alan Biley's first goal for the club. The following Saturday, Steve Powell had returned from injury, Dave Swindlehurst made his debut and the Rams went on a run over the next 11 games which included 4 wins, 3 draws and 4 defeats (11 points). Other significant improvements since that date had been the form of Barry Powell, often a victim of the boo-boys but who had played quite well in an attacking midfield role in the latter part of the season. Gerry Daly's form and fitness during 1979-80 was unpredictable, but he too had improved during the later months. An improbable escape from relegation had started to look possible, but the injury jinx had struck again on Easter Saturday when Daly, and both Powells, were injured in the game against Leeds United, and at that point, Derby were effectively doomed. The signings of Biley and Swindlehurst had proved very effective (albeit both cost the kind of fee that Derby could ill-afford in 1979-80).

Addison, though, was not exempt from blame – he was the manager and his team was going to be relegated. Seasons start in August, not February. Several of his earlier signings had not paid off – Emery had never looked like a First Division standard player, Barry Powell had started very badly, and Keith Osgood was another who took a long time to settle at Derby – like Emery, Osgood was full of heart and courage, but lacked the class to regularly contribute to a club in the First Division. Roger Davies was another who gave his all but had not been successful. Addison had also failed to address the problem goalkeeping position, where David McKellar had performed erratically for most of the season. In another stroke of bad luck, Addison's preferred first choice goalkeeper John Middleton had suffered a career-ending shoulder injury in October 1979 – destined never to play football again, his contract was due to expire at the end of the 1979-80 season and he was released in December 1980 and became unemployed. It was a sad and unlucky end to a promising career and Ilkeston Rams supporters organised a Charity Gala Dance in December 1980 to raise money for the unfortunate Middleton – the dance was attended by most of the Rams' squad as well as several of his former Nottingham Forest team mates, and the Middleton family returned to their native Skegness just 24 hours later. This represented yet another financial catastrophe for the Rams – Middleton had been signed in part exchange for Archie Gemmill in September 1977, somehow the Rams had only valued Gemmill at £20,000 in the deal and the Rams received just £25,000 plus the tenacious midfielder. Addison had spent more than £1 million, in his failed attempt to keep the Rams in the First Division.

Many journalists were reasonably sympathetic with Addison's plight – Bob Hughes, writing in the Sunday Times in April 1980 penned "In fairness (to Addison) he has not had time to rectify fully the ruinous selling of Tommy Docherty". Even Neil Hallam, who had been very critical of the club in his Derby Trader column for the past four seasons, correctly asserting, on many occasions, that the club was going backwards, had the following to say in May 1980 – "ironic isn't it, that a side facing relegation can honestly say that the darkest days are behind them. The framework of a solidly competent side has been established to reward the fans for their loyalty, and I have a feeling they will be further rewarded next season". Hallam was certainly no cheer-leader for Derby County, he was, at times, the club's harshest critic.

One man who was less effusive in his comments on the Rams was Peter Taylor. The man who, along with Brian Clough, had steered Derby to its greatest achievement, winning the Championship of England in 1971-72, a feat they had subsequently matched at Nottingham Forest (adding also a European Cup win – and soon after a second), was noticeably spiky when asked of his opinions on the Rams, following their defeat at the City Ground. Whilst Taylor had nothing positive to say about Derby's team, he was quick to describe the club's supporters as the best and most loyal in the Country – he had a point – Derby's recent 17,000+ crowds were better than several others in the First Division (Leeds United, Norwich City, Coventry City, Bristol City and Bolton Wanderers).

At youth level, the Rams were also recruiting – a new batch of promising schoolboys were signed up by Youth Development Officer Geoff Worth, including 15-year-old defender Paul Blades, from Peterborough. The signing of Blades, whilst he was still at school, was to prove an excellent piece of business for Derby County – he went on to make 166 first team appearances for the Rams before being sold to Norwich City for £700,000 after 10 years with the Rams – Worth proved his worth with that one. The Rams' quest to improve the quality and numbers of youth intake continued – for the whole of the 1970's the club had been desperately poor in its recruitment and nurturing of Youth talent, preferring to get the cheque book out, which was fine when the club was profitable and winning trophies, but this was no longer the case. Worth organised days such as 27th April 1980, at which 126 youngsters who had written to the club from all over the Country asking to be considered, were all given a trials at the Raynesway Training ground – "no expenses will be paid...but we have told them that if they make their way here they will most certainly get a thorough examination", said Worth. In the event, not one of the triallists from this day were considered good enough to make the grade.

The 1979-80 season came to an end at Carrow Road, Norwich, on Saturday May 3rd. Derby, already relegated, went down by 4-2 in front of 15,173, in a disappointing display. Several players were making their final appearances for the club – these were Gerry Daly, subject of almost constant transfer speculation during his time at Derby, Aiden McCaffrey, who had never really established himself in the side and had been unfortunate to find himself being dropped in as emergency replacement in unfamiliar positions, and Dave Langan, who had requested a transfer in January 1980 and had a difficult and strained relationship with manager Addison. The Rams line up for that final game was Cherry; Langan, Osgood,

McFarland, Buckley; McCaffrey, Steve Powell, Daly; Wilson, Swindlehurst, Biley. McCaffrey and Swindlehurst scored Derby's goals. On the bench, making his first appearance in a first team squad, was youngster **Wayne Richards**.

Richards, a left back, had been a reserve team regular in 1979-80. The Scunthorpe native had been signed as an apprentice in the Docherty era and was awarded a professional contract in May 1979, in the period between Docherty's departure and Colin Addison's arrival. He made little impact at Derby (19 starts and a further 4 appearances as substitute – usually deputising when regular left back Steve Buckley was injured or suspended) and dropped down into non-league football with Northern Premier League side Matlock Town in the summer of 1982 when his Rams contract expired – soon dropping a further rung with Heanor Town just 3 months later.

So, on Saturday 3rd May 1980 at 4.40pm, Derby County kicked a ball in the top flight of English football for what would be the last time until Saturday 15th August 1987. At the time, the expectation was of a return within 1 season – but the reality was to prove very different. Unlike most relegation campaigns, there was never any threat to the job of manager Colin Addison – his £25,000 a year contract was, at least for now, secure.

The Rams ended the 1979-80 season 21st out of 22 in the First Division table. They had won 11 games (more than both Everton and Bristol City, who finished above them, and, astonishingly, the same number as West Bromwich Albion, who finished 10th) but they had been beaten 23 times, more than any other team in the division (and 11 times more than West Brom). The goal difference, minus 20, was also worse than all but bottom placed Bolton Wanderers, and the points tally of 30 left them 5 points short of survival. Biley was the leading scorer, with 9 goals in 18 games. Player of the Year Buckley was the only ever present in the league (42 matches), and of the other players only Langan (40), made more than 25 league appearances. Addison used a total of 32 different players in his failed attempt to keep the club in Division One. The Rams slipped back into the Second Division after 11 seasons in the top flight, which included 2 League Championships.

In the Central League, Derby's Reserve team had a mixed season in 1979-80, finishing half way up the table. Falconer, Wayne Richards and Paul Bartlett led the appearances, with Billy Caskey (11) heading the goal scoring charts. Highlights of the reserves' season included 5-1 wins over both Preston North End and Bury. The Rams' Youth team finished 7th out of 10 in the Midland Youth League.

At the end of the season central defender David Webb, who had fallen out of favour with Addison, was released to join AFC Bournemouth as player coach. Webb had made just 26 first team appearances for Derby since joining from Leicester City in 1978, scoring 1 goal – he had not featured in the side since February 1980, having lost his place to the returning Roy McFarland.

In July 1980, right back David Langan was sold to Birmingham City for £350,000. This represented an excellent deal for Derby, Langan having requested a transfer and with no intention of playing Second Division football. Langan had cost the club nothing, having signed as an apprentice, turning professional in February 1975 (while the first team, managed by Dave Mackay, were heading for a second Football League championship title). Langan finished with 1 goal in his 155 games for Derby. Supporters had always liked the Irishman, but had been resigned to the fact that he would be going, and, as far as the majority were concerned, the size of the fee achieved represented another tick in the positive column for manager Addison – the Rams also already had another natural right full back on their books, although the hard-working Steve Emery was not in the same class as Langan, who was undoubtedly of First Division ability.

Addison promptly spent £150,000 of the fee received for Langan on 22-year-old central defender **Alan Ramage**, from Middlesbrough. Ramage, who combined football with a professional cricket career for Yorkshire, had been with Middlesbrough since joining as an apprentice in 1975. Whilst never in the highest class at either cricket or football, it must be noted that to be able to have played both sports at the levels Ramage did, made him an exceptionally fine all round sportsman – unfortunately, the sheer physical exertion was to end his sporting career at a very early age, and he was forced to retire from football less than a year after joining the Rams – tragically unfortunate both the player and the club, for whom once again another big money signing walked away without recouping any fee.

As a cricketer, Ramage was a right arm seam bowler who took 44 wickets in first class cricket for Yorkshire and played for the England schoolboys' team. As a footballer he was a tough, uncompromising defender who had been spotted by Jack Charlton when he was manager at Ayresome Park and had made his debut for the first team aged just 18 – Ramage was very much in the Charlton mould, he had made 77 appearances for Middlesbrough when Derby came in for him.

Although Derby had always planned to bring in another central defender that summer, Ramage was not Derby's first choice - Rams manager Colin Addison had missed out on his first choice, Bolton Wanderers' Sam Allardyce (the future England national team manager, and another rugged, tough defender), when Allardyce pulled out of a planned deal at the 11th hour and signed for Sunderland instead, the Rams having agreed a deal with Bolton and the player having given his word that he would be coming to the Baseball Ground – indeed, in November 1980 at the annual Shareholders meeting, Addison admitted, to considerable disquiet, that he had only seen Ramage play a couple of times and had relied almost entirely on the judgement of Chief Scout Alan Ashman. Because of the Ramage signing, and with Roy McFarland looking likely to be fit for the start of the 1980-81 season, Keith Osgood was placed on the transfer list.

Also, in July, Addison took steps to address the goalkeeping problem which had beset the Rams since Colin Boulton's time, some 5 years earlier, when he signed former England Under 23 International **Roger Jones** from Stoke City.

Jones was already 34 by the time he joined Derby and was already a veteran of well over 500 matches. He had started at Portsmouth in 1964 but was soon on his way to Bournemouth when Portsmouth disbanded their reserve team. From there he moved to Blackburn Rovers, then, via a short stay at Newcastle United, moved to Stoke City in February 1977. At Stoke, under the management former Rams player Alan Durban, he had been first choice until the middle of the 1979-80 season when he lost his place at the Victoria Ground to Peter Fox. He was not happy to settle for reserve team football at Stoke and sought a move, Derby's promise to make him their first choice goalkeeper being enough to persuade to move to the Baseball Ground – despite Rams manager Colin Addison describing Jones as a "short-term signing" and making it clear that Derby were also trying to sign a younger goalkeeper (which turned out to be Jaka Banovic) as competition. It helps with Jones's decision that he did not have to uproot his family, he lived in Loggerheads, which enabled comfortable travel to both Stoke and Derby.

After 2 seasons with Derby, and 59 appearances, during which he had a short spell out on loan at Birmingham City, Jones was released and finished his career with 122 appearances at York City. He was a reliable, steady goalkeeper who did well for Derby, but was one who the club simply could not afford to keep, having joined on a First Division level contract.

With Jones's signing, Derby were able to sell David McKellar and made a very tidy profit on the Scotsman when he was sold to Third Division Brentford at the start of the 1980-81 season, for a fee of £25,000 – the goalkeeper had been signed from Scottish non-league football in April 1978, for just £2,500. After leaving Derby, McKellar forged a long career in the English and Scottish leagues, going on to play for clubs as varied as Carlisle United, Hamilton Academical and Newcastle United, before ending his career as a back-up goalkeeper for Glasgow Rangers in 1992.

The following month, on the eve of the 1980-81 season, Aiden McCaffrey was sold to Bristol Rovers for £75,000 – a profit of £15,000, good business for a player who tended to be erratic and had not established himself either in his chosen central defensive position, or central midfield, where he had regularly filled in as injury cover for the Rams.

Also, in August 1980, Gerry Daly, who had planned to spend a third successive summer in the North American Soccer League, was sold to Coventry City for £300,000. Although Daly was a class player and had done well for the Rams in his early time with the club, he was becoming injury-prone and was frequently unsettled – the fee Addison achieved, for another player who did not want to play in the Second Division, represented a profit of £125,000 on the fee that Colin Murphy had paid for the player to Manchester United in March 1977.

The three deals over the summer brought in a vital £725,000. It was a lifeline, albeit the fees would be received over the course of the next 3 to 4 years rather than immediately - the wages saved (especially Daly's) also helped. However, it merely delayed the inevitable – the crash was coming. The Rams had a squad full of players receiving First Division salaries, there were no clauses which reduced the players wages in the event of relegation. Nobody had thought that far ahead – it was mismanagement of catastrophic proportions, and should have been addressed long before the bank fired its first significant warning shot, refusing to extend the club's overdraft at the end of summer 1980 – the final straw for the bank being Derby's astonishingly misguided decision to turn down a £650,000 bid for Alan Biley, at the end of July – going against their promise given when the bank had provided the funds to sign both Biley and Dave Swindlehurst, that they would be sold and the money recouped in the event of relegation.

Derby's first game at Second Division level since 19th April 1969 was a disaster. At the Abbey Stadium, Cambridge, and displaying the logo of new sponsor British Midland Airways "Fly British Midland", they were beaten 3-0 by Cambridge United in front of a crowd of 9,558. Travelling supporters, of which there were an estimated 5,000, outnumbered the home support. Derby's side that day included the two new summer signings Jones and Ramage, and comprised Jones; Emery, Ramage, McFarland, Buckley; Clark, Steve Powell, Barry Powell, Emson; Swindlehurst, Biley. Wilson was an unused substitute. It was encouraging to see Roy McFarland start the season, but it was not to last – he was soon injured and missed the next six games, but the game itself was a disaster, Cambridge having enough chances to have won by 5 or 6, hitting the woodwork twice.

For the travelling army of Rams supporters, it had been a particularly difficult afternoon. As well as seeing their team hammered by the home side, they had encountered notably heavy-handed treatment by Cambridge Police. The massed convoy of vehicles heading down from Derby to the University town had first been stopped several miles outside Cambridge and forced to wait until 1.30pm before being allowed to enter the vicinity of the town. Then, after the game, all coaches heading back to Derby were given a police escort out of the town, just 10 minutes after the final whistle.

The local police had their reasons – several hundred Rams fans had charged from the stadium after the final whistle, looking for locals with whom they could make trouble. Considering both the behaviour of hooligan supporters and the treatment of all travelling fans by local police, it was no wonder that attendances were down, and families no longer considered football matches to be safe and suitable places for a day out with children.

At the Baseball Ground, fences had been erected in front of both the Osmaston End and Popular side in the summer of 1980, at the request of the Derbyshire Constabulary. Throughout the 1970's the Baseball Ground pitch had suffered from fan encroachment and battles between rival supporters. The final straw for the Police and the club had been the final home game of the 1979-80 season, during which fans had flooded onto the pitch after the final whistle and a small minority had fought with the visiting Manchester City supporters. The fences were destined to stay in place, indeed more were to be added, at the Baseball Ground until the aftermath of the tragedy at Hillsborough at the end of the decade. To cover the expense of having the fences installed, Derby charged visiting fans £2 to stand on the terrace at the Baseball Ground, 50p more than home fans were charged. "If there were no away visitors there would be no need for fences, so it's only right we should ask them to contribute to the cost" said secretary Michael Dunford.

Gerry Daly, who had been the subject of almost constant transfer speculation over the summer, was not selected for the trip to Cambridge but did feature for the reserves, who drew 0-0 with Preston North End at the Baseball Ground on the same afternoon. Transfer listed Keith Osgood also started the season in the reserve team but came straight back into the first team when McFarland picked up his latest injury. Youngster Steve Cherry was preferred to David McKellar in goal for the reserves, McKellar would soon be on his way to Brentford.

The deal taking Daly to Coventry was completed when a fee of £300,000 was agreed the day after those first games of the season, on Sunday 20th August. The Rams, under pressure from the bank to reduce their overdraft, had no choice – the same situation that they had found themselves in with David Langan a month earlier. Both players, it should be remembered, had stated their desire to remain in the First Division and both had been pushing for a move. Daly had also been on what could best be described as a "lucrative contract" at the Baseball Ground – the best paid player at the club. Addison was frustrated with both players, saying of Coventry's bid for Daly "There is little doubt that nobody else was going to come in for Gerry in the foreseeable future, and the player had started the season injured yet again". Addison had finally agreed terms with Coventry late on the Saturday evening, after returning with the first team from Cambridge, and Daly had passed his medical at Highfield Road the following morning (despite having reported injured for Derby's first game of the season). A few weeks later, clearly still upset about the whole situation, Addison would say about Daly "if he had bothered to put himself about, and had played to his true potential, Derby might still be in the First Division"

The Rams moved to strengthen their goalkeeping department following the sale of David McKellar when they signed 23-year-old Yugoslavian-born Australia International **Vjckoslav "Jaka" Banovic** from Melbourne side Heidelburg United, for a fee of £40,000. Banovic had travelled to Derby for trials in the spring of 1980 and had impressed the Rams enough to be offered a contract. Colin Addison expressed himself pleased with the goalkeeping situation "We are now strong in a position where we were so weak…with Roger Jones and Steve Cherry also here. Jaka is aware that he will have to fight for a reserve place, never mind a League spot, and he is ready to do that".

At the time of signing for the Rams, Banovic had played 7 times for Australia. His signing presented a number of headaches for Derby's Secretary Michael Dunford, who had encountered issues with the Work Permit (a legal requirement, which was finally achieved thanks to the player's Yugolsav ancestry), and then, to comply with a rule of the time (said Dunford) "we had to convince the Department of Employment and the Professional Footballers Association that we had made every effort to sign a player of similar calibre either in this Country or from Common Market (now EU) countries". It was not so simple as just providing anecdotal evidence either, the Rams had to supply documented evidence of bids for goalkeepers in recent months to prove that Banovic's signing was not simply an attempt to bring in cheap labour. Banovic had to be paid no less than the average salary paid to the first team squad. This was an incredibly slow process – Derby had wanted to sign Banovic back in May, it had taken 3 months to complete the deal.

On Wednesday 20th August, Derby's first team took their Baseball Ground bow for the 1980-81 season, the visitors were Chelsea and the attendance a very encouraging 20,353 (comfortably above the previous season's average 19,900), boosted by several hundred from London. Addison's only team change was enforced, as Osgood replaced the injured McFarland who pulled out on the morning of the match. The Rams won 3-2 against Geoff Hurst's side, it was hardly a vintage performance, but the win was all that mattered following the debacle at Cambridge. Alan Biley put Derby one up, with a fortunate goal after Chelsea's Micky Droy's attempted clearance rebounded off the Rams striker and flew past the helpless Borota in goal. Chelsea equalised just before half time, but Derby restored their lead via an own goal, Gary Chivers turning a shot into his own net, following Emson's fine run and cut in from the left. Barry Powell scored a retaken penalty to make it 3-1 before a terrible mix up in Derby's defence resulted in Chelsea pulling a goal back, to make it a nervous last few minutes for Rams fans.

The Executive Box complex, at the back of the Ley Stand, was opened for the first time for the Chelsea game - "Patrons enjoyed carpeted, armchair comfort", according to the Ram Newspaper. The club had engaged Stadia Catering Ltd (who also looked after similar facilities at Villa Park) to provide match day catering to the Executive Boxes. Mr Thomas Edmonds was employed by the club to oversee the Boxes on match days, assisted by hostesses Nicki Dilks and Hilary Bamford. Despite the club's claims at the time of the Box development being announced, that "all would be sold on a 2 or 3 year contract before they had even been constructed", several boxes remained unoccupied and were made available for hire on a match-by-match basis at a cost of £250 per match (12 seater boxes) or £150 (6 seater boxes) – "including waitress service, car parking space and a match day programme". Gas central heating appliance engineering company Glow Worm, headquartered at Belper, were the first company to hire one of the Executive Boxes.

Down below the Executive Boxes, on the Pop Side, the atmosphere was somewhat less convivial. Chelsea supporters burst through a Police cordon and into the Vulcan Street enclosure, encountering and confronting the home support. Police later explained their initial confusion, they had found it difficult to distinguish between rival supporters as both wore blue and white. Bill X, the Ram Newspaper's terrace correspondent, felt it was no surprise that Chelsea's fans had chosen to enter the Vulcan Street enclosure rather than the designated Colombo Street section – the price was 50p less for the home section.

Police Sergeant Ron Stevenson, an officer of 25 years' service and secretary of the Nottingham Branch of the Derby County Supporters Club, was in no doubt about how he felt the "fans who come to the Baseball Ground just to bait each other". He continued - "there is no law against caning the young thugs, and if do-gooders prevent that then ask them to stand on the football terraces…they're not football hooligans, they're criminals against society seven days a week". Stevenson and his son had a first-hand view of the trouble on the Pop Side, they stood in the pen which served as the buffer zone between the Colombo Street and Vulcan Street ends of the terrace.

The Rams then won 2-1 at Luton Town, on Saturday 23rd August. It was their first away win since the 2-1 at Bolton Wanderers on 15th March. Addison was able to name an unchanged starting 11, the only change being on the bench where Wayne Richards replaced Kevin Wilson.

At Kenilworth Road, backed by well over a thousand travelling supporters paying £2.50 for a spot on the terraces, the Rams went 1 down before Keith Osgood's superb long-range free kick levelled the scores, just a couple of minutes before half time. Luton had started brightly and had looked the better side before Osgood's stunning equaliser – but from then on Derby took charge and it was no surprise when Dave Swindlehurst was able to capitalise on an error by defender Saxby to fire home the winning goal from just inside in the penalty area. In the end, Derby were very good value for their win and should perhaps have added more goals – Emson, for example, having missed 2 very good chances including an open goal after rounding the keeper at the end of a fine run from the left wing, only to fire wide with the goal at his mercy. The Rams were up and running in the Second Division.

The Luton game was marred by trouble involving Rams supporters who travelled on the newly reinstated Ramaway train, many boarding at Luton for the return to Derby without tickets. The club hit out "Derby County will not tolerate incidents like these. Certain individuals cannot be allowed to spoil a fun day out, and it is our intention to come down hard on these offenders". Meanwhile, Blue Boar Services, who ran Watford Gap and Rothersthorpe Service stations on the M1 Motorway, offered a trophy for the club with the supporters who behaved best during visits to their facilities. In recent years, Motorway service stations had refused admission to any football coaches en-route to away matches. Blue Boar's statement "we believe that fans frustrated by refusals to serve them on motorways release pent up emotions on the grounds they visit… this season we intend to make all responsible coach travelling football supporters most welcome"

The Rams had been drawn away to Queens Park Rangers, managed by former Derby boss Tommy Docherty, in the League Cup 2nd Round. Manager Addison was able to name an unchanged team for the 3rd successive game (this being long before the days of clubs fielding weakened sides for this competition). Derby set out to frustrate QPR and achieved their aim of bringing the West Londoners back to the Baseball Ground for a reply, the game ending 0-0 – QPR perhaps had the best of the game but the Rams had been very solid at the back and goalkeeper Roger Jones in particular, outstanding.

By now, Addison and Newman signings dominated the Rams' team. Seven of the players who played against QPR had been signed by the duo – only Buckley, Steve Powell, Clark and Emson were already at the club when they had arrived, in July 1979. Addison said of his remodelled squad "we have not changed for the sake of change, but simply because the squad we inherited was not good enough. From now on change will take place much more slowly". Regarding the departures of popular players Daly and Langan he said "I am adamant that no-one gets the impression that we will toss away our best players like falling Autumn leaves. In the case Gerry we received a rare offer, one not likely to be repeated...and felt that the player's form since we arrived justified nothing but acceptance in both his and our best interests and in the case of Langan, I would never had agreed to the sale had any concrete offer been made for Gerry at that time". Newman made the financial situation quite clear – "in the past supporters of Derby County became used to the club going for the highest-class players. This is beyond us for the moment, we simply cannot afford to bid in the £1 million region. Out investment has to be in younger players...that process is well under way"

There had been more change in the boardroom over the summer. Sam Longson (President) and Richard Moore (Chairman) remained in their positions, but former Chairman George Hardy and Bob Innes had left the board, with Bill Stevenson stepping up to the position of Vice Chairman. Arthur Atkins and Bob Mullholland remained on the board, and had been joined by newcomers Rex Stone, of Alida Packaging Group, and Eddie Strachan, of Chan Court Ltd.

Of life in the second tier, Steve Powell had made it clear that the players needed to adapt quickly, and could certainly not take the Second Division lightly – "Cambridge shook us rigid" he said of the opening day thrashing at the Abbey Stadium...second division sides seem to knock the ball up quickly from the back, rather than playing through midfield. And the opposition tend to chase rather than use the ball".

The Rams "A" team had suffered a chastening start to life in the Midland Intermediate League, having been thrashed 3-0 away at West Bromwich Albion and then 5-0 at Raynesway against a Mansfield Town side which comprised mainly reserve team players rather than the 15-17-year-old level players which the Rams drew from. Ron Webster, the youth team coach, had decided to put his side back up a level, having entered them in the Derbyshire Combination and then the Midland Youth League in the previous 2 seasons. Paul Blades was among the players featuring regularly for the Rams "A" team at this time and had conceded an own goal in the Mansfield defeat. Youth Development Officer Geoff Worth was especially excited about the prospects of 14-year-old Associated Schoolboy Mark Clifford and 17-year-old second year apprentice Paul Halford, a striker.

The Rams reserve team at this time featured future first team players Graham Harbey (the Matlock born 17 year old who had been signed on Associated Schoolboy forms just a year earlier, but had shown such promise that he had already been promoted to the reserve team, where he became the regular left back), Steve Spooner, Glen Skivington and Tony Reid as well as Steve Cherry, Paul Bartlett and John Clayton, who had already appeared for the senior side. They had started their Central League campaign non-too impressively, with 2 defeats and a draw.

The Baseball Ground's electronic scoreboard, which had been installed during the 1978-79 season, was taken out of service for the Rams second division campaign, for financial reasons. The contract with the company who had originally installed and sponsored the scoreboard had expired and the club could not find any companies prepared to take over the sponsorship – in its place, a half time scoreboard was re-installed in the corner of the Normanton End and the A Stand, above the boy's pen, after supporters in the Osmaston End complained that they were unable to see the main scoreboard (which was in the above the corner of the Osmaston terrace). Another problem was the public address system, which was, according to correspondent to the Ram Newspaper John M. Pepper of Kilburn "virtually inaudible…a proper PA system is a necessity rather than a luxury". Secretary Michael Dunford conceded that this was indeed a problem – "we have for three or four year tried to improve things, without success…we are advised that our tightly enclosed ground presents extreme acoustic problems". The club engaged Reliance Systems of Birmingham, with a view to addressing the issue. Several weeks later the cause of the Baseball Ground's PA problem was discovered – painters working at the stadium over the summer had unplugged many of the speakers and had neglected to plug them back in.

Also, off the field, a campaign entitled "we'll be back in '81" gained some traction. The club shop "Ramtique" was experiencing good sales of T-shirts and scarves bearing the slogan. Hundreds of fans paraded their new attire at Cambridge and Luton with woven woollen scarves displaying "Derby County – We'll Be Back" retailing at £1.99 and "We'll Be Back" badges at 75p. Less popular with supporters was the increased price of Derby's matchday Ram Newspaper, which was now 30p.

Back to matters on the pitch, and Derby's second home game of the season, against Bolton Wanderers on Saturday October 30th. Manager Addison named his 4th successive unchanged starting 11, with Wilson returning to the substitute's bench in place of Richards. Bolton had most of the game, but the Rams' run of good fortune continued when a fortunate rebound from Jonathan Clark's powerful 11th minute shot fell straight into the path of Dave Swindlehurst, who made no mistake with his left foot finish at the Normanton End. Goalkeeper Roger Jones continued his impressive form as the away side poured forward in the second half, producing a remarkable double save as he pushed out a long range shot from Cantello, then somehow managed to keep Brian Kidd's follow up out, from point blank range – of Jones, Assistant Manager John Newman said "it's fair to say that goalkeeping like this would have earned us another eight points last season". The Rams, who won 1-0, did have chances to extend their lead, with Alan Biley, who had not started the season very well, and was carrying a minor injury, missing two good ones - but on the whole Bolton's goalkeeper Dennis Peacock remained a virtual spectator for most of the game, and the away side were very unfortunate not to come away with at least a draw.

Colin Addison, in his post-game interview, summed things up nicely "It was the worst overall performance since we arrived at Derby, but I was gratified to see them grafting despite it all and keeping their heads up". Less believable was the claim of Allestree "psychic medium", Mrs Audrey Lamb (a season ticket holder in the Osmaston Stand), who claimed she was responsible for the Rams' upturn in home form since the time she had organised the exorcism of an evil spirit from the Baseball Ground pitch in February 1980 – in fact, the results gave some credence to her claims, Derby were unbeaten in 8 League matches at home since Mrs Lamb's intervention, having lost 8 of the previous 15 beforehand. Mrs Lamb, who had suffered many abusive telephone calls and taunts calling her a fake, nevertheless asked "to be left alone to get on with it...I concentrate on blocking off the goal (which Derby are defending)".

Somehow, the Rams found themselves second in the league table despite "finding it hard to string more than a couple of passes together and struggling for any sort of rhythm", according to Assistant Manager John Newman. There was no lack of effort – "without that extra effort we would never have won six points out of the last six". On the question of fitness, a cause for concern for many fans around this time, Newman said "look at all the extra running they are doing (due to) their lack of control and passing accuracy, you'll see why they are so tired towards the end of games". Nobody should have been under an illusion that the Rams, despite positive results, were in a false position – "we know the team can produce better than this", said Newman, "right now we are not producing even 50% of the skills, rhythm or control we did during our good run towards the end of last season".

The players were finding life in the Second Division very tough. Dave Swindlehurst, for example, complained that "Alan Biley and myself are not getting the ball at our feet quickly, like I was last season...everything happens in a bit more of a rush (in the second division), and accuracy is often a casualty...in the first division there is more time to play the ball around, and strikers invariably find the ball coming to their feet". On his strike partner Biley, who had come in for some criticism from supporters, Swindlehurst said "we get on well, on and off the field. I've not played with better. From the start of the season he has been carrying an injury, so we haven't seen as much from him as expected but notice how he's been decoying people away from me".

Biley, meanwhile, maintained that the Fourth Division was the hardest to play in (and he had played in all four) – "Everybody is going at it 100 miles an hour and that is the most physical league of the lot. If you can survive that and still turn on some football among the whirlwind, you might be a player someday". He preferred the first division "because of the class of player all around you, you can play some football". Of the second division – "there are some class players, just not so many".

On the same day as the win over Bolton, Derby's reserves notched their first win of the season, winning 2-1 at Stoke City's Victoria Ground, coming back from a goal down with markers by central defender Kevin Murray and winger Paul Bartlett.

The Football League Cup 2nd round replay at the Baseball Ground against QPR, on 3rd September, brought former manager Tommy Docherty back to the Baseball Ground for the first time since his controversial resignation some 16 months earlier. Also returning to their former club were winger Gordon Hill and defender Steve Wicks. Once again, as in the original tie at Loftus Road, there were no goals in regular play, and once again manager Addison was able to name an unchanged side. It was another disappointing display from the Rams, and they were eventually knocked out of the competition after a penalty shoot-out. Both sides could have legitimate claims to have won in normal time, the Rams were denied what appeared to be a clear penalty when Biley was tripped while clean through and had an Emson header hit the bar, and Rangers hit the woodwork no less than three times.

In the penalty shoot-out, at the Osmaston End of the ground, Barry Powell missed Derby's first spot kick and that was enough to secure the victory for Rangers, who scored all five of their penalties to win 5-3 (both Hill and Wicks scored) – Emery, Osgood and Biley scored for the Rams. At the end of the game Docherty ran onto the Baseball Ground pitch to embrace Hill, the Baseball Ground crowd of 16,728 were not amused.

Season Ticket sales for the 1980-81 season had reached more than 10,000 by the end of September 1980. In times of falling attendances at almost all football grounds, it was remarkable that the Rams could still count of such loyal and committed support. Season Ticket numbers at the Baseball Ground had fallen steadily since their 1969-70 peak of more than 20,000, but to take £500,000 in advance sales in the summer before a Second Division season was considered exceptionally good, albeit the "break even" figure for home attendances was calculated at approximately 21,000 for the 1980-81 season, – it was more than other large clubs in the same division, such as Newcastle United, Chelsea and West Ham United had achieved that summer. Of the Baseball Ground, Sunday Express columnist Alan Hoby wrote:

> "It is a ground which for sheer emotional impact has few equals in English football. On match days the spectators seem to tower right over the players. The fans are so close that they can hear every shouted warning, every oath, every bellowed command. The name of this tight, tribal square of strident excitement is The Baseball Ground, home of Derby County, the famous old club where greatness and glory have so often gone hand in hand"

The Rams did indeed inspire some incredibly passionate support, none more so that 21-year-old Michael Anthony Stack, who changed his surname by Deed Poll to Derby, after 18 months of legal wrangling. He had wanted to become Mick Derby-County but had been forced to settle for Mick Derby. Mick, a British Rail employee, estimated that he spent 50% of his income following the Rams – "if the League side isn't playing, and the reserves are away, then I'll travel to see the reserves...fair weather fans annoy me. I am too proud of Derby County, and the City of Derby, ever to be lukewarm about either". Other impressive displays of loyalty included a 16-year-old "Ossie Ender" from Frome in Somerset, Mark Baber, who hitch-hiked his way to almost every Rams game, both home and away. However, it was unlikely that anyone could match the record of Mr John Ayre of Spondon, who was six years old when he first saw Derby play – at Wembley in the 1946 FA Cup Final – and claimed to have missed only 16 games, home or away, since that day.

The Baseball Ground had been Derby County's permanent home since 1895 – 10,000 people saw legendary player Steve Bloomer scored both goals in the Rams' 2-0 win over Sunderland on 14th September 1895, their first game since becoming permanent tenants. Until 1926, little had changed of what had previously been Sir Francis Ley's sports ground – Ley owned the ground until July 1924 when it was purchased by the football club. The first major development of the ground was the opening, on 4th September 1926, of a new stand, known as "B Pavilion", running along Shaftsbury Crescent, at a cost of £16,000. The new stand, which was later extended and became the Main Stand, seated 3,300. Dressing rooms, which had been behind both goals in previous years, were built under the new stand, and the ground capacity at this time was 30,000. The next major developments were a cover over the Popular Side (summer 1932, at a cost of £750), followed by a new double decker stand at the Osmaston End (summer 1933) and then a similar double decker stand at the Normanton End (summer 1935).

In January 1941 the Osmaston Stand was hit and severely damaged by a bomb during a German air-raid – this did not deter fans who were so desperate to see the Rams' 1946 FA Cup tie against West Bromwich Albion that they put their lives at risk by climbing into the bomb-damaged stand. Floodlights were installed at the ground in March 1953, set on the corners of the Osmaston and Normanton Stands, and an early attempt at undersoil heating was abandoned due to cost, also in 1953. The Rams had to replace the original floodlights in 1972, to accommodate colour television coverage of their European home matches – the new floodlights cost £50,000 and were erected on pylons on each corner of the ground.

As the Rams returned to Division One, a cantilever stand was erected above the Popular Side terracing at a cost of £150,000, with the cooperation of Ley's Malleable Castings, who provided the additional land necessary to enable access behind what was originally called the Ley Stand. With the Ley Stand completed just in time for the start of the 1969-70 season, the Baseball Ground's capacity was 42,000. In the 1970's seats were added first to the middle tier of the Osmaston Stand (in 1971 – 1,500 seats which brought the ground's seating capacity up to 14,000 but reduced the overall capacity to 40,000), then to the middle tier of the Normanton Stand (in 1972 – adding 1,000 more seats), then finally in 1975-76 to the Paddock, below the Main Stand. By the early 1980's, the ground capacity was 33,700.

The Ram Newspaper reported sad news involving popular former Derby goalkeeper Colin "Bernie" Boulton, who had broken his arm playing for Lincoln City at the end of August 1980 and had confided with friends that he may never play again. Rams manager Colin Addison attempted to help by offering transfer listed David McKellar on an emergency loan. Lincoln, managed by former Rams boss Colin Murphy, were also interested in signing reserve team winger Paul Bartlett for a small fee. In the event neither deal materialised – McKellar went to Brentford on loan, a move which was made permanent the following month, and Bartlett (who had played for the first team under Tommy Docherty but had never been in contention since Addison took over) dropped out of professional football altogether, signing for non-league Boston United in December 1980. The Rams, meanwhile, were taking a look at Belper Town winger Keith Dainter, who had impressed in the recent "A" team victory over Walsall, and had signed Mansfield schoolboy Neil Banks, ahead of several other League clubs who had also been watching the 15-year-old.

The Rams' 3rd home game in a week took place on the Saturday following the League Cup exit, with top of the table Blackburn Rovers the visitors – the Rams were second in the table. There was another first for the club, Nicholas Ulfsberger of Vasby in Sweden becoming the Rams' first ever overseas mascot. His father Boris, a huge Derby fan, interrupted the family's holiday in Blackpool to bring his son to the Baseball Ground. The attendance, 18,159 with 100 at best from Blackburn, was again encouraging, as was the average for the season so far – 18,597, albeit still considerably short of the figure required to "break even", 21,000.

Manager Addison was forced into one change, Kevin Wilson replacing Dave Swindlehurst, who had picked up an injury against QPR. Once again Derby started badly with a desperately poor first half display went 2-0 down in the first half, Blackburn's tricky Irish midfielder Noel Brotherston and veteran Howard Kendall dictating the play with the Rams' midfield barely getting a kick. However, a rousing second half recovery by Derby, in which Alan Biley, in a welcome return to goalscoring form, scored twice within 12 minutes of the restart, brought the scores level at 2-2 and that is how it finished. On the bench for the Rams and brought on to replace Biley for his debut late in the game, was **Glenn Skivington**.

Glenn Skivington, a midfield player, was a low-key signing in the summer of 1980, joining from non-league Barrow AFC at the age of 18, as the Rams looked for hidden gems amongst the lower and non-leagues. He had been spotted during the previous season by Chief Scout Alan Ashman and his scouting team, playing Alliance Premier League football (1 rung below Football League status) while still studying at Barrow Sixth Form College – in fact Ashman had been so certain about the young man's ability that he had suggested Derby should have signed him several months before they eventually did, in July (after Ashman had persuaded

Colin Addison and John Newman to watch the player for themselves). The Rams eventually agreed a fee of £20,000 to the Northern Premier League club, for Skivington's signature.

Skivington had joined on a 3-year deal and stayed with the Rams until his contract expired in the summer of 1983, when he moved on to Halifax Town, before returning to Barrow via a short stay at Southend United, to see out the rest of his career. After retiring from football, he became a Solicitor. He made at total of 50 appearances for Derby (including 7 as substitute), scoring 3 goals.

At Blundell Park, against Grimsby Town on 13th September, Derby maintained their challenge at the top of the table with a 1-0 win. Grimsby were unbeaten at home since January 1980 and featured in goal former Rams "A" team goalkeeper Nigel Batch. For the first time since early August, Addison changed his starting eleven with Skivington getting his first start, replacing Jonathan Clark in midfield (Clark was named as substitute) and Swindlehurst returning from injury to replace Kevin Wilson. For the first time in the season, the Rams began to show flickers of form and did well against a Grimsby side whose sole tactic seemed to be long punts downfield into the Derby penalty area, attempting to take advantage of a swirling wind – unlike at Cambridge a month earlier, when similar tactics (albeit in better weather conditions and on a better playing surface), had completely undone them.

The only football that was played on the day was played by the Rams, with Skivington and Steve Powell impressing, and Dave Swindlehurst's 12th minute close range headed goal in a 1-0 was probably a fair representation of the game overall. The victory at Blundell Park was particularly sweet for Derby's Assistant Manager John Newman, who had been manager there before joining the Rams in July 1979. Newman, still highly thought-of at Grimsby, was presented with a silver salver before kick-off, in recognition of his services to the club. After the win at Grimsby, Derby remained in second place in the Second Division table, with 9 points – above them were Blackburn (10) and just below were West Ham and Notts County (both 8).

The Rams' remarkable away support continued to grow. From numbers down to less than a hundred during the later Docherty era, just 18 months earlier, Derby were by now regularly followed on their travels by 3000 or more. As at Cambridge and Luton, Grimsby's match day attendance for the visit of the Rams, 15,052, shattered their previous best for the season (at Grimsby this was 10,461 for their game against Preston North End). Unfortunately, the Grimsby game was marred by several incidents of hooliganism, with one fan receiving a six-month sentence in a detention centre, and four others fined £850 following a fracas in a Cleethorpes pub involving at least 100 fans. Several more trivial incidents, such as a fan tipping a cup of coffee over an innocent bystander on a train station platform, and young fans making obscene gestures towards passers-by, resulted in Derby withdrawing travel cards from several supporters.

The spectre of football hooliganism hovered over Derby, among many other clubs. Suspecting organised trouble, the Football Association decided to ban Sheffield Wednesday fans, who had rioted on the terraces during a game at Oldham Athletic earlier in the season, from travelling to the Baseball Ground for the forthcoming league game, scheduled for October 4th. Derby issued vouchers in the Ram Newspaper for the games prior to the Sheffield club's visit, and only voucher holders would be permitted onto the terraces for the match against Wednesday. Rams secretary Michael Dunford applauded the decision – "despite the compensation we shall lose money in the short term, but in the long term we, and Sheffield Wednesday and football stand to be the winners" (the Rams had been expecting around 4,000 travelling supporters from Wednesday). Sheffield Wednesday had been ordered by the FA to compensate Derby with a sum of £3000 plus VAT, yet the Rams could have expected to net £8000 from terrace ticket sales, at £2 per head.

Dunford was also insistent that only registered and accredited supporters using official club transport (in Derby's case the Ramaway trains or Roadrider coaches) should be permitted to attend away matches. Dunford insisted that "sale of alcohol on grounds is not the issue...it is outside the grounds where these idiots get tanked up, it is on British Rail concessionary trains, and in the supermarkets and the off licences that they get most of the drink that inflames them". Dunford went on to say that eventually he hoped every club would have an all seater stadia, and that an all seater Baseball Ground "with the yobs firmly kept out" was the eventual aim of the club. R.M.Taylor of Ilkeston, writing to the Ram Newspaper, disagreed with Dunford – "bars under the Ley Stand should stop selling alcohol. You find groups of 14- and 15-year olds with pints in their hand at the back, not a bit interested in the game. At half time they come into the crowd to make a nuisance of themselves, using obscene language...alcohol gives these young louts Dutch Courage".

New signing Jaka Banovic made his debut for the Rams' reserves on 16th September, in a 1-1 draw away at Burnley. Also featuring in that game was Roy McFarland, who was 2 reserve games into his latest come-back attempt and strolled through the game at half pace. Central defender Frank Sheridan scored the Rams goal at Burnley but catching the eye of Rams Newspaper correspondent Harry Brown was young Graham Harbey, at left back. Midfielder Tony Reid and defender Ian Dalziel, both reserve team regulars, received call-ups for trials with the England Youth squad – the unlucky Dalziel, however, had to withdraw due to injury.

After the seeds of hope had been sown at Grimsby, there followed two defeats which left all but the most partisan of supporters in no doubt about the true direction their club was heading. Next to visit the Baseball Ground were mid table Wrexham, on 20th September, in front of BBC's Match of the Day cameras. This was the day that the Rams' poor form and disappointing performances caught up with them, and they were beaten 1-0 by the no more than ordinary visitors. Derby could consider themselves rather unlucky to lose the game – a controversially disallowed "goal" from Biley and a Swindlehurst effort that appeared to have crossed the line before Wrexham's Mel Sutton hooked the ball clear – but it was a dreadful display overall, the only moment of real skill being Wrexham's goal, a superb 20 yard curling shot from the edge of the penalty area which left Rams goalkeeper Roger Jones grasping at thin air. The attendance, just 16,823, was another worry, albeit allowances could be made for Wrexham's very small following. The Rams had invited 10 Vietnamese Boat People to the game, showing admirable charity and support for the displaced migrants – Rams supporters sitting near them were somewhat less charitable when the Vietnamese, unaware of who was playing in which shirts and for whom, leapt to their feet to cheer Wrexham's winning goal.

Following the dispiriting defeat at home to Wrexham, the Rams lost at Orient, again by 1-0. Roy McFarland made his comeback from injury, having not played for the first team since the opening day of the season, with new signing Alan Ramage, rather than transfer listed Keith Osgood, dropping to the bench. Osgood had been listed at the end of the previous summer, but the Rams had received no enquiries for the player, despite his good form since coming back into the team when McFarland got injured – in fact only Osgood and goalkeeper Roger Jones had been credited with playing well so far in the season. Many appeared to be simply "going through the motions and there had certainly been a considerable drop off in performance levels since the good run towards the end of the First Division campaign the previous season. Youngster Skivington retained his place in midfield ahead of Jonathan Clark, who was also on the transfer list. Derby again grumbled about refereeing decisions, which seemed to favour the home side, but once again had been desperately poor and had deserved to lose the game. The defeats at Orient, and against Wrexham, left Derby down in 7th place in the Second Division table, 5 points behind leaders Blackburn Rovers. A minority of Rams supporters had once again caused trouble after the game at Orient – a correspondent to the Ram Newspaper, who happened to be on the same London Underground train as some boisterous young fans complained "I have never heard such disgusting language in public. Then some idiot smashed a train window. We were glad when they got off, shouting their "Super Rams" slogans and much else".

Colin Addison reacted to the dreadful displays in the previous 2 games by selecting 5 regular first team players for the reserves game at home to Newcastle United, the following Monday night. Jonathan Clark, Alan Ramage, Barry Powell and Alan Biley (all Addison's own signings), plus Paul Emson had incurred the manager's wrath and were made the play in the "stiffs" as a form of punishment. It did not improve the Reserves' fortune – they lost the game 4-2.

As first performances, and then results, declined, fans began to lose patience and the first rumblings of criticism of Colin Addison began to materialise. Despite the Ram Newspaper's frequent and often tub-thumping endorsement of the manager and his assistant John Newman, letters began to appear which questioned team selection and the performance of individual players. A supporters club branch complained that Addison and Newman had failed to turn up for a function one evening, and some made suggestions which at the time sounded far-fetched, such as imploring the club to bring back former player, and all-time great Kevin Hector – "is it beyond the realms of common sense to bring him back to Derby County even if it was only for this one season…he would certainly bring back many fans…it seems more than possible that Zak (Hector's nickname) could do a job in the Second Division", wrote Mark Brannan of Derby, in October 1980.

The Rams continued to recruit in the younger age groups, with Geoff Worth reporting the signing of several boys on Associated Schoolboy terms, 3 of them, who had been playing for Derby boys under 14 side, were Andy Roberts and Richard Butler (both midfielders) and striker Mark Skinner – unfortunately none of these youngsters were to go on to professional football careers, but Andrew (Andy) Garner, a 14 year old striker from Stonebroom, near Alfreton, who was already six feet tall and signed at the same time as the other boys, would go on to play nearly 90 games for the Rams first team, scoring 20 goals – it was another coup by Worth, and testament to Derby's increased activity in scouting local talent. One age group higher, the Rams' "A" team was continuing to find life tough in the Midland Intermediate League – in order to help the youngsters in their most recent game, a 3-5 loss to Coventry, coach Ron Webster drafted in several players from the reserves in a line up featuring 3 future first team players (plus Keith Dainter, still on trial from Belper Town: Cherry, Lovatt, Harbey, Beaver, Tarry, Blades, Dainter, King, Robertson, Halford, Gibson.

There followed the visit to the Baseball Ground of Sheffield Wednesday, whose fans had been banned from entering the visitor's enclosure on the Pop Side following their involvement in trouble earlier in the season. Admission to the Pop Side and the Osmaston End terracing was strictly on presentation of a voucher only. In fact, Wednesday still brought some 1000 fans with them, they simply bought seat tickets instead, and they boosted the attendance to 18,554 – much to the disgust of one Ley Stand season ticket holder who complained "all seater stadiums, not on your nelly, not after the Sheffield Wednesday riff-raff who bought seats all round us and insulted our ears with the vilest language I've heard in years". Manager Addison decided to bring Clark back into the side, with Skivington dropping out – his team was: Jones; Emery, Osgood, McFarland, Buckley; Clark, S.Powell, B.Powell, Emson; Biley, Swindlehurst.

Derby got back to winning ways against Wednesday, in a much-improved performance which was helped by a slice of good fortune as defender Grant sliced an attempted clearance into his own net on 12 minutes. Five minutes later Emson clattered a superb 25-yard drive into the Normanton End net and the Rams were cruising 2-0 at half time. Wednesday, to their credit, came out battling in the second half and pulled a goal back only for Biley to latch on to a poor back pass and lob the goalkeeper after beating 2 defenders, it was a wonderful finish and deservedly completed the scoring for a 3-1 Derby win. The Rams' improved performance was no doubt assisted by the visitors' preference to try and play entertaining, attacking football themselves - It was a fine game, the best of the season so far, and Derby climbed slightly to 5th in the league.

The Rams then faced 2 successive away games, at Watford on the following Tuesday night, then at Swansea City on Saturday 11th October. At Watford, Addison altered the formation and experimented with Roy McFarland as sweeper behind central defenders Alan Ramage and Keith Osgood. It was not a success – the team looked totally uncomfortable with the unfamiliar formation and were very lucky to be only 1-0 down at half time. The Rams were forced to revert to a familiar flat back four when Ramage was injured and substitute Jonathan Clark replaced him, and suddenly they began to play well and Osgood's header to equalise the scores was, in the end, no more than they deserved.

At Swansea, Derby lost 3-1. The Swans opened the scoring through Leighton James, after a dubious penalty was awarded for handball against Jonathan Clark, who could do little to get out of the way of a point-blank range shot. Derby's misery increased when McFarland had to come off with hamstring trouble, to be replaced by Skivington. Immediately after the break, at 0-1 down, Swindlehurst missed an easy chance to level the game and that was it for Derby – 2 more goals from former Rams winger James, who was booed and jeered throughout by Derby's supporters, secured the win for Swansea. Jonathan Clark was sent off, to round off a game he would want to forget, and the referee appeared to be looking to "even things up" when he awarded the Rams a soft penalty in the dying minutes, which was converted by Osgood. It was a strange game, with odd refereeing throughout, but what was most significant about this match was that **Kevin Hector** made his "re-debut" (and making his 530th appearance for Derby), after joining from Vancouver Whitecaps, via Burton Albion, earlier in the week. It was the Rams' legend's first game for Derby since he had played in a 3-1 defeat at Bristol City on 12th November 1977 - Hector was brought straight into the side at the expense of Alan Biley, and Addison decided to revert back to a flat back 4 – with Ramage injured (and replaced by midfielder Clark), McFarland and Osgood paired up at the back.

Kevin Hector has significant claims to be one of Derby's greatest ever players, certainly he was one of the most popular and his 486 League appearances for the Rams remains a club record, in all games for the club he appeared 589 times. Born on 2nd November 1944 in Leeds, Hector had first joined Derby in 1966, when manager Tim Ward had persuaded his board to part with a significant fee to bring him to the Baseball Ground from Fourth Division Bradford Park Avenue (for whom he had scored 113 goals in 176 games, including 44 in a single season). Hector went on to play a key role in both of the Rams' Football League Championship wins (1971-72 and 1974-75), and had played in European Cup, FA Cup and League Cup semi-finals.

At his peak Hector was fast, skilful and had tremendous balance – he could pass, shoot and always seemed to be in the right place at the right time, he was an outstanding player and was unlucky not to have won more than the paltry 2 caps he earned for England, in 1973.

After many years of sterling service to the Rams, Hector was badly treated by Tommy Docherty (for example, he was named as substitute for the reserves), and eventually left the club in 1978 to join many other former Rams players in North American soccer (with Vancouver Whitecaps, for whom he won an NASL Championship title in the summer of 1979).

Vancouver, who owned his registration, allowed Hector to return to England to play non-league football on loan for Boston United (in 1978) and then Burton Albion (1979–80). He could still play, but the pace and spark had gone from his legs by this time, so it was a shock when Colin Addison decided to bring him back to the club to play in the Second Division in October 1980, at the age of 34. With all due respect to Hector, the decision to bring him back to the club at that stage of his career smacked of desperation, it was a relatively cheap crowd-pleasing option – as things turned out, and most likely due to the increasingly desperate financial situation at the club, his second spell at Derby perhaps lasted longer than expected, he made 56 appearances and stayed until his contract expired at the end of the 1981-82 season – he continued to play football at non-league level, with several local clubs including Shepshed Charterhouse, Gresley Rovers, Belper Town, Eastwood Town and Heanor Town, and was still playing Sunday football in 1994 at the age of 50.

When Hector re-joined to Derby, he became one of only 5 players who had returned for a second spell at the club, the others being Steve Bloomer. Frank Upton, Bruce Rioch and Roger Davies.

Derby's youth team went out of the FA Youth Cup on 13th October, losing 2-0 at the Baseball Ground to Swansea City, on a skidpan of a pitch in incessant pouring rain. Ron Webster, the coach, whilst disappointed with the result, professed himself pleased with some individual performances, especially Graham Harbey, the young man from Starkholmes, near Matlock. The young Rams line up: Palmer; Beaver, Dalziel, Blades, Harbey; Reid, King, Bird, Gibson; Halford, Shackleton, substitute Mulholland.

Queens Park Rangers were the opposition on 18th October, for the third time already that season – and once again the Rams were unable to beat the West Londoners, the game resulting in a 3-3 draw. Since the League Cup ties a few weeks earlier, Rangers had sacked manager Tommy Docherty and replaced him with Terry Venables. For Derby, McFarland, Ramage, Swindlehurst and Biley were all missing – in fact, the Rams' injury problems were so severe that there was no team line up published in the Ram Newspaper, just a blank space saying "please write them in" next to the numbers 1 -12. Skivington, Wilson and debutant **Frank Sheridan** were drafted into the side. Hector continued in attack. The first half was a poor affair, with neither side showing much attacking intent, but then Derby sparked into life. Sheridan, playing in midfield in place of Steve Powell, who had dropped back into defence, had a remarkable game - perhaps the best Derby County debut for 5 years, scoring twice – the first after just six minutes, a header from Paul Emson's cross; the second an instinctive finish after chesting down a Hector flick on from Buckley's free kick -

and playing with poise, vision and hunger - while the very impressive Skivington notched 2 assists, including a superb inch-perfect pass to put the impressive Emson through to make the score 3-1. Derby were cruising – they could have gone 4-1 up when a sliced clearance hit QPR's post but instead, in sadly typical style, the Rams began to make errors at the back, 2 of which resulted in goals for the opposition. Sheridan's brace on debut made him the first Derby player to achieve that feat since Des Palmer in August 1961, and he became only the fourth to manage it, after Palmer, Ian Buxton (1959) and Tommy Powell (1948).

It was a pity that such a small crowd, just 16,021, were there to witness Sheridan's brilliant debut. So exhausted, both physically and mentally, was the young man after the match, that he lay on the treatment table for an hour after the final whistle. There appeared to be significant hope for the future – in addition to the 2 young midfielders, striker Kevin Wilson also had a fine game, being unlucky not to add a goal himself, and young winger Paul Emson had given the QPR right back Don Shanks a chastening afternoon.

East Londoner Frank Sheridan joined Derby County as a 17-year-old in the summer of 1978, having been spotted and brought to the club by Colin Murphy's Assistant Dario Gradi, but had been nowhere near seeing any first team action until Colin Addison selected him for his debut in October 1980.

Before the Rams stepped in for him, Sheridan had trials at Chelsea, Plymouth, Charlton, West Ham and Millwall – in fact Gradi had seen both him (at the age of 16) and Steve Spooner play in the same trial match at Chelsea and had offered terms to both after the game.

Sheridan was primarily a defender but could also play as a defensive midfielder and had done so often for the Rams' reserve team. He played a total of 44 times for Derby (including 2 substitute appearances), scoring 5 goals, including 2 on his debut, before leaving at the end of his contract in June 1982. He finished his football career in the South West of England, first at Torquay United where he spent 2 seasons before dropping out of professional football and joining Teignmouth.

October 18th, 1980 also marked the day when the true scale Derby County's financial problems became public. The accounts to the most recent financial year end (May 31st, 1980) showed a loss of £962,745. It was an eye-watering, jaw-dropping figure. The club attempted to mask the severity of the situation by declaring that the relationship with their bank, the National Westminster – "who have been tremendous to us amid our problems, and assuming gates do not decline to disastrous levels, then we shall hold on" – said Chairman Richard Moore, followed by the worrying caveat "unless there is an unexpected change of situation". Moore went on to say that the debt could be "wiped out at a stroke" by selling the club's 2-star strikers, Alan Biley and Dave Swindlehurst, who, between them, had cost Derby more than £750,000. However, announcing what was to turn out to be a ruinous decision, Moore declared that he and the Board felt that to sell the club's 2 most valuable assets would be a mistake.

The football club, and the Board, were clinging on, more in hope than expectation. Moore was hoping for a reduction in the MIR (bank interest rates) – "even last year, bank interest cost the club more than £1,000 a week and currently it is running at £3,000 a week". Moore, a chartered accountant, had over the summer enlisted the help of Rex Stone, another with the same specialisation and qualifications, and had appointed Stone to the role of Financial Director.

Also revealed in the annual accounts were some salary details. One Derby County employee received £900 a week for the period 1st June 1979 to 31st May 1980, and eight more received over £400 a week. In addition to wages, and the fees paid for players, the club paid out almost £78,000 in compensation to former employees who left when Colin Addison and John Newman took over as manager and assistant, including the fees paid to the former clubs of the new managerial duo. There was no way of dressing things up – it was desperate stuff. Moore and his Board had gambled everything on trying to stay in the First Division, then, when that failed, they had launched into an even greater and riskier gamble to try and go straight back up at the first attempt. It was a classic case of throwing good money after bad.

Sam Longson, the President of the football club, announced that he would be stepping down from his position and would cease to be a Director on 6th November 1980 – ending an association with Derby County which began when he first joined the board, in 1955. Longson, a self-made millionaire from a farming family in Chapel-en-le-Frith, had become Chairman in the mid 1960's and had presided over two of the most significant decisions in the club's history – firstly, in 1967, he had been responsible for recruiting Brian Clough and Peter Taylor, against the wishes of some of his fellow Directors. Longson was Chairman throughout the Clough & Taylor era and accepted their resignation in 1973, following a break down in what had been a very strong relationship, before appointing Dave Mackay as their replacement – it was the most successful era in Derby's history, the club won the Football League Championship twice and reached semi-finals of the European Cup, the FA Cup and the Football League Cup, as well as winning the FA Charity Shield.

Following the resignations of Clough and Taylor, and the subsequent removal of Dave Mackay from his position (when Mackay had failed to receive the Board's vote of confidence), Longson became unpopular with many Rams supporters but had managed to retain his position of Chairman until being replaced by George Hardy in 1977. He awarded an OBE shortly before retiring as Chairman. One of the accusations regularly levelled at Longson had been that he did not invest any of his own money into the football club – he had been presided over a time when the Rams were relatively wealthy, and football clubs in general, at the top level, made healthy profits. Clough claimed that Longson had once boasted that "he had never put a penny of his own cash into Derby County". As player's wages rose from the mid 1970's onwards, football clubs soon began to see profits turn to losses – Derby County were probably amongst those affected worst by this, as they had gone from League Champions to the Second Division so quickly that they found themselves having to deal with staff wages more applicable to a club near the top of the First Division, with gates of 30,000, rather than those of a club languishing in the league below with attendances not much more than half of that figure. Longson's influence at Derby County waned when George Hardy took the Chair, and he was perhaps fortunate to have lost the top seat when he did, as the football club began its rapid decline – his autobiography "Sam's Story" (2013) is worth a read, and offers his side of the story of the catastrophic break down of relations with Brian Clough and the subsequent appointment of Dave Mackay.

The Rams drew away at Ashton Gate against Bristol City on 25th October, a poor result against a side who were languishing second bottom of the table. Biley returned to the side, replacing Wilson who dropped to the bench, and Clark (suspended for the game against QPR) returned in place of the previously ever-present Barry Powell. It could and perhaps should have been much worse – the Rams were 2-0 down with just four minutes remaining, before two moments of brilliance from Kevin Hector brought them back from the dead – first latching onto a poor back pass from Merrick and lifting the ball over the advancing goalkeeper Cashley, towards substitute Wilson who finished with a delicate chip over spread-eagled Bristol defenders, then, in injury time, cutting in from the right he wrong-footed two defenders and played a superb reverse pass to Paul Emson, who netted a fine equaliser.

Derby had been very lucky to take a point, as manager Addison admitted afterwards – they had been second best all afternoon against an equally poor Bristol City side. In fact, one piece of accidental good fortune came about when Skivington went off and with only Wilson on the bench, there was no real choice but to drop Hector back into midfield. At the back, the Rams were beginning to look very shaky – Ramage's absence through injury unsettled the defence and Keith Osgood's form had become questionable. Steve Powell, deputising alongside Osgood (with McFarland injured again), was a far better player in midfield and was struggling in the centre of defence.

The following Saturday came another game which Derby were expected to win – the visit of struggling Shrewsbury Town to the Baseball Ground. It was a crucial match, with away games at two of the top three sides (Notts County and Chelsea) to follow. The Rams were boosted by the return of Dave Swindlehurst to partner Biley in attack, and Hector took over from the injured Skivington in midfield. Youngster **Tony Reid** was selected as substitute, the first time he had appeared in a first team squad.

Tony Reid, a Nottingham born midfield player, joined Derby County as an apprentice and signed his first professional contract in May 1980 aged just 17. He was a regular with the Rams' reserves before being called into the senior squad during an injury crisis in November

1980 and had been considered an exciting prospect before suffering a nasty knee ligament injury in November 1981, whilst still only 18.

Reid had been spotted playing parks football in Nottingham for a local club called Clifton All-Whites – Derby's Chief Scout at the time, Bert Johnson, and former Rams player Peter Daniel had watched him a couple of times and they offered the then 14-year-old Reid a schoolboy contract (he was a pupil at Holgate Comprehensive, the same school attended by Steve Buckley). After a couple of trial games at Raynesway, Dario Gradi, then Assistant Manager to Colin Murphy, offered the youngster an Apprentice deal.

He made a total of 34 appearances for the Rams (including 4 as substitute), scoring 1 goal, before being transferred to Newport County in March 1983, following a loan spell at Scunthorpe United. He returned to Derbyshire in 1985, joining Chesterfield, but another serious injury forced him out of professional football after just 67 appearances for the Spireites, and he joined Stafford Rangers then Burton Albion as a part time player.

The Rams went a goal down inside two minutes against Shrewsbury but fought back and were unlucky not to score until 2 minutes into the second half, having no less than 3 efforts cleared off the line with the goalkeeper beaten, before Biley got on the end of a Swindlehurst header from a corner to rifle the ball home at the Normanton End. Instead of going on to win the game, however, Derby faded badly and in the end were fortunate to hang on to a 1-1 draw – to a backdrop of disgruntled supporters on the Osmaston Terrace giving their team a slow hand-clap, with only the sight of a stray dog wandering onto the pitch to liven them up – "that was a display which deserved every critic and every criticism it got, it's just not good enough" wrote correspondent John Wragg of Holbrook, to the Ram Newspaper.

Two daunting-looking away games, on 8th and 12th November, found the still injury-hit Rams in better form and appeared to show signs that better days could be on the way. First, at Meadow Lane, where Swindlehurst played in midfield and Wilson stood out in attack, they held second placed Notts County to a goalless draw, then, at Stamford Bridge, where defender Alan Ramage returned from injury, they crushed third placed Chelsea 3-1.

Against Chelsea, the Rams produced their best football of the season so far and their fast, attacking game was too much for the high-flying hosts. As at Notts County, Swindlehurst played in midfield and dictated the pace and direction of the game, whilst Emson and Wilson were outstanding, giving the Chelsea defence a torrid evening. Buckley was absent, and Osgood deputised at left back. Wilson opened the scoring on 37 minutes, chipping the goalkeeper after latching onto a poor back pass. Clark, on his birthday, fired home from outside the penalty area to make it 2-0 just after half time, and substitute Tony Reid, making his first appearance for the first team having replaced the injured Emson, became another to score on his debut for the Rams (and the first Derby County substitute to score on debut) when he turned in a loose ball following a corner to put the Rams 3-0 up. The only downside from the game at Stamford Bridge was a cheek bone injury to right back Steve Emery, which required an operation the following week, and meant that both regular full backs were now injured and joined Hector, McFarland and Sheridan (broken toe) on the treatment table. The win at Chelsea maintained Derby's league position of 8th, with 18 points from 16 matches (6 wins, 6 draws, 4 defeats).

Derby received some good news at the end of October 1980 when James Fryer, the Chief Constable of Derbyshire, announced that there would be no prosecutions as a result of the police investigation into Baseball Ground affairs, which had started just after Tommy Docherty's departure as manager in May 1979. The police had submitted a file on matters to the Director of Public Prosecutions, but no charges were considered appropriate. It was a relief to Chairman Richard Moore, who said that the club had cooperated fully with the Police throughout the 17-month investigation. In the interests of balance, it must be noted that the Police had stated that the enquiry was not into the affairs of Derby County as such, but Fryer did state, when refusing to reveal the name of the original informant – "although I am not prepared to reveal the original source of complaint upon which our investigation was based, I can assure that the initial report was neither spurious nor frivolous…the content of the information was such that a full inquiry was of paramount importance in the public interest and, although the Director of Prosecutions decided not to initiate any proceedings, the inquiry was fully justified"

Supporters continued to question financial matters at the football club. Some questioned why two young players had been flown to Exeter to play in a recent Testimonial match for Exeter City's groundsman Sonny Clarke, arranged by Assistant manager John Newman who had managed the club some years before (the Rams claimed that a private charter took the players, at no expense to the club), and others wondered why the Baseball Ground's floodlights were switched on for the recent home game, on a bright sunny afternoon (this time the club said that TV coverage demanded it, and ATV, who's cameras were covering the match v QPR, had picked up the bill). The consensus was that money appeared to be being wasted, whilst the football club was clearly under tremendous financial pressure – although Derby did provide answers to many of the more detailed accusations. Rumours of outgoing transfers were also rife at the end of October 1980, although a defiant Colin Addison stated "we have no intention of selling our best assets. That would be a waste of all the work since John (Newman) and I came here". Interestingly, however, Addison did not say there would be no moves – suggesting that the club would consider bids for players not considered as key assets. One player who did leave was reserve team winger Paul Bartlett, who had made 13 first team appearances under Tommy Docherty after joining the Rams as an apprentice in 1974. Bartlett's contract was cancelled by mutual consent on 31st October 1980 after he failed to secure a move to Lincoln City, following a trial period at Sincil Bank – the player had desperately wanted to move nearer to his home in Grimsby. The Rams inserted a clause into Bartlett's release form that entitled them to pick up a fee should any league club wish to sign him. David McKellar, the goalkeeper who had been discarded by

Addison and had moved to Brentford on loan early in the season, had done well enough to earn a permanent deal with the Griffin Park club and the Rams negotiated a very handy £25,000 fee.

Secretary Michael Dunford, reporting from a Football League seminar, announced that the League was considering awarding 3 points for a win rather than the current 2 (with a draw continuing to be worth 1 point). Interestingly, the initial proposal had been that only away teams would receive 3 points for an away win, with home wins staying at 2. The clearly stated purpose of this initiative was to make football more entertaining – to encourage teams to go for wins rather than settling for draws.

Another initiative discussed was that clubs should be allowed to choose their playing time between Friday nights to Saturdays and Sundays. Typically, Dunford welcomed Sunday football especially "as restricted licencing hours on Sunday would have a most beneficial effect on the hooligan element". Another benefit would be that clubs could avoid their fixtures clashing with other local clubs – at the time Derby considered that they had lost some "fringe support" to Nottingham Forest and were anxious to avoid staging home games when Forest were also playing at home. Dunford also welcomed the idea that half time could be lengthened "to allow for on-pitch entertainment". Unfortunately, the issue of television's ban on shirt advertising remained unchanged, and TV companies continued to demand that no advertising could be displayed on players' shirts during any televised match.

Kevin Hector also had some interesting opinions on potential changes to the English game, reflecting his three years playing in the North American Soccer League with Vancouver Whitecaps. Hector's ideas included the introduction of an "offside line" 25 yards from each goal, outside of which players could not be ruled offside; a change to the points system where a point per goal would be awarded up to a maximum of three (in addition to the normal match result points; goals should be made bigger "for example a foot higher and wider…the skills of goalkeepers have increased out of all recognition"; and finally, music to Michael Dunford's ears "I would like to see all-seated stadia. I believe they would help cut down a lot of the crowd behaviour problems the game suffers".

In October 1980 a local three-piece band called Syndrome released a Derby County-themed record called "We will follow you". The record retailed at Derby's Ramtique store for £1 per copy and was also sold by Derby's record shops. Commercial Executive Stuart Robinson claimed "they're going like hot cakes at the Ramtique. It's a cert as a children's stocking filler". The song, written by Mike Storer of Sinfin, received considerable air time on BBC Radio Derby, the first verse and chorus:

> *"We will follow the Rams to the end of the earth, never shirking the whole season through,*
>
> *You will crush any foe, where you happen to go. Derby County we will follow you.*

Derby County, we're behind you, and we are strong.

Derby County, we'll soon find you, back in the First Division where you belong"

The song followed the general theme which the club were only too keen to promote – "We'll be back (in the First Division) in 1981". Performances on the field did little to suggest that this would become a reality – the Rams had struggled to string together 2 good performances on the trot and looked exactly what they were in the Autumn of 1980, a mid-table second division side, which would probably have been fine were it not for the fact that the Derby County was still living, acting and spending, like a First Division club.

Derby County Promotions, who ran the club's three lottery schemes, had branched out into organising holidays. In October 1980 one such trip was arranged, this time to the Hotel Barbados in Magaluf, Majorca. Co-ordinator Ernie Hallam reported that a fun time was had by all who had engaged in competitions such as "finding the perfect woman" and "entering a room seductively". One of the prizes was a pair of Derby County briefs. In the context of Autumn 1980, it was probably what would have been described as harmless fun – Hallam certainly considered it such "let me give you my personal opinion, backed 100% by everyone on this trip, that these are really enjoyable holidays".

Derby's reserve side continued to struggle in the Central League and came in for some severe criticism in the local press following a particularly chastening 2-0 defeat at home to Bury. The reserves had suffered from losing several of their better players, Frank Sheridan, Glenn Skivington, Tony Reid and Kevin Wilson, to the first team, covering the senior side's injury crisis – but still, 6 home games, 5 defeats and no wins was not good enough. After losing to Bury, the reserves were 3rd bottom of the Central League, with 5 points from 11 matches.

At the annual Shareholders meeting in early November 1980, the atmosphere was distinctly uneasy. Chairman Richard Moore, perhaps acknowledging the true scale of the Rams' financial problems publicly for the first time, announced that the club "may have to sell (players), but only as a last resort" (At the time, Everton were reported to have revived their interest in striker Alan Biley). Moore also adjusted the "break even" gate figure upwards to 23,000 to 24,000 but claimed that Derby's gates were holding up remarkably given the current state of English football. Bank interest charges were running at £3,000 a week but he hoped the bank would continue to support the club with existing overdraft arrangements. Moore, increasingly clutching at straws, claimed that it was difficult to forecast cash flow because "a good run in the FA Cup this season would help to ease the problem". In more positive news, Moore announced that despite a deficit of more than £1m during the previous financial year, the club had made a surplus of approximately £500,000 in transfer dealings since the end of that period (since June 1980). Instalments of fees due on players previously signed were biting (this was the era of player transfer fees being paid in instalments over the length of the player's contract) – whilst the Rams were also due some instalments from other clubs, but the deficit on this was about £800,000. In his final statement, Moore summed up the club's plight – "The Board will do everything in its power to get the finances right, but there could be no guarantee that the clubs bankers might not, at some time, call for their money" – it was the first open suggestion and admission that Derby County were by now operating under the control of their bankers.

The financial fall of Derby had been astonishing in both speed and scale. As late as 1976, just 4 years previously, the club were competing in European football, season ticket sales had brought in half a million pounds, and there was a surplus of £200,000 on deposit with the bank. There were also no less than ten International players on the books.

A tribute was paid, by one shareholder, to Stuart Webb, the former club secretary who had resigned during the Police inquiry into club affairs, some weeks after being suspended from duty by the Board. Webb, who was present at the annual meeting, received the tribute with thanks. The Chairman, Mr Moore, made no comment. Mr Webb had been busy masterminding the promotion of a pop record called "You can't win 'em all" by disco artist JJ Bardie, featuring the spoken voice of Brian Clough making an anti-football hooligan statement. Clough appeared on the Michael Parkinson TV chat show to promote the record – "I know nothing about the pop record business, but I'm assured by the experts that this will be a winner. I hope so, for football's sake". The record flopped.

In another heated exchange, the news of Sam Longson's retirement from the Board – which had led to a letter of congratulation "for what you have done, and continue to do for football", from Football Association Chairman Sir Harold Thompson – was greeted with a mixture of appreciation and, at the other extreme, one shareholder, Colin Lawrence, demanding to disassociate himself from any tribute to Longson. The embers of the fires lit following Brian Clough's resignation in 1973, and the subsequent protest movement, still lingered on.

A few of the shareholders expressed disappointment that the Board had refused to sanction from their own pockets the sum £50,000 to sign a player wanted by Addison, to which the Chairman replied that Director's guarantees at the bank already exceeded that amount. The same group of disillusioned shareholders shouted "Rubbish!" at Addison when he said that he fielded what he considered to be his strongest team on any day, and catcalled Director Bob Mulholland's plea for unity (Mulholland, as Longson's son-in-law, was never likely to be accepted by everyone).

The Rams had the opportunity to avenge their dismal 3-0 defeat on the opening day of the season, when Cambridge United visited the Baseball Ground on 15th November. What transpired, however, was a carbon-copy of the Abbey Stadium humiliation, with Derby going down 3-0 again and seemingly hitting a new low. The attendance, 15,179, was the lowest of the season so far. Manager Addison had been forced into several changes – with both regular full backs injured (and reserve right back Wayne Richards also unfit), Skivington and

Osgood filled in at right and left back respectively. Steve Powell and Alan Ramage, paired at centre back, endured a nightmare afternoon. Swindlehurst, Clark and Barry Powell were largely bypassed in midfield as the visitors' direct game was simply too much for the Rams to cope with. Emson, who had been injured in the previous match at Chelsea, was replaced on the left wing by reserve forward **John Clayton**.

John Clayton, born in Elgin in 1961, had played for Scotland Schoolboys and joined Derby as an apprentice aged 17, after completing his A Levels. He had been spotted playing for Elgin City in the Scottish Highland League. Clayton was a regular scorer for the reserves after signing his first professional contract for Tommy Docherty in December 1978. He never established himself in the first team at Derby and made just 27 appearances including 4 as substitute, scoring 4 goals before leaving to join Hong Kong club Bulova in August 1982, as part of the deal in which Barry Powell made the same move.

Clayton returned to England a year later and joined Chesterfield, then had his most successful spell in professional football at Tranmere Rovers, for whom he scored 36 goals in the 1984-85 season. From Tranmere he moved for £24,000 to Plymouth Argyle, and was also a success there – helping them to promotion from Division Three, along with Derby, in 1985-86. He continued his good goalscoring record in Holland, with Fortuna Sittard (after being transferred for a fee of £64,000), then FC Volendam before having his career ended in the early 1990's by a persistent back injury. After retiring as a player, he became a highly respected youth coach and worked at Bristol City's Academy for 17 years before taking up a Youth Development role with the Football League in 2012.

It was perhaps a shame that Clayton's career at Derby spanned such an unsuccessful period because he was most certainly a natural goal scorer and could well have flourished, had he been given a regular run in the first team.

After the humiliating home defeat to Cambridge United, the Rams travelled to Eastville to face Bristol Rovers who were, like their City rivals, languishing at the bottom of the league. Manager Addison was able to recall Emson, who replaced Clayton, but Hector, McFarland, Buckley and Emery were still out. The result was once again disappointing, a 1-1 draw with Emson getting Derby's goal.

The following Wednesday, top of the league West Ham United were the visitors to the Baseball Ground. A good crowd for a midweek game, 18,446, saw Derby score an upset 2-0 win. Roy McFarland returned from injury to replace Osgood, and Wayne Richards, another who had been out injured, came in at left back in place of Skivington. The Hammers brought a strong side, including Alvin Martin, Billy Bonds, Frank Lampard (senior, the father of future Rams manager Frank junior), Trevor Brooking and future Derby forward Paul Goddard –and were well fancied to beat the struggling Rams. The players ran out of the tunnel on a red carpet, specially laid by match sponsors Fern Carpets, who's boss (and Rams supporter) Fred Fern said afterwards "it worked, didn't it".

West Ham played most of the football and caught the eye with their intricate play and flowing moves, while Derby adopted a more direct and robust style of play, often bypassing the midfield with long balls, but the Rams were resilient and dug in with McFarland impressing and Alan Ramage having an excellent game. Roger Jones, solid as ever, dealt manfully in goal with everything the Hammers threw at him.

When Derby did attack it was often Paul Emson who caused West Ham the most problems, whilst Kevin Wilson once again impressed with his constant harassing of Hammers defenders and it was his skilful turn to evade 3 defenders which freed Barry Powell to slide the ball on to Jonathan Clark who crashed in a fine left foot shot to secure the points, 2 minutes from the end. The Rams had led since the 18th minute when Alan Biley, putting in his best performance of the season so far in his 200th Football League appearance, rose magnificently to head Emson's cross past goalkeeper Phil Parkes, it was Biley's 89th league goal of his career.

It was another example of the Rams seemingly raising their standards for perceived bigger matches, as they had against Chelsea, and to some supporters it suggested that some of the Derby players were not interested in doing the hard work required in the less well exposed and glamourous of their second division games.

Derby's reserve team finally won a home game, for the first time this season, when they beat Manchester City reserves 2-1 on 22nd November. Roy McFarland featured as part of his comeback from injury, as did Steve Carter, a previous first team regular who had been out for over a year. Goals from Steve Spooner (another who was on the comeback trail after injury) and John Clayton helped the 3rd from bottom Rams to a surprising win against City, who were 2nd in the Central League. McFarland was only selected at the last minute – due to play in the centre of defence was 15-year-old schoolboy Paul Blades, who had been playing Midland Intermediate level football with the Rams' youth team against players 2 or 3 years older than himself and had taken it in his stride. It was clear, even at such a young age, that Blades was set for a good career in football.

The Rams' injury problems were so bad that Gordon Guthrie, the trainer-physio and the man responsible for treating the sick and injured, was too busy to formulate plans for the Testimonial he had been granted by the club. Guthrie, who first joined Derby as a player when Harry Storer was the manager but never played in the first team, joined the back-room staff in the early 1960's under Storer's successor Tim Ward. By 1980, the Rams had suffered an almost non-stop injury crisis for 4 years and Guthrie had been in the middle of it, working non-stop to patch players up and get them back out onto the pitch. Secretary Michael Dunford said of the situation "we are aware of Gordon's problems (with arranging his Testimonial) and we shall help him with all the necessary preliminaries as soon as Christmas is over…he is the sort of unsung hero who really does deserve the backing of our supporters so that he can build up a nest-egg which his loyal and wonderful service has earned him"

Two players had been so dogged by injury that they were almost forgotten about. Winger Steve Carter had not played for the first team since September 1979, and forward John Duncan, who had signed from Tottenham Hotspur for a big fee in the September 1978, had managed only 36 games for the Rams in more than 2 years. Carter was making tentative steps back to fitness, and had recently appeared for the reserves, but the unfortunate Duncan, who was contracted until the end of the 1980-81 season, found himself back on the operating table in December 1980 after breaking down in a comeback attempt for the Rams "A" team – and the long term prognosis on him was not looking good. Whilst Carter had never looked much of a player in his time at Derby, a fully fit John Duncan would undoubtedly have boosted Colin Addison's Rams, and would perhaps of rendered the signing of Dave Swindlehurst unnecessary – Duncan had been a fine player, one of the best strikers in British football with a record of a goal every 2 games, before injuries had ruined his career.

What Derby's seemingly incessant injury problems had created was the need, or opportunity, for young players to get their chances. The Rams had one of the youngest squads in any of the 4 divisions with 5 teenagers appearing in the first team (Wayne Richards, Kevin Wilson, Glenn Skivington, Frank Sheridan and Tony Reid) alongside Paul Emson, Alan Biley, Alan Ramage, Dave Swindlehurst and Steve Emery, all of whom were still in their early 20's. The Rams' Youth Coach Ron Webster was also excited about several other players who were yet to make the first team – Aiden Gibson, a left winger and still an apprentice, was highly thought-of, as were Kevin Murray, Barney Bowers and Yaka Banovic, who had all stood out in the reserves.

At an even younger level, Derby's Youth team had done very well to beat a much older and more experienced Lincoln City side 5-2 away in the 1st round of the FA Youth Cup – the Rams side featured 4 players who were still only 15 and four more who were 16, well below the typical age of players in the youth competition. The victory at Lincoln was particularly sweet for Derby's Youth Development Officer Geoff Worth, who had been at Sincil Bank as Youth and then Reserve Coach before leaving to join Derby when the former Rams Manager Colin Murphy took over as boss. Lincoln started the game well and a string of fine saves from Rams goalkeeper Robert Palmer kept them in the match, and gradually central midfielders Tony Reid and David King got to grips with the conditions and began to dictate the play. Dalziel opened the scoring from the penalty spot after 25 minutes, then in the second half King scored the goal of the game to put Derby 2 up after a mazy dribble followed by a fine finish. The other Rams goals came from Reid and 2 from Halford. The win set the Rams youngsters up for another away game in the 2nd round, this time at Chester City. Rams Youth: Palmer; McCormick, Blades, Dalziel, Harbey; King, Reid, Bird, Gibson; Shackleton, Halford; substitute Doyle.

The Baseball Ground attendance dropped to 15,581 for the visit of Cardiff City, on 29th November 1980 – largely reflecting the lack of away support compared to the numbers who had travelled with West Ham the previous Wednesday evening. Once again, Derby were unable to win a game they should have been more than capable of winning – the result was another draw, this time 1-1 with Kevin Wilson scoring the Rams' goal, a fine, instinctive finish from what was only a half-chance, to send them a goal ahead before a comical own goal gifted Cardiff an equaliser. McFarland and Richards continued at full back, with Steve Powell and Ramage partnering in central defence, and Osgood on the bench. On balance, the Welsh side probably deserved to win the game, missing at least 2 good chances, with Derby failing to show anything like the style they had shown just 3 days earlier against West Ham. Supporters took offence to Barry Powell's lacklustre display – jeering him for most of the match before clapping and cheering when he was eventually replaced by substitute Keith Osgood after 68 miserable minutes. After the game, manager Addison defended Powell, stating that he had played "unknown to us, with a 100 plus temperature". Powell also received support from Nottingham Forest skipper and former Derby player John McGovern, who wrote a letter of support to the struggling Rams midfielder with the general theme "don't let them get you down" – McGovern had experienced similar issues with some of the Derby crowd in the early 1970's, and had felt moved to write sympathetically to Barry Powell, who he did not know personally.

Barry Powell had a dismal time at Derby County. An attacking central midfielder who clearly required a ball-winner alongside him, the Rams were never able, due to injuries, to field a combination that suited Powell's strengths – Steve Powell was an ideal midfield partner but Steve, when not injured himself, was most often called upon to deputise for injured defenders either at right back or centre back. In his better days, at Wolves and Coventry City, Powell had starred alongside natural ball-winners such as Mike Bailey and Terry Yorath, both of whom were happy to do the "donkey work" allowing him to get forward without worrying too much about what was going on behind him. In addition to this, Powell had found it difficult to settle at the club as he had been unable to find a house in the local area and had been commuting from Warwickshire every day – it was not until over a year after joining Derby that he and his wife Hazel eventually moved in to a house in Derby. For a player who had played four times for England Under 23's and had won a League Cup winners medal in 1974, Powell's time at Derby was a career lowlight, and nobody was more pleased than the player himself when he left to join Bulova in Hong Kong, in August 1982, with the Rams no longer able to afford his wages.

The following Saturday, 6th December, in front of just 6,120 spectators on a freezing cold afternoon, Derby won 3-0 at Deepdale, against Preston North End. Kevin Hector returned from injury, in place of Wilson, and youngster Tony Reid, by now an England Youth International, came in for the injured Barry Powell. It was another dreadfully poor game and one in which the Rams once again decided that more direct balls into the opposition box, and less touches of the ball, was the way to win games at Second Division level. Manager Addison, defiant after the game, following complaints (from both the press and Derby supporters) about a lack of quality and a lack of entertainment value, said "I want results first and foremost...this division is all about long balls and chasing. Trying to play football can get you into trouble, as we have already found out to our cost. Never pass the ball twice to get where you want it when one will do, that's the secret". The game was most notable for Kevin Hector's opening of the scoring, arriving late at the far post to turn in an Alan Biley cross for his first goal since returning to the club. Swindlehurst made it 2-0 before Biley completed the scoring just before the end of the game.

After beating Preston, Derby stood 5th in the Second Division table with 24 points from 21 matches – 7 behind top of the table West Ham and 4 behind Notts County, in the 3rd and final promotion position. Despite hardly playing well at all, and having a poor record at the Baseball Ground, the Rams somehow remained in contention near the top – and had lost only once in the previous 10 matches. Derby's erratic form was highlighted by the fact that they had taken 7 out of 8 points at stake against top 3 sides so far, and only the 2 Bristol clubs, at the bottom of the table, had a worse home record, yet only second placed Chelsea had a better away record – statistics which reflected the players' frequent protestations about crowd negativity at the Baseball Ground, several stating that they feared running out for home matches and preferred to play in away games.

Kevin Hector equalled the Rams' all-time appearance record (535, held at the time by Derby's youth coach Ron Webster, and, before him by Steve Bloomer), and scored his first goal at the Baseball Ground since returning to the club (his 194th in total), in another drawn home game, this time 1-1 against Watford on 13th December. Hector, who had cost the Rams £40,000 in 1966, had played under 6 different managers at Derby and had been ruthlessly and perhaps prematurely cast-aside by Tommy Docherty in January 1978, before Addison brought him back to the club. Watford, managed by future England boss Graham Taylor, who were struggling near the bottom of the table and with an awful away record, having picked up only 1 point from 9 away games before their draw at the Baseball Ground, featured future Rams player, 18-year-old winger Nigel Callaghan in their side. Future Derby goalkeeper was also listed in the Watford side but was left out at the last minute in favour of Steve Sherwood.

Hector gave Derby the perfect start after just 2 minutes – Biley's fine cross from the right was headed down by Swindlehurst, and Hector, rolling back the years, dashed into space to turn the ball into the net. After that, the two sides both showed some decent football in what was an entertaining game, a draw was perhaps the fair result with Watford equalising 7 minutes from time through Luther Blissett. For Derby, the game was marred by a hamstring injury to Roy McFarland early in the second half, forcing a formation change with substitute Kevin Wilson coming on to play in midfield, and Jonathan Clark moving to right back, changes which disrupted the Rams' rhythm.

The attendance at the Baseball Ground for the game against Watford was 16,484 which, while it might have been less than half of what the Rams could have expected 10 years previously, was in fact quite remarkable considering the way attendances in English football had fallen in recent years. On the same day, for example, the First Division game between Coventry City and West Bromwich Albion drew just 16,027, and Crystal Palace (15,257 v Norwich City), and Leicester City (13,998 v Middlesbrough) fared even worse. Attendances in the second division had fallen to unprecedented levels – only 9 of the 22 clubs in that league averaged over 10,000. Derby's average, at the time 17,195, made them the 3rd best supported club in the division behind league leaders West Ham (24,997) and 3rd placed Chelsea (19,890).

The return game against West Ham United, on the Saturday before Christmas, presented the Hammers with the chance to avenge their loss to Derby from just a few weeks previous. McFarland had picked up another injury, in the previous game, so Keith Osgood took over in defence. Also returning, this time from a lengthy injury, was right back Steve Emery. This time round West Ham's attractive flowing football won the day and they eventually ran out 3-1 winners in a very entertaining and high-quality game, with future Rams striker Paul Goddard on the scoresheet. Derby went ahead just before half time, Swindlehurst converting a penalty after Hector had accelerated into the box and been hauled down, only for the Hammers, who looked every inch a First Division side in waiting, to equalise 2 minutes later.

The game ebbed and flowed at 1-1 until the 78th minute when a superb goal, crafted by Trevor Brooking's 20-yard dribble and Goddard's fine finish, put the home side ahead. West Ham added a 3rd just 2 minutes from full time when Brooking, a class ahead of others on the field, scored himself with a stunning left foot shot. 3-1 was perhaps unfair on the Rams, who had given a very good account of themselves against a fine side – indeed Alan Hoby, writing in the Sunday Express, said "on this showing Derby are a danger to all the top teams in the division".

Rams fans visiting Upton Park that afternoon, of whom there were only around 200, did not experience much in the way of seasonal goodwill from the home supporters. After being directed to an area marked "Visitors Enclosure" they found themselves emerging right in the middle of a home section of terracing. After some rough treatment they were moved by Stewards into what was actually the designated visitor area but were once again outnumbered 10 to 1 by West Ham fans, several of who set about the Derby supporters – "one maniac in front of us was punching one of our friends", said A.B. and D.W of Alfreton (names withheld from Ram Newspaper publication) – "the police took no notice all game and when the game finished we were forced to stay in our places until 4.55 even though we wanted to leave 5 minutes before the end to avoid trouble…(it was) an experience we won't forget. We won't return there".

A storm was brewing via the pages of Ram Newspaper, following the resident terrace correspondent Bill X's comments in a previous edition in which he stated that Derby's seated followers are "spectators" and terrace followers are "supporters". This arose from the booing and jeering of Barry Powell during the Cardiff City game at the Baseball Ground, which Bill X asserted primarily originated from the seated areas of the stadium. Correspondents to the Ram Newspaper, including John M Pepper of Kilburn - "(his comments are) immature, offensive and Ill-considered", Ronald K Starkey of Derby - "a great club is spoiled when Bill X is allowed to hit out at seated fans, most of whom started on the terrace" and I F Burns "how on earth can it be deduced that a person who sits in the stands is less of a supporter than a man on the terraces", were typical of the fiery responses to the latest column by the controversial Bill X (described by Ram Newspaper as a terrace-ite in his early 20's and a Rams fanatic who never misses a game home or away).

In the autumn of 1980, 16-year-old Colyn Doyle became the first black player to sign for Derby County. An attacking midfielder, Doyle had performed well for the Rams' "A" team and Youth Development Officer Geoff Worth commented of Doyle "we are working on his ball control and telling him to show more aggression…when he does that he can look forward to a possible good career in the game".

An experienced Rams Reserves side hit form on December 16th with a thumping 5-0 home win over Bolton Wanderers in the Central League. First team squad members Steve Emery and Glenn Skivington (making their way back from injury), Barry Powell (looking to recover some form), Keith Osgood, Tony Reid, Kevin Wilson and John Clayton all played, and Derby's goals were scored by Wilson (2), Reid and Clayton, plus an own goal. The Rams reserves improved their league position to 17th with their victory.

On Boxing Day, the Rams thumped a battling, aggressive Oldham Athletic side 4-1 in front of just under 17,000 at the Baseball Ground (a good crowd considering that the visitors brought with them well under 50 supporters). Biley and Swindlehurst both scored twice as the Rams roared back from a goal down, with Kevin Hector pulling the strings from midfield and Paul Emson, having perhaps his best game so far, giving Oldham's right back a torrid afternoon and providing excellent service for the strikers, who certainly made the most of it. Biley's first goal, to equalise, was a delicate chip over the goalkeeper at the Osmaston End, then the same player soon put the Rams ahead with a thumping header from Emson's accurate cross. In the second half it was Swindlehurst's turn as he first cracked in a volley after good work by Emery, then made the score 4-1 after beating the Oldham offside trap and rounding the goalkeeper before theatrically cracking the ball left-footed into the empty net. It was perhaps the best Baseball Ground display of the season so far.

The Rams said goodbye to 1980 with a game at Newcastle United on Saturday 27th December and came away from St James' Park with a good 2-0 victory. Newcastle's team featured future England star Chris Waddle, and future Derby forward Mick Harford. Derby took the lead through a comical own goal by Stuart Boam, who headed a ball intended for the goalkeeper Kevin Carr directly into his own net after just 90 seconds. Derby then completely dominated the first half and added to their lead through one of Roy McFarland's finest goals for the club. McFarland, who somewhat surprisingly was playing his second game in 24 hours, ran at the retreating Newcastle defence from the half way line, flicked a pass to Steve Powell at the edge of the penalty area then received a perfect return pass and continued his run to slide the ball between 2 defenders and past the onrushing goalkeeper. It was a comfortable victory for the Rams, who had achieved 4 points in 2 days and finished the year, on the field at least, on something of a high. Newcastle's fans showed their disappointment after the game by damaging the Derby team's coach – "perhaps our crime is to have the most exclusive coach in the business…but isn't it a classic example of the mindless morons who still haunt our game from the fringes", said club secretary Michael Dunford.

The Rams' injury problems were showing signs of easing – only left back Steve Buckley and long-term casualty John Duncan remained injured and the management had the luxury of selecting the same side for the games on 26th and 27th December – it was no coincidence that Derby had won both games. What Addison would have hoped was a coincidence, however, was the fact that he himself was now absent – having suffered a nasty bout of shingles, which had confined him to his home since Christmas and forced him to miss both festive victories. Assistant manager John Newman took over team affairs in Addison's absence.

Derby's line up for the final game of the year was: Jones; Emery, Ramage, McFarland, Richards; S.Powell, Clark, Hector, Emson; Biley, Swindlehurst (6 of whom had been signed by the current manager).

Derby's full record for the calendar year 1980

Played 47, won 15, drew 14, lost 18

First Team Squad at the end of the year (appearances for the club in brackets): Hector (537), McFarland (511), Powell S (274), Buckley (127), Clark (54), Emson (52), Osgood (52), Emery (48), Powell B (44), Biley (43), Swindlehurst (36), Carter (34), Duncan (34), Jones (27), Ramage (20), Wilson (11), Skivington (9), Richards (7), Cherry (4), Sheridan (3), Clayton (2), Reid (2), Spooner (1), Banovic (0)

Chapter 1.3 - 1981

On January 3rd, 1981, Derby faced Bristol City in the 3rd round of the FA Cup. It was the 100th time the FA Challenge Cup (to give its full title) had been contested. The first final, in 1871, had taken place at The Oval in London and Wanderers had beaten Royal Engineers in a match between 2 amateur sides. The Rams had won the competition once, in 1946 - captained by Jack Nicholas, when the earlier rounds were played over two-legs for the first and only time – the FA decided to implement this two-legged system for what was the resumption of regular football after World War 2 in response to huge demand from people desperate to watch the games. In fact, Derby's opponents in the 1946 final, Charlton Athletic, had the unique distinction of being the only club to lose an FA Cup match yet still reach the final (they had lost their away leg to Fulham in the fifth round, but won the tie on aggregate). The FA Cup, after 99 years, had been won by 40 different clubs, of which 7 were no longer in existence.

It's often said that Derby have a poor FA Cup record but in fact, in the first 99 years of the competition, only 6 teams could better the Rams' 13 FA Cup Semi Final appearances (Everton and West Bromwich Albion with 18 each led the way). What was undoubtedly poor was the Rams' record after reaching the last 4 stage – they had won just 4 out of 13 semi-final ties, the most recent loss being a painful defeat by Manchester United at Hillsborough in 1976, a game often attributed to be the end of the good days for Derby County.

Bristol City, who had thrashed a dreadful Rams side 6-2 at Ashton Gate at the same stage of the competition just a year before, were struggling in the second division, and looked well set to be relegated for a second time in consecutive seasons, although they had started to improve in recent weeks under new manager Bobby Houghton. Of the Rams side from the previous season, 5 were no longer with the club (McKellar, Daly, Greenwood, Davies and Moreland). This time, Derby selected an unchanged side for the 3rd successive game (although manager Addison remained absent through his bout of shingles – and he praised his assistant John Newman – "he's a tower of strength and it made me feel better just to have him visit me after the match for an hour, to hear his verdict"), and the result was a goalless draw. Derby had the better chances against a tough, hard-working and very well organised Bristol City side whose goalkeeper John Shaw had an excellent afternoon. Hector, clean through on goal, missed the easiest of the chances as his attempted chip hit the keeper and ran wide, but Biley must also have wondered how he missed an open goal after a rare fumble by Shaw – the Rams striker fired high and wide over an open net. A good crowd, over 19,000, turned up for the FA Cup tie.

In the replay the following Wednesday, Derby's form completely deserted them, and they deservedly lost 2-0. The Rams team was unsettled by the loss of McFarland with more hamstring trouble, and Emson was also injured – Osgood and Reid deputised. City's goals, either side of half time, were no more than they deserved. For the second successive season, Derby had let themselves down in the FA Cup at Ashton Gate.

19-year-old Wayne Richards, who had stepped in at left back to replace the injured Steve Buckley, played his 9th successive game in the FA Cup replay. He had been improving on a game by game basis and showed considerable promise. Richards had been spotted playing for his father Alan's works football team in Scunthorpe in 1977, while still at school, by Rams scout Ernie Roberts. He had also been invited for trials by both Liverpool and local club Scunthorpe United but had opted for Derby who were, at the time, still one of the top clubs in English football. A keen golfer, with a handicap of 16, Richards was asked which of his fellow Rams reserve teamers he rated most highly and named Aiden Gibson "a very young fast winger in the Paul Emson mould", Frank Sheridan, Steve Spooner and John Clayton (who had already played in the first team), plus midfielder Robert "Barney" Bowers.

Belfast-born Barney Bowers was spotted by Tommy Docherty's scouts while playing for Cliftonville in Northern Ireland and the Rams had been so keen that they had paid £25,000 for his services in 1978, when the player was 18 years old. Highly rated as an energetic and all-action midfield player at reserve level, but never considered ready for the first team at Derby, he stayed at the Baseball Ground until his contract expired in 1981 without making a single appearance at senior level, at which time he returned to Northern Ireland to sign for Glentoran (turning down an offer to stay in English football, from Swindon Town). Bowers made well over 500 appearances for Glentoran, becoming one of the most popular players in the club's history, and stayed until 1995 before finishing his career with Ards in 1997. He made 1 appearance for an Irish League representative team, in 1989.

Aiden Gibson, from Newcastle-Under-Lyme, earned rave reviews as a teenager and had signed apprentice forms with Derby County in May 1980, after the Rams had moved quickly to secure his services ahead of both Leicester City and Stoke City, for whom he also had trials. Gibson was a very fast and tricky left winger and a player about whom the Rams had very high hopes. In fact Gibson was almost lost to football as a schoolboy when he went to a Grammar school which only played rugby, and the then 11 year old was nominated for County trials in that sport – fortunately for the Rams, he moved to another school and was soon recommended by a family friend to Geoff Worth at Derby, who had offered apprentice terms after half a dozen trial matches.

Steve Spooner, a central midfield player from Sutton in Surrey, joined Derby County in 1978 at the age of 17 and had appeared twice in the First Division for the Rams, co-incidentally both times against Tottenham Hotspur at White Hart Lane (in March and October 1979). He had fallen behind other young midfielders in the pecking order at the Baseball Ground (most notably Frank Sheridan, Glenn Skivington and Tony Reid), and did not make a single further first team appearance until the end of the 1980-81 season. Despite never really making the grade at Derby, he went on to play over 450 professional games in a long career in the lower leagues.

Club Secretary Michael Dunford ran a survey in the Ram Newspaper in the winter of 1980. Among the more interesting questions and responses were that most Derby supporters (over 80%) did not want the Baseball Ground to become all-seated, and 99% of respondents did not want to see football on Sundays – it was interesting that Dunford himself held the opposing view in both instances. Another of Dunford's regular objections, the continuing ban on shirt advertising, came back into focus when the Rams had worn plain shirts without the "Fly British Midland" sponsor logos for their visit to Upton Park just before Christmas – the Rams had been informed that London Weekend Television were to televise highlights of the game and the players were therefore forbidden under league rules to wear their sponsored shirts. In the event, London Weekend decided against televising the match and the Rams could in fact have worn their sponsored kit – but they had neglected to pack it. Dunford was not amused and was forced to apologise to British Midland – "in future, whatever the circumstances, (the sponsored kit) will always be in the first team luggage skip". Dunford might well have referred to the fact that up until the home game against Grimsby Town on 7th February, Derby had failed to win a single game in which they had played in plain shirts without the sponsor's logo – the 9 games without sponsored shirts (because they were being covered by TV), had produced a miserable 6 points.

The Rams youngsters were making progress in the FA Youth Cup – seeing off Chester City 3-2 at Sealand Road, to reach the last 16. They had also found some form in the Midland Intermediate League with a fine 3-2 win at Raynesway over a far more experienced Aston Villa side. Most of the side was made up of first year apprentice professionals recruited by Geoff Worth after his arrival in the autumn of 1979 – when Worth arrived at the club, he had professed himself shocked and dismayed at the paucity of talent available, the youth policy of the club having been virtually non-existent since Tim Ward's time as manager 13 years previously. Youth coach Ron Webster, speaking about his young side's cup run, said "they will be in at the deep end from now on. Among the last 16 are many First Division clubs who have long-established youth set-ups and older and more experienced sides…but there will surely be no better player in the competition than the elegant Tony Reid, who was the architect of the win at Chester and was head and shoulders the best player on the field showing vision, ball-sense, positioning and distribution well in advance of his years". Also receiving praise from Webster was 17-year-old second year apprentice striker Paul Halford, who scored 2 goals at Chester – the first was especially good, from a move started by 16-year-old full back Graham Harbey "who has infinite promise" and continued by a pinpoint cross from Dave King for Halford to head home. Reid scored the other Rams goal, another header. Rams Youth: Palmer; McCormack, Harbey, Reid, Blades, Dalziel; King, Halford, Shackleton, Bird, Gibson and the substitute Doyle (replaced Gibson, 82 minutes).

Bottom of the table Bristol Rovers, with former Leeds United and England star Terry Cooper doubling-up as player-manager, were the Baseball Ground opponents for the first league game of 1981, on Saturday 10th January. Rovers, who included former Derby player Aiden McCaffrey at centre back, already looked doomed to relegation, 8 points adrift of safety and with just 1 win all season. Barry Powell returned to the Rams side (replacing Kevin Hector) for the first time since he had been booed off the field in the game against Cardiff City 6 weeks earlier. Making a more welcome return was left back Steve Buckley, in the side for the first time since the goalless draw against Notts County on 8th November.

There could be no excuses, the Rams had to win, and they did, 2-1 – having been given a perfect start by Rovers full back Don Gillies, who, under pressure from Alan Biley, turned Paul Emson's cross into his own net after just 90 seconds, Emson's 65-yard dribble and drilled cross was one of the few moments of quality in the game. The game descended into an error-strewn affair with little in the way of entertainment, and Bob Lee equalised just after half time. Cooper, the oldest player on the field, and Tony Reid, the youngest, were the game's best players and the Rams eventually won the game with a comically scrappy goal claimed by Biley (his 100th goal in professional football), after a scramble in the Rovers 6-yard box at the Osmaston End. Just 15,015 watched the game, which had been among the poorest matches seen at the Baseball Ground for many years. The victory took the Rams up 2 places to 4th in the Second division table, with 31 points, just 1 point below Swansea and Notts County in 2nd and 3rd place respectively.

The Rams had been due to face Bolton Wanderers at Burnden Park on the following Saturday, but the referee called the game off on the Saturday morning due to bad weather (not before several supporter's coaches had already left for Bolton) - but with both sides out of the FA Cup the game was rearranged for FA Cup 4th round day, Saturday 24th January. Hector returned to the side at the expense of Reid, but both Swindlehurst and Ramage were suspended, with Kevin Wilson and Keith Osgood deputising.

Once again, Derby made the perfect start – Steve Buckley's powerful 2nd minute free kick was fumbled by Bolton goalkeeper Peacock, and Wilson picked up the loose ball to put the Rams 1 up. Derby, who dominated possession after their goal, were then the victims of a poor mistake by referee Colin Seel of Carlisle – Bolton striker Alan Gowling controlled a long pass with his arm before sliding the ball into the Rams net, as Derby's players, including goalkeeper Roger Jones, stood still anticipating the referee's whistle – the whistle never came and the goal stood, and Derby's alarming lack of professionalism had cost them the lead. In the following few minutes, the Rams lost control completely and 3 players went into the book (Hector and Biley for dissent and McFarland for a blatant and unnecessary foul). Bolton went 2-1 up after 35 minutes and despite Derby controlling long periods of the second half and missing several good chances, the home side confirmed their win with a third goal 3 minutes from time. After the game manager Colin Addison fined Hector and Biley for their part in the post-goal fracas.

A week later the Rams closed out January 1981 with a 2-2 home draw against Luton Town. Osgood and McFarland continued in the centre of defence, flanked by Emery and Buckley, with Steve Powell playing a defensive midfield role behind Barry Powell, Hector and Emson, Biley and Wilson continued in attack – Ramage and Swindlehurst were both suspended. Before kick-off club captain Roy McFarland was presented with a cheque for £100 by representatives from football magazine Match Weekly, in recognition of his being voted by its readers as Second Division player of the month for December. 16,479 attended, which represented a good improvement of almost 1,500 since the previous home game – they were rewarded with an entertaining game in which both sides preferred attack over defence, the highlights of which were televised that evening on BBC's Match of the Day programme – commentator John Motson describing the game as "the sort of stuff to pull back the crowds to football". Derby manager Colin Addison, who had been absent since Christmas, was present for his first live game since recovering from his Christmas bout of shingles.

Derby's first strike, after 8 minutes, was a contender for goal of the month – Luton's Paul Price only half-cleared Roy McFarland's free kick and the ball looped to Kevin Wilson who scored with a spectacular overhead kick which looped over goalkeeper Jake Findlay. Luton equalized when a shot took a wicked deflection of the unfortunate Steve Emery, then went a goal ahead after 56 minutes after a mistake by Keith Osgood let in winger David Moss, who squared for Ingram to score with a simple finish, although Rams goalkeeper Roger Jones was perhaps slightly slow to react. The game was far from over, however, and the Rams equalised when Alan Biley's cross from the right wing was met by the head of Kevin Hector, climbing above the much taller Price to score from just outside the far post.

The Rams dropped to 6th in what was becoming a very tight race for promotion at the top of the second division – just 4 points separated Notts County (in 2nd place) and Cambridge United (in 11th), and with West Ham already looking home and dry at the top (9 points ahead of the Rams), it had become a race for 2 places. Derby's problem was their goals against – they had conceded a shocking 38 goals in 28 games, more than any other side outside the bottom 4 (and indeed 4 more than 2nd bottom Bristol City). There was no issue in the other half of the pitch, the Rams were amongst the leading scorers in the entire Football League. Derby had been unfortunate with injuries to defenders, that could not be denied – McFarland, Ramage, Buckley and Emery had all spent considerable time injured, but even allowing for that, questions could legitimately be asked about defensive structure, balance and organisation – and to rely on McFarland at this stage of his career was a decidedly risky gamble, he was a player who struggled with injury for the previous 7 years, unfortunately.

Roy McFarland was still incredibly popular with most Derby fans, and most acknowledged that if he stayed fit, and stayed out of trouble with referees, the Rams would be contenders for promotion from the second division. Indiscipline, as well as injury, had become an issue – McFarland had been booked in the fracas following Alan Gowling's controversial goal at Burnden Park and he was closing in on 20 disciplinary points, at which point he would be suspended for 2 or possibly 3 matches. His value to the team, when on the pitch, could not be overstated – twice he had hobbled off injured, at Swansea City and in the home game against Watford, and both times the Rams' players' performance levels had nose-dived as their skipper departed. He was an inspirational leader, as well as, when fit, still one of the finest central defenders in the Country. There were other statistics which highlighted McFarland's vital importance to the team – Derby had not lost a single one of the 13 matches he had played in at the Baseball Ground since returning from his last major injury in February 1980, and since he had returned to the side from a more recent injury, for the home game against West Ham, the Rams had only lost 2 games until the fiasco at Bolton – and those were the 2 games McFarland had missed during that run.

Supporters were concerned that the team was over-reliant on the captain, Mr P Chatfield of Uttoxeter, writing to the Ram Newspaper, summed the situation up nicely – "What a difference without McFarland. His absence leaves the rest like a ship without a rudder. But if one man makes such a difference, and he does, then its about time the club found money to get a real replacement" – and, responding to some national press suggestions about McFarland's wages, Arthur Coxon of Belper said "there were snide comments about wages from the press earlier this season. It seems only Roy Mac is capable of guiding this team to promotion. If he does that then this fine club servant will be cheap at any price". However, there were dissenting voices, such as H.B. Lane of Allestree who said "Roy McFarland will cost us promotion if he keeps acting like a wild man. He might have been sent off for his foul last Saturday (at Bolton) rather than just booked, and in the match before (against Bristol Rovers) he was equally as lucky"

At an Extraordinary meeting of the Football League on 9th February 1981, two proposals were made, both of which would have a significant effect on the future of English football. The first, that each club should be permitted to play a maximum of 6 home matches per season during the weekend at another time other than Saturday afternoon (provided the change was agreed by the visiting club), was backed by Derby County. The second, to extend points awarded for a win to 3 from the 1981-82 season, was opposed by a number of clubs including Leicester City, who proposed that clubs should be awarded 2 points for a result in the first half, 2 for a win in the second half and a further 2 for an overall win – the Rams preferred a system of 3 points for an away win, but only 2 for a home win. Another proposal, which clubs were still considering, was that 50% of every transfer fee must be paid as soon as a deal was agreed, with the balance within 12 months – Derby's Michael Dunford argued that transfer fees would slump if this became a regulation. The 1981-82 season would start as late as August 29th, 1981, it was also announced, to avoid peak holiday season.

In the FA Youth Cup, the Rams youngsters had drawn Manchester United in the last 16 and the two sides met at the Baseball Ground on Monday 26th January in front of a good crowd which generated gate receipts of well over £1,000. Derby went ahead after just 6 minutes, Tony Reid scoring a fine solo goal, bursting past 2 defenders and finishing with style and confidence. However, United equalised only 6 minutes later and that completed the scoring. The young Rams most gifted players, Reid (after his goal) and winger Aiden Gibson both had relatively quiet games, Gibson still recovering from a bout of tonsillitis, particularly struggled against a hard-working United side. Paul Halford, the striker who had made his debut for the reserves just 2 days earlier and had scored twice in a 2-1 win over Sheffield Wednesday, missed Derby's best chance to win the game in the second half when clean through on goal and the Rams were indebted to 16 year old goalkeeper Ian Pass, who made four excellent saves in the second half to keep the score at 1-1 and send the tie to a replay at Old Trafford. Rams: Ian Pass; Colin Murphy, Graham Harbey, Tony Reid, Paul Blades, Ian Dalziel, David King, Kevin Bird, Mark Shackleton, Paul Halford, Aiden Gibson; substitute Colyn Doyle. Pass, from Sheffield, was a newcomer to the side, having been brought in to replace the less experienced and smaller-in-stature Robert Palmer – Pass was another who was connected to Youth Development Officer Geoff Worth, through his development work at Lincoln City – the young goalkeeper having played for a Lincoln nursery club.

In the replay the following Monday Derby's youngsters put up a real fight but eventually went down by 2-1 to an older and more experienced Manchester United side, at a windy and rainy Old Trafford. United went ahead from the penalty spot after just 5 minutes when goalkeeper Pass brought down a United forward, but Pass's excellent display kept the score to 0-1 at half time. United went 2-0 ahead immediately after the restart from a defensive error leading to an own goal, but Derby hit back immediately through Paul Halford's looping far post header and battled hard without luck until the end. It had been a very promising FA Youth Cup campaign and for the first time since Tim Ward was manager in the mid 1960's, the Rams had the makings of an impressive Youth policy.

A Derby County all time great passed away on 3rd February 1981. Sammy Crooks, one of the finest wingers of the era between the First and Second World Wars, and until very recently a regular visitor to the Baseball Ground, died in Babington Hospital, Belper. County Durham-born Crooks, who was 73 when he died, won 26 England International caps between 1930 and 1937. He played 446 times for the Rams, scoring 110 goals – and was unlucky not have won an FA Cup winners medal in 1946 when a knee injury ruled him out of the final, having played in the early rounds. After he finished playing, Crooks moved into management and played a big role in Shrewsbury Town's election to the Football League in 1950, after managerial roles at Gresley Rovers, Burton Albion and Heanor Town he became Derby's Chief Scout and remained in that capacity until sacked by Brian Clough in 1967 – among his best achievements as the Rams' scout was to persuade manager Tim Ward to sign Kevin Hector, who Crooks had watched repeatedly in the Fourth Division, from Bradford Park Avenue. He was also Chairman of the Players Union (now known as the PFA) for 14 years, in a period which spanned World War 2, and played his last official match for the Rams on September 28th 1939, at the Baseball Ground against Blackpool – he was best remembered as one half of Derby's superb wing partnership, playing on the right with Dally Duncan on the left, and was never booked or sent off in his entire career.

A small structural change took place at the Baseball Ground in early February 1981 when seats were installed in the Osmaston Terrace reserve pens, which were situated at the side of the main central terracing section. The aim of the club was to create what they described as a Family Viewing Area, and seats were initially priced at £2 for adults and £1 for children. Existing Osmaston Terrace season ticket holders who stood in the pens but preferred to sit were allowed use the seats until the end of the season. The pitch side perimeter fencing was removed from the front of the newly seated areas but remained in place in front of the central terrace.

Demolition work around the environs of the Baseball Ground, clearing out old buildings and houses to make way for car parking, spelt the end of an era for much loved local establishments Wilds Off-licence, and County Stores in Shaftsbury Crescent. "We're going to miss our little shop, but you can't stop progress" said County Stores proprietor Doris Blackshaw. Doris, a Derby County fanatic who kept a large Ram's head above her shop counter, had managed the store for 10 years and planned to spend future seasons closer to the action, as a season ticket holder at the Baseball Ground – seeing the whole 90 minutes rather than just the second half as she had been able to do whilst running her shop.

On 7th February Grimsby Town were the visitors to the Baseball Ground, and they arrived as one of the form sides in the division, having gained 17 points from their previous 11 matches – they were a club very much on the up under the management of George Kerr, having risen from the lower end of Division 4 as recently as 1978, before 2 promotions (the first under Derby's Assistant Manager John Newman) had transformed their fortunes and status.. The Rams were close to full strength, only Alan Ramage was missing from what could be considered the first choice starting 11 – Steve Powell partnered Roy McFarland in central defence, with Keith Osgood on the bench. The game drew an excellent crowd of 19,691 and Derby deservedly won an entertaining game 2-1. Dave Swindlehurst put the Rams ahead in the 13th minute, heading in a rebound off the bar after Kevin Wilson's overhead kick hit the woodwork. The score remained 1-0 until right back Steve Emery, in a rare foray upfield, ran through the Grimsby defence to score a fine solo goal on 65 minutes. Thereafter, the visitors piled on the pressure with their direct and physical approach almost paying dividends straight after Emery's goal, when Roger Jones made an excellent stop from Kevin Drinkell's shot. Grimsby's only goal, however, was a penalty in the dying minutes of the game after Buckley had committed a needless foul. The win moved Derby back up to 4th place in the second division table.

The Grimsby result turned out to be as good as it got for Derby in the 1980-81 season and after that win, they managed only 3 more victories in the remaining 13 games, of which 5 were lost and 5 drawn. It was 6 weeks before the Rams won another game after beating Grimsby, and during those 6 weeks any realistic prospect of promotion disintegrated – it would be 6 years before they were so close to First Division football again.

At Ewood Park on 14th February, the Rams went down 1-0 to Blackburn Rovers. Ramage returned to the side in place of Steve Powell and defensively Derby were quite solid, but the result was justified on balance of play against a very competent Rovers side who jumped ahead of the Rams into 4th place, on goal difference. Blackburn's goal came in the 12th minute of the game, but the main talking point was an incident in the 75th minute in which Swindlehurst, running across the Rovers' penalty area, appeared to be knocked over by defender Tony Parkes – the referee decided there was no infringement and denied the Rams what looked like a clear penalty.

Manager Colin Addison had no doubts, nor did the watching press reporters – "no ifs or buts, it was a penalty" - "The fact that (Blackburn manager) Howard Kendall chose not to add his own judgement of the incident was perhaps an answer in itself" (The Sun). "(Derby) had a strong, legitimate claim for a penalty ignored when Swindlehurst was brought down" (Sunday People). Once again, the Rams players showed a lack of discipline and dissent at a refereeing decision – "They staggered around in amazement as the referee turned down their appeals" (Sunday Express).

There were rumblings of discontent among Derby's fans at Blackburn who questioned the apparent negative tactics of their team and were especially vocal when striker Kevin Wilson was replaced by the substitute, defender Keith Osgood, on 60 minutes with the Rams 1 goal down.

Derby's reserves, who's results had been steadily improving, picked up a point in their Central League match at home to top of the table Liverpool on 17th February, to follow the 2 they had gained by beating 6th place Aston Villa, also at the Baseball Ground, the previous Saturday. Steve Cherry had returned to the side, replacing Yakka Banovic, and Wayne Richards was also back, with Steve Buckley having regained fitness and his first team left back spot. Also, back from injury was Frank Sheridan, who had broken his toe in early November. Most impressive of all was striker John Clayton, who had scored 10 goals in the past 16 reserve games, including both goals in the 2-1 win over Villa and the Rams only goal against Liverpool. The reserves had improved their Central League standing to 17th.

The following week, on 21st February, Derby's stuttering promotion campaign took another severe knock when they failed to beat Orient at the Baseball Ground, the game ending 1-1. Alan Biley made his 51st and (what turned out to be his) final appearance for the club, and Tony Reid replaced Paul Emson on the left wing, Emson having suffered a complete loss of form and confidence in recent weeks. Biley suffered an ankle ligament injury during the game, which required an operation and therefore ruled him out for the rest of the season – he had scored a total of 19 goals in his Derby career, of which 17 had been at the Baseball Ground. McFarland, who scored Derby's goal, was also withdrawn through injury and the Rams finished the game with 10 men.

For the Orient match, Derby opened their new family seating area on a section of the former Osmaston End terrace. This comprised 400 seats priced at £2 for adults and the club announced that from the start of the 1981-82 season these seats would be exclusively for the use of families – no adults would be admitted unless accompanied by a child. The new seating area was partially sponsored by Lonsdale Travel, who's Chairman Sir Fred Pontin announced - "as Derby are pressing on with their bid to stage value for money family entertainment, we are delighted to tie in…I am convinced clubs must concentrate on family viewing if the game is to restore its image". In other sponsorship news, it was announced that Fern Carpets would sponsor the Normanton Stand upper and lower tiers from the start of the 1981-82 season.

Derby's intriguing summer 1980 signing Vjekoslav "Yakka" Banovic was enduring a frustrating time after joining with the expectation of being first choice goalkeeper, only to see Roger Jones, who had been signed from Stoke City as a short-term option with the aim of allowing Banovic time to acclimatise in England, perform well week in week out to cement his first team place. Interviewed in Ram Newspaper in February 1981, Banovic expressed his frustration at the length of time the transfer to Derby had taken, which meant he had therefore missed most of pre-season training and therefore lost the chance to start as first choice goalkeeper.

His background was interesting – his family had left Zagreb (then part of Yugoslavia, now the capital of Croatia) in 1966 taking the then 9 year old Yakka to Australia (first to Adelaide, then to Melbourne), and he had started as a striker for his school football team at under 16 level before stepping in to cover for the absent goalkeeper in one game – and had been spotted and signed by the adult side Adelaide Croatia on the back of that single performance, as a goalkeeper. For 8 months he had commuted by air 250 miles each Saturday to play for his new team, while still at school. His next move was to Canada, where he signed for Toronto Metros in 1977 – this ended in disappointment when the club went bankrupt just 6 months into the young goalkeeper's contract, so he returned to Australia and after a spell with Melbourne Croatia he joined National League side Heidelburg United, by which time Banovic had become an Australian citizen and was selected for the Australia national team.

He was recommended to Derby County by brothers Bill and Geoff Bateman – Bill, who lived in Australia, had seen Banovic play and Geoff, who lived in Derby, provided board and lodgings for the young goalkeeper when he moved to the area. Since signing for the Rams, Banovic had become friends with his fellow Yugoslav (and future Serb), Notts County's goalkeeper Raddy Avramovic, who attended most Rams reserve matches to watch his compatriot play.

The Rams' number one celebrity fan of the era was Buxton-born comedian Tim Brooke-Taylor, and when he was selected for the television show "This Is Your Life" in February 1981, Derby's first team squad and management were amongst the guests who celebrated with him. Derby's players were filmed arriving for the recording on tandem bicycles, in a tribute to Brooke-Taylor's famous ITV sketch show The Goodies.

Derby's finances were boosted by sales of Lottery tickets – in fact despite a general slump in football club lottery type sales since their peak in the mid 1970's, when lotteries became legal in the UK, the Rams had continued to do well in this regard and were selling 100,000 lottery tickets per week early in 1981. Stuart Robinson, the Derby County Promotions Executive, announced that 8 people would win free holidays to the United States in the summer of 1981 – winners coming from any of the 3 different lotteries being run by the club at that time – "Bingo", "Cash Casino" and "Midland Lottery". Robinson also organised a demonstration game of Baseball, between 2 teams of American Air Force personnel from RAF Alconbury, to take place on the Baseball Ground pitch before the game against Orient on 21st February – the first public game of Baseball at the ground for more than 80 years. There was also entertainment from "Johnny Reb's All-American Marching Band – complete with pipes, whistles and majorettes" (Johnny Reb's band actually came from Mansfield...).

If the failure to beat Orient at the Baseball Ground had dented Derby's promotion hopes, the following 3 games, all away, all but ended any realistic chance of an immediate return to Division One. Successive draws, at Wrexham (2-2, on 28th February) and fellow promotion hopefuls Sheffield Wednesday (0-0, on 7th March in front of over 28,000), were followed by a dismal 3-1 defeat at Loftus Road against Queen's Park Rangers. The scheduled home game against Swansea on Saturday 14th March was postponed on the morning of the game due to a waterlogged pitch at the Baseball Ground (in fact the game had not been called off until after 10am that morning and Swansea supporters were already en-route to Derby, causing numerous complaints – Derby, however, countered that they had wanted the game to go ahead but it was the referee, in consultation with Swansea manager John Toshack, who had made the final decision).

The Baseball Ground pitch, which had a reputation for being one of the worst in the entire Football League, was described as "nearer to perfection than it has ever been" by the club, following works in the summer of 1980 involving both penalty areas being injected with sand (technically, the whole pitch was injected with sand, but the two penalty areas had received coarser and deeper treatment than the rest of the pitch), which was designed to improve drainage. The treatment was scheduled to be extended to the whole of the pitch in the summer of 1980. Of the underground drainage system, secretary Michael Dunford described it as "working 95% perfectly and only limited adjustments are necessary" – Dunford added, with the benefit of hindsight – "the new pitch laid 6 years ago (after the Rams' second League Championship victory) used finer and less well-rooted grass native to Derbyshire rather than the coarser, deeper-rooted rye grasses, which would be ideal".

Whilst the pitch did not, according to Dunford, require much attention, much of the Baseball Ground did. A 2-year improvements programme was announced in the spring of 1981, beginning with catering facilities all round the stadium, which would be "drastically improved and modernised". Also earmarked for improvements were the Ley Stand, below which would be added a club room (to which all ticket holders would be admitted free), which was to serve drinks and snacks "in a tabled, neatly furnished area" – the club had teamed up with Stadia Catering Ltd, who were providing significant funding for this part of the project, as well as the plan to upgrade most of the food kiosks around the ground – "it is hoped that the food and drinks will be of a higher standard… that is the aim of both the club and Stadia Catering". A drastic improvement of the unsatisfactory catering facilities on the Pop Side would also take place in the summer of 1981, as well as several new "Ramtique" retail outlets being added around the ground. Plans were also in place to improve toilet facilities at the Baseball Ground "a complete overhaul", but this would have to wait until the summer of 1982 due to financial constraints.

The Rams had not won for a month and had picked up 3 points in the 5 games since they had beaten Grimsby Town on 7th February. Biley, injured against Orient, Ramage, who injured a cartilage at Hillsborough against Sheffield Wednesday and had an operation later that week, and youngster Glenn Skivington (Glandular Fever) were all out for the season. For Ramage, the injury was a new and unpleasant experience – he had never suffered a major injury before, either playing football or cricket.

With 8 games to go, Derby were 9th in the Second Division, with 37 points – only 3 behind Blackburn Rovers, in the 3rd and final promotion place, but with a goal difference of just +3 (considerably worse than the Blackburn and the other 5 clubs vying for the last promotion place). It was not quite a miracle they needed, but it was getting to that stage – on average a minimum of 51 points were needed to achieve promotion. The Rams away form, so impressive before Christmas, had fallen apart in the New Year and they had picked up only 2 points from their previous 5 away games.

Assistant Manager John Newman, speaking at a fans forum, gave the first clear indication that Derby's higher-earning players could be on their way out in the summer, when asked specifically about Alan Biley and Roy McFarland – "most clubs are finding that current wages are too high for their income limits. Players have fought hard for their freedom of contract, and the fact is that if at the end of their contracts they feel they can get better wages from another club then they are free to negotiate for them…we would be delighted if both players opted to stay here but that remains to be seen" Since the club had already professed themselves willing to sell Biley before his injury, it appeared unlikely that he featured in the club's long term plans. In fact, Newman and Addison were expecting many clubs would be shedding their higher earners during the coming close season, and they were hopeful that Derby could pick up some good out of contract players to improve the balance of their squad.

It was clear that the emphasis was very much on youth development – when Addison and Newman had arrived at the club in July 1979 they had found only 3 schoolboys on the books, yet they, along with Alan Ashman and Geoff Worth, had quickly instigated a youth system, from scratch, which was already paying dividends and Newman insisted "the level of apprentice intake in summer 1981 will be the highest Derby County have ever had… we have earmarked 8 boys who will be signing apprentice professional forms and each one has already played for the club...what's more, we already have boys of 14 and 15 earmarked for apprenticeships, we are preparing some three or four years ahead" and, in a thinly disguised plea to be given more time, Newman said "next season is when all the hard work should really start to show at the Baseball Ground".

On 28th February at the Racecourse Ground, Wrexham, Frank Sheridan made his return to the first team after a long-term injury, forming a youthful midfield partnership with Tony Reid. John Clayton played on the left wing. Dave Swindlehurst (with a penalty) and Sheridan scored the Rams' goals in a 2-2 draw in front of just 6,485.

The visit to Hillsborough to face fellow promotion contenders Sheffield Wednesday resulted in a 0-0 draw, only the second goalless draw of the season – McFarland, who had missed the game at Wrexham, returned to partner Ramage in central defence. Ramage was injured during the game and was out for the rest of the season. Reid and Sheridan continued in midfield, Wilson and Swindlehurst in attack.

At Loftus Road on 21st March in the game against Queen's Park Rangers, John Clayton, who had been in fine goalscoring form for the reserves and had been drafted into the first team in place of the out-of-sorts Paul Emson, hit the bar with the score at 1-1 and the Rams had the better of an entertaining first half, Barry Powell having scored the visitor's goal. They remained well in contention until Steve Powell was adjudged to have handled the ball inside the penalty area (he could hardly have got out of the way of a fierce shot), and the resulting penalty was converted. Rangers rounded off the scoring with a 3rd in the 87th minute.

On 14th March at Raynesway, the Rams' training ground, Derby's young "A" team registered a very good win over local rivals Nottingham Forest in the Midland Intermediate League. The Rams won 2-0 against the league leaders, with goals from King and Mulholland.

On 28th March Derby played their first home game for 5 weeks, against struggling Bristol City, 21st in the table and looking likely to be relegated for a second successive season, and the lowest goal scorers in the entire football league. They were familiar rivals, this was the 7th time the clubs had played each other in the past 16 months. Significantly, the Robins had not won a single away league game all season and had not scored more than 1 goal away in any of those 17 games.

It was a poor game, played in a swirling wind in front of just 15,008, desperately low on quality and entertainment as the visitors cancelled out most of Derby's forward movement with their well drilled defence and protective midfield shield. Rams fans had begun to show discontent (including a slow hand-clap from patrons in the A-Stand) long before Dave Swindlehurst broke the deadlock in the 70th minute, when the recalled Paul Emson made his only significant contribution after escaping the attentions of his marker Paul Stephens to cross from the left – Barry Powell, having one of his best games for Derby, flicked the ball on at the near post and Swindlehurst bundled the ball home in the Normanton goal. The Rams were indebted to Roger Jones, who made a brave save at the feet of striker Trevor Tainton to secure a narrow 1-0 win.

Manager Addison had changed his formation, 4-2-4 reflected the crucial need for a win as well as the expectation of Bristol City sitting back and looking for a draw. For the first time since December 1979 the manager was able to call on striker John Duncan, and the Scotsman joined Wilson, Swindlehurst and Emson in the 4-man attack, with Barry Powell and Kevin Hector operating in midfield. Duncan, who said after his first league game in 15 months – "I was so tired I don't think I could have run for a bus at the end had I had to do so". Addison was pleased with his contribution – "his performance was a bonus and he was unlucky not to score".

John Duncan was born at Lochee in Scotland in February 1949, and started his football career at Dundee in 1966, staying there for 8 years before moving south to join Tottenham Hotspur for a fee of £125,000 in October 1974 after winning the Scottish League Cup with Dundee. He was a fine centre forward, one of the best in British football, and Tottenham's leading scorer in their successful 1977-78 second division promotion side. However, he was injury-prone, and when Tommy Docherty paid £150,000 to bring him to the Baseball Ground in September 1978 it was a risky gamble and it did not pay off – Duncan managed just 39 appearances (including 2 as substitute), scoring 12 goals in a Derby career ruined, and ultimately ended, by injury. He scored 129 goals in 269 professional games over 15 years, which reflected both his ability and injury record.

Nearing the end of his contract with the Rams in June 1981, Duncan left to take over as player-manager at Scunthorpe United and was poorly treated there, being sacked in February 1983 (after he had been accused of discussing a move to local rivals Grimsby Town) when promotion from the fourth division was in sight. He remained in management, first with Hartlepool United, then Chesterfield (where he won promotion from Division Four) and eventually (in June 1987) with Ipswich Town, where he stayed for 3 years. Three years after being sacked by Ipswich, and after a spell as a school teacher, Duncan returned to Saltergate to take over at Chesterfield for a second time, achieving promotion from Division Three and taking his side to the semi-finals of the FA Cup where they narrowly missed out on a place in the final after a controversial replay defeat against Middlesbrough. He eventually left Chesterfield in October 2000 and has since managed Loughborough University FC.

The win against Bristol City put the Rams back into contention for promotion. A combination of helpful results around the second division on 28th March meant that Derby jumped from 9th to 5th with their 2 points, 2 behind both Grimsby Town (3rd place) and Blackburn Rovers (4th) – although this was effectively a 3-point gap as the others had a significantly better goal difference than the Rams. West Ham (53), were effectively already promoted, and Notts County (44) were close to joining them. The Rams now had their rearranged home game against Swansea City (11th place but just 2 points below them in the table) to come, the following Tuesday night.

Queen's Park Rangers announcement in Spring 1981 that they wished to install artificial turf as their playing surface at Loftus Road, at a reported cost of £350,000, was accepted by the Football League committee and now required acceptance by at least three quarters of the other League clubs. Clubs who had suffered costly problems with the condition of their pitches, including Derby County, watched developments with interest – "it would alleviate the sort of pitch troubles we have been plagued with here at the Baseball Ground for so long" said secretary Michael Dunford.

Rangers' plans included transforming their stadium into an all-purpose ground – the artificial pitch was to be constructed to enable it to be lifted-up when necessary, enabling use as a boxing stadium or for pop concerts, for example. Dunford described the plans as "a revolutionary, far-reaching decision the deserves success because it is a road up which most League clubs will have to travel for survival before too long", and specifically about Derby – "we cannot any longer survive on the receipts from 21 League games plus any cup ties which may come our way, leaving the ground empty and unused most of the year...a lift-up, put-down artificial surface transforms both the possibilities and potential".

Derby's reserves produced their best win of the season at Gigg Lane against Bury on the same day that the first team laboured to victory at home to Bristol City. The second string won 4-0, with 2 strikes from John Clayton, back in the reserves after 3 outings in the first team, plus goals from Keith Osgood and 19-year-old Frank Gamble, on trial from non-league club Burscough – the Rams were considering a loan move for the Liverpool-born midfielder. Some had not done well – including Kevin Murray, the already transfer-listed midfielder of whom manager Colin Addison said, "his performance was not acceptable, so he has played his last game for the club".

Derby's rearranged game against Swansea on Tuesday March 31st was a dispiriting affair, the Rams second best throughout and deservedly losing 1-0 – Swansea's goal coming when Roy McFarland, suffering from more hamstring trouble, was unable to intercept a long through pass which ended at the feet of David Giles, who crossed for the unmarked Jeremy Charles to head unchallenged beyond Roger Jones in the Rams goal. Derby's wayward passing and questionable commitment of some players, particularly after McFarland had gone off injured, suggested that any ambitions of promotion were completely unrealistic.

Steve Powell, writing in his newspaper column after the game, was quite clear – "I was a bit concerned about the attitudes of some of our players. This was particularly true after Swansea had scored. We went to pieces, which was a disgrace". There was a suggestion that some players had settled into their comfort zone at second division level and were not sufficiently motivated to engage in a determined fight for promotion – the hope of supporters for the future rested with the half dozen or so young players who had emerged during the season, and that those who had been found wanting in both character, determination and commitment would be shipped out in the close season. D. Watson, a Ley Stand regular, summed up the prevalent mood – "I have seriously contemplated chucking the whole thing...its not the fact that we have dropped out of the promotion race, but the way we dropped out, that depresses me. The Swansea match capped the lot this season, the way the players gave in so easily was diabolical...they didn't look as though they wanted promotion. Is it the players? Or is it orders from the Board above? ...I wouldn't mind if the Rams lost every game, as long as the passion is there. I've got it, all the fans have got it". It appears clear that the Board did want (and need) promotion – financial meltdown was rapidly approaching - the failure to go straight back up, after gambling on keeping big money signings Biley and Swindlehurst despite relegation, was a catastrophe in waiting.

The club had by now resigned itself to losing McFarland in the summer – the player would be sure to exercise his right to leave the club when his contract expired in July 1981 and begin his search for a management position. McFarland, one of the highest paid footballers in the Country, had been plagued by injury and there was no way that Derby County could either afford, or justify, a new contract on the same or better terms.

The Rams played Shrewsbury Town at Gay Meadow on Saturday April 4th and somehow contrived to put on a display even more abject and disheartening than they had at the Baseball Ground against Swansea City 4 days before. Emson was dropped again (Clayton replaced him), the injured McFarland was due to be replaced by reserve team centre-back Ian Dalziel, but the unfortunate youngster was badly injured in the previously Thursday's reserve match, so Frank Sheridan – a midfielder by preference, was drafted in, and Duncan was not considered capable of a second game in such a short space of time. On the bench, making his first appearance in a matchday first team squad, was young winger Aiden Gibson.

Shrewsbury were poor, but Derby were worse, especially in the second half when lack of application and discipline was again evident – only Steve Powell, appeared to have the required urgency and determination. Swindlehurst was sent off for a ridiculous head-butt (retaliating to an elbow in the face which went unpunished), and the home side won the game 1-0. Gibson replaced Kevin Wilson on 68 minutes for his Rams debut. After the game hospital scans revealed that Gibson, who had suffered a very heavy challenge seconds after coming on when chasing back (before he had even touched the ball) but had unwisely played on through the pain, had suffered a broken ankle and was out for the rest of the season.

Despite what was acknowledged as one of the poorest displays ever seen by a Derby County side, a group of young Rams fans waited outside the ground and cheered the team coach as the players boarded to leave the Shrewsbury ground – it was an astonishing display of loyalty and one that should have ashamed some of the players. Others were less convinced – Four "Ossie Enders" from Ashbourne, Tim Woods, Ray Barker, Sid Moore and John

Rathbone said "for the first time in five years we wondered whether we are mugs to be spending money…on following the Rams home and away…(Shrewsbury) certainly made us think…when there is less than 100% commitment on the field there will be less than 100% from the fans too".

Manager Colin Addison accepted that the game at Gay Meadow had finally put paid to promotion hopes and said after the match "there was no pride in performance from too many of our players and they should not have to be reminded of their responsibilities to our supporters". Of the season, he said "the truth is that the team hasn't been good enough over the season…the balance wasn't right…but lack of cash and unfortunate injuries which ruined a couple of exchange deals which would have helped us enormously, thwarted us". Of the coming summer, he said - "John and I will be putting in a lot of time even though there is no hard cash, and we will be forced to sell…what we need above all in the second division are battlers…the example of Steve Powell has been tremendous and he will provide the cornerstone of the team next season".

David Swindlehurst summed up the players' view – "its been a season I'll be glad to forget". Swindlehurst had suffered without his strike partner Alan Biley, who's injuries, illness and (according to some reports) desire for a move away and more money, had brought about a loss of form. Swindlehurst himself had been troubled by ligament problems and ankle injuries and had suffered at the hands of many uncompromising second division defenders – towards the end of the season his patience had worn thin and frustration had boiled over into indiscipline and suspensions. He was, however, a real favourite with Derby supporters, who recognised him as one of the very few true class players still on the books, willing to give 100% to the cause every time he pulled on a Derby shirt. Biley, who was finally walking again with the aid of crutches after injuring his left ankle, had his plaster removed 6 weeks after being injured in the game against Orient – he looked unlikely to be fit for pre-season, and even less likely to be staying at Derby.

Aiden Gibson was a very highly rated young prospect who the Rams picked up aged 16 in May 1980, ahead of several other interested clubs. A natural left winger, he had pace and skill but was very unlucky with injuries during a short professional career, both at Derby (where he broke both ankles, one on his first team debut then the other in a comeback game for the reserves) and then at Exeter City who he had joined after leaving the Rams in July 1982. He never started a first team game for Derby and his 3 appearances were all as substitute. After leaving Exeter, the Newcastle-under-Lyme born Gibson moved back to the midlands and played non-league football for Stourbridge and Willenhall Town. Drifting out of football altogether, he became a Chartered Surveyor.

With 5 games to go, the Rams were 9th in the league with 39 points from 37 games – theoretically they were still in contention for promotion, Swansea City (now in 3rd place), were only 2 points better off albeit with a game in hand – but their recent performances suggested anything but a promotion push, and they had 2nd placed local rivals Notts County to play next, at the Baseball Ground on Saturday 11th April.

A good crowd of just under 18,000 were in attendance for the game against Notts County, who were by that stage odds-on for promotion to Division One (where they had last played in 1926), under the management of Jimmy Sirrell and coached by Howard Wilkinson, and looking certain to finish 2nd behind runaway leaders West Ham – in fact County were on course to complete a magnificent and at the time unparalleled journey from 4th division to 1st under the same management. Duncan returned to the side and played in attack alongside Wilson, with Swindlehurst suspended. It was a lively game and Derby gave as good as they got, the 2-2 result was probably fair – recalled Keith Osgood's penalty and Wilson's goal the markers for the Rams. Notts County's team featured former Rams midfielders Don Masson, who had been excellent for the Magpies all season, and David Hunt, plus future Ram 21-year-old Trevor Christie. The game turned out to be John Duncan's last for Derby – his contract expired at the end of the season and he was released to join Scunthorpe United as player manager.

After the Notts County game there were unfortunate skirmishes outside the Baseball Ground as some Derby fans attacked cars carrying Notts supporters away from the game – bottles were thrown, and cars were jumped on and kicked.

With Derby all-but certain to remain in the second division for the 1981-82 season, the club announced that season ticket prices in most areas of the Baseball Ground would be increased by £2 (representing an increase of around 4%) – Terrace tickets would be £30, Osmaston and Normanton Stands £48, Ley Stand from £52 to £65, Main Stand £52 to £76. There were also discounts for families buying tickets together in the new Family Viewing areas. The club was to "dramatically cut its coat according to its cloth in all departments, it's the only way we can keep solvent in a period where both the running costs are spiralling and inflation is still running into double figures", said Michael Dunford – "we must all accept that the next 12 months are going to be vital so we shall have to roll up our sleeves and work harder…we cannot afford to be out of the top flight a moment more than is absolutely necessary"

With the Rams losing £3,000 a week, Chairman Richard Moore, whilst acknowledging that economies needed to be made in all departments of the club, said in April 1981 – "no player considered crucial (by manager Colin Addison) to next season's promotion push will be allowed to leave this summer unless support dwindles alarmingly or the situation changes drastically and unexpectedly in some other way, for example we receive an offer for a player which is higher than our own valuation" and "only two senior players are likely to be involved in any outgoing transfers, plus Roy McFarland (who would be leaving on a free)".

The club's overdraft at the bank at the end of the 1980-81 season totalled just under £1 million. Moore remained adamant that without the transfer dealings of the previous season

– Biley, Swindlehurst, Barry Powell and Emery in particular, the club would now be "running on an even keel". However, there was no way the £1m deficit could be made up from income – inflation and the current recession ("biting deeper than anyone anticipated") had made the position even more difficult to retrieve. Drastic cost-cutting would have to take place, and it was by now inevitable that players would have to be sold "the only way to reduce our crippling overdraft". Praising the still quite remarkable support, despite the largely dreadful displays on the field for 2 seasons, Moore added "(at 17,000) our support is an amazing figure and has prevented a difficult and awkward situation from spilling over into crisis proportions. It is not easy, but without this support it would be a disaster".

One very real problem of this time, often misunderstood by supporters, was that any player whose contract ends had to be offered a new one of at least equal in length and financial value as the old. If one is not offered (such as in the case of Roy McFarland), then the club lost its right to a fee and the player had to be given a free transfer. The Football League had negotiated this with the Professional Footballers' Association. This, said Moore, was fine for clubs staying in the same division, but for relegated clubs like the Rams it was nothing but a millstone around the neck – it meant that Derby had to offer First Division terms, should they wish to ask a fee for any player who was the subject of transfer negotiations. In practice this meant that a player could ask for high wages from another club, but if nobody offered equal to what he was getting from his current club, that club was stuck with the player on the wages he was currently on – in Derby's case, most of the squad were on First Division wages.

It was obvious that youth (as well as selling the more valuable players) was the key to survival, and Moore applauded Addison and John Newman for developing a promising youth policy from scratch and bringing through several very promising youngsters. The scouting network was also praised, something else that had been largely neglected for the past 15 years.

Miss Derby County 1981 was crowned on 8th April at a Rams social event staged at Bertie's Cabaret Club in Derby, 22-year-old model Jane Allen from Littleover picked up the award, and won a holiday courtesy of Lonsdale Travel, beating runners-up Jackie May from Spondon and Louise Gray from Chesterfield. Hazel Bark, from Alfreton, won the "Rams fan of the year" award, and there was a special "merit award" presentation to Mr and Mrs Fred and Betty Martin, caretakers at the Baseball Ground.

Also winning an award was Derby's goalkeeper Roger Jones, who was crowned player of the year at the club's annual awards night on 21st April, at Romeo's & Juliet's in the City – with well over 1,000 fans in attendance. Manager Colin Addison revealed that Jones was also his own choice for the award, describing him as "a great professional and a tremendous guy". Everton manager Gordon Lee, who had managed the goalkeeper at both Blackburn Rovers and Newcastle United, described Jones as "the best goalkeeper I have ever worked with".

Jones, with characteristic humility, said "I had a great chance to win the award, I'm the only one who hasn't been injured".

On Saturday 18th April, with nothing to play for, Derby defeated a very poor Newcastle United side 2-0 at the Baseball Ground. Most notable was the very small attendance, just 13,846, which reflected a general lack of interest in a game which counted for nothing, as well as a growing anger amongst supporters about the way Derby's team had been performing – by now support was down to just the hardest of hard-core. Mick Harford, the future Rams striker, featured for Newcastle. John Clayton replaced John Duncan, who had played his last game for the club a week before, for the Rams.

Along with Clayton, fellow youngsters Tony Reid and Kevin Wilson also impressed, and Paul Emson finally appeared to be back at something approaching his best form. Wilson put Derby ahead on 41 minutes after Barry Powell's corner was headed back from Emson to Clayton, who teed-up his fellow striker for a cool finish. Roy McFarland scored Derby's second, also from Powell corner, in the second half.

Supporters in the Rams new Family Viewing seated area, on the former Osmaston Terrace, did not enjoy the game against Newcastle – they were subjected to a tirade of abuse and hurled missiles from the visiting supporters standing in the nearby Colombo section of the Pop Side. Secretary Michael Dunford insisted that "steps will be taken to obviate any possibility of a repetition…this experience has alerted us to a danger which will not be tolerated when August arrives"

On Easter Monday the Rams travelled to Boundary Park to play Oldham Athletic, and Steve Buckley made the headlines with a retaken right-footed 25-yard free-kick which went past the home goalkeeper before he had chance to move, putting Derby 1-0 up after 24 minutes – his first goal of the season. In what turned out to be the best performance since the Christmas period, John Clayton made the score 2-0 after 77 minutes when he ran onto a through ball from Kevin Wilson and coolly clipped the ball past the onrushing keeper, it was Clayton's first ever goal in League football. Frank Sheridan deputised at centre back as McFarland was not considered capable of a 2nd game in 3 days. It was too-little, too-late as far as promotion was concerned, but the performances over Easter had been promising, and the youngsters in the side continued to show promise.

With 2 games to play, the Rams (on 44 points) were still theoretically in the promotion mix, in 6th place – but with Blackburn (on 46 from 40 games), and Swansea and Luton (both on 45, with 3 games to play), Derby were long odds-against – although the remaining games were against 4th bottom Preston North End and 3rd bottom Cardiff City.

The game at Cardiff City on 2nd May was another low point. In front of 7,577 (which included an impressive contingent from Derby, numbering over 1,000) a 0-0 draw was played out. Derby, who dominated the game, were unlucky not to win and played some attractive football – they created at least 5 clear goalscoring chances in the first half alone, and somehow failed to convert any of them – Cardiff goalkeeper Ron Healey had a superb game. In the second half, the home side fought back and had a goal ruled out for offside. Steve Buckley and Frank Sheridan played in central defence with Wayne Richards at left back and Keith Osgood at right back. Young reserve midfielder Steve Spooner came into the side for his 3rd first team game (and his first since October 1979). It was a young side – Richards, Sheridan, Spooner, Tony Reid, Kevin Wilson and Paul Emson all started the game, and John Clayton was the substitute.

Steve Spooner, born in Sutton, Surrey in 1961, had joined Derby as an apprentice under the management of Colin Murphy, having been spotted playing in the same trial game as Frank Sheridan, and offered terms on the spot by Murphy's Assistant Dario Gradi. He had played 2 first team matches as an 18-year-old in the First Division before dropping down the pecking order in the Colin Addison era. He eventually made just 8 appearances for the first team at Derby and was released to join Halifax Town in 1981. After leaving Derby, his career flourished at a lower level and he became a key player for Halifax, Chesterfield, Hereford United, York City and Mansfield Town. After finishing his career at Rushden & Diamonds he went into coaching and worked extensively for Birmingham City, where he became Lead Professional Development Coach.

The final home game of season 1980-81 was against Preston North End, managed by England World Cup winner Nobby Stiles, originally scheduled for Saturday 25th April but played on Wednesday May 6th after the initial game was postponed due to unseasonal bad weather. It was to be Roy McFarland's 521st and final game for the club (although he was to make a surprising comeback in desperate times, 3 seasons later after returning to the club as Assistant Manager). McFarland had been with Derby since August 1967, the night that Brian Clough and Peter Taylor had waited at the then 19-year-old's house until he got out of bed and signed for the Rams from Tranmere Rovers, for a fee of £27,000. There was little doubt then, or now, that he was one of the truly great players in Derby County history, and few who saw him play would doubt that he was one of England's all time finest central defenders. He was also a menace to opposing defences, especially from set-pieces, and had scored 48 goals, a considerable number of these being headers from corners.

McFarland had been cruelly cut down in his prime with a snapped Achilles tendon at Wembley in 1974, aged 26 in a game against Northern Ireland (while partnering his Rams team mate Colin Todd for only the second time), while playing for England, but after missing 11 months of all football had fought back to win 4 further caps, in 1976 and 1977. His eventual total of 28 England caps could well have amounted to 100 had it not been for injuries. Even now, at 33 and the end of his career, with failing hamstrings, Colin Addison was moved to say - "could you weld new legs onto footballers this man would still be the best in Europe". The Rams could not afford to match the terms of his expiring contract, so he moved on, as was his contractual right, to explore opportunities in management. To many, it seemed highly unlikely that they would ever again see such an accomplished defender in a Derby shirt – a man who's honours with the club read: Second Division Championship, Texaco Cup, two Football League Championships, Watney Cup, FA Charity Shield, European Cup and FA Cup Semi Finals.

In a parting message to Derby supporters, McFarland acknowledged the severity of the club's financial situation but praised the current youth policy and scouting network – "wider and more efficient than I have known in my 14 years here…it could take three or four years for you to see the full benefits of this youth policy, to see the birth of the new Rams, but you'll see it" (in fact, it was to be 5 years before the club began to climb up the football ladder again).

The game itself, played in front of just 15,050 (including 500 invited VIP Junior Rams, sitting in the Ley Stand as guests of the club) saw the Rams once again lack skill and determination, and it was a sad and disappointing anti-climax on which to say farewell to the great Roy McFarland. Relegation-haunted Preston (who were staging a late rally in their battle to avoid the drop, having won 6 points from their previous 8 including draws against promoted Notts County and promotion contenders Blackburn Rovers), showing a desire barely seen from Derby's players in months, won comfortably, 2-1 at the Baseball Ground, with Swindlehurst getting the Rams' consolation goal – the result, and the performance, was hardly a shock, but it was an embarrassment – sadly, it proved to be a taste of what was to come when the new season started, in August.

Derby's team for that final game of season 1980-81 – Roger Jones; Keith Osgood, Steve Buckley, Roy McFarland, Frank Sheridan; Tony Reid, Steve Spooner, Kevin Hector, Paul Emson; Dave Swindlehurst, Kevin Wilson, and substitute John Clayton.

Derby's reserves had suffered a mixed run at the end of their Central League season. Since thumping Bury 4-0 at Gigg Lane at the end of March they had played 9 games in 30 days to catch up with a fixture backlog caused by winter postponements, and had won 2, drawn 2 but lost 5 (in fact, 5 of the last 6 matches, 4 of which were away). They had started April well, beating Blackpool at Bloomfield Road, then Sheffield United at the Baseball Ground, followed by a very impressive draw at Old Trafford against Manchester United, but had then gone into something of a tail-spin, with defeats at home to West Bromwich Albion and Coventry City, and away at Newcastle United, Huddersfield Town and Nottingham Forest.

Towards the end of the season, the reserves struggled to field a consistent team as injuries and suspensions to first team players regularly robbed the reserve side of its better players. Yakka Banovic and Steve Cherry tended to alternate in goal, and the regular full backs were Lovatt and Richards. At centre back Ian Dalziel, regarded as one of the better prospects, had been injured at the start of April, and Frank Sheridan was, often, away with the first team – leaving Graham Harbey, a full back, and Steve Spooner, a midfielder, to fill in. Jonathan Clark, who had fallen completely out of the first team reckoning around the turn of the year, was a regular in midfield, as were youngsters Frank Gamble, on loan from Burscough, and Barney Bowers. Paul Halford and John Clayton often played in attack although the latter was regularly removed for first team duty. Former first team regular Steve Carter, still at the club but having seen no first team action since September 1979 due to injury, made sporadic appearances, but by that stage it was clear he had no future with the Rams.

The Rams' "A" team finished the season with a flourish when they reached the Midland Intermediate League Cup Final after beating Coventry City 2-0 in the semi-final at Raynesway, Gamble and King scoring the goals in the second half. The youngster's league season ended with 12 wins and 5 draws from 26 matches, and 29 points.

What would certainly be returning for next season was the Ram Newspaper. The profit made on the newspaper had more than doubled since the previous season (1979-80). In fact, the matchday publication was one of the few success stories of the 1980-81 season – in its 10-year history, only once before had it contributed more financially than it had this season, and a higher than ever proportion of the average gate were buying it. The Newspaper, which was voted eighth-best matchday publication in the Country by The Wirral programme collectors club in 1981, was produced and edited by Harry Brown – despite the occasional grammar and syntax error, it was a quite remarkable publication for a one-person operation. For the Preston game, which had been postponed from Saturday 25th April and rearranged for Wednesday 6th May, 2 separate issues of Ram Newspaper were produced, with entirely different content.

What had been quite remarkable during the 1980-81 season was the level of support that Derby had continued to receive. Season ticket sales totalled 9,675, which was the 9th highest in the Country and by far the highest outside the First Division. For comparison, the top club for season ticket sales for this season was Manchester United, with 20,427, followed by Manchester City (17,224) and Liverpool (16,902). Local rivals Nottingham Forest, who had recently won the European Cup twice, had 16,742 season ticket holders, and Leicester City, in the First Division, had just 6,195. Derby's nearest rivals outside the First Division were Sheffield Wednesday (6,127) and runaway Second Division champions West Ham (5,830). On the other hand, Derby's total of 9,675 was less than half of the number they had achieved ten years previously, in 1970-71 – but back then, they were one of the best sides in the Country and just a year away from becoming Champions of the Football League.

As well as McFarland, John Duncan and Steve Carter were also released as their contracts expired. Both had been signed by Tommy Docherty, and both had their Rams careers ruined by injury. Great Yarmouth born winger Carter, who joined the club as part of a deal taking Don Masson to Notts County in August 1978, had made just 35 appearances for Derby (including 1 as substitute), scoring 1 goal. Although he had technically arrived on a free transfer, Carter was in fact another example of catastrophic transfer dealings at Derby in the mid-late 1970's, tracing back to the signing of winger Leighton James for £300,000 in November 1975 (at the time, a club record fee) – James had been an early casualty of

Docherty's feverish buying and selling and had been exchanged in October 1977 for Masson, who, at 33 years old (compared to James who was just 24) was somehow valued at the same figure - £180,000, meaning no cash changed hands. Within a year, Masson had gone to Notts County on a free transfer, with the Rams receiving Carter as part of the deal – from beginning to end, this chain of events resulted in Derby writing off £300,000. Added to the £150,000 fee paid for Duncan, these two players being released for nothing represented a straight £450,000 loss to the club.

Also released at the end of the season were reserve players Barney Bowers and David Tarry. All other players were retained although Jonathan Clark remained on the available for transfer list.

The club received a welcome financial boost with the temporary transfer, at the end of April, of Barry Powell to Portland Timbers of the North American Soccer League, for the NASL summer 1981 season. Not only did Derby receive a payment of around £250,000, they also saved Powell's wage of around £500 a week. The player was scheduled to return to Derby in September, but Timbers, who wanted to sign the player permanently, were given first option should he become available for a permanent deal – at the time neither Powell, nor Derby, wanted to take this option.

Powell's temporary move, added to the savings made by the release of McFarland, Duncan, Carter, Bowers and Tarry, meant that the club's wage bill was reduced by not far short of £2,000 a week (at least until Powell returned from the USA). The club appeared ready to cut their losses on Alan Biley, who was by this time openly looking for a move away, and a deal with West Bromwich Albion for cash plus midfielder David Mills looked to be on the cards – whether or not the out-of-favour but highly-rated Mills, who had cost Albion £500,000, would be prepared to drop down to the Second Division remained to be seen. Ron Atkinson, Albion's manager, had Biley near the top of his short list. Biley's injury, in the game against Orient, marked the end of Derby's previously impressive goalscoring record – the team had scored just 10 goals in the 10 league games since then. There were also rumours that full back Steve Buckley may be one of the players deemed surplus to requirements, with the promising Wayne Richards appearing ready to step up – Buckley, it was felt, would command a sizeable fee.

It was announced that the Rams would make a pre-season tour of Finland, to begin around 10th August – "every year some three dozen of our fans use their summer holidays to follow Derby County on our pre-season tour" said Michael Dunford. Dunford also announced that corporate sponsorship had held up well despite relegation, in fact this had generated not far short in 1980-81 of what it had in the previous, First Division, season. In the negative column was revenue from away matches, which was down £120,000 on the total received in the First Division a year earlier – big gates at the likes of Old Trafford, Anfield, Highbury and the City Ground had been replaced with away games at places like Cambridge, Orient,

Bristol Rovers, Blackburn, Cardiff, Oldham and Shrewsbury. At the time, visiting clubs received 30 pence for every adult in the ground and 15 pence for every junior.

Derby County Promotions, who ran the club's three lottery games, donated a sum to the football club which was more than £25,000 down on the previous 12 months – there had been recent negative press coverage about lottery scams and fiddles, and whilst there was no suggestion whatsoever that Derby, or any Football League club, were involved in any wrongdoing, it had nevertheless hit buyer confidence hard and sales had fallen dramatically in recent months. In response to this, Derby County Promotions decided to rename their "Cash Casino" and "Midlands Lottery" to "Money Maker" and "Double Chance" respectively. The Rams had around 1,000 active agents, selling their lottery tickets mainly to family and friends.

By the time football resumed at the Baseball Ground, on Saturday 29th August 1981, for the League Division 2 meeting with Orient, much had changed. Tragically, Wendy Osgood, wife of Rams defender Keith, died in hospital on 21st August 1981 – a month after giving birth to the couple's second baby. The players heard the news when they arrived back at Heathrow Airport, following their pre-season tour of Scandinavia. Derby's final pre-season match, a friendly against Wolverhampton Wanderers at Molineux on 23rd August, was a sombre affair and only began after a minute's silence as a mark of respect.

The Baseball Ground had undergone a change as the almost the entire Osmaston Terrace was converted to an all seated Family Seating Area for the start of the 1980-81 season, only a very small pen, for the use of season ticket holders who preferred to stand, remained as terracing. Colin Addison, the manager, hoped that this would increase the level of vocal support as all standing spectators would now be housed on the Pop Side and the Normanton Terrace – the younger, more vocal support would be likely to congregate on the Pop Side. Three separate ticket offices would be operating for the new season – the main office in Shaftsbury Crescent, and one each behind the Osmaston and Normanton Stands. The planned club room in the Ley Stand was also completed and ready for use from the first match of the new season, comprising a free to access room with refreshments and a bar, a Ramtique kiosk, and a colour TV broadcasting the day's football results after the match.

On the Pop Side, the patrons benefitted from a new Ramtique shop beneath the Ley Stand, new catering kiosks, and of perhaps most benefit, there would be no more problems with viewing during televised matches as the TV gantry which, when in situ, had caused restricted viewing from some areas of the Pop Side, was permanently removed and new, unobtrusive, structure was built to replace it.

Ramtique IV, the fourth incarnation of the club's main souvenir shop, was built next to the main matchday ticket office. It replaced the demolished former shop which was situated on Shaftsbury Crescent. Other Ramtiques were now situated in the Ley Stand, behind the Pop Side, under the newly seated Osmaston End and at 39 Osmaston Road in the City. The

Ramtique shops did suffer a loss to local rivals when manageress Maureen Hubbell, a lifelong Rams fan, left to take on a similar role at Nottingham Forest.

A storm of almost monsoon proportions, on Thursday 9th July, caused a significant flood at the Baseball Ground, leaving every carpet ruined, drains blocked, and the manager's office, board room, trophy room and kitchen two feet deep in sewage-contaminated water. Also affected were the dressing rooms, the boiler room, the secretary's office and the players' lounge. All electricity was put out of order. New carpets were eventually installed by Fern Carpets, managed by friend-of-the-club Freddie Fern, and all expenses and costs were covered by insurance.

Approaching the Baseball Ground, things had undergone a significant change as a huge space was created by the demolition of Cambridge Street and surrounding areas, behind the Osmaston End, and terraced houses facing the main entrance, on Shaftsbury Crescent, and on Vulcan Street, behind the Normanton End, had also been demolished. Much of the now cleared land would be used for matchday car parking, creating around 600 new spaces. The area behind the Osmaston End, where Cambridge Street once stood, was to be covered with tarmac to create an all-weather football pitch.

This was to be the first season of three points for a win – brought in with a view to encouraging more attacking football. The Rams had not supported this move, preferring an alternative plan to award more points for away wins, but a large majority of Football League clubs had, and the legislation was passed.

The Rams were rated by bookmakers at 10-1 against winning promotion, only Queen's Park Rangers, and relegated clubs Leicester City and Norwich City, were favoured over Derby. A syndicate of 20 Pop Siders, led by 19 years old Stuart Ryan of Derby and his friend Mick Mulhall of Chaddesden, paid £20 each into a pool to back the Rams, sacrificing their planned weekend in Blackpool over the summer to make the bet.

Derby County's new kit, a smart affair by manufacturers Patrick (UK) Ltd, based in Aldridge (near Walsall), was described as practical and comfortable by the players. The club signed a three-year deal with Patrick to supply all the kit until the end of the 1983-84 season and the deal involved a substantial payment for the right to display the Patrick name on the player's shirts. Patrick's managing director, Mr Everitt Plater, a football fan himself, had also signed similar deals over the summer with First Division Southampton and Swansea City, as well as Second Division Wrexham – he remarked "the Rams may be Second Division at the moment but in outlook and ambition they remain a First Division club with a First Division ground...we expect to be involved with them as a First Division club, without a doubt". Patrick were also to supply replica kits "at reasonable prices" – "now they know that the Patrick kits will be used for three years, there is no risk of them going out of date", said Michael Dunford – "we are well satisfied with the deal and have come out of it almost certainly as well as many First Division clubs in the shirt sponsorship sphere".

Previous shirt sponsors, British Midland Airways, were unable to renew their agreement "due to current economic restraints" but remained closely connected with the club in other, smaller, ways, including advertising on Rams' lottery tickets. Patrick (UK) Ltd became the first sports goods manufacturers to sign shirt sponsorship deals with Football League clubs. The new first team kit remained white and navy blue, and the change kit remained amber and navy blue, but the shirts were now without collars. Every player had Patrick football boots individually fitted.

The sponsors also announced that the clubs they sponsored, Derby, Southampton, Swansea and Wrexham, would compete for "the Patrick Cup" during 1981-82, with details and dates to be announced. Despite protestations from many clubs, most notably Liverpool, Nottingham Forest and Southampton, sponsors names on shirts remained barred from use for all televised matches. The Rams had blazed that trail as long ago as 1974, and the saga still rumbled on, 7 years later – the Rams had, back then, missed out on a £250,000 fee from Swedish car manufacturer Saab, when they had been unable to overturn the ban. The new style Patrick replica shirts retailed at Derby's Ramtique outlets at £8.50 for adults and £6.20 for children, with shorts at £3.85 and £2.95, and socks at £1.70 and £1.20.

TV Comedian Tim Brooke-Taylor, a long-time Derby fan, was appointed to the Board of Directors. Living and working in London, Brooke-Taylor was not to be a working director, and would miss some board meetings, but he would be operating in a networking capacity, using his many and varied contacts in the entertainment and publicity industries to promote the club. He joined Chairman Richard Moore, vice chairman Bill Stevenson, and directors Arthur Atkins, Bob Mulholland, Rex Stone and Eddie Strachan, on the Board. Club Patrons were announced as W.Critchlow, R.Crisp, C.W.McKerrow, F.Cholerton, W.Stevenson (Belper) Ltd, Bowmer & Kirkland Ltd, Strachan Knitwear and Vitrev Packaging.

Chairman Richard Moore was due to remain in office until November 1982. He had been in office since being elected by his colleagues in August 1979 for a two-year period, but his term had been extended by a Board decision in November 1980. There was no system of automatic rotation of the position of Chairman (as there had been in the past), and the position was decided by election every two years – Moore, should he so wish, would be able to put his name forward for another term.

The Rams had lost their final pre-season friendly by 2-1 at Wolverhampton, in front of 6,221. The game was played with considerable intensity and Derby were certainly better value than the defeat suggested – Steve Powell, the new club captain (who had signed apprentice forms for the Rams exactly ten years previously, and was the Rams' youngest-ever debutant), put them ahead on 16 minutes, volleying home an Alan Ramage flick on from a Kevin Hector corner – also involved in the goal was new signing Mick Coop, who played at right back. Pender (23 minutes) and £1 million striker Andy Gray (77 minutes), won the game for Wolves – both goals coming as a result of individual errors by Derby defenders, and fighting on the terraces unfortunately demonstrated that this element remained a menace to football, even on Sundays. out of season.

The Rams lined up in a 4-4-2 system, with Roger Jones in goal, a back four (right to left) of Mick Coop, Steve Powell, Alan Ramage and Wayne Richards, a midfield four (right to left) of Kevin Hector, Steve Spooner, Tony Reid and Paul Emson, and Dave Swindlehurst partnering Kevin Wilson in attack. After 80 minutes, substitutes John Clayton and Steve Emery were introduced.

Lack of cash, however, had already hampered the preparations of Colin Addison and John Newman. They had wanted to sign 25-year-old winger Alan Birch from Chesterfield just before the season started, but with no cash to spend and only players in exchange to offer, the North Derbyshire club had preferred a rival bid from Wolves. Birch, a prolific goal scorer as well as a very creative player, had scored 58 goals from the wing in 261 matches for Walsall and Chesterfield up to that point, and could have been just what the Rams needed. Also, Steve Buckley, who did not feature in the pre-season match at Molineux, looked likely to be sold – something that had been widely expected since promotion back to the First Division became out of the question towards the end of the previous season – Buckley had turned down the offer of a new contract from Derby, preferring to look for a move away, with Brian Clough's Nottingham Forest reputedly interested in signing the left back.

The only new addition, 33-year-old defender or defensive midfielder Mick Coop, turned down the offer of a 2-year contract at Coventry City in order to sign for Derby in July 1981. Grimsby-born Coop had been with the Highfield Road club since joining as an apprentice in January 1966. He had also played a summer season in the North American Soccer League, with the Detroit Express club, in 1979. He had played nearly 500 games for Coventry – "he could prove to be as great a bargain as Roger Jones has undoubtedly been in goal", said Colin Addison. Coop's signing, uninspiring at the time, was not to prove successful and he was at the Baseball Ground for only 6 months before his contract was cancelled, by mutual consent.

Colin Addison's name was linked with the managerial vacancy at his old club West Bromwich Albion, following Ron Atkinson's move to Manchester United. Addison was adamant – "I took no notice…I wouldn't want to go and let someone else cash in our John Newman's and my blood and sweat". Assistant manager John Newman turned down offers from Chesterfield, Gillingham and Plymouth Argyle during his first 18 months with Derby.

Alan Ramage, who was a professional cricketer with Yorkshire, as well as a professional footballer with Derby, had taken the decision to focus on football with the Rams, and had turned down Yorkshire manager Ray Illingworth's plea not to join the footballers for the start of pre-season training, on July 28th – "I am a Yorkshireman and proud of my county cap, but I have a growing affection as well as loyalty for the Rams and I want to be a key part in their set up…I get the bulk of a good living from Derby County so I have to give them my almost undivided attention throughout the year", said Ramage, who, along with his wife Alison, opened a video tape hire shop on Ashbourne Road in Derby.

Roy McFarland and John Duncan, released at the end of the 1980-81 season, both stepped into management straight away, with Bradford City and Scunthorpe United respectively, they joined five other former Derby County players in managerial roles with Football League clubs – Alan Durban (Sunderland), Ritchie Barker (Stoke City), Bob Saxton (Blackburn Rovers), David Webb (Bournemouth) and Bruce Rioch (assistant to Frank O'Farrell at Torquay United).

Also leaving the Baseball Ground in the summer of 1981 was Jonathan Clark, who left for Preston North End, having fallen completely out of favour at Derby and on the transfer list for the whole of the previous season. Clark's departure was not lamented by Derby supporters, frustrated by the player's lack of consistency and tendency to go missing for periods during games. Most supporters felt that the Rams had better, and younger, midfielders on the books – especially Tony Reid, who had stepped into Clark's number 7 shirt with considerable comfort.

Alan Biley, who had been seriously injured and missed the last months of the season, was sold to Everton in July 1981 – he had been chasing a move back to the First Division it was no shock when he left the Baseball Ground. He struggled at Everton, making only 19 appearances, and had left for Stoke City on loan within a season.

Over the summer, Derby had sent the six players considered most promising of all on the club's books, to the Lake District country estate of Brathay Hall, the former home of poet Wordsworth, on the banks of Lake Windermere. The six, all aged 16 to 17, were Rob Palmer, Paul Bancroft, Mark Frid, Paul Blades, Colyn Doyle and Nick Mihic. Mihic, Bancroft and Doyle were all Derby Boys players. Alongside them were boys of a similar age from Everton and Ipswich Town, and they endured "hell and blisters" during outward bound activities such as mountaineering and rowing. The Rams' Assistant Manager John Newman, and Youth Coach Ron Webster, travelled with the boys – "everything we have been hammering into our youngsters was concentrated here, it was a superb grounding for the boys, and we are delighted with it". The Daily Mail, also following proceedings, were focussed on Derby's young black player Colyn Doyle who, they said "went into the course a sheep and came out a lion". Doyle said – "lots of my pals are out of work, and only four of the group I left school with have jobs. Those who haven't are envious…most of them go to youth clubs, if they get bored, they rob shops and just do anything to enjoy themselves". In addition to the six who attended the outward-bound course, brothers Jimmy and David Collins from Liverpool constituted a total of eight who became first-year apprentices in the summer of 1981.

Three of the 1980-81 apprentices signed full professional terms in the summer of 1981, they were Paul Halford, Dave King and Colin Murphy – all of whom had made a good impression at reserve level the previous season. The six who survived from the previous season's apprentice professional intake were strikers Mark Shackleton (from Holbeach) and Ian Mulholland (Newcastle-on-Tyne), midfielders Chris Ball (Somercotes), Stuart Beaver (Kirkby-In-Ashfield) and Kevin Bird (North East), and defender Graham Harbey (Starkholmes, near Matlock). A Rams Youth XI lost to local side New Villa Reserves in a pre-season friendly, and the New Villa side's 18-year-old midfielder Des Gordon impressed so much that he was invited to trial with Derby's reserves. Derby announced that their newly-formed Under 18 side, the Colts, would play in the Derby City League during 1981-82, with home games being played at Raynesway.

Another youngster who showed tremendous promise in the reserves pre-season fixtures was 20-year-old Liverpool born striker Frank Gamble, who had joined Derby on a one month trial from Cheshire League club Burscough but had impressed so much that he had been offered immediate professional terms – "he sparkled with rare promise and made an immediate impact" said reserve coach Richie Norman. Unfortunately, Gamble suffered a broken toe in a pre-season game, and was out for about a month. His key attributes – ability to play on either wing, powerful and accurate shooting, had alerted the Rams Chief Scout Alan Ashman. The young man with the strong scouse accent had to be persuaded to tuck his shirt in, and to wear shin pads, when he became a professional footballer – at Burscough he had not needed shin pads – nobody at that level could get near enough to kick him.

Before the Wolves friendly, the Rams first team squad had toured Sweden and Finland. They had flown to the North Sweden town of Lulea from Heathrow, via Stockholm, on Sunday August 9th, and had stayed at Alvsbyn for their four day stay in Sweden. Days were long and training hard – there was no strong beer for sale anywhere other than one shop, and no sales at all after 7pm. There was also no night life. The team was followed throughout the tour by 25 Rams supporters.

In the first game on 12th August, the Rams demolished a somewhat undistinguished Lulea 6-0, Dave Swindlehurst scoring a hat-trick, Kevin Wilson and Steve Spooner getting the other goals. The following evening, Alvsbyn IF provided much sterner opposition and Derby were held to a 1-1 draw – Alvsbyn's goalkeeper Birger Johansson, wanted by Malmo, was outstanding.

The following night, after a long coach journey to Oulu in Finland, Derby played Finnish Champions OPS Oulu (who had been drawn to play Liverpool in the European Champions Cup), and won handsomely by 3-0, courtesy of another Swindlehurst marker, plus one from Paul Emson and an own goal. After flying south from Oulu to Turku, the players were given some respite before their next game, on Tuesday 18th, against TPS Turku, who proved to be decent opposition – Derby narrowly winning via a Wilson goal, 1-0. The final match, on 19th was against current Finnish League leaders KPT Kukio, who had won 15 successive matches and proved to be by far the best side the Rams had met on tour, but Derby got themselves 2-0 up and restricted the home side to just one in reply, courtesy of some gutsy defending. The tour ended with the devastating news of the death of Keith Osgood's wife, Wendy.

Derby's tour party: Jones, Cherry, Emery, Richards, Coop, Ramage, Osgood, S Powell, Reid, Spooner, Skivington, Sheridan, Emson, Hector, Swindlehurst, Clayton, Wilson

The Rams reserves suffered a mixed pre-season, with several who would be considered regulars away with the senior team's Scandinavian tour. They lost a Bass Charity Vase semi-final game at home to Leicester City, 0-2, then beat Stoke City in the 3rd place play off match 3-2 (fighting back from 2-1 down at half time). They then lost 1-0 at home to Shepshed Charterhouse (managed by ex-Rams forward Frank Wignall) and rounded off their pre-season with a thumping 5-0 win against Ilkeston – goals coming from Gamble (2), Woods (2) and Dalziel. Steve Buckley, expected to leave the club soon and consequently omitted from the First Team tour, played in all the reserves' pre-season matches, as did future first team players Yakka Banovic, Graham Harbey, Ian Dalziel, Aiden Gibson, Frank Gamble and newcomer Ilkeston-born forward Andy Hill, who had been signed from Kimberley Town in June 1981. An error with the Football League's fixture computer left the Rams reserves without a match on the first scheduled Saturday of the season, they were selected to play Bury at home, which was not possible as the First team were due to play at the Baseball Ground on the same day.

First team action began for real on 29th August 1981 against Orient, managed by Jimmy Bloomfield, at the Baseball Ground. Mick Coop made his Rams debut at right back in a 4-4-2 formation, with Steve Emery on the bench. Derby lined up with Jones; Coop, Ramage, S Powell, Richards; Hector, Spooner, Reid, Emson; Wilson, Swindlehurst. Keith Osgood was absent following his personal tragedy, contract rebel Steve Buckley was left out due to ongoing transfer speculation and negotiations. The other changes from the final game of 1980-81 were McFarland (left the club), Frank Sheridan and John Clayton (not selected). Orient's experienced side including England Under 23 International goalkeeper Mervyn Day, ex West Ham defender Tommy Taylor, and former England internationals Stan Bowles and Peter Taylor. The game began after a minute's silence as a show of respect for Wendy Osgood.

The first shock was the attendance – just 12,423, which included just 96 on the visitors terracing from Orient (and not a single visiting fan in a seat). It was almost 3,500 down on the number for the same fixture back in February. It was Derby's lowest home crowd since 11,031 watched the end of season game against Plymouth Argyle, in 1967 (in which Rams current assistant manager John Newman turned out for the visitors) – just before Brian Clough and Peter Taylor were appointed, in fact after that game manager Tim Ward, trainer Ralph Hann and chief scout Sammy Crooks were dismissed. Derby's players ran out onto the pitch to the tune of the Dambusters theme – for many years this had been the music accompanying the Rams, but it had been dropped a few seasons previously, nobody could remember why – but most people were glad it was now back.

The second shock, although perhaps not so much as the size of the crowd, was the result – Orient winning the game 2-1. Derby were dreadful and were flattered to only lose the game by one goal – only Swindlehurst appeared to show the necessary determination and it was unfortunate that he sliced a penalty wide at the Normanton End after 26 minutes, by which time the Rams were already 2-0 down. Kevin Hector got the consolation goal, after goalkeeper Day dropped a Mick Coop cross.

Frustrated fans on the Pop Side chanted "what a load of rubbish" and "sack the board" throughout the second half of the Orient game, and for the first time since he had joined the club, manager Colin Addison was subjected to press speculation regarding his job security – The Sun reporting on 2nd September that Addison "was given full boardroom backing" following "crisis club Derby's disastrous home defeat to Orient".

Mick Coop was born in Grimsby in 1948 but grew up in Leamington Spa, Warwickshire. As a schoolboy he was an outstanding cricketer and footballer, and Coventry City moved quickly to offer apprentice terms to secure him in 1962, after leaving school aged just 14. He made such progress that by January 1966 he was offered professional terms, making his first team debut that season. Coop was Coventry's regular right back for the next 8 years, before briefly losing his place and going out on loan to York City in 1974-75 – he returned to win back his first team spot at Highfield Road and went on to make 499 appearances for the Sky Blues, including many at centre back. In the summer of 1979, Coop went on loan to Detroit Express of the NASL, and in July 1981 he rejected a new deal at Coventry in favour of an offer from Derby County, who paid £20,000 for the services of the then 33-year-old.

After just 18 games with Derby, he agreed an early contract termination and retired from professional football, before making a brief comeback with non-league AP Leamington. He went on to coach at Highfield Road under former team mates George Curtis and John Sillett – his 1987 youth team won the FA Youth Cup, then became an antiques dealer. He is considered one of Coventry's greatest ever players and came close to England Under 23 honours in the late 1960's, only missing out when manager Noel Cantwell refused to support his selection. He became Coventry's penalty-taker and missed only twice from the spot in his career. Mick Coop endured a torrid spell at Derby, suffering with poor personal form in a very poor and badly organised side (in which he was often made scapegoat by frustrated supporters) – neither the player himself nor the club would look back with any fondness of those miserable six months.

Derby won their first points of the new season on Tuesday 1st September in front of just over 5,000 (including some 1,300 from Derby), at the Abbey Stadium, against Cambridge United. It was the first time that the club had won 3 points from a single game, and goals from Steve Emery (selected ahead of Paul Emson), and Dave Swindlehurst, were the deciders in a 2-1 win. Steve Buckley returned to the side, despite continued transfer speculation, and Addison juggled his formation – with Coop and Richards remaining at full back, Buckley partnering Ramage in central defence, and Powell and Emery in midfield. Wilson was left out, and Hector partnered Swindlehurst in attack. Emery's opener was a stunning 25-yard shot, and the Rams were reasonably comfortable until 2 minutes before half time, when the home side equalised. Derby showed good character to battle back after the break and Swindlehurst's goal, a scrambled affair after a corner, from which Hector's overhead kick was saved, then Ramage's shot hit the post before the big striker found the net, gave them a deserved 3 points. The Rams share of gate receipts for this game amounted to just £1,300 (by way of contrast, Nottingham Forest received £15,000 for their away game at Old Trafford, in the First Division). After the game, 12 Rams fans found themselves stranded in Cambridge when a group of local fans upturned their minibus outside the Abbey Stadium. Rams manager Colin Addison offered to take some of the fans back to Derby on the team coach – "he couldn't have been more helpful, but we couldn't all fit in, so we stuck together and after assistance from the local police we finally got back to Derby at 4 in the morning"

On Saturday 5th September at Gay Meadow, Shrewsbury Town shattered any illusions that Derby supporters may have had about the season ahead. The Rams capitulated 4-1, in front of just 4,373 (for which Derby received a share of only just over £1,000). It was a nightmare day for Derby County, and probably spelt the beginning of the end for manager Colin Addison. Shrewsbury, who had lost both of their previous games, hit the Rams for 2 goals in the space of 5 second half minutes, after Swindlehurst had levelled the game 1-1 soon after the restart. Derby had played some reasonable football, but the way they had caved in when the home side went into the ascendancy was a clear warning sign – it appeared that the Shrewsbury players, whilst less naturally talented, simply had more desire to win the match.

Colin Addison and John Newman were coming under pressure from supporters for the first time since their appointment in July 1979 – they had been fortunate to get a very long honeymoon, more than 2 years, and had some justifiable reasons for the continued poor results and poor performances - but there was no sign of improvement. They had no money to spend on new players now, but they had spent a huge amount in 1979-80 and, Swindlehurst aside, the players they signed had proven poor value for money. They had suffered injuries to key players, but so did all the other teams. The plain facts were that they had taken on a reasonably poor First Division side and, two years down the line, had created a reasonably poor Second Division side. Newman said, in September 1979 – "the young players must accept the challenge and start proving themselves or look for another job…the experienced players must live up to their reputations or face playing football elsewhere. We don't intend to let two years of blood, sweat and tears go down the drain without putting up a fight, we're definitely on our own now".

Finances, by now close to breaking point, came back into focus in September 1981 when it was announced that an Extraordinary General Meeting of shareholders would be held to consider the issue of £30,000's worth of non-voting shares. This became necessary if Derby County FC Ltd were to remain a public company, under the revised 1980 Companies Act, and so remain in a position to raise cash from the public, the club needed to raise their share issue from the present £20,000 to £50,000 by March 1982.

Despite the financial situation, the Board took the decision to purchase the freehold of the cleared land at Shaftsbury Street and Harrington Street. Previously, the football club had a nine-month rental agreement with Derby City Council, to use the land for car parking. The Board's considered opinion was that despite the current hardship, they had to give the club the best opportunity to develop and expand the Baseball Ground in future, and had they turned down the chance to buy this land, the chance would be gone forever. Derby City Council, whilst encouraging and supportive to the Board's bid, had to secure the best value for their ratepayers so there had to be an equitable financial return for them. Car parking around the Baseball Ground had always been a major problem – evidenced by the long waiting lists for any available space in the small Vulcan Street car park. The new areas could house 600 cars in secure, fenced-off space. The club offered one, two or three seasons car park tickets at £29.90, £57.50 and £82.80 respectively, or on a match by match basis at £1.50.

Meanwhile, the club's Executive Box complex was struggling to sell its facilities. Priced at £150, £225 or £250 per match for 6, 10 or 12 seated boxes, sales were slow as Derby's stature fell, both on and off the pitch.

Matchday attendances were also a major concern – the picture was gloomy, and the 12,433 at the first home game of the season, plus the numbers for the 1980-81 season, looked reminiscent of Derby's previous period in the Second Division – in the two seasons following relegation from Division One in 1953, gates fluctuated between 7,766 and 18,917. The 7,766 figure for the final home game of 1954-55 against Hull City (with the Rams already relegated to Division Three North), had been the smallest crowd since March 8th, 1939 when only 6,157 turned up for a match against Chelsea. The lowest crowds in the season prior to the current one were 14,139 v Newcastle United in 1980-81 but the first signs of the real decline had been in Tommy Docherty's final season as manager when just 15,935 watched the First Division game against Ipswich Town, in February 1979 – at the time that was the smallest crowd that Derby had registered since they had been promoted to Division One in 1969.

Supporters were not happy with changes at the Baseball Ground, especially former Osmaston Terrace inhabitants, who bombarded the club with letters of complaint after they had lost their beloved "Ossie End" to the new Family Seating Area and were now "crammed in like sardines" on the Pop Side. Mick Williams of MIckleover complained – "all you can see from the Pop Side is the passive main stand". Club secretary Michael Dunford said in response – "we would have extended the Pop Side, taking many yards of the visitors (Colombo) enclosure this summer, had the £25,000 cost not made it prohibitive, but I can promise we will do just that as soon as we have the cash available".

The structural changes at the Baseball Ground over the summer of 1981 left the capacity restricted to 32,000, of which exactly half, 16,000, was seated. Of the 16,000 terrace spaces, they were divided at the time as such: 4,500 reserved for visiting supporters (at the Colombo end of the Pop Side), 800 reserved on what was left of the Osmaston Terrace (season ticket holders only), 1,200 reserved in the Pop Side season ticket area (known as the "Pop Side Pen") – however, only 300 standing season tickets had been sold for the Ossie End and Pop Side, leaving 1,700 spaces unoccupied, meanwhile the 9,000 terrace spaces for "pay at the gate" spectators were crammed into the remaining areas – the Pop Side Vulcan terrace, and the small Normanton Terrace. It represented a miscalculation by the club – despite the crowd total for the game against Orient being barely over 12,000, the Pop Side Vulcan section had crowds "packed in like sardines" (according to several witnesses), while 96 Orient fans stood in the Colombo section, large enough to hold 4,500. There was some easing of pressure on the Pop Side for the Leicester City match, despite the attendance being over 16,000, but it was still uncomfortably tight for room – Secretary Michael Dunford suspected that many had bought seats or the Leicester game, being anxious not to relive the dangerous crushing they had experienced during the previous match – "don't blame us…fencing is costly to erect and costly to move", said Dunford, "we may have to use the Pop Side Pen, which can hold 1,200, as an overflow area when crowds in the Vulcan section are tight". Derby's seating areas were a different matter altogether – whilst the terraces remained packed almost to capacity, vast sections of empty seats were evident all around the Baseball Ground.

The Family Seating Area on the former Osmaston Terrace, undoubtedly planned with the best of intentions, was proving something of a mixed-blessing. The club had stated that tickets for this area would only be sold to adults who were accompanied by children, but this was clearly not the case and the club said, after the Leicester City home game – "in the pre-match rush, it's hard for our staff to monitor everyone who buys a ticket for these seats". What had happened, was that supporter's intent on baiting rival visiting fans, standing just yards away, had infiltrated the Family Seating and caused trouble, harassing the visiting supporters as well as upsetting the families with children who had bought tickets specifically to avoid this kind of trouble.

The days of professional footballers being considered "just one of the lads" was by now already a distant memory. Seat prices at the Baseball Ground were prohibitive, and with the UK Government talking about a 4% wage increase limit in the autumn and winter of 1981, and some employees taking a pay cut just to keep their jobs and not join the three million unemployed, luxuries like football season tickets were obviously going to be sacrificed. Football players, meanwhile, were earning bigger and bigger salaries – the new contract laws, discussed previously, were biting and the players now held most if not all the power in contract negotiations. Clubs like Derby County, with constantly falling income and players on relatively high wages, especially suffered. Michael Dunford insisted that the clubs had no choice but to "get tough" in contract negotiations, as Derby had in the case of Steve Buckley.

Buckley, who had been at the club since January 1978 and had been a reasonably consistent performer in a declining side. His contract expired in the summer of 1981 and he had turned down the offer of a new deal from the Rams (of course, the deal had to be the same or better than the First Division contract he had previously been on). Buckley, feeling that he could earn more elsewhere, held firm over the summer and Derby County, in no position to increase their offer (even if they had wanted to), refused to negotiate further – and were proven to be correct when Buckley eventually signed the contract he had been offered in May 1981, just after the start of the new season.

Sheffield Wednesday's loss was Derby County's gain when Wednesday manager Jack Charlton turned down the opportunity to sign 20-year-old former Ilkeston Grammar School pupil Andy Hill, following trials. Derby County stepped in quickly to offer professional terms to Hill, who had recently passed his accountancy exams – "I don't aim to stop that until I'm Chartered, you can't take anything for granted in football", said Hill. Reserve coach Richie Norman was pleased at how the player had adapted to full time training – "he has good close ball control and is positive in the air, but he must work up more aggression in the box". Hill made his debut for the Central League side against Burnley on 2nd September, laying on John Clayton's winner with an excellent run and cross. He had starred in Ilkeston and Heanor Schoolboy sides and had played for Derbyshire's Under 19 team and had been playing part-time for Kimberley Town (managed by former Rams defender Geoff Barrowcliffe) when he was spotted and recommended by Derby scout Jack Nesbit.

Derby's reserves started their Central League campaign with a win at home to Burnley, followed by a defeat at home to Leeds United. Basic defensive errors marred the Leeds defeat, and the Rams should have won the game, having several good chances aside from the 2 goals they scored in a 2-3 defeat, Kevin Wilson finishing a half-chance very well for the first, but missing an open goal in a mixed display. A new name in the Reserves, as well as Andy Hill, was 16-year-old Neil Banks – still at school, having just finished his O-Levels, the Shirebrook boy was already well over 6 feet tall. Like Hill, he showed admirable intelligence, declaring "I am carrying on with my studies to ensure that I'm qualified for an alternative career if things go wrong". Banks became Paul Blades's regular central defensive partner for Derby's "A" team. Recently bereaved Keith Osgood turned out for the reserves in both the first two games of the season, as did first team squad members Glenn Skivington, Frank Sheridan, John Clayton and the recently recovered from injury Aiden Gibson.

The Rams' second home game of the season was against recently relegated Leicester City, managed by former Glasgow Rangers boss Jock Wallace, on Saturday September 12th. Barry Powell, back from his summer in the NASL, returned to the side in place of Steve Spooner, and Steve Buckley, the contract-rebel now back in the manager's good books, reverted to his natural left back position to replace Wayne Richards. A better crowd, 16,046, was encouraging – Leicester brought with them 2,400 standing supporters and just short of 500 seated. Leicester's side featured future Derby players Mark Wallington and Ian Wilson, as well as future England star Gary Lineker (who came on as substitute).

Derby, playing at a far higher standard then seen in the previous 3 games, were 3-0 ahead by half time. Hector opened the scoring after 5 minutes, after Swindlehurst had flicked an Emery corner over the goalkeeper at the near post, leaving the veteran with a free header from inside the 6-yard-box. Buckley crashed home a 30-yard free kick after half an hour, and a scrambled clearance from another corner rebounded off Ramage into the net for goal number three, a minute before half time. After the break Leicester fought back and reduced the arrears on 63 minutes with a fine strike from Melrose, but a resolute Derby held firm for a 3-1 victory, with the returning Barry Powell perhaps their best player.

The game against Leicester City was controversial for non-footballing reasons. ATV, the regional television network, spent around £14,000 to film the game for TV, but before transmission (in fact immediately after the game) it was banned from screens, because Rams goalkeeper Roger Jones's shirt displayed the name of the sponsor, Patrick, on the front. The outfield players wore plain shirts without the logo. The Rams objected to the cancellation of the broadcast, but ITV Sports boss Gerry Loftus would not relent, citing Football League regulation 61, banning any shirt advertising from televised matches.

Derby insisted that the incident was an accident and not a premeditated flouting of the rules. In fact the Rams were clear in their defence, stating – "when we were informed on August 6th that the Leicester game would be screened by ITV we followed the normal procedure, we informed advertising agent Harold Bermitz who booked £5,000 extra in advertising hoarding space for his clients – would we have allowed angry repercussions from this vital source of extra income, and risked football league punishment, for the doubtful privilege of getting our shirt sponsors screen time?". Training staff were informed that sponsored clothing was not to be worn for this match but there was clearly a human error somewhere down the line, as the outfield shirts were correct, only Jones's goalkeeper jersey was wrong. Jones, who due to superstition only put on his jersey as the teams ran out of the tunnel, did not notice. Michael Dunford, reaching his Director's Box seat 6 minutes into the game, spotted the error right away and sent word to Gordon Guthrie on the bench to change the shirt – "in the manager's opinion there was not considered adequate opportunity to switch the shirt until half time" said Dunford.

The issue of sponsor advertising on TV sports was reaching its bitter conclusion around this time. A week before the Derby v Leicester game, the BBC had banned coverage of a European Championship boxing match between Alan Minter and Tony Sibson, because Minter wore DAF Trucks advertising on his shorts. However, the same day as the game, ITV allowed coverage from the First Division game between Ipswich Town and Liverpool, despite coverage clearly showing Liverpool's trainer wearing a track suit emblazoned with the club sponsor Hitachi's logo.

In fact, Derby County considered themselves hard-done-by by the ATV network – during the Friday night sports programme, before the Leicester game, the Rams had come under considerable criticism for their poor start to the season, with comment from local journalists Gerald Mortimer (Derby Evening Telegraph) and Neil Hallam (Derby Trader), both of whom were critical of the club. The club were invited onto the programme to reply, but both Chairman Richard Moore and manager Colin Addison declined the invitation. ITV cut the journalists' comments short and edited out Hallam's referral to an alleged "take-over-bid" by former Aston Villa chairman Doug Ellis – a matter which both the Trader and the Telegraph had recently reported on. Co-incidentally, or otherwise, both Ellis and Head of ATV Sport Billy Wright were present at the Derby v Leicester game, in the same Executive Box.

On 19th September, at Hillsborough, Derby drew 1-1 with Sheffield Wednesday in front of more than 24,000. Once again, the Rams started quickly and took the lead after only 2 minutes – a short corner from Emery was smartly chipped into the box by Coop, deceiving goalkeeper Bolder, leaving Steve Powell to head into an unguarded net. They held firm until the 85th minute when former Derby winger Terry Curran's cross was headed home by Gary Megson – it was the only real chance that the Rams had allowed the home side all game. Curran, on his day the finest winger outside of the First Division, and being touted for an England call-up, was marshalled with admirable competence by Buckley, and Barry Powell once again had a fine game. It was a good point, but the Rams probably deserved all 3 – the Sunday People, summarising the game, wrote – "Sheffield Wednesday, would-be First Division aristocrats, were cut down to size by Derby's humble brand of honest professionals...they were so carried away with their 100% start to the season that star forward Terry Curran – number of international caps nought – was announced to the crowd as "the England Superstar"".

The reserves picked up their second win of the season, a 4-2 victory over Sheffield Wednesday at the Baseball Ground on 19th September – they had impressively gone 4 goals ahead and the two late Wednesday markers were no more than consolation goals. The very impressive Frank Gamble, returning from a broken toe injury, scored twice, and fellow forwards Andy Hill and John Clayton scored the other two. It was a significant improvement on previous results, 0-3 at home to Stoke City and 1-4 away at Liverpool – only Hill and winger Aiden Gibson had looked impressive in the two defeats. Gibson had been absent for three months after breaking a bone in his ankle on his first team debut the previous season – like Gamble, he was considered a fine prospect and was expected to step up to the first team in the short term.

Down the age groups, Derby's "A" side had lost to Shrewsbury Town, fast becoming a bogey team and all level, at Raynesway – Ian Mulholland scored the Rams' goal in a 1-2 defeat. After that loss, the youngsters beat an older and more experienced Mansfield Town side 2-

0, with 2 late goals from Mark Shackleton and Mulholland. Goalkeeper Robert Palmer had a particularly good game against Mansfield, including 2 fine saves late in the game.

Mulholland, a second-year apprentice, had struggled for consistency in the previous season after moving down from the North East, but had been in fine form so far this season, scoring in all four of the "A" team's Midland Intermediate League gams so far. Youth Development Coach Geoff Worth admitted he had had doubts about Mulholland and had wondered if he had made a mistake but was now starting to see the ability and quality that had made him snap the youngster up in the first place. Youth Coach Ron Webster concluded that home sickness had contributed to the issues last season – "he was missing his mates", said Webster.

The Rams made a coaching appointment in September 1981 when they appointed former England International Alan Hodgkinson as specialist goalkeeping coach. Previously, there had been nobody performing that role – manager Colin Addison commented - "It's a specialist job needing specialist coaching". Hodgkinson was working with the four goalkeepers on Derby's books – Roger Jones, Steve Cherry, Yakka Banovic and Robert Palmer.

The following Wednesday evening, the Rams went down 0-2 at the Baseball Ground to Bolton Wanderers. The attendance marked a new low – just under 12,000. Before the game, Derbyshire County Cricket Club, led by captain Barry Wood, paraded on the pitch with their recently-won Nat West Knockout Trophy. The game was a fiasco for the Rams – Bolton had not won a single point during the season so far and were completely devoid of confidence, but two gifted goals handed them all three at the Baseball Ground. The visitors were a hard, rugged unit who battled well, but they did not have the same footballing ability as Derby and should have been comfortably beaten.

Roger Jones was injured – "having suffered a groin strain doing exercises at home", so young Steve Cherry deputised in goal and had a poor game – the first goal, after 13 minutes, was particularly poor as Cherry lost the flight of a Brian Kidd corner and allowed it to run across the face of goal to Gerry McElhinney, although Derby's defenders were also not blameless. It was 2-0 to Bolton by half time, after a long ball was worked quickly from Kidd to future Derby midfielder Trevor Hebberd, who played in Chris Thompson to score easily, and should have been more but a combination of poor finishing and the woodwork came to Derby's aid.

The Rams gave the ball away so much that it became an embarrassment and supporters again showed their frustration – which boiled over into unacceptable territory when a linesman appeared to be struck by a missile thrown from the Pop Side, causing Derby's trainer Gordon Guthrie to be called over to assist the stricken official, and the club were reported to the Football Association. The result saw Derby drop to 13th position in the league table.

Season Ticket sales were distressingly poor, down 18% on sales at the same time a year earlier. The club, anxious to boost numbers, began to offer "football on hire purchase", with a scheme that allowed patrons to pay £10 now and the balance in monthly instalments – "the recession is biting deep, and we have hard evidence that scores of fans are missing because they haven't the ready cash to splash out £50 plus on a season ticket…what we are doing is testing the widespread credit market, to see if it might apply to football" said Michael Dunford.

In the National and local press, the pressure was piling on to Colin Addison and John Newman. Typical reports were "the most harassed and haunted management team in English football had a face to face confrontation yesterday with their chairman to ask the startling question – "are our jobs under threat from Brian Clough and Peter Taylor?" – and they are likely to quit the club unless they get the right answers from chairman Richard Moore". The reports referred to a meeting on the Monday prior to the Bolton defeat, widely reported as a "clear the air" between Moore and the management duo. The focus was recent press speculation about a take-over bid involving Doug Ellis, with stories suggesting that Clough and Taylor would join him at the Baseball Ground. Moore said - "I know nothing more than I have read in the papers". In fact, none of the Board had been approached by Ellis, or anyone else, regarding ownership of the club. The situation at Derby was so bad by this time, that any consortium or individual planning a take-over would surely have their sanity questioned – an investment of £1million would be required to acquire a controlling interest, and £750,000 would immediately be swallowed up by the club's overdraft.

Addison and Newman retained the confidence of the current board, that was clear – whether or not the fans shared the board's opinion was by now a matter for debate – an article by John Barber in a supporters club publication had been highly critical of Addison's management, and neither the Derby Evening Telegraph nor the Derby Trader were convinced that Addison remained the right man for the job.

Derby faced Queen's Park Rangers in their second successive home match, on Saturday 26th September, and picked up their 3rd win of the season, by 3-1. The crowd was even smaller than had turned up for the midweek defeat to Bolton – just 11.246, the lowest at the Baseball ground since 1967. Frank Gamble made his first team debut, on the right wing, and Keith Osgood made his first appearance of the season for the first team, at full back. The Rams lined up: Jones; Coop, Ramage, S Powell, Osgood; Gamble, B Powell, Reid, Emson; Hector, Swindlehurst – with Sheridan on the substitutes bench.

Derby had a great start, with Kevin Hector scoring what was at the time the fastest goal in club history, timed at 14 seconds – no opponent touched the ball which went from Barry Powell to Paul Emson, via Dave Swindlehurst to Hector. Rangers equalised early in the second half, but a second goal from Hector and another from Alan Ramage secured the victory.

The QPR result left Derby with a record of played 7, won 3, drew 1, lost 3 (10 points) and it illustrated what the Rams were by then, an inconsistent, mid-table Second Division side. Worse was to follow – Derby were only to win 3 games over the next 4 months, and as miserable Autumn turned into freezing winter, Colin Addison's time as manager was approaching its end.

Frank Gamble was born in August 1961 in Liverpool and signed permanently for Derby following a brief spell on loan from Burscough. A gifted although mercurial player, he was predominantly a right sided attacking winger and did not enjoy tracking back – consequently, he made 8 only appearances for Derby (including 1 as substitute) and scored 2 goals, and eventually walked out of the club in November 1982, in the middle of his contract, dropping out of professional football to join Barrow as a part-timer, before following manager Vic Halom to Rochdale in December 1984. After 2 successful seasons at Spotland, with 9 goals in 46 appearances, he again dropped out of league football and signed first for Morecambe, and then Southport.

Gamble had off-field issues, and stories of drug abuse and theft followed him around – at Rochdale, it was an open secret that his team mates did not leave valuable items lying around in the dressing room when he was about. It was a shame, because he was clearly a very talented footballer and could have played many more games in the Football League, had his attitude matched his ability.

After beating Queen's Park Rangers at the Baseball Ground on 26th September, Derby endured a miserable run. Successive league defeats to Charlton Athletic and Newcastle United sandwiched a League Cup loss to West Ham United, and in total 6 of the next 10 games were lost, and 2 drawn.

Defeat at The Valley against no better than average Charlton Athletic, by 2-1, turned out to be the final first team appearance for young midfielder Steve Spooner (who replaced Frank Gamble in the starting line-up) – he would be on his way to Halifax Town 3 months later. Steve Cherry continued to deputise in goal for the injured Roger Jones, and Kevin Wilson replaced Kevin Hector in attack. Paul Emson scored the Rams' consolation goal, in front of just 6,686. It was a dire Derby performance, not helped by injuries to Swindlehurst, who was replaced at half time by Gamble, and both Barry Powell and Spooner, who were slowed by knocks received earlier in the match. Paul Emson had put the Rams ahead, but two goals by former Derby striker Derek Hales won the game for the home side. The lack of spirit and determination from Derby's players was shocking, even by recent standards.

There had been more national media attention on the Rams' finances after in the week before the defeat at Charlton. On Tuesday 29th September The Sun reported – "Derby put almost a whole team on offer as Addison feels the pinch", going on to claim that Derby were asking less than a quarter of a million pounds in total for ten players – Kevin Wilson, Paul Emson, Steve Emery, Keith Osgood, Frank Sheridan, Wayne Richards, John Clayton, Steve

Spooner, Jaka Banovic and David King. It was certainly a shock, but taken in context, it had to be considered that Derby's professional staff of 42 players (including 14 apprentices) was amongst the biggest in England. Some players were already under offer – Emson had turned down a £50,000 move to Preston North End, after the Rams had wanted him to go, and Steve Emery was the subject of a firm enquiry from Bolton Wanderers, with the same fee being discussed. Derby's bankers, Nat West, were putting the club under pressure to reduce its overdraft and players had to be sold – the club had no choice. Costs had already been cut with many non-playing staff losing their jobs over the summer, and travel and overnight hotel costs (first team and reserves) plus other internal savings, which had resulted in the end of season 1981-82 overdraft forecast being improved from £1.4 million to £900,000. It was a thankless task, however, with bank interest rates reaching record high levels of 16%.

Meanwhile, the club's major shareholders, in whose hands any recovery plan would sink or swim, had decided to block a planned share issue which would have raised vital funds but in turn would have opened the door to potential new investors who may instigate a bid for control, such as Doug Ellis. Brian Clough, who's name had been linked with a return to the club, perhaps in an ownership capacity, had already laughed off the rumours – "too daft for words". What was a matter of fact was that the club's player wages had more than doubled in the period 1975 to 1980, from a quarter of a million pounds to more than half a million – the Rams had not started the wage spiral, but they had participated in it, either willingly or without any other option.

The club's youth policy was called into question – five of the ten players listed for sale were part of Colin Addison's much-praised youth scheme (Richards, Spooner, Clayton, Sheridan and Wilson). They had all shown promise, said the manager, but had not performed consistently enough to hold down a regular place in the second division. On the other hand, a new, younger crop of players were being groomed to step into their places – Addison named left winger Aiden Gibson, forwards Andy Hill and Frank Gamble, and defenders Graham Harbey and Paul Blades. Tony Reid, the 18-year-old midfielder, was named by the manager as the best of all the club's young players – Reid, by this time, was already established as a first team regular.

The Rams "A" team captured the Midland Intermediate League Cup at the end of September 1981 (the final had been carried over from the previous season), with a victory on penalties over Wolverhampton Wanderers – the youngsters were a goal up inside half an hour after Mulholland latched onto Halford's pass to finish neatly, and held the lead until the 88th minute when Wolves equalised against a tiring Derby defence. After a goalless extra time, the Rams won the shoot-out 5-3, Beaver, Bird, Harbey, Dalziel and goalkeeper Banovic all scoring from the spot. On 10th October the youngsters scored a notable victory over local rivals Nottingham Forest at Raynesway, winning 4-1 with a hat-trick from Colyn Doyle – including 2 goals in two minutes – the second being a fine solo effort after a mazy dribble through the visitor's defence.

The reserves were also doing well, with away wins at both Manchester United and Preston North End in the Central League. Kevin Wilson, recently placed on the available for transfer list, scored a hat-trick at Deepdale in a 4-0 win. Paul Blades made his debut for the reserves in a 2-0 win at Old Trafford, scoring one of the goals. After 7 games, the Rams' reserves were 6th in the Central League, with 8 points (at this level, there was still only 2 points awarded for a win).

In the 2nd round of the Football League Cup, Derby had drawn West Ham United, flying high at the top of the First Division. The first leg, at the Baseball Ground on 7th October, was watched by 13,764 and the Rams went down 2-3 after battling hard against a far more skilful Hammers side. Derby took the lead on 8 minutes when Scottish International full back Ray Stewart's back pass evaded his own goalkeeper Tom McAlister and rolled into the Normanton End goal. Kevin Hector scored his 200th goal for the club, with a typical instinctive finish – only Steve Bloomer, with 337, had scored more goals for the Rams. Derby held the game at 2-2 until an inexplicable hand ball by Alan Ramage, suffering a spell of wretched form, gifted the visitors a penalty which was converted.

In the second leg, three weeks later, 2 goals from future Rams striker Paul Goddard won the tie for West Ham by an aggregate score of 5-2. Colin Addison had still failed to win a single cup tie in his time as Derby County manager. At Upton Park, Derby had shown considerable fight after conceding a poor goal when they reacted too slowly to a quickly-taken free kick – but poor finishing cost them dearly and they were clearly second best. It was an uncomfortable night for Derby's supporters, who found that the designated visitors enclosure at Upton Park was not only right next to the rowdiest West Ham supporters' section, but also shared the same W.C and food kiosk. "we could not even go to the toilet or snack bar or toilet without the fear of being spotted and beaten up. None of us could enjoy the match, even though Derby did give an excellent performance" said Pete Simcox of Chaddesden.

On Saturday 10th October the Rams travelled to St James's Park to take on Newcastle United, and were easily beaten 3-0, with goals from Imre Varadi (2) and Kenny Wharton. Derby's team for this game: Cherry; Coop, Ramage, Sheridan, Buckley; B.Powell, S.Powell, Skivington, Emson; Hector, Swindlehurst and substitute Clayton. Newcastle, managed by future Rams' boss Arthur Cox, cruised to victory over a lacklustre Derby side which, Steve Powell apart, looked disinterested from the start. Despite missing a penalty, most observers felt that the Rams were lucky to escape with only a 3-goal defeat.

After the game, Powell wept in the dressing room, unable to accept the attitude of his team mates – "the lad was upset with our performance. He had given us 100%, he sweated blood for the club, and I want to be on record saying that", said manager Colin Addison. Powell, who always wanted to play in midfield, had been struggling manfully in a defence that was statistically the worst in the Second Division – with Ramage (who was substituted at St James's Park, sparing him for further misery, and new signing Mick Coop enduring particularly torrid times. Reserve right back, Middlesbrough-born John Lovatt, who had impressed his coach Richie Norman - "tough tackling is his strength" appeared poised to step up to replace the struggling Coop. It was the tenth consecutive league game without a clean sheet, and 22 goals had been conceded in the past 11 matches. At the other end of the pitch there was no compensation – only 14 had been scored by Derby over the same period. Addison could not get the balance right – already in the season he had used 20 different players.

The Derby Evening Telegraph was by now forecasting that the Rams were heading for a relegation fight – "Survival in the Second Division is becoming the prime objective this season. It may well be the only target and the air of crisis surrounding the club is inescapable" – wrote the paper on October 5th – along with veiled suggestions that it could be time for a managerial change. The Rams were 6th from bottom of the Second Division after the defeat at Newcastle, with 10 points from 8 matches.

Chairman Richard Moore announced a £350,000 "survival scheme" at a Board meeting on 14th October 1981. The scheme, approved in principle by the club's major shareholders but requiring formal ratification at an Extraordinary General Meeting, which was to be held as soon as possible, involved an issue of additional voting shares and loan schemes – the £350,000 raised would be used to reduce the club's indebtedness to Nat West Bank to what Moore described as "within manageable proportions". This appeared to be an "about-turn" from the shareholders' previously stated position. Headlines in that week's national press claiming that a cheque issued by Derby County had bounced were true, but out of context – it had indeed happened, but some ten months previously.

Supporters were growing increasingly frustrated with the apparent delaying of the share issue. Stephanie Brownson, writing to Ram Newspaper in October 1981 – "uppermost in the minds of supporters is the issue of new shares, which could give Derby County the financial fillip it so badly needs. I understand that this has been blocked by the main shareholders...is one man to deny the club even this chance? Is this the beginning of the end? Is it the irresistible force against the immovable object, because if this is the case Derby County is surely doomed and Mr Majority Shareholder will find that his shares are not worth the paper they are written on"?

One of the players who the club were determined to keep, David Swindlehurst, handed in a transfer request on 13th October. Swindlehurst had suffered with inconsistent form, as had the whole team, and had missed two penalties already in the season. He had battled hard and never appeared to be lacking in effort but had not scored for 7 matches (contrasted with his strike partner Kevin Hector, approaching 37 years old and having scored 5 in 8 games so far in the season) and, it appeared, he knew the ship was sinking – "the club is drifting", said the big striker. It was a major blow for manager Colin Addison – he had placed Swindlehurst at the top of his "must keep" list and recommended to the board that the transfer request be turned down. Further bad news came in the form of injuries to Frank

Gamble, who broke a toe for the second time in the space of 3 months, and Kevin Wilson, who was involved in a car accident.

The Football Association decided to take no action regarding the coin throwing incident in the Baseball Ground game against Bolton - but issued a strong warning that should a repeat occur, there will be a heavy fine and possible closure of part, or even all, of the ground for a period.

The Rams met Blackburn Rovers at the Baseball Ground on October 17th. The visitors dominated possession and looked the better side after going ahead on five minutes when Fazackerley, unmarked at the near post, turned an in-swinging corner towards the equally unmarked Keeley who headed home from close range. Barry Powell equalised for the Rams against the run of play, with a fine free kick on 54 minutes. The attendance was yet another new low – just 10,572 turned up.

A week later, Derby won for the first time in a month, when they beat Crystal Palace 1-0 at Selhurst Park. In a much-improved display, the Rams played some fast, intricate passing football and should have won more comfortably, hitting the woodwork twice and missing several other good chances. Dave Swindlehurst scored the winning goal, his first for 9 matches, and the defence looked more solid than previously – Frank Sheridan, who had replaced Alan Ramage 3 games previously, settling in to a partnership with Steve Powell in a vastly improved defensive display. As well as Sheridan, fellow youngsters Tony Reid and John Clayton were beginning to establish themselves in the side. The win at Selhurst Park took the Rams up one place in the league table, to 16th.

It was a memorable day for Rams fan David Probert, from Orpington in Kent, who was turned away from the visitor's enclosure because the Palace stewards did not believe that someone with that his Kentish accent could be a Rams follower. Two coach loads of Derby fans on their way to Selhurst Park were caught up in a "Ban the Bomb" march taking place in Central London – and missed most of the game.

During the final week of October 1981, more details of the proposed new finances, share issues and cash injections began to emerge. On Monday 26th it was announced that the Rams had turned down Dave Swindlehurst's request for a transfer. The decision had been taken by the club's new board of Directors, headed by new Chairman Bill Stevenson – who had replaced Richard Moore, who voluntarily (and gladly) stepped down from the role. The new financial package, it was announced, would introduce well in excess of the originally targeted £350,000 – whilst it would not solve all the problems, it would considerably ease both the overdraft at the bank and interest payments "revitalising the club's standing with our bankers" said Stevenson – "and should soon allow the management more manoeuvrability in their search to strengthen the playing staff". Stevenson stressed that the club needed better gates than it was getting – after 10,572 turned up to see the game against Blackburn Rovers, for example, Blackburn received £3,000 of the share of turnstile receipts and the Rams were left with just £5,072.

The new Board of Directors, which was set to underwrite the proposed finance being injected included John Kirkland, Chairman of local firm Bowmer & Kirkland (and son of the late former club Director Mr Jack Kirkland, heavily involved in the resignation debacle of Brian Clough and Peter Taylor in 1973) who was by this time the club's major shareholder – Kirkland had agreed to play an active inside role in the club's affairs. Richard Moore, the previous chairman, stayed on the Board, and was joined by Rex Stone (the new vice chairman) as well as Kirkland.

There were also, according to the Ram Newspaper, to be three new faces on the Board (due to restrictions in the number of Directors allowed by Derby County's Articles of Association, there could currently be no more than eight serving Directors, so an extra-ordinary general meeting of shareholders was required to ratify these changes). These new men were Fred Fern, owner of carpeting company Fern Carpets (and already a significant sponsor and supporter of the club), Frank Cholerton, head of a local electrical wholesale and retail operation and another lifelong Rams supporter, and Mick McGarry, a North East-based bookmaker and formerly vice chairman of Grimsby Town, who had recently fallen out with his fellow directors at Blundell Park.

Leaving the board was Arthur Atkins, although he did agree to continue in a supervisory position with responsibility for the Baseball Ground pitch, working with Groundsman Bob Smith and his assistant Ricky Martin – a role he had carried out for the past 3 years. Despite Atkins's continued involvement with practical matters of the pitch, his departure caused considerable rumours that all was not well behind the scenes – the Derby Trader suggested a rift between Atkins and Director-designate Frank Cholerton. Cholerton, after various stories emerged regarding money, finally did not join the board.

Something had to be done about falling attendances, and it did not help that a significant section of Derby's supporters felt ignored. The unpopular decision to put seats onto most of the Osmaston Terrace was cited as a major reason for reduced crowds – G.Tomlinson of Derby, for example, wrote – "The Baseball Ground is just not the same without the Ossie End terrace...the Ossie End was covered with seats without reference to the fans themselves. Some of the people who have thus been kicked out have been Ossie Enders season after season for years. Then you (the club) calmly tell us it's going to be covered with seats. A lot of your fans do not like standing on the Pop Side, nor can they afford to sit down, so they don't bother coming anymore...and why is Bill X no longer writing in the Ram. It seems you no longer care about the terraces".

Bill X, who had asked to be stood down from his column-writing duties, added to the general discontent – "what a dog's ear the club has made with their once highly attractive stadium for standing fans. The ridiculous Family Seating area of the Osmaston End has completely killed off the atmosphere which was once so good...haven't we got enough seats already without putting in more". It was also common knowledge that away supporters were infiltrating the Family seats, and many unruly West Ham fans had done so at the recent League Cup tie. "The club went to great expense to build fencing around the Ossie End then, in the midst of a cash crisis, pull the whole lot down for unwanted seats. This really is a cause of great discontent among terrace supporters, many of them have quit coming in protest". J.L.Gould of Derby added – "(the club) upset scores of Ossie Enders by arbitrarily taking away their space to put in Family Viewing seating which isn't even a quarter full most games...scores I know have stopped following the Rams in disgust, they won't be packed into the Pop Side and can't afford a seat. Please rectify this daft decision".

On Saturday 31st October Derby entertained Grimsby Town at the Baseball Ground. A marginally improved crowd, up over 1,000 from the previous home game, saw a 1-1 draw. Aiden Gibson, the substitute, replaced Paul Emson for what turned out to be his last appearance for the first team. John Clayton, looking increasingly at home in the first team, scored Derby's goal. Grimsby's team featured former Derby apprentice goalkeeper Nigel Batch, future Ram Mike Brolly and Trevor Whymark, who had played twice on loan for the Rams.

It was a strange game. After a dull first half, Derby came out with all guns blazing after half time and for 20 minutes played perhaps the best and most attacking spell of football seen at the Baseball Ground in five years – hitting the woodwork three times. Des Anderson, the former Rams assistant manager, watching from the Directors Box said - "it was brilliant stuff, imaginative, attacking football", however, what was missing was decisive finishing. Paul Emson, who had turned his full-back inside-out during that spell was inexplicably taken off and replaced by youngster Gibson, and the Rams completely lost the initiative as substitute struggled to meet the pace of the game. The Rams, who had led 1-0 since Clayton's 20-yard strike on 35 minutes, left themselves wide open to a sucker punch, which duly arrived in the 4th minute of injury time. The 94th minute equaliser, and the questionable substitution, did not bode well for manager Colin Addison's future at the Baseball Ground.

At Kenilworth Road against top-of-the table Luton Town on 7th November the Rams went down 2-3. It was Derby's 4th league defeat in the previous 8 matches, and they had only won 1 of their last 8 in all competitions. It was, however, a decent performance from the Rams against a quality home side. Dave Swindlehurst, suffering from a swollen knee, failed a pre-match fitness test, so Kevin Wilson (who had not played in the past month due to the after-effects of a car crash) started in attack alongside Clayton, and there was a further setback when Tony Reid was injured within two minutes of the start and had to be replaced by substitute Keith Osgood. The Rams went 0-2, and then 1-3 behind but battled on and fought back well on both occasions – Town's third goal came courtesy of a rare error by goalkeeper Roger Jones, who misjudged the flight of a corner. Derby's first goal was especially well taken, with Osgood striding onto a pinpoint through ball from Steve Buckley and finishing with some style, the second coming from Clayton, in the final minutes.

The following from Derby was quite impressive but would have been more but for a mix-up with *Roadrider* coach bookings, which resulted in two bus-loads of Rams fans being unable to travel to Kenilworth Road. One who did see the game, but uncomfortably, was Adrian Moss of Belper, who had been forced to remove his steel-tipped boots (which he had to wear for medical reasons) – "come in bare-footed or go and buy a new pair of shoes", insisted the Police at the Kenilworth Road turnstiles (at the time, it was relatively common for people wearing heavy boots to be instructed to remove them before entering visiting terrace enclosures – the term "bovver boys" had been coined to describe such fans). Adrian, upset and clearly not a "bovver boy", was taken to find the Derby team coach where Steve Powell took pity and loaned the young fan his training shoes.

Popular former Derby striker Billy Hughes returned to the area in November 1981, to take over as licence holder of the Rising Sun pub on Friargate in the City. Hughes, who preferred to settle in Derby rather than his native North East, had recently left North American Soccer League side San Jose after a contractual dispute – still with a soft-spot for the Rams he said – "I'm still super fit and I'd help the Rams out for nowt...I was happy here, with so many friends in the area" Hughes had been the club's top scorer when manager Tommy Docherty surprisingly sold him in the autumn of 1978.

Also, in November 1981 the Baseball Ground was put to a different use when more than 2,500 people turned up to watch Derby County's "Fireworks Spectacular" – a 30-minute firework display, a marching band, and a penalty shoot-out by the first team players were the entertainment on offer. Michael Dunford had long suggested that the ground must be used for more than just football and he announced that a pop concert in the spring or early summer of 1982 was now on the cards.

The Rams reserves extended their unbeaten run to 10 matches with an away win at Bloomfield Road against Blackpool, and a 1-0 defeat of Aston Villa at the Baseball Ground – moving them up to second place in the Central League table, behind only Liverpool. Attendances at home reserve games had more than doubled since the previous season - 470 paid to watch the Rams' second-string play Everton in October 1981. Outstanding during the run had been Graham Harbey, the 17-year-old who had been starring in a sweeper role behind central defenders Paul Blades and Glenn Skivington. The improved form of goalkeeper Yakka Banovic, and the fast-blossoming Andy Hill were also of note. Banovic appeared to have leap-frogged Steve Cherry in the club's goalkeeper rankings – Cherry, the First Team goalkeeper when Roger Jones was injured a few weeks earlier, now found himself on the transfer list, and playing Midland Intermediate League football. Despite the club's apparent lack of faith in Cherry, one man who continued to champion the cause of the young goalkeeper was Gerald Mortimer, the Derby Evening Telegraph's football reporter, who said "after watching (Cherry) against West Brom "A", I hope no club comes up with the money to sign him. Cherry looks better at this stage than John Turner and Nigel Batch did, and they are building good League careers. Cherry could still play an important part in the club's future".

Another who appeared to be pushing for a First Team place was 19-year-old defender or midfielder Ian Dalziel. Dalziel, from Seaham near South Shields, had joined the club as an apprentice in 1978 and was now in his second year as a professional. He had been approached by several other clubs while playing for Durham County Boys but had opted for the Rams because he felt the path to a full- time career in football was clearer.

Others were not so fortunate – three apprentices were released in October 1981 – Ian Mulholland, Stuart Beaver and Kevin Bird, all three were close to their 18th birthdays. All three had played at Central League level but had played mostly at "A" and Youth Team levels. With youth unemployment so high at this time, it was particularly tough on the youngsters, but the Rams' horrific financial situation ensured that only young players who could possibly generate a fee in the future could be kept-on.

It took an almost full first team strength Wolverhampton Wanderers reserve side to end the Rams' second string's unbeaten run, on October 14th (a day when there were no First Division games because of the England National team's World Cup Qualifying match against Hungary, taking place that same weekend – the result of which qualified England for their first World Cup Finals appearance since 1970). Wolves striker Andy Gray, who they had signed for £1 million, scored 2 goals for the home side in a 3-1 win although the young Rams, with Andy Hill again outstanding, pushed their far more experienced and costly opponents to the limit in another fine performance – Dalziel and Lovatt also looked like first team players in the making.

Another sub-11,000 Baseball Ground crowd saw 5th from bottom Derby beat 2nd from bottom Wrexham 2-1 on Saturday 14th November. Steve Emery came into the side to replace the injured Tony Reid in midfield – the unfortunate Reid was out for 2 months. Frank Sheridan and Steve Powell continued at centre back and John Clayton continued his partnership with Dave Swindlehurst in attack. Mascot for the day was the author's sister, 9-year-old Sara Forsyth, of Ashbourne.

The game itself was desperately short of quality, Derby's recent improved form disappeared, and they were lucky to beat the gritty but inferior North Wales side in a game chosen for TV coverage by ATV. Wrexham almost broke the stalemate on 43 minutes but Dowman hit the post when he should have scored, then almost immediately Steve Buckley drove forward from left back and hit a powerful shot from 30-yards out, which dipped and swerved beyond goalkeeper Niezwkiecki in the Osmaston End goal. The Rams winner was a lucky one – the goalkeeper saved a Barry Powell shot but could only deflect it into the path of John Clayton, who's effort was going wide until deflected into his own net by the unfortunate Ian Edwards – the same player who had netted the visitor's goal with an unmarked header. Watching the game from the stands was Nottingham Forest manager Brian Clough, with his reported summer target Steve Buckley again being the subject of the former Rams manager's attentions. Buckley, who claimed he was unaware of Clough's presence, said after the game – "I'm very happy at Derby but any player worth his salt keeps an open mind about his future. You must do what you think is best for your present club, as well as for yourself...I was upset that all the rumours about (Clough's) interest in me in the summer didn't turn out to be true"

On Saturday 21st November Derby were easily beaten 4-1 at Carrow Road against Norwich City. Norwich's superiority was complete – Kevin Hector described them as "the best side I've seen in the Second Division", and they went ahead in the first minute, while the Rams lost their best player, skipper Steve Powell, through injury. Norwich dominated the game, with the Rams' midfield completely ineffectual and lacking any bite. Derby's consolation goal was scored by substitute Keith Osgood, but the 4-1 scoreline flattered them – Norwich could easily have won by 6 or 7 goals. The result dropped the Rams 3 places in the league table, they were now 17th.

New Chairman Bill Stevenson, in his first major interview since taking the Chair, announced that with gates averaging around 12,000, the club was heading towards an overdraft well in excess of a million pounds by the end of the season – this was despite the new board injecting funds into the club by way of personal loans, as demanded by the bank. The board was also "in the process of accumulating a further cash injection" according to Stevenson. There was no cash for new players but the Chairman was aware that a new player or two could revive flagging public interest, but the funds were simply not there "the club will be back on a slippery slope if the utmost care isn't taken in the future...a large cash injection does not set our trading balance to rights, our expenditure exceeds our income"

As far as attendances were concerned, it was only to get worse. On Wednesday 25th November just 8,470 turned up to see the Rams beat Cambridge United 2-1 at the Baseball Ground – it was the lowest crowd for a Derby County first team home game since 1965, including just 51 in the visitor's enclosure. Manager Colin Addison, without injured skipper Steve Powell, partnered Steve Buckley with Frank Sheridan in central defence, bringing in Wayne Richards at left back. Summer signing Mick Coop, who had endured a torrid time at right back, was dropped in favour of Keith Osgood. Dave Swindlehurst put Derby ahead just before half time, with one of the best goals of the season, a 30-yard left foot shot into the top of the Normanton End goal. In the first half, the Rams played some of their neatest football of the season but lacked a cutting edge. Disturbingly, however, Derby looked lethargic and poorly-organised after the break and allowed Cambridge back into the match – until John Clayton's well-placed header, against the run of play, gave the Rams a 2-goal lead. The visitor's consolation, a few minutes before the end, was an own goal by the otherwise excellent Frank Sheridan.

One scheme which was proving successful was the *Ramarena* – Derby County's newly named Sports and Social Club at the club's training centre on Raynesway, under facility manager Phil Jones. Since opening fully in September 1981, it had been adopted for use by many local clubs including 5-a-side Football, Jogging, Netball and Badminton. The weight training and fitness area was proving particularly popular with local gym enthusiasts. Various football leagues made use of the all-weather pitches including a shift-workers league which operated on Tuesday afternoons, to suit night shift workers. The Ramarena also played host to a regular "home match disco" which started at 8pm after every Saturday Derby County home match.

Also thriving was the Derby County Supporters' Club Norwegian Branch. In fact, in the whole of Scandinavia only Manchester United had a bigger supporters club in that region than the Rams. Secretary Arnstein Hernes told Ram Newspaper in November 1981 – "most leading English clubs have supporters club branches in Norway, but Derby County's is flourishing and strong, compared with most others. Our 130-strong membership is on par with that of the First Division Championship days...once a Ram, always a Ram"

Derby played at home again on Saturday 28th November, with Chelsea the visitors. Before the game, six young soldiers from the Royal Signals stationed in Derby's twin-town Osnabruck, led by Signalman Andrew Green of Leabrook, did two "laps of honour" around the Baseball Ground following their 450 mile walk from West Germany to raise funds for local charities. The Rams were again without captain Steve Powell, and Steve Emery was also absent injured and replaced in midfield by Keith Osgood – they also lost left back Wayne Richards with a head injury in the first half.

For most of the game, Chelsea simply outclassed the Rams – only some very poor finishing denying the visitors a comfortable victory, but despite all the dominance, they managed only a single goal and were dealt a hammer-blow by Derby in the final minute of the game when John Clayton's over-hit corner was chipped back into the box for Osgood to bravely dive through a sea of legs to equalize at the Osmaston End. Osgood had provided a warning to the visitors just five minutes before his equalising goal, when he headed a left-wing cross against the crossbar.

The football on the pitch, sadly, was not the main story on 28th November. Midway through the second half a smoke bomb was thrown into the Family Seating Area by Chelsea fans, and then supporters from Chelsea sparked a near-riot after Osgood's equalising goal, and the Rams were driven to declare that from now on visiting supporters would be actively encouraged to stay away from the Baseball Ground. The first action was to increase the price for terrace tickets in the visiting Colombo enclosure to £4, and, also that any game in which a large visiting contingent was expected would be admission by voucher only. Alcohol sales in all areas of the Pop Side were stopped.

Also seated areas would be segregated, meaning that visiting spectators wishing to sit down would not be able to freely select the area in which they wanted to sit. For the "all voucher" games, visiting supporters would be restricted to seats on the former Osmaston Terrace – now the Rams Family Viewing Area, again at £4 per match. "we appreciate that our actions may be construed as ripping off visiting supporters", said Michael Dunford, "but we are allowed to dictate our own policies and in no way can we tolerate a similar situation to that which prevailed at the Chelsea game...the reason that the Family Viewing Area seats will be allocated to visiting supporters is because there are only 60 season ticket holders for this area compared to more than 33% season tickets in every other stand. The decision was therefore simple, rather than inconvenience the majority it was better to ask these 60 people to accept alternative seats (for the voucher games)".

Any future match between Chelsea and Derby at the Baseball Ground would be strictly voucher only, except for 12 Directors Box tickets (one of which for this particular fixture, had accommodated Olympic gold medallist Sebastian Coe) and 50 tickets provided for Chelsea's players and officials, friends and families. Derby also requested that the Football League schedule any future match between the clubs for midweek early evening kick-off, to discourage Chelsea supporters from attending. The Ram Newspaper received a threatening letter with a London postmark, reading – "If Chelsea receive some kind of FA ban as a result of the after-match scenes grossly exaggerated by Mr Dunford in the press, Derby supporters should go to Stamford Bridge in April (for the return fixture) at their peril. That is not a threat, it is a fact"

13,964 was the official attendance on 28th November. Derby County had expected, and made police provision for, 15,000. Precautions should have been more than adequate for the visit of Chelsea, who's supporters at that time had a reputation for trouble-making around visiting grounds. In fact, the visiting hooligans were able to make trouble in all stands, all around the Baseball Ground – police were not able to get to them in the stands and instead found themselves attacked from all directions by hundreds of marauding Chelsea supporters within the 4,000 who had travelled from London. The Police made it clear that a very large proportion of the 4,000 were involved in the trouble – not simply a "mindless minority".

From the perspective of Derby's Pop Side supporters, they had been surprised to find that no Chelsea fans had entered the home Vulcan Street section of their terrace (despite the price being 70p cheaper in this section compared to the Colombo Street area). The first real signs of any trouble had come when Chelsea supporters began spitting and throwing beer from the balcony of the Ley Stand above, into the Pop Side. Derby supporters responded in kind as Chelsea fans were escorted back to their section of the ground. A fire was lit and swiftly extinguished at the Normanton End, and numerous red flares were let off in the Osmaston End – both potentially disastrous in the wooden stands. "The horrors that something like that could cause are unbearable to even contemplate", said correspondent Bill X in Ram Newspaper.

After the match, Chelsea supporters exited the Ley Stand and waited outside the Pop Side exit, "congratulating" the Rams on their late equaliser courtesy of flying boots, bricks and fists. This initial mob was soon joined by what Bill X described as "an absolute herd of Chelsea fans" coming from Shaftsbury Crescent, having exited the Colombo terrace. There was supposed to be a police escort, but according to Rams fans on the scene, only 1 male and 1 female officer were waiting for the Chelsea supporters. "The depth of venom displayed by so many Londoners in so many parts of the ground was football hooliganism at its very worst", said Bill X.

6 days after drawing with Chelsea, on a Friday night, the Rams went to Ninian Park to face fellow mid-table side Cardiff City. Kevin Wilson replaced John Clayton in attack – Clayton having failed a pre-match fitness test, and Buckley and Sheridan continued their makeshift centre back partnership. Just 5,515 attended the game, and the Rams lost 1-0 to the mediocre home side, dropping to 16th place in the Second Division on 22 points – 19 behind leaders Luton Town and 6 ahead of bottom-of-the-table Bolton Wanderers.

After a dull and disappointing first half, in which Cardiff went ahead through a Wayne Richards own goal, and Kevin Hector missed a gilt-edged chance to level the game, the Rams' form completely disintegrated in the second half in yet another embarrassing non-performance. Manager Colin Addison conceded – "we barely turned up for the second half". The Derby Evening Telegraph asked – "have the players got the club in their blood and in their hearts?" – it was a fair question, and the answer appeared perfectly clear. Two milestones were reached at Ninian Park – Dave Swindlehurst played his 300th Football League game (including 64 for Derby, with 19 goals), and Steve Buckley his 150th for the Rams (with 8 goals). Derby's team for what turned out to be their final game of 1981 was: Jones; Coop, Sheridan, Buckley, Richards; Osgood, B.Powell, Hector, Emson; Swindlehurst, Wilson; substitute Skivington.

After the defeat at Cardiff, Derby caused something of a surprise by signing highly-rated young defender Richard Money on loan, initially for one month, from Liverpool. That Liverpool had allowed Money to go to the Baseball Ground on loan, rather than elsewhere, was testament to manager Bob Paisley's admiration for the Rams and his genuine wish that "our old friends Derby County" get back to the top flight again. Derby had expressed a desire to take Money on a permanent deal "for the first stage in our improved financial climate inspired by our so-often criticised Board, who have made it possible for the management to now build on a side which has so much potential...fans can now expect quite a little activity in and out, as far as players are concerned" (Michael Dunford). For the first time in quite a while, Dunford was able to announce that money was available again "not millions, but still substantial...the time is over for bouncing cheque rumours, the cash is beginning to flow again, it's only a dribble, not a torrent, but the pipes have been unblocked". There were strong rumours early in December 1981 that Dave Swindlehurst, perhaps the Rams' best player and almost certainly its most valuable, was set the leave the club to free up funds to allow manager Colin Addison to bring in new players.

Money, the 22-year-old former Fulham defender, had been chased by most of the top clubs in 1980 before he opted to join Liverpool. He made 14 appearances in the First Division with the Reds in 1980-81 but had barely featured in the current season and was clearly disappointed not to have made the grade at Anfield – "now I will prove them wrong….I am most impressed with the management and set-up (at Derby), I want First Division football and I will help your former League Champions to get it back". Manager Colin Addison said – "if we'd had £300,000 to spend a few months ago we would have been in (for Money) before Liverpool. Bob Paisley has been great allowing us a month's loan initially until we can lay down the hard cash".

Leaving the Baseball Ground on loan in November 1981 was Reserve team skipper Steve Spooner, who had fallen completely out of favour since starting the season in the first team and had been allowed to join Halifax Town on an initial one-month loan, with a prospective transfer fee of £5,000 agreed should The Shaymen wish to make the deal permanent – as eventually happened on 21st January 1981 (at Spooner and new wife Lynne's wedding reception). Spooner's team mates in the reserves were still flying high in the Central League, in 5th place with 24 points from 19 matches (2 points for a win). Only Liverpool, Everton, Wolves and Nottingham Forest were above them in the table. Glenn Skivington typified the spirit of the Rams youngsters – playing in the First Team away at Cardiff on Friday 4th December then turning out for the reserves against Huddersfield Town the following day, due to a sudden injury crisis in which Andy Hill, Graham Harbey, Paul Blades and Neil Banks were all unavailable. Recently married Frank Gamble, just back from his honeymoon, scored the only goal in a 1-0 win over Huddersfield at the Baseball Ground.

On Saturday 12th December 1981, Derby were scheduled to face 2nd placed Oldham Athletic at the Baseball Ground. This game, along with the next 4 scheduled League games, all fell victim to the severe winter weather of 1981 – games at home to Barnsley (scheduled for Boxing Day) and Shrewsbury Town (scheduled for January 9th), and away to Watford (scheduled for December 19th) and Rotherham (December 28th) were all postponed in one of the harshest spells of winter weather for decades. The Rams were destined not to play League football again until January 16th, 1982 when they visited Brisbane Road to play Orient.

Keith Osgood, who had lost his young wife in tragic circumstances in the summer of 1981, left Derby at Christmas. He had expressed a desire to move closer to extended family and was allowed to join Orient for a fee of just £20,000. In the circumstances, it was the decent thing for the football club to do, and it also freed-up a space on the wage bill for the Liverpool loanee Richard Money, but financially it was yet another disaster – Addison had paid £150,000 for the defender just 2-years previously.

Chapter 1.4 - 1982

On January 2nd, 1982, Derby faced Bolton Wanderers at Burnden Park in the 3rd Round of the FA Cup. It was the first game they had played since losing to Cardiff City almost a month earlier in a Second Division fixture. There were two debutants in the Rams' side, loan signing **Richard Money** and reserve midfielder **Ian Dalziel**. The game turned out to be Mick Coop's final appearance for Derby.

Bolton, 3 places below the Rams in the league table, proved far too resilient and determined for Derby and progressed to the 4th Round courtesy of a 3-1 win in front of just under 10,000 spectators, Barry Powell scoring Derby's consolation goal. The Rams' first line-up of 1982 was: Jones; Coop, Money, Buckley, Richards; Dalziel, B.Powell, S.Powell, Gamble; Swindlehurst, Clayton; substitute Emson.

Richard Money was born in October 1955 in Lowestoft. A childhood Norwich City fan, he started his career as a junior at Scunthorpe United aged 18 and made 173 appearances for the club over 4 seasons before being signed by Fulham in 1977. At Craven Cottage, he received rave reviews for his defensive performances, earning him an England "B" cap, and was constantly the subject of speculation linking him with a move to one of the top First Division clubs. Eventually he signed for Liverpool in 1980, for a fee of £333,333, and played in a European Cup Semi Final, despite only making 14 appearances for the Anfield club. Bob Paisley decided that Money was not going to make the grade at the very top level and made him available for transfer in the summer of 1981.

He joined Derby County on loan in December 1981, with the intention being to make the move permanent, had the Rams been able to find the necessary transfer fee – instead he played just 6 matches for Derby before returning to Anfield. Money eventually left Liverpool permanently for Luton Town in April 1982, after spending the previous month on loan at Kenilworth Road. He stayed only a year at Luton before a short stay at Portsmouth, then returned to Scunthorpe to finish his playing career.

After 465 League appearances as a player, Money went into management with Scunthorpe, then became Youth Coach at Aston Villa and Assistant to Frank Clark at Nottingham Forest – following Clark to Manchester City in a coaching role, having forged an excellent reputation as an Academy and Youth Coach. He returned to the front-line management win Sweden with AIK and Vasteras SK, then in Australia with Newcastle Jets. Most recently he managed Cambridge United, Solihull Moors and Hartlepool United.

Ian Dalziel joined Derby County as an apprentice, becoming a stalwart of the talented Central League reserve side at the Baseball Ground before making his debut for the first team in January 1982. Born in South Shields, Dalziel was predominantly a defender but could also play in midfield, and he never let the Rams down when the first team called. In total, he made 28 appearances (including 2 as substitute) for Derby, scoring 2 goals – his longest run in the side came in the Autumn of 1982, when he was a regular on the left-hand side of midfield, occasionally filling-in at left back. He was released on a free transfer at the end of the 1982-83 season and was promptly snapped-up by John Newman, who was by then managing Hereford United – forging a successful career at Edgar Street and making 150 appearances for the club, before moving back North first to Carlisle United and then to non-league Gateshead. He had a spell as Assistant Manager at Morecambe in the early 2000's.

On 19th January 1982 at an Extraordinary General Meeting, Derby County's Shareholders voted to accept a proposed issue of 60,000 new shares, valued at £10 each. Additionally, the Football Club's Articles of Association were amended to allow up to 12 Directors to serve at the same time, meaning that Director-Designate Fred Fern could be formally appointed.

In response to lower gates, Derby City Council withdrew several "Park and Ride" bus services for Derby's home games. Services from Mickleover and Mackworth (the 500 and 502) were amalgamated, as were services from Breadsall and Chaddesden (507 and 514). The 501 service from Allestree was withdrawn completely. Fares remained unchanged, at 35p for adults and free for children.

The Rams finally returned to Second Division action on Saturday 16th January 1982 with a visit to Brisbane Road to play Orient. It was 43 days since they had last played a league game, due to the severe winter of 1981-82 (and the Orient game itself was also under threat from the weather and only went ahead after banks of snow were swept off the pitch and piled behind each goal), and they had not won a game since November 1981. A crowd of just 4,598 watched yet another Rams defeat, this time by 3-2, the result dropping the club to 17th in the Second Division – the Third Division appeared to be looming, just 7 seasons since the club had been Champions of the Football League. **Andy Hill** made his first team debut for Derby, in place of John Clayton, Steve Emery replaced Mick Coop (who was on his way out of the club) and Keith Osgood made his debut for Orient after leaving the Baseball Ground in December.

What was apparent at Orient, and indeed had been for most of the 1981-82 season so far, was a lack of discipline and commitment which was embarrassing to watch – the experienced players appeared to be the most-guilty. Also, there were question marks over the ability of the young players – were they good enough for Second Division football? Orient went into a 2-goal lead, but Derby fought back, and debutant Andy Hill scored with a fine header from a left-wing corner, then home full back Henry Houghton, under pressure from Paul Emson, pushed a back pass beyond his own goalkeeper Mervyn Day to level the scores. It was not enough, and Orient went on to win the game as Derby's performance level again dipped well below acceptability.

Andy Hill joined Derby in June 1981, while training to be an accountant and playing semi-professional football for Kimberley Town. He had been set to join Sheffield Wednesday, but the Hillsborough club changed their mind at the last minute. He was born in Ilkeston in November 1961 and had shown remarkable promise in the Rams' reserve team – soon being promoted to the first team and making his debut early in 1982. Hill only stayed at the Baseball Ground until September 1983, and only scored 4 goals in 28 appearances, but one of them was amongst the most famous of all Rams goals – against Nottingham Forest in a 1983 FA Cup tie victory. He moved on to Carlisle United after leaving Derby, then dropped out of professional full-time football with Boston United, Shepshed Charterhouse and Hinckley Athletic, in 1987.

Football returned to the Baseball Ground for the first time in almost 2 months when the re-arranged home fixture against Oldham Athletic was finally played, on Saturday 23rd January 1982. Oldham's team featured future Rams player Paul Futcher in central defence, and the attendance was 10,171. The game turned out to be manager Colin Addison's final match in charge of Derby County.

Derby dominated the game from start to finish in a match which made a mockery of the respective league positions of the two clubs – the Rams (17th) looking a far better side than 2nd placed Oldham. In fact, due to a succession of poor misses, Derby won by only 1-0 but might have had five or six. Hector (twice), Money, Barry Powell, Dalziel and Hill all missed when scoring would have been easier. It was not until the 80th minute when Swindlehurst wrong-footed Futcher after receiving a throw from Emson, then crashed home a right-footed shot from 20-yards at the Osmaston End to deservedly put the Rams ahead.

On Monday 25th January 1982, manager Colin Addison was dismissed from his position. The Board of Directors took the decision to advertise for a Managing Director, who would take over responsibility "for all affairs connected with the running of the club and will, of necessity, be knowledgeable in football and management. He will be offered a substantial shareholding in the club. The appointment of a new team manager will be the responsibility of the new managing director". Derby, therefore, looked set to be become the first club in England whose board of Directors was prepared to hand over complete control to a professional footballing man. Directors, throughout the history of English football, had always performed the hiring and firing responsibilities – the Rams Board were also proposing that the new man assume responsibility for administrative and commercial activities.

Bill Stevenson, the club Chairman, said that there would be no rush to appoint the new Managing Director. Speaking specifically about Brian Clough, who's name was predictably linked with the post – "we never aimed this at one man, we deny that we did. Had Brian Clough applied, of course there is no doubt his chance for the job would have been very good, but as he says he will be staying at Forest, it appears there will be no application". Stevenson denied approaching Clough "on the quiet", which would have been a breach of the Gentlemen's Agreement between League chairman, which forbid an approach. "Brian's statement that he remains where he is will disappoint hundreds of our fans because he is highly respected and intensely popular in our City and throughout our County, but we can do no more than advertise the job"

As for outgoing manager Colin Addison, he professed himself "sad, disappointed and relieved". He thanked Derby County's "wonderful supporters, who have given me so much encouragement over the past 2 ½ years". Addison said that the team required a couple of new players "there is no way the club is in its rightful position…just a small infusion of new talent will send them up the table". Addison claimed he had left behind "some wonderful young players for my successor. I know he will be bequeathed many good things, so I reject that I was a total failure…the pressure never worried me, I have never lacked faith in my ability, never been frightened of any job. But in the end, all the pressures, the tremendous ill-luck, the injuries, the never-ending imponderables, the problems and tragedies that went on and on, defeated me….the financial situation was a millstone round my neck almost from the day I stepped first through the door…I admit that one or two of my early signings were mistakes".

Speaking about his Assistant John Newman, Addison said that he had advised Newman to stay in to continue the work if the time came that he (Addison) had to go, presuming the Board of Directors allowed it. Newman, for the time being, remained at the club – albeit only temporarily, it appeared at the time. Derby faced three games in a week, including difficult-looking away trips to Watford and Rotherham United, and Newman reluctantly agreed to handle team affairs for these three games. Newman, and the Board, had only one objective – to keep Derby County in the Second Division.

Addison, in context, was remembered as a warm-hearted and likeable man who always tried to make himself available to answer supporters' questions with impressive frankness. He did, however, fail, and his partnership with John Newman was never entirely convincing. They did inherit a squad which had been decimated by Tommy Docherty (who, it must be remembered) was under pressure to revitalise an ageing and ailing outfit and bought hurriedly to bolster resources. However, Addison shot himself in the foot almost immediately by spending most, if not all, of the available cash on signings which proved, almost to a man, to be poor investments. Better players, like David Langan and Gerry Daly, were rebellious and left the club as soon as they had the opportunity, this was also not Addison's fault, but he had no resources with which to replace them.

In addition to his mistakes in the transfer market, Addison made a glaring error in not upgrading the goalkeeping position soon enough, waiting until after relegation to sign Roger Jones despite David McKellar proving clearly unreliable for a First Division campaign, and there being no adequate experienced goalkeeper in reserve. What he did undoubtedly do, to his credit, was to encourage and develop young players – several of whom were looking like exciting prospects, especially midfield player Tony Reid. Colin Addison was a nice guy, who tried his best and received excellent backing and goodwill during his time at Derby

County but, in the end, he had failed, and nobody could realistically query the Board's decision to wield the axe – 1 win in the previous 5 games was simply not acceptable.

Colin Addison eventually lost his job because of poor results, nothing more and nothing less. Despite winning his last game in charge of the club, his overall record was simply not acceptable:

1979-80 in the First Division, played 42, won 11, drew 8

1980-81 in the Second Division, played 42, won 15, drew 15

1981-82 in the Second Division, played 20, won 7, drew 18

His overall record of 100 points from 104 league games represented a poor return from a manager who was backed by his Board to the extent that he broke the club's transfer record on three occasions in the 1979-80 season, the deals in question being Barry Powell, Alan Biley and finally Dave Swindlehurst. Under Addison, the Rams' home form was unimpressive – just 23 wins from 52 league games at the Baseball Ground – but it was away from home where results really hit hardest, just 10 wins from 52 away games and only 45 goals scored.

The undoubted highlight of Addison's career at Derby came very early in his tenure, when the Rams beat European Champions Nottingham Forest 4-1 at the Baseball Ground on 24th November 1979. The decline at the Baseball Ground since Dave Mackay left the club was depressing – Mackay had averaged 1.16 points per game (marginally less than Derby's most successful manager Brian Clough, who averaged 1.18) – subsequent managers Colin Murphy (30 points from 35 games), Tommy Docherty (69 from 78) had fared no better than Addison, albeit with all of their matches being at First Division level.

The evening after Addison's dismissal, 26th January, Derby travelled to Vicarage Road to play 3rd placed Watford. John Newman took temporary charge of the team and made only one change from Addison's final team – bringing in Wayne Richards to replace Paul Emson on the left side of midfield. Newman's first selection as caretaker-manager was: Jones; Emery, Sheridan, Money, Buckley; Dalziel, Hector, B.Powell, Richards; Swindlehurst, Hill; substitute Emson.

The game was a disaster from start to finish. Goalkeeper Roger Jones had a nightmare evening, as the Rams fell to a 6-1 defeat. Jones's performance was so bad, being directly responsible for at least 3 of the goals, that he never played for Derby again and eventually moved to York City in the summer of 1982 – John Newman preferring to the young Yugoslav Yakka Banovic. Graham Taylor's Watford side ran Derby ragged for 90 minutes and could easily have won by even more, they simply outclassed the Rams.

There was no bite in midfield, as had been the problem all season – Kevin Hector and Barry Powell simply were not that kind of player, both preferring to get on the front foot and attack, at languid pace. One could not expect young Dalziel to influence a game like this, and

Richards, a reserve full back playing in midfield for the first team, was simply not the answer. Central defenders Sheridan and Money simply could not cope with the home side's continual pressure. Derby's consolation goal was a surprising one, a diving header from substitute Paul Emson.

John Newman could hardly have had a worse start to his managerial career at Derby. After the embarrassing thrashing at Watford, his team managed only 1 win in the next 8 games, which included 4 defeats. In fact, after Addison got the sack, the Rams managed just 5 victories in the last 22 games of season 1981-82, they did, however, manage 8 draws and the 23 points gathered was just, in the end, enough to keep them in the Second Division – thanks largely to a run of 7 games with only 1 defeat, between mid-March and mid-April.

The Ram Newspaper dated 30th January 1982 featured a prospectus relating to the proposed issue of 60,000 ordinary shares with a nominal value of £1, to be issued for a price of £10 each. Of interest to potential investors was the trading results for the past five years of The Derby County Football Club Limited, a summary of which is below:

1977 – operating profit £201,723, net transfer fees minus £173,732, net profit after tax £38,679

1978 - operating profit £84,562, net transfer fees minus £469,054, net loss after tax minus £352,084

1979 - operating loss minus £38,793, net transfer fees plus £81,628, net profit after tax £217,218

1980 – operating loss minus £172,742, net transfer fees minus £829,840, net loss after tax minus £962,745

1981 – operating loss minus £320,156, net transfer fees plus £513,191, net profit after tax £127,223

At the end of the previous financial year, 31st May 1981, the company was £923,607 in debt. The Baseball Ground itself was valued at £323,331 and other land and buildings owned by the company was valued at £92,776. The club was also operating at a loss, due largely to bank interest payments.

Prospective investors were invited to apply to purchase shares in The Derby County Football Club Limited, in writing to the Baseball Ground office, attaching a postal or money order with the appropriate payment.

The 1980 result, a loss of £962,745, reflected the huge amount of money gambled on maintaining the club's first division status, in Colin Addison's first season. When that failed, the Board had opportunities to salvage most if not all, of that loss by selling their highly valued players, Biley and Swindlehurst (in addition to Langan and Daly, who were sold). For reasons best known to themselves, the Board (under the Chairmanship of Richard Moore), decided not to take what would have been a conservative approach – and they were now paying the price for what, with hindsight, turned out to be a disastrous decision.

Reaction to Addison's sacking, in the Ram Newspaper dated 30th January, seemed to back the Board's decision, often with the caveat that Addison seemed to not have the full backing of his playing squad. A typical example being Don Ferryman of Chaddesden's letter: "It has to be said that the team Colin Addison built has played some absolute rubbish the season…the squad weren't obviously behind him 100% and the much maligned Board deserve our congratulations for what they did (sacking him)…maybe his bad signings made our Directors warn of squeezing the till absolutely dry…but what a job the man did with his fine Youth policy".

R.Y.Wilmot, of Long Eaton, wrote: "I have never seen so much rubbish from Rams sides as since Colin Addison took over" and went on more in hope than expectation: "if we can have Cloughie back our gates will be 25,000".

Another season ticket holder: "Andy Hill and Ian Dalziel have come into the side to give performances we have no right to expect considering their lack of experience, yet their sheer enthusiasm and pride in their Derby County shirts is forcing us to note them in contrast to the lackadaisical displays from some of their colleagues, who give the impression that their only interest is in Friday's wage packet"

Tom Symonds, a Popsider from Derby, wrote: "the end of Colin Addison's term was inevitable, but did he have the support of the players? …the attitude of some individuals was the cause of great concern among travelling fans on the way back from the FA Cup defeat at Bolton…usually we have all dug deep for the cause of Derby County football club (when asked for vocal and financial support), in return we only ask for 100% effort, it is now our turn to ask the club for something in return, a bit more effort from the players and a little bit more professionalism from them. A bit of pride in playing for Derby County while they are representing us and the City of Derby. Too many players seem for forget they are paid good money to do something many of us would give our right arms to do"

On Saturday January 30th, John Newman took charge of his first home match as Derby's manager – albeit no more than caretaker manager at the time. The visitors were Sheffield Wednesday, managed by England World Cup winner Jack Charlton and coached by former Derby County assistant Frank Blunstone, placed 6th in the Second Division and one of the best supported clubs outside the top flight. Due to the possibility of crowd trouble, and Wednesday supporters' recent poor behaviour (as well as the near-riot during Derby's previous high-profile home game against Chelsea), admission to the Pop Side and Normanton terraces was by voucher only, and no seats were put on sale on the day of the match. One person who did attend was former manager Colin Addison, who watched from the stands as his former team won 3-1.

Fighting back from a goal down, an injury-hit Rams side (featuring only three players who could be classed as senior – skipper for the day Buckley, Hector and Barry Powell) showed admirable grit and determination. Goalkeeper **Yakka Banovic** made his first team debut and despite some early nerves, showed signs that he could become a long-term solution at number one – especially with his bravery and willingness to come off his line. The unfortunate Ian Dalziel was carried off injured after just 12 minutes, and was replaced by Glenn Skivington, who put in a fine display. Man-of-the-match, however, was Frank Sheridan – he brought the score to 1-1 with a fine header at the Osmaston End early in the second half and his aerial dominance helped secure Derby's position when Wednesday did attack. In the second half Kevin Wilson, with his best display for the first team so far, scored twice and showed skill and bravery with a non-stop display in which he ran freely at the visitor's back four. Wilson's partner in attack Andy Hill also put in an enthusiastic and promising performance.

Unfortunately, there was some trouble inside the Baseball Ground, despite Derby's ban on visiting fans – some Sheffield Wednesday supporters had managed to buy tickets for the Family Seating area on the former Osmaston Terrace, and they showed their frustration at events on the pitch by kicking the backs of seats and throwing them at Derby fans sitting in the Osmaston Lower Tier.

Vjekoslav "Yakka" Banovic made a total of 38 appearances for Derby County, between 1980 and 1984, when his contract expired. He had joined the Rams from Australian side Heidelberg United, after being recommended to the club by his former junior coach Bill Bateman, and despite being born in Yugoslavia (in Bihac, which is now part of Croatia, in 1956), played twice for the Australian National team, just prior to joining the Rams. After leaving Derby Banovic returned to Australia and joined one of his former clubs, Melbourne Croatia. During a career which lasted 17 years, he also had a spell in Canada with Toronto Metro FC in the North American Soccer League, but the Rams were his only other club outside Australia. He lived in Geelong and ran an indoor sports centre for 20 years after finishing with full time football and retired to the small town of Whyalla in 2011.

Banovic almost missed his first team chance at Derby altogether. After being put into the "A" Team, finding himself behind Roger Jones and Steve Cherry, and being left out of the summer 1981 tour, his instinct was to leave the club and return home to Australia. "I was well known in Australia", he said, "playing for the National team in front of thousands. The one Saturday morning I was playing at Raynesway in front of six men, a dozen youngsters, one lady and a dog". Eventually he was glad to have stayed, as John Newman made him first choice for the first team, and the Baseball Ground crowd made him a firm favourite.

The Rams' reserves continued their excellent Central League campaign with a 4-1 victory against Leeds United at Elland Road on 23rd January. Their season had been equally disrupted by the harsh winter and the victory at Leeds was the first time they had played since beating Huddersfield Town 1-0 at the Baseball Ground on December 5th, 1981 - when

Frank Gamble had scored the winner. At Elland Road Kevin Wilson bagged a hat-trick and John Clayton scored the other goal for Derby – the result left the reserves 5th in the Central League, behind only Everton, Liverpool, Nottingham Forest and Wolves. They had lost only twice in the past 16 games and were winning considerable plaudits under the leadership of reserve team manager Richie Norman, the former Leicester City left back who had appeared in four Cup Finals during a distinguished playing career.

Norman, who starred in the Northumberland County Boys team had joined Leicester from Northern League club Ferryhill Athletic in 1958 and went on to feature in the 1961 and 1963 FA Cup Finals, and the 1964 and 1965 League Cup Finals, during a golden era for the Filbert Street club. He was eventually replaced in the Leicester side by future Rams defender David Nish and joined Peterborough United in 1969 and then went into management at Burton Albion and coached at Coventry City and in Toronto, Canada, before joining the Rams staff in 1978, a Tommy Docherty appointment.

Around this time, Derby had a reasonably settled reserve side with Yakka Banovic in goal, John Lovatt and Colin Murphy at full back, and the very promising pairing of Glenn Skivington and Paul Blades at centre back. David King, Frank Gamble, Kevin Wilson, Paul Bancroft and Aiden Gibson were also regulars and Paul Halford often stepped in up front when John Clayton was summoned for first team duty. Blades, Gamble and Gibson were considered exceptional talents, and several others had a chance of making good careers in professional football. Of these three, Paul Blades most certainly fulfilled his potential. Gibson was incredibly unlucky with injuries, and Gamble – perhaps the most gifted of the lot, proved to not possess the attitude and dedication required to make a success at the top level.

After beating Sheffield Wednesday at the Baseball Ground, the Rams travelled to Milmoor to play Rotherham United on the following Tuesday night. Skivington replaced the injured Dalziel in the starting eleven, the rest of the team being unchanged. Once again Derby were unfortunate with injury as right back Steve Emery was stretchered off after just 4 minutes following a ferocious tackle by Gerry Gow, to be replaced by Wayne Richards – Gow was sent off, but the damage he inflicted was not limited to Emery – he had already launched into Barry Powell with almost as much ferocity, even before the Emery assault. The substitute played a key part in Derby's goal, the first of the game – Richards ran through the Rotherham defence before hitting a fierce low drive which goalkeeper Ray Mountford could only parry into the path of Andy Hill, who finished with ease. At 1-0 at half time, the Rams looked comfortable and perhaps should have been ahead by more.

The second half was a different story. Rotherham's hard, uncompromising approach was too much for Derby's young side and, led by Emlyn Hughes, the home side took control of the game. Andy Hill was injured as a result of another fierce challenge just two minutes into the second half, and despite Yakka Banovic's penalty save from Ronnie Moore's spot kick, the home side eventually scored twice to win the game 2-1. There was further bad news after the match when it was revealed that Emery would be out for the rest of the season, and Richard Money announced that he would return to parent club Liverpool as there had been no progress on the plan for Derby to sign him on a permanent basis.

Money returned to Anfield despite a generous offer from Liverpool to extend his loan at Derby. It was a big blow – Money looked like a good talent and had performed well, becoming popular with supporters in his short time with the Rams. He said before leaving that he would be happy to sign a long-term permanent contract at Derby, but with finances remaining in such a mess at the Baseball Ground, this was not likely to be forthcoming, especially considering Money's likely first division salary requirements.

On Saturday 6th February Derby played Leicester City at Filbert Street and urged on by a good contingent of travelling supporters, in fine voice from start to finish, put in a decent performance but ultimately went down 2-1. The Rams had asked for the game to be postponed because they simply did not have enough fit players, but the Football League refused the request. Running out of options, caretaker manager John Newman turned to 26-year-old defender **Brian Attley** from Swansea City, who signed on the Thursday before the game and had barely met his team mates before pulling on his shirt at Leicester. Steve Powell, barely fit and having not played since the start of January, was forced to turn out due to lack of numbers, and this decision proved costly when the club captain had to be withdrawn injured on 50 minutes to be replaced by another debutant, reserve team defender **John Lovatt**.

When Lovatt made his debut as substitute, he became the 28th different player to be used by Derby so far in the season, and the 8th debutant after new signings Mick Coop, Brian Attley, Richard Money, and reserve team players Frank Gamble, Ian Dalziel, Andy Hill and Yakka Banovic.

Leicester went ahead from the penalty spot, but a resolute young Rams side refused to give up and fought back to equalise through Paul Emson, who converted a straightforward rebound after Leicester's future Derby goalkeeper Mark Wallington could only parry Kevin Wilson's shot – Wilson had beaten three players before letting fly. Derby held on until five minutes from the end when poor marking from a corner (which was wrongly awarded, replays showed that the ball had touched a Leicester player before going out of play) allowed the home side a gift of a winning goal. The Rams' line up at Filbert Street was: Banovic; Attley, Skivington, Sheridan, Buckley; S Powell, Hector, Swindlehurst, Emson; Wilson, Clayton; sub Lovatt.

Brian Attley, born in Cardiff in 1955, started as an apprentice at his home town club and helped the club to promotion from Division Three in 1975-76 before joining rivals Swansea City in February 1979. At the Vetch Field, he won successive promotions (Division Three in his first season then Division Two in 1980-81). He joined Derby County for a fee of £25,000 in February 1982, becoming John Newman's (then still only caretaker manager) first signing

– Attley was something of an emergency purchase by the Rams, they were desperately short of defenders and regular right back Steve Emery had suffered a broken leg a few days before. He came to Derby with a glowing reference from former Rams, and current Swansea City winger Leighton James, who said of Attley: "Brian played for us 32 times in our promotion run last season, and was the best full back in Division Two…I do believe that Swansea's loss will be Derby's gain"

He did reasonably well for Newman but was not rated by his successor Peter Taylor, who loaned Attley to Oxford United in March 1983 – Attley was eventually released from his contract at Derby in the summer of 1984 and went into local non-league football with Gresley Rovers (by that time managed by former Derby player Roger Davies), then Stapenhill in 1986. In total, Attley made well over 200 appearances in the Football League.

John Lovatt became a reserve team regular after joining the Rams as an apprentice. Hailing from Middlesbrough, Lovatt was a right back and came into the first team side during a severe injury crisis in the spring of 1982 but featured in only four games, two as substitute, after manager John Newman signed Brian Attley to play in Lovatt's preferred position. He was released by Derby in August 1983 and moved back to the North East, joining non-league Whitby Town, then moving to Guisborough Town to play part time football.

The Rams' Share Issue was generating interest from the public, although perhaps not to the extent that club Directors had hoped for. Mick Derby, the young man from Chaddesden who had changed his name in honour of the football club, bought "a substantial amount" of shares – "it's my savings, I've invested in my club", he said.

Caretaker-Manager John Newman followed-up his permanent signing of Brian Attley with a loan deal for John McAlle – the veteran Sheffield United central defender joining on February 11th, initially for one month. Leaving the Baseball Ground the same week were apprentice Colin Murphy – the 18-year-old having made the decision to take up a job outside football, and goalkeeper Roger Jones, who had lost his confidence and his place following the shellacking at Watford and moved on to Birmingham City on loan for a month. Another player potentially on the move was Steve Buckley – the full back being subject of interest from his former club, Luton Town. Meanwhile, Derby's former manager Colin Addison had not taken long to get back into the game, having already been appointed as manager of Newport County.

Distressing news came when it was revealed that defender Alan Ramage would never play football again, following his latest injury in the autumn of 1981. Ramage was able to continue with his cricket career at Yorkshire County Cricket Club, having proved his fitness with three weeks of hard training.

On 13th February Derby entertained Charlton Athletic at the Baseball Ground and a crowd of 10,846 saw loan signing **John McAlle** make his debut. He lined up alongside Buckley,

Sheridan and Skivington in a back four, with Attley playing in midfield. The visitors side featured former Derby striker Derek Hales.

Charlton, managed by Alan Mullery, took the lead midway through the first half, and from then on seemed content to sit back and try to absorb pressure, allowing Derby to control much of the possession – a tactic which came within a minute of achieving victory, until Frank Sheridan stole a yard in front of his marker and headed home a nicely-flighted cross from Kevin Hector in the 89th minute to end the scoring at 1-1.

Liverpool-born John McAlle spent much of his career at Wolverhampton Wanderers, form whom he signed apprentice forms in July 1965 at the age of 16. He made his first team debut 3 years later and became a regular during the 1970-71 season and was the Molineux club's first choice centre back throughout most of the 1970's, winning the League Cup in 1974 and playing in the 1972 UEFA Cup Final. Wolves eventually signed Emlyn Hughes to replace McAlle in 1979 and he left the club in August 1981 to join Sheffield United for a fee of £10,000 – having made well over 500 appearances for Wanderers, the fifth highest appearance-maker in the club's history.

After winning the fourth division championship at Bramall Lane in 1981-82, he joined Derby County initially on loan for 1 month to cover an injury crisis in February 1982. After signing a permanent contract in April, he stayed at the Baseball Ground until March 1984 when he retired from football aged 34. He was inducted into Wolverhampton Wanderers' Hall of Fame in 2015 and at the time of writing, works in matchday hospitality at Molineux.

The Rams lost 3-0 to Queens Park Rangers on the plastic pitch at Loftus Road on Saturday 20th February. It was yet another low point – Derby failed to register a single shot on the hosts' goal and were flattered to only lose by 3, Rangers missing a host of chances and a more realistic scoreline might have been 5 or 6 nil, having had as many as 23 attempts on goal.

John McAlle, the defender on loan from Sheffield United, was scathing about the pitch after the game, saying: "if that's the future of football I'm glad my career is nearly over". John Newman, however, had no excuses: "blaming the pitch is looking for an excuse. We keep letting in goals wherever we go. There could have been five, six or seven this time". Newman was also correct in his assertion that Rangers would have beaten his Derby side on any playing surface – they were simply too good for the Rams, who had not won away since October 1981.

Regarding the plastic pitch, Queen's Park Rangers had become accustomed to receiving complaints from visiting teams, and had considered abandoning it but commercial benefits made such a decision impossible – the pitch had cost £200,000 to install but was generating in excess of £100,000 a year through hosting non-football events, such as pop star Rod

Stewart's proposed two concerts at the venue, for which the supposed fee was £20,000 a time.

John Newman was so upset with his team's lack of determination and concerned for its lack of confidence at Loftus Road that he instructed his first team to turn out against Walsall in what was originally scheduled to be a Midland Intermediate League fixture on Wednesday 24th February. "I felt we needed a serious run-out on grass before (the next League game) Newcastle. The squad is in limbo, stuck in a rut"

The game against Walsall at the Baseball Ground ended in a 3-0 win for Derby, but there was yet more bad news on the injury-front as Andy Hill, who was returning to action after being out for a month with an ankle injury, picked up a knock on his other ankle and hobbled off after just 10 minutes. Kevin Wilson scored twice, and Paul Emson got the other goal in a comfortable win.

After a poor run, with only one point from their previous four games. Derby's reserves returned to form with a fine 2-0 win over Manchester United at the Baseball Ground on 20th February. A young side, featuring four 17-year-olds, were always in charge in the game but did not take the lead until 17 minutes from the end when central defender Paul Blades, lurking on the edge of the penalty area for a Derby corner, picked the ball up and turned a defender before cracking home a fine shot. Derby's second goal was scored by Frank Gamble, from the penalty spot. Catching the eye was 15-year-old forward Andy Garner, still a pupil at Alfreton's Mortimer Wilson School – Garner had made his debut for the reserves 3 days earlier, in a goalless draw against West Bromwich Albion.

Derby were back in action at the Baseball Ground on 27th February where an encouraging crowd of 12,257 saw a 2-2 draw against Newcastle United., with John Lovatt starting at full back and Attley moving into midfield, Hector missing from the previous week's team. In charge at Newcastle was Arthur Cox, who would go on to become a popular and successful manager of Derby County. On the wing for the Magpies was future England star Chris Waddle, then just 20 years of age but already terrorising Second Division defences.

In an entertaining game, with fortunes swinging one way then the other, Derby went ahead twice but were pegged back by the determined visitors on both occasions. Derby, in patches, played some skilful one-touch football and looked better than their league position suggested. Emson's fine finish from Clayton's long ball which caught the Newcastle defence square was the pick of Derby's goals, Kevin Wilson scored the other.

On 6th March Derby received yet another thrashing away from home when Blackburn Rovers beat them 4-1 at Ewood Park. McAlle partnered Skivington at centre back, with Lovatt retaining his place at right back. John Clayton continued in attack in what turned out to be his 23rd and final starting appearance for the club – having made his debut way back in October 1978 when Tommy Docherty was manager – it had been a dismal period for the talented and promising young striker to have started his professional career in – in the 27 first team matches in which Clayton was involved, he was on the winning side only 5 times, the last of which had been more than 3 months previously in a home win over Cambridge United.

Just seven days after they had played with such determination and promise against Newcastle, the Rams capitulated at Blackburn. Frank Sheridan's one-match suspension did not help but the manner of the defeat was alarming, and Derby were 4-0 down and looking for the bus home long before Dave Swindlehurst's right footed shot gave them a consolation goal. This, the Rams ninth successive away defeat, with just 8 goals scored and 28 conceded. In all competitions they had lost 12 consecutive away games – 9 in the League, 2 in Cup competitions, and a competitive friendly at Walsall in January, when the weather had been so bad that the club felt match practice was essential, and Derby's first team had gone down 0-1 to the Third Division side.

Derby were statistically the worst side away from home in the entire Football League, a total of 39 goals conceded was the worst of all 92 clubs, and the Rams had gained points from just three away fixtures – victories at Cambridge and Crystal Palace and a draw at Sheffield Wednesday. Derby's all-time worst run away from home was the 10 successive defeats in 1954-55, a season which saw them relegated to the Third Division for the first and so far, only time in their history.

On the financial front, there had been a show of faith from the club's beleaguered Directors, who had provided a cash injection of more than £200,000 between them in early March 1982. The cash was essential, although to describe it as enough to keep Derby County solvent would perhaps be overstating the position. Additionally, just over £25,000 had been raised by the share issue, from more than 1200 individual investors (each one listed in the Ram Newspaper dated 10th March) – this was far less than had been hoped-for, and the interest from business and commerce in particular had disappointed Derby's Directors – although given the state of the club's finances, it could hardly have been a shock that anybody with an ounce of business acumen would think very carefully before investing their money. In an attempt to engage the industrial and commercial sectors, Derby County opened its doors on the morning of Saturday March 13th to enable potential investors to inspect the Baseball Ground's facilities – an event which was hosted by Commercial Executive Stuart Robinson, Secretary Michael Dunford, and Manager John Newman.

Increasingly desperate for working capital, the Board of Directors explored the possibility of selling the club's Raynesway Training Centre, with several potential buyers interested – most notably Derbyshire County Cricket Club and Derbyshire County Council. The discussions with the Derbyshire CCC involved a potential combining of training facilities between the two clubs. Also up for sale was the club's most valuable playing asset Dave Swindlehurst, who was the subject of bids for his services from Crystal Palace, the first of which had been rejected by Derby but more activity was expected on this front – regardless of the Board's most recent investment, pressure to service the bank overdraft interest payments ensured that nothing and nobody was off limits in the quest to balance the books.

Rex Stone, the former Vice Chairman, resigned from the Board in early March 1982 citing the poor health of both he and his wife. Stone was also unhappy about inside information leaking from the Baseball Ground boardroom to the media – this undoubtedly played a major part in his decision. Stone, managing director of Heanor firm Alida Packaging Ltd, had been the architect of Derby's most recent financial rescue operation and left with the good wishes of his boardroom colleagues. He was replaced on the Board by 38-year-old building contractor Brian Holmes, owner of Heanor-based ABC Construction. Holmes, whose father had been a junior at the Baseball Ground in the 1950's, was also financially involved with local non-league club Heanor Town and had been approached to join the Rams board by John Kirkland.

Also stepping down from the Board was television star and Rams supporter Tim Brooke-Taylor. Both he and Rex Stone were made honorary vice presidents of the club. Brooke-Taylor had resigned because he was unable to join the rest of the Board in making substantial cash deposits into the club, and therefore felt it would not be fair for him to have an equal say in the Boardroom.

At the start of March, John Newman was named as permanent manager, having been caretaker since the sacking of Colin Addison. Newman, who was under contract until the end of the following season, agreed to maintain his existing terms, which had been negotiated when he became Assistant Manager in the summer of 1979 – in fact, not one member of the coaching or administrative staff received a pay rise in 1981-82. Whilst Newman was perhaps a sensible choice, he was also the fiscally-prudent one – the club simply did not have the means to recruit a manager from outside, as there was no money for compensation payments to other clubs and wage demands from a new manager. Newman, for his part, had been reluctant to stay at Derby following the sacking of Addison – feeling that the club was heading backwards and not wanting to be the man associated with another relegation. It was Addison himself who had persuaded him to stay, as he felt that Derby were close to turning a corner and did not want the benefit of his and Newman's hard work to be fall to someone else.

Derby now faced two crucial home games in a week, both against relegation rivals just below them in the table. After the thrashing at Blackburn, and the dreadful away form all season the Rams, with 30 points from 28 matches and standing 15th in the Second Division, simply had to take points from these upcoming games, against Shrewsbury Town and Crystal Palace. Newman appealed to his players, several of whom appeared less than interested in the fate of Derby County: "players with contracts coming to an end this summer, players who might feel a move would help their careers...we need 110% in loyalty, effort, determination and enthusiasm, anything less from any one person could mean disaster"

Back at the Baseball Ground for a Wednesday night game at home to Shrewsbury Town, public interest fell to yet another new low when only 7,518 turned out to watch a 1-1 draw. John Lovatt, dropped to the bench to accommodate the returning Frank Sheridan, turned out for the final time for the Rams – he was to be released in the summer and dropped out of full-time football. The game was played in foul weather on a pitch coated with liquid mud, which neither side managed to get to grips with. Shrewsbury's team featured future Rams players Steve Cross and Steve Biggins as well as Colin Griffin, who had been a youth player at Derby before moving to Gay Meadow in 1976.

The Rams had conceded some terrible goals so far in the season, defensive lapses costing them many of the 57 they had conceded in 31 games so far, but none was as bad as the equaliser they gave away on 79 minutes in this game, when Brian Attley and Yakka Banovic each stood waiting for the other to claim the ball, under no threat from attacking players, meanwhile Shrewsbury's Atkins nipped in to prod the ball home. It had been a desperately poor game, summed up in the almost tragi-comic nature of the visitor's equaliser - with Derby perhaps just about deservedly ahead through Kevin Wilson's far post header after Dave Swindlehurst had flicked-on a corner.

The Rams had not won a single game since beating Sheffield Wednesday at the end of January – a run of 7 games in which only 3 points were gained. Third Division football appeared to be staring Derby County in the face, and nobody seemed capable of preventing what seemed to be the inevitable – indeed, supporters by that stage were readying themselves for a first season at third-tier level in 25 years.

John Newman had already made his mark on the team and was showing somewhat less faith in youth than his predecessor and former boss Addison – John Lovatt and John Clayton were two of Derby's highly rated young players who were discarded during the Newman regime, and more would follow. Newman had shown, by the signings of John McAlle and Brian Attley, that he wanted more experience in his team.

Just when it seemed that things could not possibly improve, Derby pulled off a surprising 4-1 home victory over Crystal Palace on Saturday 13th March 1982. Newman selected a more experienced side than had been the case for most of the season: Banovic; McAlle, Sheridan, Skivington, Buckley; Attley, B Powell, Hector, Emson; Swindlehurst, Wilson; and was rewarded with goals from Buckley (who was Derby's only representative in the season's Second Division select side, as elected by his fellow players), Skivington and a brace from Kevin Wilson. Almost 3,000 more on the gate than for the previous home game just 3 days before was also encouraging. It was a fine game, providing good entertainment for the supporters. Palace, featuring former Derby defender Steve Wicks, played a full part in the attacking nature of the match. The Baseball Ground crowd were treated to the introduction before kick-off of former star player Charlie George, who, it was revealed, was in talks to re-join the Rams – George, and John Newman (who walked around the ground with him) received a rapturous welcome from Derby's supporters.

The Rams were unexpectedly excellent on this occasion, and despite going a goal down on 17th minute when McAlle diverted a shot beyond the reach of Banovic for an own goal, they went on to put the visitors to the sword with four clinical finishes. Buckley's 22-yard free kick which flew in via the crossbar into the Osmaston goal started the comeback on 20 minutes – excited fans jumped the hoardings in front of C-Stand to join Buckley's celebrations - then 19 minutes later the Rams went ahead when Skivington headed home a Barry Powell corner and the score remained at 2-1 to Derby until the 78th minute when Kevin Wilson profited from Swindlehurst's skilful back heel which the striker volleyed into the roof of the Palace net. Wilson added his second and the Rams' fourth on 83 minutes when his diving header beat the goalkeeper, after Emson had crossed from the right.

The form and progress of Kevin Wilson was cause for considerable optimism. Comparisons with a previous occupant of Derby's number 10 shirt, Kevin Hector, proved wide of the mark but in recent weeks Wilson, who had scored twice in recent victories over Sheffield Wednesday and Crystal Palace at the Baseball Ground, was beginning to look a considerable talent – and had played in nine of the previous ten games. Having appeared to have dropped out of the first team reckoning earlier in the season, Wilson had fought his way back to senior level with some fine performances for the reserves, including a hat-trick at Elland Road against Leeds United's second string. He was joint leading scorer with 6 goals (the same total as Dave Swindlehurst), with four coming in the previous three games at the Baseball Ground. He had also scored twice in the hastily-arranged first team game against Walsall in the Midland Intermediate League, just before the Second Division fixture against Newcastle United. He was leading scorer for the reserves, with 9 goals in 9 appearances – suggesting ability above reserve level. In all senior matches for the club, Wilson's record was 13 goals in 46 appearances (7 as substitute).

On 16th March Derby followed up their recent trend of bringing back ageing, but still popular former star players when they signed 32-year-old Charlie George from Bournemouth, having featured in just 2 games for the South Coast club following his return from playing in Hong Kong. George had been away from the Baseball Ground for just over three years, having been sold to Southampton on 21st December 1978, and had been given a contract to the end of the season, with the option for the club to extend it should they so wish. George, a true star of the game, albeit a fading one, was heavily-marketed by the club, who hoped to cash in on a boost in ticket sales and merchandise. George himself received considerable endorsements from sponsors, including a Datsun Bluebird car from Ken Ives Garage in Littleover. His record in his first spell at Derby was magnificent – 54 goals in 135 matches in all competitions – but he had been somewhat injury-prone, managing a total of just 374 senior appearances since his 1969 professional debut.

Looking to follow up on their success the previous Saturday against Crystal Palace, Derby travelled to Blundell Park to face bottom of the table Grimsby Town on 20th March. The Rams' away form was dreadful – they had lost their previous 11 away games in all competitions (9 in the League) and had not won on the road since 24th October 1981. A marvellous away contingent, some 2,000, travelled from Derby to see **Charlie George** make his second debut for the Rams – in a throwback to happier times, George replaced Kevin Hector in the starting line-up.

On a waterlogged pitch which suited the home side's long ball style, Derby failed to present much of a challenge and their best chance was thwarted by mud, as a through ball to Kevin Wilson stuck fast on the surface at the crucial moment. The game was decided when poor marking by Derby allowed two Grimsby players to beat the offside trap, narrowly played on by the badly out-of-sorts Barry Powell, and the ball ended up in the back of Yakka Banovic's net – George, who had looked classy on the ball, albeit operating at a leisurely pace in an attacking midfield role, despite the surface – was booked for protesting about the goal. The mud, so deep that it dragged players' boots off their feet on more than one occasion, ensured that entertainment was largely off the agenda. It was Derby's tenth successive away defeat, in what was becoming a desperate battle to avoid relegation.

After the defeat at Grimsby, Derby stood 15th in the Second Division with 34 points from 31 games – just four points ahead of Orient, who occupied the final relegation spot, and one of 9 teams who were all battling to avoid the drop.

Charlie George was one of the true stars of English football in the 1970's. A natural entertainer and crowd-pleaser with truly superb skill and talent, he had first signed for Derby after a contractual dispute with Arsenal alerted Rams manager Dave Mackay to George's availability – the Rams were reigning Champions of the Football League and were at that time an attractive proposition for even the very best players, of which George was most certainly one.

Born in Islington in 1950 and growing up as an Arsenal supporter, George was spotted by The Gunners while playing for Islington Schoolboys and signed youth forms at Highbury in May 1966. He turned professional in 1968 and made his debut at the start of the 1969-70 season, finishing that season with an Inter-Cities Fairs Cup winners medal after Arsenal beat RSC Anderlecht in the Final. His greatest season was 1970-71 when he scored the winning goal in the FA Cup Final against Liverpool, a win which secured the League and FA Cup double. As Arsenal's great side of the early 1970's began to break up, George was involved in several contractual disputes with the club and was dropped and transfer-listed by manager Bertie Mee in the 1974-75 season after the two had fallen out. He was idolised by Arsenal supporters, and a recent poll ranked him 9th in the club's list of 50 best all-time players – he scored a total of 49 goals in 179 matches for the club.

After appearing certain to sign for Arsenal's North London rivals Tottenham Hotspur for a fee of £100,000 (the deal got as far as a press conference at White Hart Lane, at which Spurs were due to present the player as their new signing), George eventually signed for Derby in July 1975 – the lure of European Champions Cup football being too much for him to resist, and made his debut in the 1975 FA Charity Shield game at Wembley, which the Rams won 2-0 against FA Cup holders West Ham United. In three and a half years at the Baseball Ground, he became one of Derby's most popular ever players, scoring a hat-trick against Real Madrid in a European Cup tie in October 1975, and another in a UEFA Cup win over Irish side Finn Harps in September 1976, the Rams' record all time win, a remarkable 12-0 scoreline.

In 1977, as Derby's rapid decline gathered pace, George went on loan to Australian club St George's Budapest. He had become rebellious at the Baseball Ground and fell out with Colin Murphy, Mackay's successor as manager. Eventually he became another of the many Derby players of the 1970's to join the North American Soccer League, signing for Minnesota Kicks and scoring 9 goals in 18 games in the 1978 season. He returned to England with Southampton in December 1978 and had a loan spell at Nottingham Forest but could not agree a permanent deal at the City Ground. After 52 appearances with Southampton he again left English football, this time signing for Hong Kong club Bulova in the summer of 1981, staying there for a year.

In 1982, by now aged 32, he joined Bournemouth and played just 2 games before re-joining Derby County, struggling at the lower end of the Second Division and by now managed by John Newman, but played only 11 times before returning to Hong Kong. He later attempted comebacks with both Dundee United and Coventry City, but his time had gone, and he made no competitive appearances for either club.

In total, George scored 34 goals for Derby in 106 appearances over two spells. He remains a legendary figure to those who were fortunate enough to see him in his prime at Highbury and his early days at the Baseball Ground, and now works in a hospitality role at Arsenal.

Manager John Newman was permitted by the Board to bring in Everton's full-back John Barton just before the transfer deadline, on Thursday 25th March. 27-year-old Barton had not been a first team regular at Goodison Park, having played just 30 games in the First Division, but was a reliable reserve who had been with the club since his youth. Meanwhile, Somercotes-born Chris Ball, an apprentice at the Baseball Ground, left the club to seek a career outside football after being told that he would not be receiving a full-time professional contract.

At an EGM of the 22 clubs of the Central League, arguably the Country's premier reserve team league, it was decided that starting in the 1982-83 season matches would switch from their traditional Saturday afternoons to mid-week. It was a purely financial move – clubs had complained that they were struggling to find enough playing personnel to field three full teams on Saturdays (youth team football also took place on Saturdays). It appeared inevitable that clubs would now cut down their playing staff – clubs were no longer available to carry players on first team wages in their reserve sides, as the recession bit deeper and player wages continued to rise. There was also a proposal that the Central League be extended to two divisions of 16 teams – meaning fewer matches, less travelling and consequently less expenses. Clubs expressed concern at declining standards of the Central League, with fewer senior professionals and a big increase in the number of apprentices featuring in reserve teams (this was especially the case at Derby). With "retained lists" (players who would be retained under contract) due to be published in just a few weeks' time, it seemed certain that the biggest pruning exercise in the game's history was about to take place – with all football clubs feeling the pinch caused by player's excessive wage demands, since the introduction of freedom of contract. Neil Hallam, writing in The Derby Trader, summed up the mood of the clubs: "a great deal of addled thinking, vested interest and pious humbug went into the creation of the contractual freedom now enjoyed by professional footballers, and the result is that there will be a lot less to share the enjoyment when clubs respond to their exploitation by announcing retained lists in the next few weeks"

Derby County Football Club Limited's share issue closed on 20th March 1982 and raised a total of just under £80,000, adding almost 2,000 new shareholders. Added to the Directors' personal cash injections, the club's bank balance was improved by £280,000. Amongst the new shareholders were manager John Newman, secretary Michael Dunford, chief scout Alan Ashman and several players including club captain Steve Powell.

Charlie George's second home debut, on Saturday 27th March 1982 against league-leaders Luton Town, attracted a bumper crowd of 15,836. Making his debut for Derby was right back **John Barton**, who had joined from Everton as manager John Newman sought to bring experience and reliability to Derby's decidedly suspect defence.

The Rams presented each child sitting in one of the two Family Enclosures (Ley Stand and Osmaston Stand) with a personally-signed colour photograph of Charlie George – an occasion perhaps more appreciated by the adults, since the photographs were handed out by bikini-clad Derby County Promotions models Ann Hennesy and Elaine Gipp. Several letters of protest about these proceedings were received by Ram Newspaper, from several unnamed supporters including "Woman Supporter, Manchester (name and address withheld)", who wrote: "I am not, let me stress, a spoilsport, a feminist nor even a left-wing activist but I am sick to death of Derby County's inability or unwillingness to promote anything without using very undressed women or girls to do it. You go on about the Rams being a family club, you open a family enclosure for kids and parents...but then every chance you get you seem to parade girls in scanty bikinis all over the place...why on earth did almost undressed girls in bikinis distribute the pictures (of Charlie George) to youngsters?...football will stay exclusively a male preserve if you insist on promoting, and catering for, male tastes". Opposing views came from the likes of Cecil Schofield of Littleover: "in my house we all read The Sun and admire the page three pin-ups. The promotions girls were decently dressed and very attractive. What do your critics want? No glamour at all?", and Roy Barrett of Derby who wrote: "rubbish missus! My girlfriend and her mum and sister who sit in the Ley Stand with me enjoy the lasses and any pin-up pictures in The Ram".

Luton came to the Baseball Ground with a fine away record, having lost only twice away from Kenilworth Road in the season so far, the last time being as long ago as November 1981 at Newcastle – they had been one of the best sides at Second Division level over the past three years, narrowly missing out on promotion in 1980-81, and had scored 50 goals in 29 games so far in the current campaign under their attack-minded manager David Pleat. Their team was without Derby connections, bar midfielder Brian Horton, who was a serious contender for the Rams' managers job before Jim Smith was appointed in 1995.

The game was a fiercely contested goalless draw, with very few clear-cut chances at either end, in which Derby gave as good as they got and fully deserved their point. It was only the third time they had kept a clean sheet all season – debutant Barton settling down after a shaky start at right back. The Rams could have won it when Kevin Wilson's shot was superbly saved by goalkeeper Jake Findlay, but Banovic had been equally acrobatic when stopping Stein's goal-bound effort. Derby had three reasonable shouts for a penalty – the most convincing being when Frank Sheridan appeared to be pushed in the penalty area, but the referee remained unmoved and a draw was probably the right result on balance.

John Barton was born in Birmingham in 1953 and began his football career as an amateur with local clubs Boldmere St Michael's, Paget Rangers and Sutton Coldfield Town before moving into senior non-league football with Worcester City in 1976, aged 23. After interest from several First Division clubs, he eventually joined Everton in 1979 for what was then a record fee for a non-league player, £25,000.

Everton manager Howard Kendall released him to sign on a free transfer for Derby County on transfer deadline day in March 1982, and he went on to make 82 appearances for the Rams, including 1 as substitute, scoring one goal. He was released from his contract at the Baseball Ground at the end of the 1983-84 season, with Derby relegated to the Third Division, and took up the role of player-manager at Kidderminster Harriers – going on to forge an impressive career in management at senior non-league level, at Kidderminster, Nuneaton Borough, Burton Albion (for four years, 1994 to 1998) and Worcester City.

Meanwhile, a deal was agreed between Derby County and Derby City Council in which the football club were paid £135,000 for the Ramarena social and training area, with the facility leased back to the club on a short-term basis. It was also a matter of record that the Raynesway Training Ground was already owned by the Council, with the football club having a long lease (with 65 years remaining), at an annual rental of just £168 – the proviso being that the football club was not allowed to develop the land without the Council's permission. The council was also leasing to the club some ground adjacent to the Baseball Ground, which was being used as car-parking and the club had originally wanted to buy but did not have the money.

Ray Cowlishaw, for the City Council, reported that the Ramarena was listed in Derby County FC Ltd's books as being worth considerably more than the £135,000 it was being sold for. Council leader Mick Walker denied that the authority was subsidising Derby County – they were simply helping the club with their cash-flow problems and getting "a valuable asset" for a fair price – the money paid for the Ramarena would not compromise spending on other projects, said Walker. The City Council were providing substantial assistance to the football club by charging a nominal rent for use of the Ramarena – the true rental value was estimated at £11,000 per year.

Derby finally ended their dismal 10 league game losing run away from home on Saturday 3rd April at Wrexham, when they held the North Welshmen to a 1-1 draw. It was a vital point – Wrexham were one of the sides just below the Rams in the league table, just four points and four places behind them. Manager Newman was able to name an unchanged side with newcomers Barton, McAlle, George and Attley retaining their places and adding a more experienced and solid look to the side.

The Rams started on the front foot and missed several good chances in the first half as Charlie George showed his class with some exquisite touches, with Brian Attley adding some much-needed steel to the midfield. They should have gone in at half time with more than just Paul Emson's 29th minute goal to show for their dominance. Unfortunately, the second half did not follow the same pattern and Dixie McNeill equalised for the home side on 53 minutes. Wrexham could have won the game and only a stunning reflex stop by Yakka Banovic kept the score at 1-1. After what had gone before away from home, a point was more than satisfactory.

John McAlle, who had played 9 games during an extended loan spell from parent club Sheffield United, signed a permanent deal early in April 1982 – the Rams paying a £10,000 fee to the Blades for his services. Derby's suspect defence had certainly been stiffened by the inclusion of the experienced former Wolves player and young Frank Sheridan, especially, was benefitting from a wise older head alongside him. McAlle was one of four over 30's in the squad, along with Charlie George, Kevin Hector and the out-of-favour Roger Jones.

On the injury-front, the Rams were still suffering. Steve Emery was out with a broken leg inflicted by a wild challenge from Rotherham's Gerry Gow – Emery's challenge was to be fit for the start of the following season and with just one year left on his contract, his future looked uncertain. Steve Powell, the club captain, had played just 1 ½ matches since November 1981, having left the field with a knee muscle injury in the same Rotherham match in which Emery's leg was broken – Powell's injury had necessitated an operation. It was hoped that he could play some part in the first team before the end of the season. Teenage midfield prospect Tony Reid, about whom Derby had very high hopes for the future, had been out since the game at Luton on 7th November 1981 with damaged knee ligaments – he began his comeback with a "A" team game in early April 1982 but was not expected to play first team football again until the following season.

Derby's reserves bounced back to form with a 3-0 victory over a far more experienced Wolves side on 3rd April, goals from David King, Paul Bancroft and Andy Garner securing only a third win in the previous 13 matches – taking them to 8th place in the Central League. The performance in the reserves' previous home game, on Tuesday 29th March, was described by John Newman as "a shambles" – the result being a 3-1 loss to struggling Bury. Both Nottingham Forest and Coventry City had scored 4, and Aston Villa 3, against them in recent weeks.

The Rams followed up their hard-won point at Wrexham with another point at Oakwell against Barnsley on Easter Saturday, 10th March. Once again Derby were un-changed and the side showed improved cohesion and considerable determination to hold the Yorkshiremen to a goalless draw.

Barnsley were much the better side in possession, and it took another fine performance from Banovic in goal, plus resolute (and often last-ditch) defending from McAlle, Buckley and especially Barton to secure the point.

Kevin Hector, appearing as a substitute at Oakwell, equalled Jack Parry's all-time-record for Football League appearances for Derby – 483. Hector's total of 586 appearances in all competitions was also a club record.

There had been confusion before the match when Derby's officials arrived at the ground to see Yorkshire TV cameras in position – the Rams had not been informed that the game was being televised (it had been a late decision by the TV company) and they had only brought with them their Patrick-sponsored shirts, which were still banned from being seen on television. A call to the Baseball Ground resulted in a member of staff setting off up the M1 with a replacement kit, but embarrassingly this turned out to be last season's Le Coq strip. Eventually Youth Coach Ron Webster made the dash up to Oakwell with the correct strip which arrived ten minutes after kick-off – the Rams changed at half time, therefore playing the match in two different kits.

On Easter Monday Derby took a vital step towards survival in the Second Division when they beat Emlyn Hughes's fourth placed Rotherham United side 3-1 at the Baseball Ground. There was another encouraging attendance – just over 14,000, and for the fourth successive game John Newman named an unchanged side.

Glen Skivington gave the Rams the perfect start after just 90 seconds when he capitalised on a poor attempted clearance from an Emson corner, scoring with a well-controlled volley. Rotherham then fought back with their aggressive and direct approach causing Derby's defence considerable problems and, with the Rams finally getting some lucky breaks, hitting the woodwork twice and missing a penalty awarded after an error by Banovic. Eventually, the Rams established some control and Wilson headed-home John Barton's pinpoint cross from the right, before a moment of eccentric class from George set up Buckley to add a very well-worked third. Barton, and Brian Attley playing in front of him, had brought some much-needed stability and balance on the Rams' right – an area of the pitch which they had particularly struggled for much of the season.

The 3-1 win took Derby on to 40 points with 7 games to play – 5 points and 6 places above Crystal Palace in the final relegation spot. Safety was by no means guaranteed, but it looked slightly more likely than it had done a month before. The Rams' problem was goal difference – their minus 14 was amongst the worst in the division – and the three sides currently occupying the relegation positions all had 2 games in hand compared to Derby. Of their remaining games, Derby had 4 at home which, given their results so far that season, was cause for optimism.

Derby's youngsters were making good progress in the Midland Intermediate League Cup. On Saturday 10th April they beat Aston Villa "A" 4-3 in an exciting game at Raynesway, with most of the attention focussed on Tony Reid, who was playing in his third come-back game following the serious knee injury suffered the previous November. In their previous Cup game, the Rams had beaten Nottingham Forest "A" 1-0 and were now top of their group. Barry Powell also featured in the game, attempting to prove his fitness after a few weeks out – the Rams side also featured three schoolboys. The game was settled by two goals from Jimmy Collins, a third from Nicky Mihic and a late winner by Mark Frid. Rams "A": Palmer; McCormack, Harbey, Banks, Mihic, J Collins, Reid, B Powell, Chapman, Frid, Bancroft; sub D Collins. Meanwhile, Derby's reserves won 3-0 away at Stoke City four days later, Barry Powell also featuring in this game and scoring one of the goals, the others being from Frank Gamble and Paul Blades. Kevin Hector, who had not started a first team game for over a month (being substitute in the previous 5 matches), also played for the reserves at Stoke.

A second home game in a week, this time against mid-table Norwich City, resulted in a miserable 0-2 defeat in front of 12,508 at the Baseball Ground. The Rams were unchanged for the fifth successive game (the joint-longest unchanged sequence since 1974-75 when Derby became League Champions for the second time). The visitors dominated the game, especially in the first half, and became the first side to defeat the Rams at the Baseball Ground in 15 matches (since First Division West Ham had won 3-2 early in October 1981). The lead was only one goal until virtually the last kick of the match, when Norwich scored their second. The Rams' best chance of the game falling to Kevin Wilson, who chipped goalkeeper Chris Woods but saw his effort narrowly clear the bar.

Dave Swindlehurst, who had recently become a target for barrackers and had a particularly poor game against Norwich, presumably disappointed at his proposed departure from the Baseball Ground, allowed his temper to boil over into V-signs at Rams fans in the Paddock and Main Stand, after fans objected to Kevin Wilson being substituted rather than him, late in the game. In fact, Swindlehurst had turned-down a proposed move to Crystal Palace, a fact that only became clear after the Norwich game.

Sponsors for the Norwich match, Eastern British Road Services, paid for 70 orphaned and deprived children to attend the game, seating them in the Osmaston End Family Seating Area. After the game, the youngsters, many of whom were residents of the Dr Barnardo home in Derby, were introduced to manager John Newman and some of the Rams players. Members of the Heanor Branch of the Derby County Supporters Club walked 12 miles from the Jolly Collier's pub in Heanor to the Baseball Ground, finishing with a lap of the pitch before the Norwich game. The group was led by branch chairman Tom Carr, vice chairman Tony Stone and secretary Phil Sheffield – they raised £60 which was donated to the club.

Derby finally won a game away from home on Saturday 24th April 1982, when just over 11,000 saw them beat Chelsea 2-0 at Stamford Bridge, with goals from Charlie George (his first goal for Derby since 23rd September 1978, when he had scored the Rams' second in a 2-1 First Division win over Southampton at the Baseball Ground) and Barry Powell (back in the side following a month-long injury lay off). It was the first time the Rams had won a game away from the Baseball Ground since 24th October 1981 – exactly 6 months, and 15 games, previously.

The game was low on quality, but manager Newman's decision to move George into attack in place of Wilson, who dropped to the bench, was key to the result. Powell opened the scoring on 54 minutes with a superb 20-yard volley after George headed a John Barton cross into his path. George's goal came courtesy of a swerving free-kick six minutes from time, after Dave Swindlehurst had cleverly manoeuvred the defensive wall to make a gap for the shot.

Fewer than 100 Rams supporters attended the game, the smallest travelling support for the club in recent memory – the majority preferred not to test the threats from a section of Chelsea's support, issued after Derby had banned them from the Baseball Ground following their near riot during and after the fixture in November 1981.

Derby County's Roadrider patrons, who had travelled to London for the game on the club's official coach (there was only one), were instead diverted from Stamford Bridge and the passengers set down at a nearby tube station, and advised to take the Underground to the stadium – the coach operators Kinch of Mountsorrel decided not to risk damage to their vehicles by entering the vicinity of Stamford Bridge (trouble had been expected), and instead paid the Underground fares for their passengers. Derby County officials also took the threats seriously and the players left their coach at midday and travelled to Stamford Bridge in taxis, frustrating the Chelsea mob which had assembled to "welcome" their arrival.

Vice Chairman John Kirkland announced at a meeting of new Shareholders that the "break-even" gate figure for season 1982-83 would be 11,000, down from 1981-82's 15,000. This drastically reduced figure was calculated because the number of playing staff (apprentices and professionals) would be cut by around a dozen. Season ticket prices for 1982-83 were to be kept the same as the current season, the second successive price-freeze.

Questioned about the cost of signing Charlie George, manager John Newman said that the deal had paid for itself thanks to increased interest and attendances and had also provided extra funds which had been used to finance the signing of John McAlle. Another shareholder asked Derby County sold players at below their value – citing the example of Keith Osgood, who had been bought for £150,000 in 1979 and sold for £20,000 just over two years later. Newman stated that "the bottom had fallen out of the transfer market because there is little money about, many a player who's value was right at £150,000 two or three years ago is now going for £20,000 and clubs are considered lucky to get that, some are up for free" Newman also reminded the guests that the Rams had benefitted when Brian Attley had been signed for just £20,000, and John Barton on a free transfer.

Chairman Bill Stevenson reminded the hundreds of small shareholders that their views could best be heard via the Shareholders Association (of which three members were also Directors of the football club) – Shareholders Association chairman Dick Joell confirmed that there was indeed a close liaison with the club's Directors: "our views are regarded as important", said Joell.

Considering that inflation in the UK at the time was in double figures, it was a brave move to peg season ticket prices at 1980-81 prices. With 7,000 season ticket holders, Derby County were the best-supported club in the Second Division (and better than quite a few in the First Division). Several discount schemes were also made available based on early purchases, and interestingly a 10% discount to anyone holding £100 or more worth of shares in the club. Car parking season tickets were reduced to £15, reflecting the disappointing level of take-up of the new spaces created around the Baseball Ground – car parks on Vulcan Street and Harrington Street were to be merged, increasing the number of spaces to 200 vehicles. Season tickets were to be on sale from May 17th, 1982 and were priced at £52-£76 (Ley Stand and Main Stand seats), £48 (Osmaston and Normanton End seats) and £30 for any of the terraces. Family Seating on the Osmaston End was priced at £40 for adults and £20 for children. Match day prices would be £1.80 (terracing) to £3.80 (most expensive seats).

After some consideration and following several serious incidents of crowd misbehaviour during the season it was decided that, for the 1982-83 season, visiting seated supporters were to be segregated from home fans for the first time – in a fenced-off section of the lower tier of the Osmaston Stand.

Disgruntled former "Ossie-Enders", still annoyed at having their favourite standing spot replaced by Family Seating Area, had begun to take up residence in C-Stand – around 50, mainly younger fans from Alvaston, Belper and Ripley, now regularly sat at the end of C-Stand, next to the Normanton Stand and right above the small section of terrace which remained at the Osmaston End, reserved for season ticket holders. The chant of "C-Stand, C-Stand" had become prevalent in recent months. More former Ossie Enders were encouraged to join the group for the 1982-83 season – "get your season tickets and make sure you're at the far end", was the message. Traditional, mainly older C-Stand patrons were not amused, and many relocated over the summer, further to the right, towards the middle of the Main Stand.

Following victory at Chelsea, the Rams faced two successive home matches – a Wednesday evening meeting with Barnsley (with whom they had drawn at Oakwell just 18 days previously), followed by a crucial game against relegation rivals Cardiff City, who came to the Baseball Ground on Saturday 1st May.

Barnsley, managed by former Leeds United and England player Norman Hunter, featured future Republic of Ireland manager Mick McCarthy in central defence. Playing with considerable style, the Yorkshiremen were too good for Derby and the 0-1 defeat flattered the Rams – Barnsley's only reward for dominating the game being a goal on 20 minutes resulting from a defensive error. Late in the game, Derby came close to snatching a point that they had not deserved when Swindlehurst headed down an Attley corner to Wilson, who's first-time shot cannoned off the underside of the Barnsley bar and bounced to safety. A crowd of 11,296 watched the game, and Derby remained 14th in the Second Division.

A dreadful game at the Baseball Ground, not helped by a swirling wind, ensued when Derby and Cardiff City drew 0-0 in front of just over 10,000. Derby had the better of what few chances there were, and Dave Swindlehurst hit the inside of a post with a header from Barry Powell's free kick with the best of them. Charlie George also had an effort cleared off the line. The point took the Rams on to 44 from 39 matches, and they remained 14th in the table.

After a poor return of just one point from their last two games, both at home, the Rams now faced two away matches in the space of four days – on Tuesday 4th May against relegation rivals Bolton Wanderers at Burnden Park, then on Saturday 8th May against Oldham Athletic at Boundary Park.

At Burnden Park, a punctured ball - after a sliced Glen Skivington clearance had landed on the pitch-side railings, failed to brighten the mood of the travelling Rams fans as a last kick of the game winner gave the home team a 3-2 victory and dropped Derby into the relegation zone. Derby should have hung on for what would have been a crucial point, but lack of professionalism caused their ultimate downfall. Three minutes from time, with the game at 2-2, Kevin Wilson nipped the ball off a defender's toe and went clean through on the goalkeeper but for reasons best known to himself tried the walk the ball into the net and allowed the defence chance to get back and cover. The Rams had been ahead twice, through Brian Attley then Charlie George, but a battling Bolton replied both times.

Derby travelled to Boundary Park following the morale-sapping last-ditch defeat at Bolton but performed admirably against a very useful Oldham Athletic side. Kevin Wilson put the Rams ahead, following up on Barry Powell's shot which the goalkeeper could only parry. The Rams looked comfortable with the 1-0 lead until a highly controversial penalty was awarded against them, after a tackle which appeared to take place a yard outside the box was given as a foul by referee David Owen, who was quite a way behind the play – the linesman, much closer to the incident, had not flagged for a foul. Banovic was booked for protesting, and Oldham scored from the spot-kick - then tempers really boiled over as Kevin Hector appeared to be fouled in the home side's penalty area, with the referee waving play-on.

A tremendous turn-out by Derby supporters, well over 1000, many wearing fancy dress, gave excellent vocal support to the team for the full 90 minutes, and turned their attention on referee Owen after his controversial performance. Trouble had been narrowly averted before kick-off when an officious steward discovered that around 50 Derby supporters were in the wrong seats, too close, he said, to home fans who were sat dotted around a three-quarters empty stand (the attendance was just 4,296) – ordering them to leave their seats and enlisting the help of the local constabulary. Fortunately, the police inspector in charge was able to quell the increasing threat of violence, and the fans moved 20 yards to their left.

The results at Bolton and Oldham left Derby 5th from bottom of the Second Division with 45 points from 41 matches. Neither Wrexham (41 from 41), not Orient (36 from 40) could catch Derby, who had one game to play. Only Cardiff City, 4 points behind but with 2 games left and the same goal difference (minus 16) and Shrewsbury Town (equal on points and games played with the Rams, but with a considerably worse goal-difference), could overtake Derby. Because Bolton, who had finished their League programme with 46 points, had a worse goal difference than the Rams, a single point from the home game with Watford would guarantee Second Division survival. With home form, previously so solid, beginning to look decidedly suspect (no goals in the previous three home games, and one point from nine), supporters were understandably nervous about a game against the division's best team. More worrying news came when Frank Sheridan was suspended by an FA Disciplinary Committee and would not be available for the game.

Steve Buckley, the club's acting captain (Steve Powell had hardly played in the past 6 months due to injury) was voted player of the year. It was Buckley's second such award in three seasons. Goalkeeper Yakka Banovic, who had only come into the side in the spring, was runner-up, and young striker Kevin Wilson finished third. The trophy, a sculptured ram, was presented to Buckley at the annual awards night which took place at Tudor Court in Draycott on May 11th, 1982. Other award winners were supporter of the year Mick Derby, the man who had changed his name in honour of the club, and South East Derbyshire Supporters Club, who won supporters' branch of the year.

The final game of the 1981-82 season, against already promoted Watford at the Baseball Ground, took place on Saturday 15th May and attracted a crowd of 14,946. Kevin Hector made his 589th and final appearance for the club, almost 16 years after he had made his debut in a 2-1 defeat away at Crystal Palace (on 17th September 1966), and scored his 201st goal – his first since September 1981, although he had been a substitute rather than a starter for most of John Newman's tenure. The Rams' place in the Second Division the following season was by no means assured, and they required one point to guarantee survival. The Derby side for that final, vital game was: Banovic; Barton, McAlle, Skivington, Buckley; Attley, Hector, Swindlehurst; Hill, Wilson, Emson.

Hector, who had been so poorly-treated when he first left the Baseball Ground in 1978, that he had sworn never to visit the ground and the club loved (and never did, until the manager who cast him aside, Tommy Docherty, had departed) – was this time leaving without any bitterness or acrimony, at the age of 38. "Zak", as he was known by his adoring Rams supporters, was departing as the all-time leading League appearance holder and one of the club's greatest ever goal scorers. He was then, and still is now, considered one of Derby's all-time greats – alongside the likes of Steve Bloomer, Dave Mackay and Roy McFarland. Before the match, Hector was presented with a gift from the club to commemorate his record number of appearances.

Fences were erected in front of the Normanton Terrace for the Watford game, following police and public anxiety about potential pitch invasions in what was a vital match – they had been taken down previously and good behaviour from patrons of that part of the ground had convinced the club to leave them down.

Watford, who were completing their astonishing rise from Fourth to First Division under future England manager Graham Taylor, featured in their side winger Nigel Callaghan – who would go on to become a favourite at the Baseball Ground some years later.

The Rams started brightest but missed several good chances to take the lead – including a penalty, awarded when Andy Hill was pushed over, which was missed by Kevin Wilson. Eventually, a spectacular goal by Steve Buckley put Derby ahead, and they led until Hector fouled Callaghan in the Rams penalty area on 54 minutes – Luther Blissett converted the spot-kick. Another foul, this time by Glen Skivington, close to the penalty area, resulted in Ian Bolton putting Watford 2-1 ahead from a direct free kick.

At this stage, disaster was looming, and the Rams were potentially heading for Division Three – but nerves were settled four minutes later when Emson's pacey run and pass found Wilson, who scored with a deflected shot. Within another 6 minutes, Derby were safe when Hector headed-home Wilson's cross to put them 3-2 ahead. Two excellent saves from Yakka Banovic kept the Rams in front before, with 88 minutes on the clock, the referee blew his whistle for an offside decision and supporters streamed onto the Baseball Ground pitch, wrongly believing that the game had ended. Eventually, the pitch was cleared of excited fans and the final two minutes were played.

Following the game, referee George Tyson reported Derby County to the Football League due to the pitch invasion. It was later reported that 130 seats were broken in C-Stand as fans went across the pitch and approached Watford supporters in a threatening manner – fortunately the visiting fans did not retaliate, and major trouble was avoided. The Rams had finished season 1981-82 with 48 points and were finally able to draw a veil over what had been a traumatic campaign.

John Newman's record as manager since taking over from Colin Addison was less than impressive – 5 wins in 22 games, with 8 draws and 9 defeats yielded just 23 points from a possible 66. Only 27 goals scored compared to 35 conceded was also disappointing. In fact, Newman's record was worse even than his predecessor that season – Addison's team having picked up 25 points from 20 matches. With hindsight, the club should perhaps have shown Newman the door at the end of 1981-82, but this was never on the cards – Newman was working for Assistant Manager wages and still had a year of his contract to run - financial prudence was perhaps the main reason for keeping him in the manager's chair.

Derby finished 16th in the Second Division, with 48 points from their 42 matches – 23 points behind Norwich City who finished third and were promoted alongside Luton Town and Watford – and 4 points ahead of Cardiff City and Wrexham, who were relegated along with Orient.

The club's decline had continued during 1981-82, and if anything had gathered pace. Since they won the Football League Championship in 1974-75, Derby had finished lower in the League each consecutive season bar one (1977-78) over the next 7 seasons – they had also not won a single FA Cup tie since 1978:

1974-75 – 1st place in the Football League, FA Cup 5th Round

1975-76 – 4th / Semi Final (down 3 places)

1976-77 – 15th / Quarter Final (down 11 places)

1977-78 – 12th / 5th Round (up 3 places)

1978-79 – 19st / 3rd Round (down 7 places)

1979–80 - 21st / 3rd Round (down 2 places)

1980-81 – 28th / 3rd Round (down 7 places)

1981-82 – 38th / 3rd Round (down 10 places)

Considering that the lowest Derby had ever finished in the football league pyramid was 46th (in 1955-56) the club appeared heading towards an all-time low.

Leading the appearances chart for the Rams in 1981-82 was Player of the Year Steve Buckley, with 40. The only others who made more than 30 starts that season were Paul Emson, Dave Swindlehurst, Barry Powell and Frank Sheridan. Kevin Hector appeared 31 times, but 4 of these were as substitute. Kevin Wilson led the goalscoring chart with 9 (from

20+4 appearances), followed by Swindlehurst with 6 then Buckley, Hector and Emson (5 each).

The Rams reserves finished season 1981-82 with 3 wins from their last 5 matches, including a thumping 5-2 win over Bolton Wanderers at the Baseball Ground in which Frank Gamble scored twice. By the end of the season, regular players included goalkeeper Steve Cherry (who had taken over when Yakka Banovic moved up to the First Team), defenders John Lovatt, Paul Blades and Graham Harbey, wingers Aiden Gibson and Frank Gamble plus forwards Andy Hill and John Clayton.

Lovatt, with 37 games, led the appearances chart for the reserves, with Harbey, Blades, David King, Gamble, Clayton, Hill, Wayne Richards and Cherry also playing 20+ matches. Gamble (12) led the goal scorers, followed by Kevin Wilson (9) and Clayton (8).

As things turned out, around 91% of 1981-82's season ticket holders renewed their ticket for the following season, raising more than £170,000. Of the 9% who had not yet renewed by the time 1982-83 kicked off, with a home game against Carlisle United on 28th August 1982, many had requested that the club hold their seats while they see how the team started the season. It was another terrific response from Derby's loyal supporters – some clubs had reported up to 40% falls in season ticket sales over the summer of 1982. Chairman Bill Stevenson said: "football faces a critical season. Fans must be coaxed back by good football on the park, and by good behaviour from the fans. At Derby County we need both". On the second front things had started badly when the Rams played a pre-season friendly game at Banbury, in which proceeds went to aid victims of a recent terrorist bombing in Hyde Park, London. The team coach, while parked outside the Southern League club's ground, had a window smashed by local vandals. Derby won the game 2-0. Violence had also occurred on and off the pitch at Wembley Stadium during the recent Charity Shield match between Liverpool and Tottenham Hotspur.

The Rams looked set to be well supported once again on their travels, despite the generally dreadful away form of recent seasons. Just over 600 fans had been members of the Derby County Travel Club in 1981-82, and almost all of them renewed their membership for 1982-83, at a cost of £1 -the membership gave patrons the opportunity to travel to away matches on the club's official RoadRider transport.

There had been a change in Derby's commercial department over the summer of 1982, with Stuart Robinson being replaced by Stuart Crooks, who had been appointed Commercial Manager. Crooks had excellent Rams credentials, being the son of Sammy Crooks, Derby's superb winger from the inter-war years, who had been capped 26 times by England. Crooks' added another with excellent Derby pedigree when he appointed Susan Leuty, whose father's cousin was the fine Derby defender Leon Leuty as his secretary.

As well as the Charity friendly against Banbury, Derby won private pre-season friendly matches against West Bromwich Albion, Walsall and Chesterfield, and drew at St Andrews against Birmingham City. The final summer 1982 friendly, a public match at the Baseball Ground against Sunderland, was won 1-0. John Newman declared himself happy with his players: "I have never seen any squad worked harder in training, nor do I recall any group of players responding so well to all asked of them…no promises from me but I expect Derby County to make progress from the recent doldrums, both on the pitch and off it". Newman promoted Chief Scout Alan Ashman to the position of Assistant Manager over the summer – another internal (and therefore cost-effective) appointment. Most neutral observers rated the Rams as a mid-table side at best, with some bookmakers making them favourites to be relegated. The best price to be had on Derby achieving promotion was 33-1. Neil Hallam, in his Derby Trader column, was slightly more upbeat about their chances: "Derby County may surprise this season and end up some way from the relegation zone. I don't see them challenging for promotion but with reasonable luck with injuries they could prove the worst is over"

When First Division Sunderland, managed by former Derby midfielder Alan Durban, visited the Baseball Ground on 21st August 1982 for Derby's final pre-season friendly, Derby appeared a reasonable coherent unit and played quite well to win 1-0. The first half was even, with Kevin Wilson hitting the bar from a reasonable opportunity after Dave Swindlehurst had crossed, but Derby had the better of the second, which was capped by new signing Mike Brolly's excellent goal – a chip over four defenders and goalkeeper Chris Turner, from the edge of the Osmaston End penalty area. Supporters also appreciated a late cameo appearance as substitute by Durban, still popular with Rams fans. Derby's line-up: Banovic; Barton, Attley, S.Powell, Foster, McAlle, Brolly, Skivington, Wilson, Swindlehurst, Reid, and substitute Dalziel.

The fixture computer threw up an unusual situation for the start of 1982-83 – Derby were scheduled to play five of their first eight Second Division games at the Baseball Ground (and four of the first five). The Rams, however, had a very poor recent early season record and had not won on the opening day of a campaign since 1974, when they had beaten Chelsea 1-0 at the Baseball Ground. Their best return from the opening five matches since that 1974-75 season had been in 1980-81 when they had won 3 and drawn 1. More typical were the 6 seasons from 1974-75 to 1979-80, in which Derby had never won more than one of their opening five games.

Starting from 1982-83, referees were instructed by the Football League to send off players adjudged guilty of professional fouls. Also, to be clamped-down on more severely were time-wasting and taking free kicks from the wrong place. FIFA instructed that goalkeepers must follow the four-step rule – if they take more than four steps with the ball in hand, a free kick should be awarded to the opposition.

In August 1982 the Rams' full time and apprentice professional squad comprised of 30 players, of whom 11 were youngsters who had never appeared in the First team. Amongst the 19 senior professionals were new signings George Foster (from Plymouth Argyle) and Mike Brolly (from Grimsby Town). Compared with the same time a year before, the players no longer with the club were Steve Spooner (now Halifax Town), Frank Sheridan (surprisingly transferred to Torquay United in June 1982, to link up with former Rams player Bruce Rioch – now manager at Plainmoor. After only a handful of games for Torquay, the unlucky Sheridan suffered a ruptured spleen having been hit by a fiercely-struck free-kick, effectively ending his professional career), Mick Coop (retired), Roger Jones (released and joined York City during the summer of 1982), John Clayton (transferred to Bulova, Hong Kong in summer 1982), Alan Ramage (retired due to injury), Wayne Richards (released and joined Matlock Town, summer 1982), Kevin Hector (released in May 1982, and considering offers from several clubs), Keith Osgood (now Orient), Barry Powell (released on a free transfer to join Bulova, Hong Kong in summer 1982). Sheridan, Jones, Clayton, Richards, Hector and Powell therefore being the players who left Derby County since the end of the 1981-82 season, in addition to Charlie George, who's short-term contract had ended after the season had finished. Also leaving Derby during the summer of 1982 were reserve teamers Aiden Gibson (who had been very unfortunate with injuries), David King, Neil Banks, Ian Mulholland and Paul Halford.

The release on a free transfer of Barry Powell was yet another hammer-blow to Derby's balance-sheet. Powell, who had never been popular with supporters, had cost £300,000 when Colin Addison signing him from Coventry City in the autumn of 1979. After he left, Powell issued a parting-shot at Rams fans: "the pitch at the Baseball Ground is very near the terraces and a lot of individual abuse comes through loud and clear as you are struggling. It depresses you and doesn't help. It's well known in dressing rooms around the country that Derby's crowd can be rough on their own players at the Baseball Ground. I rate it as one of the reasons why home performances have not been good enough recently. A lot of players last season were happier playing away" . Nobody seemed upset that Powell had left, not least the player himself – but on the books, his transfers represented a straight loss of £300,000.

George Foster and **Mike Brolly** both made their debuts in the opening game of season 1982-83, in a team which also included fellow John Newman signings John Barton, John McAlle and Brian Attley, plus Yakka Banovic (who had been at the club since before Newman was manager but had only ever been selected for the first team by Newman). The first side of the season also included club captain Steve Powell and young midfielder Tony Reid – both of whom had missed most of the previous season with injury. The other four players in that first matchday squad were Glen Skivington, Dave Swindlehurst, Kevin Wilson and Paul Emson (who was named as substitute) – therefore only Wilson and Emson remained from the pre-Colin Addison era. Compared to the team that opened the previous campaign, just Steve Powell, Reid, Wilson and Swindlehurst also featured in the opening game of 1982-83. The previous season's Player of the Year Steve Buckley was injured and unavailable for the start of the season but had pledged his immediate future to the Rams by signing a 3-year contract in the summer of 1982. Also still out was the unfortunate Steve Emery, who had suffered a broken leg on February 1st, 1982, then compounded the injury when he fell from his crutches on a wet patch of steps at the Baseball Ground on 31st May – Emery was aiming to be back in first team contention by late November.

The game against newly-promoted Carlisle United, managed by Bob Stokoe, on 28th August was another opening day catastrophe as the Rams, playing like a group who had never met each other before, let alone played football together, went down 3-0 – the visitors' first goal coming as a result of goalkeeper Banovic dropping a routine cross from a corner. At least the attendance, 11,207, was encouraging and above the stated break-even figure of 11,000. Since season ticket sales were around 6,400 it was easy to calculate that around 4,800 had purchased a matchday ticket – a good number considering the general apathy which was prevalent around both Derby County and football in general at that time. What was certain, however, that if the Rams continued to put in such abject displays as they had done that day, attendances would fall, and fast.

George Foster was born in Plymouth in 1956 and joined his hometown club Plymouth Argyle as an apprentice in 1974, starting out as a full back but soon graduating to central defence. He was twice Player of the Year at Home Park, in 1978 and 1980, winning a promotion in 1974-75. After 212 appearances, he fell out of favour at Argyle and went on loan to both Torquay United and Exeter City (where he won Player of the Year despite playing just 28 matches for the club) – he had been disappointed when a Football League Tribunal valued him at £185,000 in the summer of 1981, a fee which Brighton & Hove Albion, who had bid for his services, refused to pay.

Derby manager John Newman spotted Foster whilst on loan for Exeter and signed him for £40,000 in June 1982 – a deal which precipitated the sale of young centre back Frank Sheridan to Torquay during the same month. Foster did not have a particularly happy time at the Baseball Ground and he moved to Mansfield Town at the end of the 1982-83 season, becoming a very popular player with the Stags and making 373 appearances – he was appointed player-manager at Field Mill in February 1989 and led the club to promotion out of the Fourth Division in 1991-92, after leaving Mansfield he managed senior non-league club Telford United from 1993-1995. Foster made 649 league appearances in a 20-year playing career and was a fine player at lower league level – but had perhaps been found wanting at Second Division level in a struggling Derby side.

Foster became a respected scout and worked at Wolverhampton Wanderers and Coventry City, before being appointed Academy Manager at Stoke City in April 2007. He also scouted for Hull City and Port Vale before taking up a role as European scout for Swansea City in 2014.

Mike Brolly, born in Kilmarnock in October 1954, was a junior player with his hometown club, who offered him a professional contract, but he chose instead to move to London and sign for Chelsea in October 1971. He never established himself at Stamford Bridge, making only 8 appearances before moving to Bristol City in 1974.

After City had been promoted to the First Division in 1976, Brolly was allowed to join Grimsby Town and it was at Blundell Park where he established his reputation as a reliable winger – featuring in well over 250 league games for the Mariners and achieving two promotions, during which time he played under John Newman's management. Newman stepped in to offer him a deal when his Grimsby contract expired at the end of the 1981-82 season.

Brolly, 27-years-old when he signed for the Rams in July 1982, featured prominently in his one season at the Baseball Ground, scoring 4 times in 42 matches, but was released at the end of the 1982-83 season and joined Scunthorpe United, before dropping out of professional football and playing for senior non-league clubs Scarborough and Boston United.

Things went from bad to worse on Tuesday 31st August when Derby travelled to The Shay to play Halifax Town in a 1st Round, 1st Leg Milk Cup (as the Football League Cup was branded that season) tie. Newman selected an unchanged side from the one which had been well beaten at home the previous Saturday and the result was another defeat, this time 2-1 with Swindlehurst getting the Rams' consolation goal. There was more bad news when Kevin Wilson was forced to leave the field through injury. The attendance, 2,820, was amongst the smallest ever to watch a competitive game involving Derby County. It was the Rams' 13th successive cup tie defeat – the last cup game Derby had won was in August 1978, more than 4 years ago, when Gordon Hill scored the goal in a 1-0 win over Leicester City at Filbert Street, in the same competition.

Season 1982-83 could not have started more miserably – the losing sequence continued when on the second Saturday of the season, 1st September, when the Rams went down 4-1 on the artificial surface at Loftus Road to Queen's Park Rangers. Kevin Wilson was injured, and Paul Emson dropped from the squad and into the side came Frank Gamble, with Andy Hill named as substitute. Gamble scored Derby's consolation goal and Swindlehurst was sent off for what appeared to be two rather minor fouls. The worst news for the Rams was yet another injury to Steve Powell, who suffered a twisted knee and did not emerge for the second half.

From the first three games of the season, Derby had lost 3 and conceded 9 goals, and scored 2. At this stage, John Newman's record as manager read: Played 25, won 5, drawn 8, lost 12 – everything pointed towards a change being necessary, and each time it appeared that things could get no worse, they did.

Derby's reserve squad, still managed by Richie Norman and coached by Ron Webster, for the Central League campaign of 1982-83 comprised, in August 1982, of Steve Cherry, Mark Shackleton, Daryll Chapman, Paul Blades, Andy Garner, Andy Hill, John Lovatt, Frank Gamble, Ian Dalziel, Colyn Doyle, Paul Bancroft and Graham Harbey – five of whom had already played first team football, and 3 of whom would go on to do so. Only Shackleton, Chapman, Doyle and Bancroft were destined to never play for Derby's first team. Central League games for this season kicked off at 7pm on Tuesday evenings, and would not clash with first team matches.

The reserves started their campaign on 7th September against Rotherham United at Millmoor and won 2-1. Derby went into a 2-goal lead in the first half but were on the rack for much of the second half and had goalkeeper Steve Cherry to thank for restricting the far more experienced home side to just a single goal, with 18-year-old Graham Harbey also impressing at left back.

Derby's youngsters, the "A" side, started their 1982-83 Midland Intermediate League campaign well, with 2 wins and a draw from their first three matches – at Gay Meadow on 11th September, where they drew 1-1 against a far older Shrewsbury Town side, Daryll Chapman scored the Rams' goal in a fine performance. The team that day was: Palmer, McCormick, Harbey, J Collins, Ride, Blades, Chapman, Doyle, Garner, Bancroft, D Collins and substitute Shackleton.

Derby picked up their first points of the season when they beat Chelsea 1-0 in front of 8,075 at the Baseball Ground on Wednesday 8th September with the winning goal coming courtesy of Steve Buckley's penalty – Buckley having returned from injury to replace Steve Powell in the side. Ian Dalziel also started the game, in place of Tony Reid, and added much-needed bite with his tough-tackling in a defensive midfield role. Andy Hill replaced Frank Gamble in attack. The Rams suffered yet another injury when John Barton suffered a thigh strain and had to be substituted at half time. Chelsea's supporters were banned from attending the match, following serious trouble at the corresponding fixture in the previous season.

The victory over Chelsea at the Baseball Ground on 8th September was to be the last time Derby would win a League game for almost three months - a run of 14 Second Division matches without a win. From the start of 1982-83 season until Christmas, the Rams played 24 matches and won only 4, two of which were League Cup games against Fourth Division sides Halifax Town and Hartlepool United.

The Rams' third home league game, on Saturday 11th September, resulted in a 1-1 draw with Middlesbrough – the crowd on almost 1,000 more than had seen the previous Wednesday's game against Chelsea reflected the fact that visiting supporters from Teesside were welcome. Derby had injury problems - both Steve Buckley and John Barton missed the game, with Ian Dalziel filling as part of a back three alongside George Foster and the increasingly error-prone John McAlle, and Tony Reid back in midfield – Brian Attley dropped back from right midfield into a defensive midfield role. The visitors went ahead but the Rams battled-back and Dalziel equalised from the penalty spot – Derby had good chances to win the game, with goalkeeper Platt making a fine save from Andy Hill, and Paul Emson missing a simple chance.

After the Middlesbrough game, Derby stood 16th in the Second Division with 4 points from 4 matches. It was a familiar story – there was no real sign of improvement from the previous season and a long battle to avoid relegation once again looked on the cards.

Boisterous behaviour amongst the younger element now sitting in C-Stand (having had their beloved Ossie End terrace taken away from them, to be replaced by Family Seating), led to the ban of alcohol sales in the Main Stand during the hour before kick-off and at half time. The Board, and Secretary Michael Dunford, felt that "consumption of alcohol contributed to bad behaviour and bad language", and had received complaints from B-Stand season ticket holders. "no-one objects to enthusiasm, even chants, but we do not require obscene chanting from the stands...or loutish behaviour near or around season ticket holders and we cannot afford any structural damage to seating...the board are ready to implement certain structural alterations in the (main) stand" said Dunford, failing to acknowledge that his own decision to restructure the Osmaston Terracing had led to the young fans relocating to C-Stand in the first place.

Derby's third successive home game took place on Wednesday 15th September 1982 when they faced Halifax Town, managed by Mick Bullock, in the second leg of their first round Milk Cup tie. The National Diary Council had pledged just under £4,000 per club to sponsor the Football League's cup competition, with a benefit for smaller clubs being that each club received an equal share of the 20% pool collected from all gate receipts – meaning that if Liverpool played Manchester United in front of 40,000, for example, every other club would benefit equally. The total investment by the sponsors was estimated at over £400,000.

The Rams went into the game down 1-2 from the first leg after their dismal display at The Shay. The away side featured young striker Bobby Davison, who had scored 20 goals during the previous season, and was in the goals again in the current campaign. Also playing for Halifax was Steve Spooner, who was now captain of the side having signed from Derby almost a year earlier. The Rams had both Barton and Buckley back from injury, and Wilson, who had also been injured, returned to the matchday squad as substitute.

Derby eventually won the tie 5-2 on aggregate in front of an encouraging crowd of 8,534 – the game went to extra time, having been level on aggregate after 90 minutes. Buckley scored twice (once from the penalty spot), Skivington, Hill and substitute Wilson (who had replaced the injured Dalziel) got the other three goals. It was the first time for almost six years that the Rams had scored more than four in a match – the last time being an 8-2 thrashing of Tottenham Hotspur in October 1976. Derby were drawn to face Hartlepool United in the next round.

On Saturday 18th September Derby faced what looked, on paper, their toughest test so far in the season with an away game against recently relegated Leeds United at Elland Road. Leeds had started quite well on their return to the Second Division and had 8 points from their first 4 games, 4 more than the Rams. John Newman was forced to leave out McAlle, who had looked desperately poor so far that season and was now suffering from gastro-enteritis and replace him with 17-year-old debutant **Paul Blades,** still an apprentice professional.

Derby went a goal down early on, then their cause was made even more difficult when Blades' partner in central defence George Foster went off injured after 18 minutes after a crunching tackle by Leeds forward Frank Worthington (who's studs made painful contact with the Rams' defender's hip), then Glen Skivington, who dropped back into central defence to replace Foster (Paul Emson, the substitute, replacing him in midfield) was sent off for pulling Worthington's shirt (now classed as a professional foul) just 4 minutes later – the clever and experienced Worthington having got away with the foul which provoked Derby's youngster into reacting.

The Rams did, however, battle on manfully with ten men against a clearly more talented side, and Mick Brolly equalised with a fine chipped finish, capping a fine individual display. Derby then had several good chances including a Kevin Wilson goal (after he had robbed goalkeeper John Lukic) which was mysteriously disallowed by referee Mr Owen, not a favourite with Derby following controversial decisions against them the previous season - plus a 30-yard strike from Emson which ricocheted back off the angle of post and bar. Leeds denied the Rams a deserved point with a winning goal 9 minutes from time.

The loss at Elland Road (where the Rams had an abysmal record, with only two goals scored there in 11 First Division seasons – and just 1 victory, in 1974-75), unfortunate as it may have been, was Derby's 74th defeat away from home in their previous 128 League games (since the start of 1976-77, when the club's decline began). During this period, they had won just 17 away league games, and drawn the other 37, scoring 111 goals and conceding 237.

Paul Blades was born in Peterborough in January 1965 and attended Walton School in the City, being scouted by Derby County and joining the club as a trainee in 1980 at the age of 15. He made his debut for the first team in September 1982, whilst still an apprentice but did not really establish himself in the Rams' side until Arthur Cox took over as manager in the mid 1980's. Blades was one of the few survivors of the traumatic Addison-Newman-Peter Taylor years, but was almost lost to Derby in 1983 when Taylor told him to find a new club. A natural centre-back, he was often called up to cover at right back and replaced both Charlie Palmer and then the injured Mel Sage in successive promotion seasons.

Blades enjoyed three seasons in the First Division with the Rams before leaving for Norwich City in July 1990, after 166 league appearances and one goal for the club. Norwich made him their record signing at £700,000 and he came close to an FA Cup Final appearance in

1992. After Norwich, he moved to Wolverhampton Wanderers for another substantial fee, this time £325,000 and made 117 appearances for them before ending his professional career at Rotherham United in 1997. He later played non-league football for Hednesford Town.

The most successful of all of Colin Addison's youth recruits, Blades was a reliable and popular player in the 1980's at the Baseball Ground, and the only player who remained on the books throughout the entire decade, playing a big part in both promotions during the 1980's. His brother Steve was also on Derby's staff.

Blades's debut at Leeds pleased both manager and youth coach Ron Webster. It was certainly a baptism of fire to be marking former England International Frank Worthington and Newman said "(Paul) was in at the deep end and I was very pleased with how he coped". Webster reminded Ram Newspaper that he had forecast two years previously that Steve Cherry, Tony Reid and Ian Dalziel would make the senior side – he added both 18-year old left back Graham Harbey and 17-year-old centre back Neil Banks ("he's still at school but he'll really develop under full time training, a real midget he is") to that list.

Derby returned to the Baseball Ground on Saturday 25th September to play Blackburn Rovers, managed by former Derby player Bobby Saxton (94 games between 1964 and 1968). Derby stood 4th from bottom of the Second Division with four points from five matches, and Rovers 4 places and 2 points ahead. John McAlle returned from his illness to replace Paul Blades, Steve Powell made his latest comeback from injury and Dave Swindlehurst (returning from suspension) and Frank Gamble started in attack in place of Andy Hill and Kevin Wilson.

Derby were dire and lost the game 2-1, despite going a goal up on 50 minutes when Dalziel scored at the Osmaston End. After going ahead, the Rams performance level disintegrated and fans felt that the scoreline flattered the Rams by the end - it was perhaps the worst they had played so far in a wretched start to the season. It was still September, yet relegation already seemed to be staring Derby in the face. There were problems all over the pitch but none more so than in central defence where the Foster and McAlle partnership was simply not working – "as compatible as Arthur Scargill and Barbara Cartland", wrote Neil Hallam in the Derby Trader. Graham Richards, on BBC Radio Derby, was equally scathing after the game, describing Derby as "simply dreadful", and the eloquent Gerald Mortimer in the Derby Telegraph wrote – "I thought the Rams would show a steady improvement this season and that they would be a more workmanlike side. I was wrong".

Off the field there were more rumblings about finances. The Board were once again forced to dip into their pockets to resolve what was described as a "temporary cash flow problem" – later revealed to be a shortfall in payments from the club for extra policing. The cause, low attendances at the Baseball Ground, was unlikely to be rectified with the standard of football and results on offer so far in 1982-83. Just 9,361 had watched the Blackburn Rovers game – some 1,639 less than the stated "break-even" figure. Rumours persisted around the City that the football club was close to bankruptcy. The Ram Newspaper was by this time a smaller publication than it had previously been – often just eight pages (and reduced in price to 30p, rather than the usual 35p for twelve pages). It was all part of the cost-cutting strategy which the club had no choice but to implement.

The cost to police football was rising, as trouble continued to be a regular occurrence both inside and outside stadiums. Writing in Ram Newspaper in October 1982, A.L.T from Basildon, Essex (name and full address withheld) complained that he had witnessed, while standing on the Popside, "a number of yobs" throwing coins at a linesman and had, when he suggested that they should stop, been subjected to "a mouthful of foul language plus a number of hefty blows round my head". After complaining to the police, A.L.T was told that there would be no further action, since no witnesses came forward. Derby County were spending around £2,000 home game to ensure enough police protection to make the ground considered safe by the authorities. This was not negotiable – without this policing the Baseball Ground would be closed.

In the summer, just over 400 season ticket holders from the previous season had asked for their seats to be held while they checked how well the Rams started the 1982-83 campaign, rather than committing there and then to renew their season tickets – by the start October 1982, just half a dozen had decided to go ahead and renew. The disastrous start to the current season was costing the club dearly, and there was no sign of improvement – either off the pitch or on it – in early October Eddie Strachan resigned from the board of directors. Strachan had been the director with direct responsibility for the affairs of Derby County Promotions and had been on the board since the summer of 1980. After Strachan's resignation, Derby's board comprised just chairman Bill Stevenson, vice-chairman John Kirkland and directors Mick McGarry, Fred Fern and Brian Holmes.

The Rams reserves thumped Manchester City 5-0 at the Baseball Ground in their first home game of the season. Several first teamers were finding their way back from injury and featured in the game – Steve Powell, Tony Reid, Frank Gamble and Dave Swindlehurst all coming through the match unscathed. Paul Emson, out of favour with the first team, also played. Gamble scored a hat-trick (and could have had several more) but the goal of the game was a 30 yarder from Graham Harbey. The reserves lined up with Steve Cherry in goal, John Lovatt, Harbey, Paul Blades and Jimmy Collins in defence, Powell, Reid, Paul Bancroft and Emson in midfield and Swindlehurst partnering Gamble in attack. Substitute was David Collins. Meanwhile, Rams "A" were themselves thrashed 6-2 at Raynesway against Leicester City. Derby's youth recruitment, significant during Colin Addison's reign (especially in his first season), had all but dried up again by this time – one exception was Mark Ahearne, a pupil at Merrill School in Shelton Lock, who signed associated schoolboy forms in the autumn of 1982.

The Reserves' match against local rivals Nottingham Forest at the Baseball Ground was rescheduled for Sunday November 7th, having originally been scheduled to be a mid-week game (as were all Central League matches from 1982-83). It was felt that a Sunday kick-off (very rare in those days) would present the best chance of attracting a good crowd – Forest had made the first move by arranging the City Ground fixture for Sunday 3rd October, where a crowd of 1,164 saw a young and inexperienced Rams side perform well against a far more experienced Forest team, eventually going down 1-0 with the goal coming from Peter Ward on 37 minutes. As well as Ward, the Forest side featured Willie Young, Ian Bowyer and future Derby forward Calvin Plummer. Derby's youngsters, particularly Paul Bancroft and Jimmy Collins in midfield, Darryl Chapman in defence and Steve Cherry in goal, put on a very encouraging display.

The week before they had lost at the City Ground, Derby's reserves had also been in Nottingham, that time at Meadow Lane where they lost 5-4 to Notts County. In an entertaining match, the Rams, fielding an experienced side including Steve Powell, George Foster, Glen Skivington and Paul Emson, had trailed 4-1 after just half an hour but fought back to level at 4-4 before a last-minute winner cost them a point. Especially sharp for the Rams were forwards Frank Gamble and Andy Hill – Hill scored twice, Gamble once with the other by Emson. Promising full-back Graham Harbey suffered a setback when he damaged knee ligaments during the game, necessitating at least six weeks out.

On the first Saturday of October 1982, Derby travelled to Valley Parade to face Charlton Athletic. They had won just one league game and had lost 4 of the other 6 – the situation was becoming critical, the Rams looked doomed already, supporters found it difficult to imagine a more depressing situation. BBC Radio Derby described the game as "a relegation battle", with Charlton just four places above the second from bottom Rams. Newman juggled his team and moved Powell back into central defence to partner Foster, dropping McAlle – the result was a more solid-looking back four.

A crowd of 4,685 (including an impressive 500 plus from Derby) scattered around the cavernous stadium watched a 1-1 draw in pouring rain, with the lively Frank Gamble getting Derby's goal when he latched onto a weak back pass and finished neatly on 54 minutes. Some pride was restored as the Rams put together a much more determined display and could perhaps feel aggrieved to only come away with one point. Derby's jittery display after going ahead, when they resorted to rushed square and backwards passing – as they had been prone to do whenever taking the lead under the management of John Newman – eventually cost them the points as the home side equalised just six minutes from the end – after a succession of nervy passes across the Rams' penalty area let the Charlton in. Lacking in creativity in midfield, albeit more resolute than of late, only Mick Brolly looked to have attack-minded intentions and the skill to make accurate forward passes.

Charlton's late equaliser, disappointing as it was, was also predictable - Derby had conceded 21 goals in the second half with Newman as manager, and 12 within the last 20 minutes.

Four of the previous five goals conceded had come in the closing minutes of games. Gamble's goal at The Valley was only the fourth that Derby had scored from open play in the seven League games so far.

Derby's supporters' morale was at an all time low. Letters to Ram Newspaper around this time were typified by A.R.Morley of Wirksworth – "I simply cannot but write my disgust at the performance of the Rams against Blackburn Rovers…the almost continual decline is wearing thin on my nerves…if I was a Rams player or on the coaching staff I would be ashamed of myself…fans should walk out before the end if we get any more performances like this". Robert Rooney of Codnor wrote – "since the slide started in April 1976, one long downward spiral, culminating for me in the defeat by Blackburn Rovers…what is the point of coming every week and hoping that four talented players, two promising youngsters and a mixture of has-beens and never-will-be's will stem the tide?". Even club secretary Michael Dunford admitted "it has been so depressing here at the Baseball Ground during the last ten days that it easily rates as the most upsetting in my career"

Derby had a break from Second Division action on Wednesday October 6th when they faced Fourth Division Hartlepool United in a Second Round, First Leg Milk Cup tie at the Baseball Ground. The attendance, 7,656, was perhaps higher than could have been expected given the opposition and represented a significant boost to Derby's cash situation. The Rams won 2-0 – a cup run was essential for finances, especially if they could win and then draw a home time in the next round (from the third round onwards, Milk Cup ties were played over a single tie, with extra time and then penalties to decide the winner if needed).

Derby went ahead after 18 minutes when Hartlepool goalkeeper John Watson fumbled a Swindlehurst cross into his own net, an own goal of almost comedic proportions and a huge slice of luck for the Rams. As had become depressingly familiar during John Newman's tenure, Derby then slipped back into negative habits and allowed the fourth division team to get on top in the game and it was against the run of play when Swindlehurst rattled a left foot shot into the Normanton goal 11 minutes into the second half to put the Rams 2-0 ahead. Nervous and negative, Derby somehow managed to hold on to their two-goal advantage to give themselves some hope of progressing after the second leg – although Hartlepool were the better side and played more adventurous and attacking football at the Baseball Ground.

Including the Milk Cup ties, the average attendance at the Baseball Ground so far in the season was 9,245 – only once had there been a crowd of five figures, and that was for the season's opener against Carlisle United – a 0-3 defeat, which set the tone for the weeks to follow.

On Saturday 9th October Derby entertained Cambridge United at the Baseball Ground, the second game there in a week. Manager John Newman again paired Foster and Powell in central defence, leaving out McAlle, with Barton at right back and Dalziel at left back. Frank

Gamble started in what turned out to be his last appearance for Derby. Cambridge included future Rams defender Floyd Streete in their side. Once again, the attendance was far below what was needed to break even, this time 8,135 (generating match day receipts of just over £5,000), although the fact that the Rams had played two home games in 4 days undoubtedly helped. Mick Brolly, one of the very few bright sparks of the early season, scored Derby's goal in a 1-1 draw – a scuffed volley at the Normanton End which somehow found its way into the Normanton End goal, after Swindlehurst had crossed from the right - the Rams were fortunate that Reilly missed a penalty for the visitors.

Substituted against Cambridge, 21-year-old Frank Gamble walked out of the Baseball Ground after the game and never returned, rendering his contract void. He later said he had felt lost and confused by the turmoil at Derby – "everybody at Derby County is afraid. It is a club full of fear. There are some very unhappy people". Gamble returned to his native Merseyside to be with his wife and child, and then, as a free agent, joined non-league Barrow a month later. A talented but troubled individual, Gamble could have made a success of his Derby County career had he been around in less turbulent times, and had his dedication and attitude been up to the level required by a professional sportsman.

Reaction to Gamble's decision was negative – club captain Steve Powell said "anyone who lacks the heart to fight for Derby County should leave. Good riddance, I say", and manager John Newman added "remarks about frightened men are plain daft, the boy is hardly qualified to comment on the general state of football, he's only been in the game two minutes". Even the national press picked up on the story with Lynda Lee-Potter writing in her Daily Mail column – "is Frank grateful (for his highly-paid job in football)?...no he is not, he's back with his in-laws, jobless, homeless and on the dole saying the daily grind took the fun out of the game and during training somebody shouted at him...I hope his wife is banging his crackpot head against his mother-in-law's door...going to work is rarely fun and most of us put self-discipline above the indulgence of being able to spend a state-subsidised day laughing our heads off"

After drawing with Cambridge at the Baseball Ground, Derby faced two difficult-looking away games in a week – on 16th October at Grimsby Town, then the following Tuesday evening at Barnsley. The Rams did better than expected, gaining a point from both matches – both being drawn 1-1

Before the Grimsby game, the Rams managed to do a deal with North American Soccer League side Seattle Sounders to sign former England youth and under-21 international midfield player Gary Mills on an extended loan, until April 1983. It was a complicated arrangement – Mills was still contracted to Nottingham Forest, for whom he had played in the 1980 European Cup Final victory over Hamburg, but under complicated agreements in force between the Football League and the NASL at that time, he was not allowed to play for Forest during the 1982-83 season and instead he turned out for the Rams, becoming a vital player in the battle to avoid relegation from the Second Division.

At Blundell Park, where Dave Swindlehurst, on the occasion of his 100th first team appearance, scored his third goal of the season, a superb 25-yard piledriver after just five minutes, and was later sent off alongside Grimsby's Joe Waters for reacting to the latest of several fouls from behind, manager Newman recalled John McAlle to partner George Foster in central defence, moving Steve Powell to his preferred defensive midfield role. Steve Buckley was injured, so Ian Dalziel filled in at left back. New signing **Gary Mills** made his debut, in the centre of midfield, replacing the badly out of form Brian Attley.

The point gained at Grimsby moved Derby up one place in the Second Division, to 20th, and Swindlehurst's goal was his 24th for the club. Following his sending off, for the second time in the season, Swindlehurst was banned by the Football Association for the forthcoming away matches at Wolverhampton Wanderers and Sheffield Wednesday.

Three days later, at Oakwell, Derby were unchanged, and Mike Brolly scored his third of the season to secure a third successive 1-1 draw – the Rams were now 19th in the league, with 8 points from 10 matches. Unfortunately, the big story that 19th October evening was not Derby's hard-won point, but news that six cars belonging to club players and officials were broken into, whilst parked on the Cambridge Street car park – with both the first team and the reserves playing away, it was normal for cars to be left there awaiting the return of the team coach. Alan Ashman, the assistant manager, had both a set of golf clubs and several personal football dossiers "which have taken years to compile" stolen. Ian Dalziel had cassette tapes stolen and his car's sun-roof smashed, and Paul Emson, Steve Cherry and Tony Reid also had property stolen. This was the second time in recent weeks that players' cars had been targeted, following a similar incident whilst a match was in progress at the Baseball Ground.

With five draws in ten Second Division matches, the Rams were becoming the draw specialists of the division. This might have been acceptable in the previous 2-points for a win system, but with 3 points now being awarded, clubs had to win games to stay competitive.

Paul Emson, who had become a regular fixture as Derby's substitute (having been named as number 12 seven times already in season 1982-83), was the subject of transfer talks, with Port Vale interested in taking the winger to Vale Park – wages were a stumbling-block, but the deal appeared close to completion.

Gary Mills was born in Northampton in 1961 - a talented performer at both football and rugby union (he played at England schoolboy level in both sports), he was also a very promising sprinter and ran the 100 metres in 11 seconds as an English school's championship finalist. He signed youth forms with Nottingham Forest, becoming their youngest ever debutant at the age of 16 in 1978. He was also the youngest player to appear in a European Cup Final, in 1980, but could never establish himself as a permanent member of Brian Clough's team and had made just 58 appearances in four years when he was allowed to join Seattle Sounders of the North American Soccer League. Whilst at Forest, he was capped by England at under-21 level.

After one summer season in the NASL, he joined Derby County on loan and made 23 appearances for the Rams, scoring 2 goals. Forest had wanted him back, but NASL rules of the day prevented him from playing for them during the 1982-83 season. He eventually returned to the City Ground and stayed until 1987 before moving across Nottingham to Notts County, then moving to Leicester City where he played 200 games before returning to Meadow Lane to finish his full-time playing career.

In 1996 Mills began his managerial career as player-manager at Grantham Town, enjoying considerable success there, and later at King's Lynn and Tamworth. He had a spell in Football League management at Notts County before returning to the non-league With Alfreton Town, Tamworth and York City. He also managed Gateshead and Wrexham, and most recently back at York City in 2017. He was still occasionally turning out as a player in senior non-league football as recently as the 2009-10 season, in his late 40's.

On 20th October it emerged that Derby County's board of directors were discussing and considering a proposed financial package which, it was suggested, "if concluded, secure the future of Derby County Football Club".

The Rams reserves, 5th in the Central League table, suffered a 2-0 defeat at the hands of Manchester City, for whom Phil Boyer scored both goals – only some fine defending from Banks and Blades kept the visitors from scoring a far more convincing win. A week earlier, an experienced Derby side (containing 8 players with first team experience) had beaten Sunderland 2-0 to maintain their respectable start to the season – the side for the victory over the Black Cats was: Cherry; Lovatt, D Collins, Skivington, Banks, McAlle, Reid, Bancroft, Hill, Wilson, Emson and substitute J Collins.

Returning to the Baseball Ground on Saturday 23rd October, Derby suffered a chastening 4-0 defeat against Leicester City. The only positive from the day was a season's best attendance of 13,191 – boosted by a large contingent from Leicester. Steve Powell missed the game, Brian Attley stepping in for the club captain. It was a day to forget for goalkeeper Yakka Banovic, as Leicester's future England striker Gary Lineker scored a hat-trick, with Alan Smith getting the other. In goal for the visitors was future Rams goalkeeper Mark Wallington, and Ian Wilson, who had a short loan spell at Derby later in his career, also played. Leicester looked competent and workmanlike, but the Rams were abject – the future looked black for Rams fans, it was the worst performance by their team in many years. It was a particularly bad time to put in such a dreadful display - as well as the presence of the prospective new chairman, there had been considerable corporate interest in this game with all 20 executive boxes filled for the first time in the season.

The Leicester game was marred by sporadic outbreaks of trouble in the Osmaston End Family Seating Area, as rowdy fans infiltrated the seats and scuffles broke-out. The Rams board responded by announcing that in future anybody wanting to use the Family Seating would have to pre-register at the ticket office, where an official permit would be issued. The club received several complaints from upset parents who complained about "bad language and aggressive behaviour by young people who had no right to be in that section"

Before kick-off against Leicester, Mike Watterson was introduced to the Baseball Ground crowd. Watterson was bidding to buy a majority share in Derby County Football Club Limited and was eventually confirmed as the club's new chairman on November 1st, 1982. Along with Watterson, a familiar face also joined the board – Stuart Webb, the former secretary who had left the Baseball Ground in the furore surrounding the police investigation into club affairs in 1979. Webb, a marketing and promotions expert with significant interests in the travel industry, had first joined the club's staff in the early 1970's during Brian Clough's tenure as manager. Watterson's proposal included a significant cash injection, necessary to keep the club solvent, plus some funds to strengthen the team on the pitch – although doubts remained as to whether John Newman would remain in position long enough to be the man to spend them.

The return leg of Derby's Milk Cup tie was played at Victoria Park against Hartlepool United on 25th October. The Rams led 2-0 from the home leg, and desperately needed the income a cup run would provide. Banovic, after his horror-show against Leicester City, lost his place to Steve Cherry (who made his first appearance for the first team for just over a year). Paul Blades replaced Brian Attley – Attley's form having completely deserted him. Derby lost the game 4-2 after extra-time but progressed to the third round thanks to the away goals rule after a 4-4 aggregate result. Brolly and Wilson scored the Rams' goals. It was a shocking display from Derby, who were once again outclassed by a fourth division side containing several part time players.

There followed two successive very difficult-looking Second Division away matches, at Wolverhampton Wanderers on Saturday 30th October, then at Sheffield Wednesday on Saturday November 6th. Defeats in both matches sealed manager John Newman's fate once and for all, although Derby were already looking for, and talking to, potential replacements and had been for several weeks – putting an end to a miserable spell in charge. Newman had not really wanted the job in the first place and had to be persuaded to stay on by his predecessor Colin Addison.

Kevin Wilson scored the Rams' consolation in a 2-1 defeat at Molineux, where Derby's improved display against their promotion-chasing opponents gave some cause for hope, with most observers feeling that a draw would have been fair reward for the Rams' endeavours. The game was not a classic, and only a disputed penalty separated the two sides in the end. Then a crowd just under 18,000 at Hillsborough saw the Rams beaten by league leaders Sheffield Wednesday in a game in which saw another battling display receive no reward. Another disputed penalty decision went against Derby and the 2-0 scoreline flattered the home side.

Derby's reserves, who had no fixtures between 19th October and 2nd November, returned to action with defeats at home to both Bolton Wanderers (2-3) then 5 days later to Nottingham Forest (1-2). Against Bolton, the Rams had been desperately poor and had been deservedly beaten by their younger but more determined visitors, Bancroft and Attley scored Derby's goals but the neither Attley nor his first team colleague Tony Reid impressed in midfield.

On Sunday 7th November the Baseball Ground staged its first ever competitive Sunday game when Derby's reserves met local rivals Nottingham Forest, who included nine players with first team experience, compared to Derby's 4. Forest raced to a 2-0 lead by half time (and could have had 3, but Banovic saved a penalty after 44 minutes), but Derby fought back in the second half, inspired by Dave Swindlehurst – working his way back to match-sharpness after a 2-game suspension. Swindlehurst eventually scored to make it 1-2 with six minutes left. Derby's team: Banovic; Lovatt, D Collins, J Collins, Banks, Blades, Chapman, Bancroft, Garner, Swindlehurst, Emson and substitute Shackleton. At a lower age group, Derby County "A" had won their previous three games, against Wolverhampton Wanderers, Port Vale and Birmingham City (all at Raynesway), scoring 11 goals and conceding just 2 in the process, with Frank Gamble and Andy Garner in particular, amongst the goals.

Between the first team games at Molineux and Hillsborough, Mike Watterson was confirmed as the club's new chairman. Former chairman Bill Stevenson and directors Brian Holmes, and shortly afterwards, Mick McGarry all resigned from the board in order to facilitate Watterson's take over, leaving only John Kirkland and Fred Fern as directors surviving from the previous regime – serving alongside Watterson and the newly-appointed Stuart Webb.

Mike Watterson, born in Chesterfield in 1942, was 40 years old when he negotiated a controlling stake in Derby County Football Club Ltd and became its chairman. He was already a professional snooker player, having turned professional in January 1981, with a highest break of 107 achieved in qualifying for the 1982 snooker World Championships – his best performance as a professional was an appearance in the last 16 of the 1983 International Open.

In his early 20's, Watterson had been a car dealer, but his passion was snooker and he who first approached the Crucible Theatre in Sheffield with a view to staging the World Championships in 1977 – the tournament is still hosted at this now-iconic venue. After his successful promotion of the World Championship event, he also founded and promoted several other snooker tournaments including the British Open, the International Open and the World Cup, becoming a key figure in the establishment of snooker as a mainstream sport. He also managed several of the top players of the 1980's including Cliff Thorburn, Kirk

Stevens and Silvino Francisco. Watterson also founded the BDO World Darts Championship, which he originally staged at the Heart of the Midlands nightclub in Nottingham and later at Jollies in Stoke on Trent. He was also involved in the promotion of floodlit cricket and indoor bowls. Most recently, he worked as a commentator on snooker events for both Eurosport and Sky Sports.

After leaving Derby he had a brief involvement with his hometown football club Chesterfield FC, which he saved from being wound up in the High Court by settling debts totalling £91,000, becoming chairman at Saltergate for a short period in the mid 1980's.

Within hours of Watterson's appointment as chairman, Stuart Webb's appointment to the board of directors was confirmed. Webb, the former general secretary, had played a key role in developing the Rams into a successful operation off the field in the early to mid-1970's. He had resigned in August 1979 and said of the situation back then "I felt I could not work with that board when some of them had brought in the police behind the back of the then chairman George Hardy". After leaving Derby County, Webb had linked up with holiday industry expert Sir Fred Pontin and expanded his travel business Lonsdale with branches opening in Ashbourne and Ashby. Specialising in sports travel, Lonsdale were appointed by UEFA as official travel agents and the company had recently taken Liverpool FC to Japan to take part in the World Club Championships – they had also been heavily involved with Nottingham Forest and Manchester United's recent European trips. He was also a committee member with Derbyshire County Cricket Club. Webb joined the board as a commercial consultant –"to offer my time and experience" and was not offering finance nor guarantees.

John Newman's contract was terminated the day after defeat at Hillsborough, on Sunday 7th November 1982, with Derby bottom of the Second Division having accumulated just 8 points from 13 matches, and only one win and just ten goals scored, and just one clean sheet. Newman became the fifth manager in six years to part company with the club – he had been manager since January 1982, firstly on a caretaker basis and then appointed formally in March. Newman's sacking was not a shock, but the name of his successor most certainly was.

Peter Taylor was appointed manager of Derby County on Monday November 8th, 1982. The immediate impact of Taylor's, formerly assistant manager to Brian Clough at both Derby and Nottingham Forest, appointment was a spike in ticket sales – around 200 were sold within 48 hours of the announcement (at £32-£50 for seats and £20 for terraces), a very welcome cash boost. Mike Watterson, the new chairman, received some 500 letters of support congratulating him on his managerial appointment. Taylor signed a 2-year contract – "that should be long enough to find out on both sides whether my appointment was the right one for Derby County".

Asked why he had returned to football with the Rams, Taylor said – "I was sitting at home enjoying retirement when Stuart Webb phoned asking if me if I would see Mike Watterson about returning to Derby. Anybody else but Stuart and I would have refused but when I heard he was going back to the club himself I was interested…quite a few people have tried to lure him back to the game in the last three years, I was one of them…they came to my home, you know the rest, Football is all about passion you see. The Derby job kept me awake at night, whereas none of the other offers I received did. This is the only club I would have given up my retirement for. The chairman and Stuart Webb were vital keys in that decision".

Taylor had retired from football after leaving Nottingham Forest at the end of the 1981-82 season. His friend and partner Brian Clough having negotiated, on his behalf, a sizeable pay-off from Forest. The pair, friends and colleagues since the 1960's, parted ways on the best of terms – that, however, was soon to change when Taylor shocked football by returning to the Baseball Ground, announcing "I would have come back for no-one but Derby County".

The incoming manager was promised carte-blanche to strengthen the team however he saw fit, although Watterson's comment "so much was needed simply to keep the club afloat that perhaps not enough remains to enable Peter to make substantial excursions into the transfer market" suggested that Taylor would not be operating at the millions of pounds end of the market, as he had become accustomed to at the City Ground. On 13th November, the occasion of Taylor's first home game as manager, everybody passing through the turnstiles at the Baseball Ground was handed an envelope in which to donate to a "help buy a player appeal" – the club being finally able to guarantee that every penny donated would be given-over to the purchase of new players. Taylor's first job after being appointed was to put together a back- room team "that will be second to none in calibre…if we get it right behind the scenes in the dressing room, we'll be half way to getting it right on the park".

Peter Taylor was born on 2nd July 1928 in Nottingham, playing junior football for Christchurch and Mapperley Methodists before joining Nottingham Forest in 1942. A goalkeeper, Taylor never established himself in the Forest side and joined Coventry City in 1945, staying at Highfield Road for 10 years but playing only 86 first team matches. He was sold to Middlesbrough in 1955 for a fee of £3,500 and it was at Ayresome Park where he established himself as a first team player and where he formed a close friendship with striker Brian Clough, who was six years his junior. Aside from Clough, the other major influence on Taylor's career was Harry Storer, Coventry City's (and later Derby County's) manager.

Taylor's first experience as a manager was at Burton Albion in 1962, building a successful side which won the Southern League Cup in 1964. His friend Brian Clough, by now manager of Hartlepool United, appointed Taylor as assistant manager in 1965 and they rebuilt what was at the time one of the weakest of all football league squads into a side capable of challenging for promotion from the Fourth Division. In May 1967 Clough was approached by

Derby County and accepted the job with the proviso that Taylor was also appointed as his assistant. Between 1967 and 1973 Clough and Taylor built the finest side Derby County's history, winning the second division title in 1968-69, the first division title in 1971-72 and reaching the semi-finals of the European Cup in 1973.

After their acrimonious departure from the Baseball Ground in October 1973, Clough and Taylor moved to Brighton & Hove Albion before parting company in July 1974 when Clough agreed to replace Don Revie at Leeds United while Taylor, settled on the south coast, preferred to stay on as manager at the Goldstone Ground. They were reunited in July 1976 at Nottingham Forest and repeated their stunning achievement at the Baseball Ground by winning promotion from the second division then becoming champions of the football league in 1977-78. They then surpassed their Derby success by winning the European Cup in 2 successive seasons, 1979 and 1980, before Taylor retired in May 1982 after several of the duo's more recent signings, especially Raimondo Ponte and Justin Fashanu, proved to be poor investments. Without Taylor, Clough was unable to replicate the astonishing successes the pair had achieved, although Forest continued to be a significant force at domestic level throughout the 1980's.

Peter Taylor never worked in football again after leaving Derby County in April 1984 at the age of 55 and he died suddenly aged 62 while on holiday in Majorca. He and Clough had not spoken to each other since 1983 – much to Clough's regret. Brian Clough dedicated his 1994 autobiography to Taylor, saying "To Peter. Still miss you badly. You once said, 'when you get shot of me there won't be as much laughter in your life'. You were right"

The Rams' first game with Peter Taylor as manager was the third round Milk Cup tie at St Andrews against Birmingham City, bottom of the First Division, on Wednesday 10th November. Taylor had been in situ for only 48 hours, so the team was largely selected by Alan Ashman, who for the time being remained as assistant manager. The only changes from Newman's last side, which had lost at Sheffield Wednesday the previous Saturday, were McAlle and Swindlehurst who returned to the side in place of Skivington and Wilson. Steve Buckley played his 200th senior game for Derby, becoming the 28th post-war player to reach that landmark.

Taylor, watching from the dugout alongside Gordon Guthrie and Richie Norman, was left with no illusions about the scale of the task ahead as the Rams went down 3-1, Swindlehurst getting the consolation goal in a dire game with neither side showing any kind of rhythm or cohesion, but the real story was Derby's ill-discipline – both Steve Powell and John McAlle were sent off and they finished the game with nine men. It was the first time in his career that Powell had received a red card, and Derby had now lost five games in a row.

Alan Ashman's tenure as Derby's assistant manager appeared to be hanging by a thread as it became public that Peter Taylor had identified former Rams star Roy McFarland as the man he wanted as his number two. McFarland had become the first Derby player to exercise his right to leave the club under newly-established freedom of contract laws in the summer of 1981 and had joined Bradford City as player-manager, leading them to an immediate promotion from the fourth division in 1981-82, but had got into a contractual dispute over bonus payments at Valley Parade and was keen to link up with Taylor at the Baseball Ground. Bradford City, however, were in no mood to facilitate McFarland's return to Derby and demanded a fee of £200,000 to release him, chairman Bob Martin describing his manager as "certain to be England's manager one day" – Martin was especially unhappy that Derby's approach had come on the eve of his club's Milk Cup tie against Manchester United. From Derby's perspective - "I have nothing to say on the subject", said Taylor "I need a number 2 and a number 3. If circumstances force me to look elsewhere then I have other ideas and irons in the fire. One always must have contingency plans.

As well as McFarland, Derby were also interested to hire his assistant at Bradford, Mike Jones. Jones, born in Sunderland, had joined Derby as a junior in November 1964 when aged 17 and had played in the Rams' reserves before moving to Notts County in July 1969 – after 101 league appearances for County, Jones had moved to Peterborough and then via a player-manager spell at Kettering Town, back to Notts County as player-coach. His first job as a league manager was at Mansfield Town in 1979, before he linked up with McFarland at Valley Parade, McFarland describing him as "one of the best coaches in the game".

Peter Taylor's first home game in charge was against Bolton Wanderers at the Baseball Ground on Saturday 13th March, a game which attracted a crowd of 10,999 (including just 121 visiting supporters). It was a bottom of the table clash – Bolton, for whom former Derby player John McGovern was player-manager, were one place above rock-bottom Derby in the Second Division table, and the Rams missed three straightforward chances to secure three points, the game ending 0-0. Steve Powell, the Rams' captain, had to leave the field injured early in the game.

The draw against Bolton ensured that Derby had recorded their second worst first third of a season ever, only 1962-63 had been worse, and that season they had won 1 and drawn 5 of their first 14 matches, compared to won 1 drawn 6 so far in 1982-83. The attendance of near 11,000, almost all of whom were home supporters, suggested that the appointment of Taylor had drawn almost 3,000 extra on the gate.

Taylor, in his post-match interviews, did not hold back. He told the Derby Evening Telegraph - "I knew we were bad, but frankly on the evidence I've seen it's worse than I thought...one player was an absolute disgrace...two or three who gave their lot aren't good enough and I've told them so...no manager discusses his players by name in public, except in exceptional circumstances...I make no apologies (to the fans), if they stick around, they will see the improvements over the next few weeks, I can't say when, I haven't a magic wand, but we'll be giving them their money's worth before too long".

There was more straight-talking in the Ram Newspaper dated 20th November – "I have no time at all for reflections on past glories...we're in too much trouble out there on the pitch for that...I'd like to say that we are bottom of the league because confidence has been drained, but I can't because in my opinion the confidence factor has played little part. Nor have injuries – every club must face up to them and I have no room at all for that sort of excuse...we are where we are because the team is not good enough. Because of a series of mediocre performances...the skill factor is mainly missing but even more important, not enough people are prepared to get hurt for Derby County...we are mainly missing almost all the ingredients you must have in a successful side"

There was considerable speculation about the identity of "one absolute disgrace and two or three who aren't good enough". None of them were Dave Swindlehurst – the big striker who had been subject to significant interest from European Champions Aston Villa, said to be preparing a £100,000 cash plus a player bid, which would have certainly tested the resolve of the previous regime – but not Mike Watterson and Peter Taylor, who saw Swindlehurst as one of the club's very few prime assets and had suspended all discussions with regards to a transfer and it appeared that the player, who appeared on his way out of the Baseball Ground just weeks earlier, would be sticking around for the time being at least.

With regards to Watterson, some disquiet surfaced at a Shareholders Association meeting on Monday 15th November. Both he and fellow director John Kirkland had assured supporters and shareholders that money would be made available to Peter Taylor to strengthen the team, and that the club's bankers were assuaged. Watterson said "I have not put any money in so far because it has not yet been necessary. My board is committed to helping the manager financially" Watterson also claimed that his position would be easier if he had full control of the club – resignations from the board meant that he did not have 51-52% of the shares as had been set out in the original deal, but work was in progress to purchase former director Mick McGarry's shares. Stuart Webb added "the Chairman has guaranteed the club at the bank and has given us stability. We need better cash flow from attendances, sponsorships and promotions to increase the cash available to Peter Taylor for players".

Derby County Football Club's accounts for the year ended 31st May 1981 were also discussed at the shareholder's meeting. There were some surprising revelations, especially that travelling and matchday expenses had reduced from £143,415 in the previous period, to £79,441 in the current figures. John Kirkland explained the savings as "all part of the club's drastic cost-cutting exercise, the team stays overnight before games only at Newcastle and Carlisle, for example". Also falling was the wage bill, down around £70,000 from the previous period to £535,000. Another interesting announcement at the meeting came from former director Eddie Strachan, who revealed that only four people outside the current board of directors had contributed more than £1,000 to the previous Spring's share issue – consequently, Strachan criticised the decision to put out collection boxes at the

Baseball Ground before the previous home match as "most of the (share issue) support came from fans on the terraces...so why go to the same people with an idea like this"

Kirkland defended accusations that the accounts reflected poor management by the board – "costs were pruned and directors themselves put in their own cash to sustain the club", and refuted suggestions that the Directors responsible had resigned rather than face the situation – "had it not been for the men who resigned from the board and who left both their guarantees at the bank and their cash in the club, we would not have been around to allow the takeover to have taken place", going on to name the former directors who had "kept faith" – Bill Stevenson, Brian Holmes, Richard Moore, Bob Mullholland, Eddie Strachan and Rex Stone.

Referring to the appointment to the board, without financial guarantees, of Stuart Webb, former director Eddie Strachan (who had personally invested £20,000 into the club) said "if directors now join the board without guarantees it is my view that if it is good for Derby County, and I think Mr Webb is, then so be it". Webb was also welcomed back to the club by Barrister and Radio Derby commentator Graham Richards said "we're delighted to have him. He would never have gone but for an abortive and useless exercise with the police. He was the best secretary in the Football League without doubt and I hope his career as a Derby County director is a long one". Asked how much Derby needed as a financial injection to operate in the short term, Webb replied "in my view, about a quarter of a million pounds".

John Kirkland also explained that Derby County had appealed against their annual rates bill of £67,000 to the Inland Revenue, with the hearing expected before Christmas – he hoped that the club would be able to claw back some of the money before March 1983, citing Leicester City (a club with similar facilities yet a rates bill of just £27,000) as an example.

Derby County's trading loss for the year ended 31.05.81 was £428,159. After donations from Derby County Promotions and transfer transactions (mainly the sale of Alan Biley), the deficit was cut to £123,927. As a result of the cut-backs, economies and cash injections the bank interest on the club's overdraft was cut by more than £20,000 – however it still cost £127,789 to service the overdraft during the year, reflecting the very high interest rates of the time.

An interesting Sunday Times survey in October 1982 regarding the current financial situation in football reminded readers that despite the deep recession and general depression, when thousands of businesses had gone bankrupt, it remained a fact that only Accrington Stanley had gone bust in the Football League during the previous 20 years. With regards to attendances at football, whilst they were down by almost 50% compared to their peak of 41 million fans in 1948, the cinema had lost 90% of its audience over the same period. Hunter Davies, the author, concluded that the game was losing its traditional working-class support – down 40% in the last ten years, mainly because of poor facilities for terrace fans, but better facilities elsewhere in grounds was maintaining middle class interest. "working class wives", concluded Davies, "encourage their husbands to stay at home and watch football on the telly, and who can blame them when you look at the primitive conditions on the terraces"

The new manager's first foray into the transfer market was to bring 35-year-old Archie Gemmill back to the Baseball Ground, on an 18- month contract. Gemmill, who had been captain when Derby last won the championship of the football league in 1974-75, and had also skippered Scotland's 1978 World Cup squad, was brought in as "a tried and trusted player of class and an inspiring leader". Gemmill was immediately appointed captain, replacing Steve Powell. Most recently, in the summer of 1982, he had been playing in the North American Soccer League with Jacksonville Teamen and for Wigan Athletic at the start of the 1982-83 English season - on a non-contract basis, meaning there was no transfer fee involved when he signed for Derby. Gemmill had continued to live in Derby after leaving the Rams for the first time, just after Tommy Docherty arrived as manager.

Taylor was soon back into the market, securing Wolverhampton Wanderers' former England centre forward John Richards on a month's loan. Of his new signings, Taylor said "we've got to instil some grit, guts and passion here, that's why I have re-signed Archie Gemmill and obtained John Richards on loan...I will make no panic signings...if this job is to be done right it will be done in my time, its my reputation that's on the line, and the future of this great club"

John Richards was not Taylor's first choice as a loan striker. He had approached Brian Clough with a view to take Nottingham Forest's out-of-favour centre forward Justin Fashanu, and Clough had agreed but the player himself refused to move to the Baseball Ground. When Richards heard about this, he went straight to his manager at Wolves, Graham Hawkins, and engineering his own move to Derby. The proposed signing of Fashanu would have represented a first for Derby County – the deal would have been made possible by individual sponsorship from outside the club, as had been the case with Newcastle United's signing of Kevin Keegan.

A second successive home game, on 20th November against 6th in the table Oldham Athletic, drew a very good attendance of 11,775 for the second debut of **Archie Gemmill**. Loan signing **John Richards** also started, and Brian Attley came back into the side – the players left out were Andy Hill and Kevin Wilson, and Steve Powell missed the game through injury. Oldham, managed by Joe Royle, featured in their side 18-year-old future Scottish International goalkeeper Andy Goram, and soon-to-be Derby defender Paul Futcher.

Derby performed much better than they had so far in the season, with Gemmill dictating the tempo of the game from the centre of midfield. Oldham were at times hanging on desperately as the Rams pressed forward towards the end of the game, which was drawn 2-2. The visitors went ahead but the Rams hit back with two quick goals at the Normanton

End, first from Swindlehurst and then a well-controlled Dalziel volley from Richards's knock-down, and looked comfortable until a defensive error let in Oldham for an equaliser they had scarcely deserved, just 7 minutes from the end – the unfortunate George Foster putting the ball into his own net when attempting a goal-line clearance.

Archie Gemmill began his football career at St Mirren in 1964 at the age of 17 and forged a good reputation despite suffering a series of injuries including a broken ankle in 1966 before being spotted by Preston North End, who paid £13,000 for his services in 1967. Peter Taylor, Derby's assistant manager, was a big admirer of Gemmill and convinced Brian Clough that the 5'5" Scottish midfielder was the man to drive the Rams on to major honours.

Famously, Clough drove to Gemmill's house and refused to leave until the player had agreed to join Derby – even sleeping overnight in the spare room – and a deal was eventually done over breakfast the following morning, with Derby paying a fee of £60,000. It turned out to be a masterstroke despite supporters' initial reservations at Gemmill being brought in to the side to replace the popular Willie Carlin. He played in both of Derby's league championship winning sides, in 1971-72 and 1974-75, and was captain for the latter, deputising for the injured Roy McFarland.

Gemmill left Derby when Tommy Docherty became manager in 1977, the two had not got on, a dispute dating back to Docherty's time as Scotland team boss. He re-joined Clough and Taylor at Nottingham Forest, becoming the third former Derby title-winning player to make that move (after John O'Hare and John McGovern) and played an important part in Forest's rise to become a dominant force in English football, although he was dropped for the 1979 European Cup Final and became unsettled after that.

After Forest Gemmill joined Birmingham City, playing 97 games there before moving into the NASL with Jacksonville Tea Men. In September 1982 he joined up with former Forest team mate Larry Lloyd at Wigan Athletic and made 11 appearances before Peter Taylor made him his first signing at Derby County, bringing him back to the Baseball Ground in a player-coach capacity in November 1982. Gemmill retired from football when his contract expired at the end of the 1983-84 season, he had done more than anyone else to try and keep the Rams in the Second Division, but towards the end of his spell had fallen out with Peter Taylor and briefly lost his place in the side.

With 43 caps and 8 goals for Scotland, Gemmill was a prominent international player in the 1970's, although his appearances tended to be sporadic and he made his debut as early as 1971, and his final appearance ten years later. He scored one of the iconic World Cup Finals goals, against Holland in the 1978 tournament.

After retiring as a player, he returned to Nottingham Forest to work as a coach under Brian Clough, and became a manager in his own right at Rotherham United in the mid-1990's. He also managed and coached in Scottish National age-group football and achieved some success when his Under-19 team finished runners-up in the 2006 UEFA European U-19 Championships.

John Richards was born in Warrington in 1950 and spent almost his entire career with Wolverhampton Wanderers, during which he won two League Cups and appeared in the 1972 UEFA Cup Final. He was capped once by England, in 1973, and played at Under-21, Under-23 and "B" level for the National side. Having started as a professional in 1969, he became Wolves' all-time leading goal scorer, with 194 – a record which was subsequently broken by Steve Bull.

At the age of 32 and no longer in the first team picture at Wolves, Richards heard that Derby County were desperate for players and promptly signed on loan, initially for a month, after Peter Taylor became manager in November 1982, becoming Taylor's second signing – and despite only playing ten games (scoring 2 goals), played an important role in Derby's revival and ultimate survival in the Second Division during 1982-83. Richards eventually left Wolves to move to the Island of Madeira, where he had a successful 2 years playing for CS Maritimo in the Portuguese league, scoring 23 goals in 44 matches. After retiring as a player, he went into local Government before being appointed a director at Molineux in the mid-late 1990's.

After a drawn-out and heavily-publicised saga, Derby County finally appointed Roy McFarland with the job title Team Manager, and Mick Jones as McFarland's assistant (Taylor had never been one to get involved on the training field, this would be the domain of the new men) - they had been Taylor's choice since his appointment and the club had gone to considerable effort and expense to get the duo away from Bradford City, to whom they were under contract. McFarland and Jones had put together a good record at Valley Parade, with promotion from the Fourth Division in their first season (1981-82) and a good start to the current season – 7th place in Division Three. They had been in charge for 62 matches at Bradford, winning 34 and losing only 12, so it was no wonder that Bradford's chairman Bob Martin did not want them to leave.

At the same time as McFarland and Jones were appointed, Ken Gutteridge was appointed as chief scout, with additional responsibility for the Rams "A" team (where he would be assisted by Jack Wilmot and Brian Newton). Gutteridge had been recommended to Derby by Brian Clough and Peter Taylor in 1979, before the appointment of Colin Addison as manager.

In the back-room reshuffle which saw McFarland, Jones and Gutteridge appointed, only physiotherapist Gordon Guthrie survived. Ron Webster left the club, after 22 years at the Baseball Ground as a player and the youth coach, as did former chief scout and assistant manager Alan Ashman (who had first worked for Derby in 1977), and reserve team manager Ritchie Norman, who had been with the club for 7 years after being appointed by Dave Mackay. There were also new faces in the boardroom, with Trevor East and Bill Hart joining Mike Watterson, John Kirkland, Stuart Webb and Fred Fern on the board.

The McFarland affair was far from over. Bradford City complained that their manager had been illegally poached, and the Football League Commission found in their favour and fined Derby £10,000 for alleged breaches of League regulations 59 and 80. Derby County appealed against the verdict, on the basis that they were neither happy with the verdict, nor the way it had been reached – citing the fact that relevant witnesses, including Peter Taylor, had not been called. There was considerable, and mostly negative, national media coverage of Derby's appointment of McFarland – the BBC, for example, describing the Rams as "pirates".

In late November 1982 the Mail on Sunday newspaper ran a story which described Derby's new chairman Mike Watterson as a "puppet and a front man" for Rotherham United's chairman Anton Johnson. Johnson, who under Football League rules was not allowed to be involved with two clubs, had been part of the original takeover discussions at Derby County, as had Alastair Ward, but, according to Watterson, had dropped out when the deal was done. By this time, Watterson had purchased £30,000 worth of shares in the club from former director Mick McGarry "but Anton has no stake in Derby County...and more money will be coming into the club". The chairman was said to be considering legal action against the newspaper and against a Lancashire radio station which had described him as "a pirate". Watterson also claimed to have been misquoted when he was accused of threatening to liquidate Derby County to clear his and the club's name from the charges brought about by the Football League Commission relating to Roy McFarland.

Following the negative media coverage, McFarland was jeered by a section of the home support as he followed his team onto the field when Derby visited Turf Moor to play Burnley on 27th November – to which the 1,000 plus visiting Rams supporters responded with chants and applause in support of their returning favourite. McFarland, Mick Jones and Gordon Guthrie took charge of the Rams team, with Peter Taylor absent watching a player (which turned out to be Halifax Town's Bobby Davison).

Paul Blades replaced the suspended John McAlle in the centre of defence, partnering George Foster. Loan signing John Richards scored Derby's goal in a battling 1-1 draw. Derby had to weather almost constant pressure in the first half on a muddy pitch – Burnley hit the woodwork twice and missed several good chances - and were fortunate to only be 1 goal behind by the time Steve Buckley's free kick 9 minutes from time was headed on by Swindlehurst, named "Buxted Turkeys Rams Player of the Month" for November, to Richards, who found space between two defenders to bury a header into the Burnley net and secure a vital point for the Rams – it was the third league draw in succession. Blades's performance drew praise from Roy McFarland, who knew a bit about the art of central defending – "he gave a cool, cultured and convincing display...there is no doubt he has rich potential, if handled correctly".

Blades, it was later announced, was to be signed by the Rams as a full-time professional when his apprenticeship ended on his 18th birthday, in January 1983.

The Rams were becoming draw specialists – the result at Turf Moor was their eighth draw in 16 matches and was the equal highest number of draws in the entire Football League. This though, was not good enough – Derby were two points adrift at the bottom of the Second Division. Since Peter Taylor had been appointed, the side was unbeaten in League games, all three having been drawn.

On Wednesday 1st December, Peter Taylor made his first cash signing when Derby agreed to pay £80,000 for the 23-year-old Halifax Town striker Bobby Davison. On the recommendation of Roy McFarland, Taylor had watched Davison once, the previous weekend, and decided immediately "this lad is an interesting player, full of youthful promise, exciting potential and a flair for scoring goals". Davison said, "I'm delighted to be here where there is a big club atmosphere, the move is right for me in every way". Roy McFarland was in no doubt about what Davison would bring to Derby – "the one thing above all is Bobby can stick goals away, this quality we saw in him last season (against Bradford City) when he was very impressive against us". At the time he signed for the Rams, Davison had scored nine goals for Halifax so far during the 1982-83 season – the Rams' leading scorer so far was Dave Swindlehurst with 7 (4 in the league), and the Second Division list was headed by Fulham's Gordon Davies and Leicester City's Gary Lineker (14 goals each), whilst the Football League's leading scorer was Third Division Reading's Kerry Dixon, with 17.

The board finally lost patience with the rowdier contingent congregating in C-Stand and the Osmaston Paddock stopped the sale of seats on a match-b-match basis, re-designating that section of the Main Stand for season ticket holders only from December 1982. "The board have decided they can no longer tolerate season ticket holders of long standing being alienated by the language and disorderly behaviour of the youngsters who have been crowding into the C-Stand since early this year", said Michael Dunford. The fact that C-Stand was not too far from the Director's Box no doubt also had a significant bearing on the decision. Dunford revealed that Derby County were still in arrears for policing bills from the previous season, and that the police were allowing the club to pay in instalments rather than demanding payment in full. "raucous behaviour, bad language and jostling by no more than a minority of a hundred or so youngsters" in this area was causing increased police costs.

On 4th December, the Rams finally won a league game when they beat Rotherham United 3-0 at the Baseball Ground. It was only the second league win of the season, and the first since they had beaten Chelsea 1-0 almost 3 months previously. An excellent attendance, more than 13,000, saw Derby finally put on a good performance, and the debut (as substitute) of **Bobby Davison**, the young striker signed earlier that week from Halifax Town. Rotherham, managed by Emlyn Hughes, stood half way up the Second Division, with 22 points compared to Derby's 11, presented an uncompromising, tough task - as well as Hughes himself, their side also contained Gerry Gow, who's wild tackle had resulted in Derby's Steve Emery suffering a broken leg the previous season. Roy McFarland, on his return to the Baseball Ground received a tremendous reception from the crowd when he took to the field with Derby's players before kick-off.

The Rams were excellent, and dominated the game from start to finish, with Archie Gemmill and Mike Brolly controlling the midfield and a positive approach which saw Derby looking for forward passes whenever the opportunity arose – unlike earlier in the season. Dave Swindlehurst, clearly benefitting from having the experienced John Richards alongside him, scored twice, either side of Ian Dalziel's excellent left-foot strike from the edge of the penalty area at the Normanton End. The victory lifted Derby off the bottom of the Second Division table, with 14 points.

Bobby Davison was born in South Shields in 1959 and began his football career as a striker at Huddersfield Town in 1980, making only two first team appearances before transferring to Halifax Town in August 1981. After a few weeks at Leeds Road, he was spotted by First Division Arsenal, who took him on trial for a month and wanted to extend the arrangement, but Huddersfield refused – a decision which left Davison unhappy. He was a success at fourth division level with Halifax, scoring 29 goals in 63 appearances, and had played against Derby County in the Milk Cup early in the 1982-83 season, scoring three times over the two legs, before Peter Taylor stepped in with an £80,000 bid in late November 1982, making Davison his first (and best) cash signing for Derby – the recommendation had come from assistant manager Roy McFarland, who had tried to sign Davison for his previous club Bradford City, before he had linked up with Taylor.

Davison became a big hit at the Baseball Ground and was loved by supporters for his effort, speed, enthusiasm and goals, especially thriving after Arthur Cox's arrival as manager – he scored 98 in all competitions for the Rams between November 1982 and November 1987, in 239 appearances (including 3 as substitute). He scored 20 or more goals in each season between 1984-85 and 1986-87, his best return being 26 in 1984-85 – Derby's best since Ray Straw had scored 37 in 1956-57 – and was the main spearhead as the Rams powered to two successive promotions.

Derby rejected bids for Davison from First Division clubs Watford and Oxford United during the 1986-87 Second Division championship season, and he stayed to score 22 as the Rams returned to the top flight after 7 years away. Eventually, much to the disappointment of Rams supporters, he was sold to Leeds United in November 1987 for £350,000 and he went on to score 35 in 110 games for the Elland Road club, achieving cult-hero status as he helped them win promotion to the First Division in 1989-90 under the management of Howard Wilkinson. Derby had not forced Davison to leave, but the player expressed a desire to join Leeds should the opportunity arise, and manager Arthur Cox was not a man to hang on to players who were not 100% focussed on the task in hand. Before joining Leeds, Davison turned down the chance to sign for a German side.

After losing his first team place at Leeds United to Lee Chapman, Davison was allowed to leave on loan and returned to Derby County, where he scored 8 goals in just 10 games in a successful attacking partnership with Ian Ormandroyd. There was talk of a permanent return for the then 32-year-old, but by that time Derby had money to spend and opted for other targets – Davison eventually moved on to Leicester City, then Sheffield United and Rotherham United where he finished his full-time playing career in 1995.

In February 1998 Davison was appointed player-manager at non-league Guiseley, where he stayed 2 years. He was later assistant to former Rams defender Colin Todd at Bradford City, then joined Sheffield United as a coach. The Blades announced in February 2008 that they had taken ownership of Hungarian side Ferencvaros, and appointed Davison as chief coach – a role he retained until October 2009 when he was replaced by another former Derby defender, Craig Short. He has recently worked in a coaching capacity with Leeds, Crystal Palace and England National age-group squads.

Bobby Davison was perhaps Derby's most popular player in the 1980's and fully deserves his revered status amongst Rams supporters of the era. He is often cited as Peter Taylor's legacy to the football club, but it should be remembered that Roy McFarland also played a significant role in bringing him to the Baseball Ground.

Things were beginning to look brighter at Derby County, and when the FA Cup 3rd round draw paired them with local rivals Nottingham Forest, excitement around the City and the club was tangible – it would be the first meeting between the Rams and Forest since 1980, and the first at the Baseball Ground since Derby's shock 4-1 victory in the autumn of 1979. The Rams had sold another 250 season tickets since Peter Taylor's arrival, and secretary Michael Dunford suggested that the number could reach four figures by Christmas following the recent improved performances and results on the field and the Cup draw.

Ticket prices for the Forest game were to be increased , causing a few grumbles in the letter pages of the local press. At the time, the capacity of the Baseball Ground was restricted to 31,500, and the visitors had requested almost 10,000 for their own supporters. A sell-out crowd would generate gate receipts in the region of £80,000, which would eclipse the previous club record of £65,000 taken for the European Cup Semi Final second leg against Juventus in 1973 – after expenses and the shares claimed by Forest and the FA Cup pool, it would mean a £25,000 windfall for Derby County.

The game against Forest was to be admission by ticket only with prices increased from normal matchday levels to £3.50 from £2.70 for the most expensive seats, and to £2 from £1.80 for the terraces. Tickets went on sale to Derby supporters on Sunday 19th December, with priority vouchers being issued to fans attending the home match against Crystal Palace the day before. Peter Taylor, in public at least, was keen to play-down the "Clough v Taylor" sentiment and said, "any game between these local rivals is a big game, regardless of the managers involved".

Increased interest and optimism extended to the corporate areas of the Baseball Ground, with all Executive Boxes sold for the two upcoming home games – a far cry from a few weeks previously, when the club were struggling to give them away. Michael Dunford – "ironically, we could have sold three dozen this week for the Forest cup match...so priority will be given to applicants who are prepared to take over a box for the whole season, we must protect our long-term interests". Dunford also appreciated the gesture made by match day stewards, gate staff and programme sellers who all took a voluntary wage cut, as cash liquidity remained an acute issue at the club – even though the amounts involved were little more than a drop in the ocean compared to the mess of Derby County's finances.

The convincing win over Rotherham United on 4th December, following three battling draws, appeared to herald the start of better times. Unfortunately, in the short-term at least, that was not to be, and the Rams failed to win any of their next 5 matches – losing 3 and drawing 2 and did not win another game until the visit to the Baseball Ground of Queen's Park Rangers on 3rd January – 5 days before the scheduled FA Cup 3rd round tie against Nottingham Forest.

Derby's Youth Team also landed a plum cup draw after beating non-league Willenhall Town away in the second round of the FA Youth Cup – they were drawn to play Manchester United in round three, with the game scheduled to be played at Old Trafford on Monday 20th December.

On 11th December the Rams met Fulham, one of the best sides in the Second Division that season, at Craven Cottage and they were just seconds from extending their unbeaten run under Peter Taylor to five matches, with Fulham scoring four minutes into injury time at the end of the game to go 2-1 ahead. The home side had led 1-0 before Steve Buckley's deflected 66th minute free kick wrong-footed goalkeeper Peyton, then Derby should have gone ahead when Brian Attley was unable to steer a rebound from John Richards's fierce shot wide of an open goal – before 18-year old Cliff Carr won the game for Fulham, heading home a cross to deny the Rams a deserved point and leave them second-bottom in Division Two, by virtue of goal difference.

Taylor and McFarland had decided to change the usual pre-match arrangements and had taken the team to London by train rather than coach (as Taylor and Brian Clough had often done with Nottingham Forest) – the first time a Derby side had used this method for several years.

Returning to the Baseball Ground on 18th December, another very impressive attendance, this time a season's high 13,207, saw a 1-1 draw with Alan Mullery's Crystal Palace on an icy surface which inhibited movement and prevented much skilful football from being played. The Rams went ahead through the impressive, hard-working John Richards, who finished well after Dave Swindlehurst had laid on the opportunity – and then appeared to have been denied a clear penalty with the score at 1-0, when Richards was pushed in the back. Palace, however, fought back strongly and perhaps deserved more than just their equalising goal. Other results went against the Rams and they dropped back to the bottom of the Second Division table, with 15 points.

Both Derby and Crystal Palace had wanted the match moved forward to Friday 17th, with an evening kick off. This was because any game played on the final Saturday before Christmas was traditionally one of the poorest-attended fixtures – the Football League turned down the request, made a fortnight previously, and given the excellent gate which the game attracted, both clubs were grateful that they did – only 160 travelled to support the visitors, meaning that Derby's home support was back above the 13,000 level, albeit undoubtedly boosted for this game by the incentive of vouchers for the forthcoming Nottingham Forest FA Cup tie, which were distributed on the gate. The Rams had been caught unawares by the large crowd and had not provided enough operational turnstiles, meaning many supporters missed the kick-off, having waited in long queues to enter the ground – Michael Dunford later claimed that five of the appointed gate staff had called in sick on the morning of the match, causing the problem.

Peter Taylor spoke at the annual shareholders meeting in the week before Christmas 1982. He described Derby as "a magic football city" and said that Derby County would be playing First Division football again in two years, "if three conditions were met" – firstly, attendances back to 20,000 level – "our pre-Christmas Saturday crowd of over 13,000 was proportionally the best in the Country. No other place could do that for a club at the bottom of the Second Division". He also requested cash for new players – "with half a million to spend we could end up in the top six this season, even now...but I have no cribs, the chairman and Stuart Webb spelled out the grim financial position to me before I agreed to come...I am happy to go for players in the £50,000 to £100,000 range and within our wage bracket". His third condition was "relegation must be avoided this season...we were in a state when I came...even if we finish fourth from bottom, we will have achieved the first stage and I will be delighted".

Taylor emphasised that his search for new players was ongoing and more moves were in the pipeline, to follow the permanent signings of Archie Gemmill and Bobby Davison, and the loan signing of John Richards. "I know what I can spend, and I know what I want. Last week I drove 1,000 miles in search of players and next week I'm prepared to up that to 2,000 if necessary. It's now a buyers-market and players' demands are more realistic in the current financial climate, now is the big chance to get the players needed at prices and wages the Rams can afford". Regarding the current playing staff, Taylor added – "we are delighted with the current players and their response", and in a thinly-veiled dig at the previous manager – "whether some are good enough or not for what we need, the fact remains I cannot understand how they were allowed to get into the mess they did, they deserved better than that"

Derby had been thwarted in their bid to sign Chesterfield midfielder Danny Wilson, when their £85,000 plus a player offer had been turned-down – but there was still some hope that the deal could be revived, with the Spireites appearing ready to negotiate. Aston Villa, meanwhile, remained interested in Dave Swindlehurst, but the club's respective valuations were still far apart. Swindlehurst's contract at Derby was due to end in May 1983 and he would then become a free agent – "I believe Dave would then be looking for pastures new" said Peter Taylor "so even though I don't want to lose him, the position seems to be that it would be better for both club and player if we parted before then"

Yakka Banovic had been placed on the transfer list – "he came to see me and say he was not happy with his position in the reserves. Now I had only been here four weeks and Steve Cherry was doing quite well in the first team, so I considered his timing to be diabolical, he was putting me under pressure I didn't need, so I put him on the list" said Taylor. Gary Mills, who was under contract with Derby until March, at which time he was due to return to his NASL club Seattle Sounders, was not a favourite of Peter Taylor – "I'm not happy about (the Mills situation) but that was what I inherited. Meanwhile, he is as available as the next man to get into the side if his form warrants it…there are one or two contracts that I would like to end but I can't just kick them out of the door. Contracts are contracts".

John Richards, described by Taylor as "a wonderful influence off the park as well as on it" was unlikely to be at Derby for the long term – "I'd give my right arm to keep him, but he could probably command a bigger salary elsewhere, and I'll miss this great, great character…this is where Bobby Davison comes in, and I'll be looking for a younger striker too…Bobby is one for the future, a player in whom I have great faith".

Taylor had great faith in Ken Gutteridge, whom he had appointed as youth coach. He had taken Gutteridge with him when manager of Brighton and described the new man as "a first-class organiser who knows how to find and pursue top talent…we must find home-grown players and we will, we already have the best junior set-up in the Second Division". With regards to the young talent already on the books, Taylor said "you only have to look at Paul Blades, not 18 until January and doing well in the first team. We are delighted with him, we could be on to a real winner here, there's a good deal of hope among our youth".

Regarding the forthcoming FA Cup tie with Nottingham Forest, Peter Taylor said "I'm looking forward to it mainly for the cash we'll earn from it, it will be a great occasion and I'll enjoy it when it comes, but our main concern is to get up that league table, that's our bread and butter"

Chairman Mike Watterson told the meeting that the club was negotiating ex-gratia payments with Ron Webster, Richie Norman and Alan Ashman, who had all been dismissed by Peter Taylor – "I do it my way, and with my own men around me…and neither Ron nor the others have a part to play in that". The matter of John Newman's dismissal was currently in the hands of solicitors, but "we will treat the payment for Ron Webster in a generous manner, given his 24 years association with the club". Another former manager, Colin Addison, had been paid £25,000 during the year ended 31st May 1982, which included an ex gratia payment for the ending of his contract.

Watterson revealed that when he had arrived at Derby the club had creditors to the extent of £220,000 and there was an £840,000 overdraft at the bank. The creditors were now being met and the overdraft had been converted to a loan which had been opened at a level of £793,000, to be repaid over a ten-year period at the sum of £11,000 per month. Already since the loan had been opened, it had been reduced to £785,000 and the club's current account was now in credit. Derby County, he said, "was now not only solvent but in good working shape". Of the new directors, Watterson said "Stuart Webb has been invaluable to me, the amount of time he has given has been incredible…Trevor East has done a considerable amount of work with us in the last few weeks…Bill Hart is a man of integrity who I have known for some years and who has seen it no problem to make substantial loans to Derby County". He was also sorry that circumstances had caused both Bill Stevenson and Brian Holmes to resign during the takeover. Generally, interest in the club was on the up and season ticket sales were now well over 6,000 – with 150 having been sold before the home game against Crystal Palace, followed by nearly 200 more during the following week.

Trevor East, an ex-Bemrose schoolboy and lifelong Rams supporter had started his career as a television reporter for ATV Sports in the 1960's and made his breakthrough when recruited as a presenter for the ITV Saturday morning cult-TV classic Tiswas between 1974 and 1975. He had made the acquaintance of Mike Watterson when made responsible for ITV's snooker output and later tried and failed to take the coverage of snooker's World Championships from the BBC to ITV. After being poached by Sky Sports in the early 1990's, East became an integral part of Sky's dominance live football in the UK. He later became a director of Setanta Sports and has been ranked in the top 30 of most influential people in UK media.

It was also revealed that Steve Buckley had suffered a broken toe in the December 4th win over Rotherham United, but had played on and subsequently played in two more games before an X-Ray picked up the injury – Buckley now had his right leg in plaster and would be out of action for a month – "this has been a dreadful season for me injury-wise, my worst ever. Now I'm going to miss the Forest match".

With Christmas Day and Boxing Day falling on Saturday 25th and Sunday 26th December 1982 (in those days football was generally not played on Sundays), the Rams did not play again until Monday 27th, when they faced a daunting trip to St James' Park to face resurgent Newcastle United, a side containing Terry McDermott, Chris Waddle and Kevin Keegan, in front of a crowd of more than 30,000, which included around 300 from Derby. For the Rams, Tyneside-born Bobby Davison made his first start for the club, partnering John Richards and Dave Swindlehurst in three-pronged attack – Mike Brolly dropping to the bench. Somewhat surprisingly, Gary Mills, about whom Peter Taylor had been so disparaging at the recent shareholders meeting, returned to the side.

The Rams battled bravely, especially after Ian Dalziel had been sent off for protesting a dubious penalty decision given against George Foster, who had been adjudged to have brought down Keegan – Dalziel was unfortunate to be the player sent off, as he had hardly been involved in the heated behaviour following the decision. Steve Cherry saved Keegan's penalty and Derby held the scoreline at 0-0 until Howard Gayle, on loan from Liverpool, scored the only goal of the game on 65 minutes. The result left the Rams five points adrift of Bolton Wanderers in the "safe" 19th place in Division Two.

After the game Roy McFarland was angry, but not at Dalziel nor the referee – "George Foster was directly responsible. He should not have responded as he did when the referee gave a penalty…it created a hostile atmosphere. In the end the referee responded by making young Ian suffer when he didn't deserve to be sent off". Foster was later fined by the club.

Derby's travelling supporters had a miserable day – first their RoadRider coaches were held up and they were left standing around in biting wind and pouring rain outside St James' Park after the end of the match, then they arrived, pre-booked, at a Service Station on the A1 to find it locked up and in complete darkness.

The Rams' Youth team played their FA Youth Cup tie at Old Trafford in front of a crowd of 3,382 on 20th December – battling to a deserved 2-2 draw against a side containing Northern Ireland international striker Norman Whiteside. Andy Garner, the 18-year-old forward, put Derby ahead on 6 minutes, a lead which they held until the 57th minute when United equalised, the home side then taking the lead through a Ride own-goal and looked set to win the game until Garner seized on a poor back pass and earned Derby a replay. Derby's Youth team: Palmer, McCormick, Harbey, Blades, Ride, J Collins, D Collins, Bancroft, Ackroyd, Garner, Clifford and substitute Roberts. The replay, originally scheduled for 23rd December, was postponed due to bad weather and eventually rescheduled for January 10th, 1983. Following the game, the Rams' Liverpudlian youngsters, twins Jim and David Collins, were signed as full-time professionals.

Unlike the youth team, Derby's reserves were suffering frustration at the lack of fixtures – having managed to play just twice since November 9th, thanks to a combination of a smaller league (the Central League having been split into 2 divisions) and bad weather. On November 30th they had lost 2-0 at home to Middlesbrough, and on 14th December they thrashed Preston North End 8-1 at the Baseball Ground, leaving them 9th in their 16-team league, with 8 points from 11 games (2 points for a win).

Derby's final match of 1982 took place on Wednesday 29th December when they took on Shrewsbury Town at the Baseball Ground. Once again, the attendance topped 13,000 (and once again the gate operators failed to cope with demand, causing the kick off to be delayed by five minutes whilst latecomers were admitted) and, as at St James' Park, the Rams fielded an attacking side with Swindlehurst, Richards and Davison all starting, Derby's team in full: Cherry; Attley, Dalziel, McAlle, Foster, Gemmill, Mills, Brolly, Davison, Swindlehurst, Richards and substitute Barton. Shrewsbury featured future Rams players Steve Cross and Ross McLaren, plus former reserve Colin Griffin.

The game was notable for Bobby Davison's first goals for the Rams, he scored both of Derby's 2 in a 3-2 defeat, but once again the unconvincing partnership in central defence of George Foster and John McAlle cost the Rams dearly as defensive errors allowed Shrewsbury a 2-goal lead after just 17 minutes. The Rams fought back and were unfortunate to still be 2-0 down at half time – with two Swindlehurst headers and a Gemmill shot all cleared off the line, but after the break the visitors went 3-0 ahead with a goal which looked like it should have been ruled out for offside – a long ball down Shrewsbury's right found the visiting player standing a clear 3 yards goal-side of Derby's defenders, who stood waiting for a linesman's flag which never came. Manager Graham Turner ran jubilantly onto the Baseball Ground pitch in celebration, which only added to the hostile atmosphere in the crowd.

The Rams made a tactical switch with Gary Mills moving into the left-wing position and, sparked by that, it became the Davison show, as he struck two goals in five minutes to announce himself to the Baseball Ground crowd – first a header from Gary Mills's cross, then a spectacular 25-yard lob into the Normanton End goal. Derby pressed for an equaliser with excellent vocal backing from supporters, but it was not to be. Also, in attendance was Nottingham Forest manager Brian Clough, taking a look at his side's FA Cup opponents.

Peter Taylor was unhappy with both the result and the performance, saying "there are some players here who are hardly up to Southern League standard, and I have told them so. Some simply freeze under pressure although that does not happen come Fridays when they are grabbing big pay packets". Taylor did repeat his assertion that Derby, bottom of the table, would not go down – "there is plenty of time yet for us to get this right and beat the drop, that is the priority this season…panic and despair are useless…I want some results to keep our support coming and to earn us the cash to buy as I want and need. The players here are giving their lot, but effort is not enough…there could be several coming in, or none, but we'll stay up…we're beginning to see who gels with whom and who doesn't"

Before the Shrewsbury match, 2,000 terrace tickets were put on sale for the FA Cup tie against Nottingham Forest – these would be the final tickets sold for the match, all seat tickets had already been sold. Ian Dalziel, Derby's young midfield player, received a boost with news that his suspension for being sent off at Newcastle would not begin for 14 days, meaning he would be eligible for the Cup tie. Considering that the Baseball Ground infrastructure had struggled to cope with recent crowds of 13,000, there was some anxiety about how the expected 30,000 plus would be handled – it was announced that gates would open at 1pm for the big game, and spectators were urged to arrive early to avoid queues.

Supporters were also reminded that policing costs were a major problem for Derby County (and most football clubs at that time) – for example, when Crystal Palace brought 160 supporters with them, in a crowd of 13,207 on December 18th, it had cost the club £2,000 to pay for policing. With more than 30,000 tickets sold for the FA Cup tie, the Rams were facing a huge cost to provide security and safety and requested that supporters be on their best behaviour and refrain from baiting the 10,000 expected from Nottingham.

Hopes were high that Chesterfield's Danny Wilson would soon be a Derby player, with the two clubs having returned to the negotiating table and hoping to revive a proposed player-plus-cash deal.

Chapter 1.5 - 1983

On New Year's Day 1983 Derby travelled to Boundary Park to play Oldham Athletic. With Dalziel missing, John Barton came back into the side at full back, Gemmill, Mills and Brolly again forming a midfield three. Gemmill, with a penalty and Dave Swindlehurst scored the Rams' goals in a 2-2 draw – the Rams being very good value for their point and perhaps deserving all three, in an attacking and entertaining match, backed by tremendous following of around 2,000 from Derby.

Swindlehurst had put the Rams ahead, heading home John Barton's right-wing cross, and John Richards should have made it 2-0 just before half time when clean through on goal. Unfortunately, defensive errors allowed Oldham to score twice within seven second half minutes, but Derby, playing with verve and determination, fought back and deservedly levelled on 83 minutes when Bobby Davison was brought down and Gemmill converted the spot kick.

Before the big FA Cup tie, Derby had a vital Second Division match to play against Queen's Park Rangers at the Baseball Ground, on Bank Holiday Monday 3rd January. Support was growing for Peter Taylor's improving side, and this time more than 14,000 attended, including Kirk Stevens, the Canadian snooker player who was managed by Rams chairman Mike Watterson, and were rewarded with the Rams' 3rd League win of the season, as goals from Gary Mills and Dave Swindlehurst secured a 2-0 win against their high-flying visitors, in what was comfortably the Rams best display of the season so far.

Once again Archie Gemmill, by far the best player on the pitch and performing as well as he ever had for Derby, controlled both the pace and the flow of the game. Mills, wearing the number 11 shirt and putting in a display of First Division quality, opened the scoring with a 25-yard drive into the Normanton goal, and QPR had their moments as Steve Cherry made a couple of excellent saves before Swindlehurst settled matters in the second half, finding space to get in front of defender Bob Hazell to head home the Rams second. Encouragingly, Derby's back four had begun to look a more cohesive unit, with George Foster and John McAlle both playing well.

Things were looking up – the four points taken from the last two games lifted the Rams off the bottom of the Second Division, with 19 points from 23 matches. Since Taylor had come in, they had played 10, won 2, drawn 5 and lost 3 and attendances had risen from around 8,000 to a high point of 14,007 for the visit of QPR.

There was also excellent news for Derby's terrace supporters with the news that the Family Seating Area on the former Ossie End terrace was to be removed, and the area restored to a terrace in time for the home game against Leeds United, scheduled for 22nd January. Season ticket holders for the Family Seating were offered replacement seats in the C-Stand or Osmaston Paddock. The board's decision, said to be because demand for terrace space was increasing rapidly since Peter Taylor's arrival, was "not an admission that the original decision (to put the seating in) was wrong". It is reasonable to conclude that recent issues with fan behaviour in the C-Stand also played its part.

On the morning of the Cup Tie, BBC Radio Derby ramped-up the excitement by broadcasting a documentary entitled "The day Derby won the cup", featuring a series of interviews by local freelance writer Anton Rippon, in which he engaged six of the surviving seven of the Rams' 1946 FA Cup winning team – Peter Doherty, Raich Carter, Jack Howe, Jack Stamps, Reg Harrison and Jim Bullions (the other survivor, Dally Duncan, lived on the South Coast so was unavailable). Sadly, Vic Woodley, Jack Nicholas, Leon Leuty and Chick Musson had all passed away. Rippon's narration, and use of original BBC radio commentary, provided an evocative and stirring start to the current Rams big day.

Jackie Stamps, the Rams' burly centre forward from the Cup winning side, remained a regular fixture at the Baseball Ground despite being totally blind. Stamps was able to follow the match by the sound of the ball and crowd reactions, and the assistance of his friend Clive Reid, who sat next to him in the Paddock. Stamps was appointed an Honorary Vice President of Derby County at the start of 1983.

Most pundits were convinced that Forest, fourth in the First Division, would have too much for Derby, 21st in the Second Division. Former Rams and Forest forward Frank Wignall – "Forest should win by two or three clear goals", Charlie George – "I'd give my eye teeth to play in this match...my heart tells me Derby could win, I'd be over the moon with that...but my head tells me it must be Forest", John McGovern – "Forest's class will see them through in the end, but they may need a replay", John Middleton – "I know from experience, Forest don't like playing here...Forest to win but it won't be easy", Colin Murphy – "I would not be surprised if the game goes to a replay...I must favour Forest though", Alan Hill – "Nottingham Forest will eventually go through".

Of those not preferring Forest, Jimmy Gordon, the former Rams and Forest coach (and a close associate of both Brian Clough and Peter Taylor) – "This is one game I personally did not want to happen, I would rather not commit myself", Colin Addison – "A draw, either 0-0 or 1-1", and then there were two who backed the Rams to pull off a shock result – Henry Newton and John O'Hare, both of whom played for both clubs. Doreen Shadbolt, a Uttoxeter-based clairvoyant and medium, predicted on BBC Radio Derby that the Rams would defeat Forest 2-0.

The Ram Newspaper was enlarged to 20 pages and printed in full colour for the occasion, with the front cover featuring both team line-ups either side of the FA Cup itself – Forest's team listing featuring future Derby players Steve Sutton, Steve Hodge and John Robertson, plus former Ram Colin Todd, whilst the Rams side featured former Forest players Archie Gemmill and Gary Mills. The referee was George Courtney of Spennymoor, County Durham – one of the top officials of the day.

Peter Taylor was unable to field his first-choice side, as neither John Richards nor Bobby Davison were eligible for selection. Richards, on loan from Wolverhampton Wanderers, was ruled out because manager Graham Hawkins refused to allow his player to be cup-tied, which was particularly odd given that he had agreed to extend his player's loan spell at the Baseball Ground. Davison had played already that season in the FA Cup, for Halifax Town, and was therefore ineligible. Also missing was Steve Buckley, out with a broken toe on his left foot, and still in plaster. Steve Powell remained out, with a long-term injury, although he had not played much part in the revival under Taylor. Youngsters Kevin Wilson and Andy Hill came into the side to replace Richards and Davison, with Ian Dalziel named as substitute. Neither Wilson nor Hill had been involved in the first team since Taylor's first game in charge, when he had been so scathing of many of the players, one of whom he had described as "an absolute disgrace" and others as "not good enough". Dalziel, a wholehearted trier who had become useful covering several positions, was one of the players that Taylor did appreciate.

Derby's record in the FA Cup was generally poor – in fact they had not won an FA Cup tie since 1978 when they had beaten Birmingham City in the 4th round at the Baseball Ground, before going out to West Bromwich Albion in the next round – since then they had scored only three goals and conceded fourteen in the five subsequent ties. However, they had mainly been drawn away in the third round – and they had won 7 and drawn 1 of their last eight home 3rd round ties and, encouragingly, had not lost a home 3rd round tie since 1966, when they had been beaten by Manchester United.

The Rams and Forest had not met in the FA Cup since 23rd January 1936, when Derby won 2-0 at the Baseball Ground in front of a crowd of 37,830 – gates had been locked closed at 2.15pm with thousands locked out. Halford put the home side 1-0 ahead, netting from a Crooks cross after 17 minutes, and Bowers put the tie beyond Forest's reach when he ran on to Napier's high through-ball to beat the offside trap and score Derby's second on 76 minutes.

In the event, the attendance was 28,494 – the highest at the Baseball Ground since 27,783 attended a First Division game against Manchester United on 2nd February 1980, and the Rams lined up with Swindlehurst in midfield, and youngsters Wilson and Hill in attack. It was a makeshift team and certainly not Taylor's preferred line-up, but the two youngsters gave Forest's defenders a torrid time in the first 20 minutes with their eager running – Hill having a couple of good chances to score, but lacking composure at the vital moments. Nottingham-born Steve Cherry, the boyhood Forest fan in the Rams goal, then did well to keep out a Mark Proctor header before Gary Mills almost scored direct from a corner – Steve Hodge clearing off the line with goalkeeper Sutton beaten.

Somehow the score remained goalless at half time but on 57 minutes Wilson, despite having injured his right foot in collision with Steve Sutton in the first minute of the game, almost broke the deadlock when his shot hit the post, following good work from John Barton.

Wilson's moment was still to come, and on 65 minutes he was pulled down just outside the penalty area by Forest's big central defender Willie Young. Dave Swindlehurst ran over the ball from the resulting free kick, deceiving several in the Forest wall, and Archie Gemmill stepped up to curl his shot beyond the reach of Sutton into the Osmaston goal, to put the Rams deservedly ahead.

Derby continued to dominate the game, although Cherry had to react quickly to turn away one long-range shot from Brynn Gunn, and made the game safe right at the end when Ian Bowyer was robbed of possession with most of the Forest players stranded upfield, and Mick Brolly powered forward with Hill in support, the youngster making no mistake with his opportunity to write his name into Derby County history with what turned out to be his last goal for the club. 2-0 to the Rams, and game over – Derby's vintage performance had been simply too much their illustrious neighbours in every department, with former Forest men Mills and Gemmill the best players on the pitch.

Fans in the stadium had been generally well-behaved although there were pitch invasions originating from the unfenced Paddock seating following Derby's goals. After the game Michael Dunford issued a warning to supporters – "we do not wish to fence in (the seating areas) but if there is any repeat, they will have to be installed". Groundsman Bob Smith sat in the stands watching as hordes of jubilant Rams supporters celebrated on the Baseball Ground pitch for half an hour after the final whistle – the pitch was already sodden following a week of almost continual rain and was now a quagmire. The game had been in danger of being postponed on the Friday evening, because of the state of the pitch.

In the away dressing room after the game, Clough jabbed his finger at one of his players, accusing him of taking a bribe from Taylor. Forest's players described it as the angriest they had ever seen their manager. The two former friends' relationship had by now irretrievably broken down – Clough considered Derby his domain and Taylor was supposed to have retired, describing his ex-partner as "a rattlesnake" and "a snake in the grass" and then famously - "If I was driving along the A52 between Derby and Nottingham and saw Taylor broken down, thumbing a lift, I wouldn't pick him up, I'd run him over" – to put these remarks into context, Clough deeply regretted them and wished he could have taken them back before Taylor's sudden death a few years later.

Clough had placed so much emphasis on this game, that he had said to his central defender Willie Young before the match "just do one thing for me Willie, play well in this match and I won't ask another thing of you". After the game Clough saw Young talking to Taylor before getting on the team coach – "did you shake hands with that shithouse Taylor?", he demanded, running to the front and back of the bus shouting and pointing – "that's the last thing you ever do at this club".

Taylor's influence was paying handsome dividends off the pitch as well as on it. The last seven home league games had been watched by 98,396 spectators at an average of 12,770, and the last four alone by 53,431, an average of 13,357. The Forest cup tie, with extra payments to the away club and FA pool, plus extra policing and staffing, netted Derby only around £4,000 in the end. There was another bonus when the Rams were drawn at home again in the fourth round, this time against Chelsea, in a tie scheduled for Saturday January 29th, 1983. The attendance for the Forest match was the first time the Rams had attracted more than 20,000 since the opening home game of season 1980-81. The club responded to increased interest by increasing terrace matchday prices from £1.80 to £2.00 – "to ease congestion, as giving change at the gate causes so many delays", said Michael Dunford.

The Forest had also passed relatively peacefully off the pitch, where less than 30 arrests out of a crowd of over 28,000, could be considered a big positive in those days. After the match, however, Derby could well have been reported to the Football Association for invasions of the pitch by fans during the match, however the incursions were dismissed by referee George Courtney as sheer exuberance and without malice, and he decided to let the matter pass. A meeting of Second Division clubs had decided to trial an idea proposed by Leeds United in which visiting clubs would bring their own stewards to control their supporters at away grounds – Derby had done this at Molineux for the game against Wolverhampton Wanderers, and Leeds would be doing the same at the Baseball Ground on January 22nd, Derby's first home match since the FA Cup victory over Nottingham Forest.

After the excitement of the FA Cup tie came a bread-and-butter Second Division fixture at Brunton Park against Carlisle United on Saturday 15th January. Gemmill and Wilson were injured, and Paul Blades came in to partner Foster at centre back with McAlle moving into midfield in place of Gemmill. John Richards and Bobby Davison returned to the side, with Hill, who had scored Derby's second goal against Forest, dropped from the squad.

It was very much a case of "after the Lord Mayor's Show", as the Rams crashed 3-0 to a hard-working, direct Carlisle side. Derby started well and looked the better side, with some good chances missed, particularly Davison's header which he directed wide when it looked easier to score. However, once they had gone 1-0 down on 16 minutes following a rare error by Steve Cherry, the Rams became nervy and allowed the hosts to dominate – with Derby's back four looking particularly suspect, young Blades having a difficult afternoon against Carlisle's physicality and eventually being substituted, with McAlle moving back to centre half. By the time the Rams crafted another chance, when Richards chipped the goalkeeper only for the ball to stick in mud on the goal-line, they were already 3-0 down and well beaten.

The defeat at Carlisle on 15th January 1983 was the Rams' fourth loss in their last 7 matches and returned them to the bottom of the Second Division with 19 points. It was not good enough, and Roy McFarland said after the game – "there are players here who shouldn't be. Two or three just don't want to play". One of the players who the management had wanted to keep, John Richards, returned to his parent club Wolverhampton Wanderers when his loan deal expired after the match at Carlisle, having made 10 appearances for the Rams –

the clubs had started discussions to extend the loan deal, but an injury crisis at Molineux put paid to that, it was a blow for the Rams – "he's a magnificent character on and off the field and did a great job for us", said Peter Taylor.

Peter Taylor, however, knew that the tide was turning, he had seen enough in the games against QPR and Nottingham Forest – from this point, Derby were about to embark on what was a quite astonishing run in which they remained unbeaten in the league until May, spanning 15 matches. He had already identified the position which needed strengthening, and the player he wanted to help achieve it – in fact that man, Oldham Athletic's central defender Paul Futcher, had played against the Rams just a couple of weeks previously.

For the second time in three seasons, the Rams Youth Team were knocked out of the FA Youth Cup by Manchester United, for whom Norman Whiteside starred, when they lost their third-round replay 1-0 at the Baseball Ground on 10th January. The visitors had the better of the game, unlike in the original tie at Old Trafford, which Derby had dominated, and would have been disappointed to only score one goal, just after half time – Robert Palmer having made some spectacular saves to keep Derby in the game. The Rams did push forward in the final minutes to try and force a replay, but to no avail.

On 22nd January, Leeds United, under player-manager Eddie Gray, were visitors to the Baseball Ground. Leeds featured future Derby player Kenny Burns. For Derby, captain Archie Gemmill returned to the side after missing the defeat at Carlisle through injury. Also, back from injury was Steve Buckley, and Kevin Wilson, who had played so well in the win over Nottingham Forest, was back in the side. The attendance, 17,005, was the highest for a league game at the Baseball Ground since February 1981.

The game itself was a tremendously exciting affair which ended 3-3. Leeds looked a very good side, perhaps First Division quality, but the Rams pushed them all the way. The visitors went ahead and led 1-0 at half time, but Bobby Davison levelled the scores when he converted Gary Mills's cross, a fine shot which deceived goalkeeper Lukic with its pace. Unfortunately, soon after Davison's goal, Derby's back four then presented the visitors with two chances, both of which were taken, and Leeds led 3-1 after 62 minutes and the game appeared to be over.

Derby were not finished, and heads did not drop as they undoubtedly would have done earlier in the season. Lukic was penalised for taking too many steps with the ball in hand, and from the resulting free-kick Gemmill tapped the ball sideways to Dave Swindlehurst, who hit a fierce shot through Leeds's defensive wall and into the net at the Osmaston End. Then came the crescendo, on 87 minutes, when Derby were awarded what appeared to be a dubious penalty as Mills fell over under an innocuous challenge -Gemmill slotted home the spot-kick, injuring his hamstring in the process, and made the final score 3-3.

The excellent entertainment on the pitch was unfortunately not the main story of Derby's game against Leeds United. Leeds supporters sitting in the upper tier of the Osmaston Stand had ripped out seats and thrown them, and other objects – including, according to Ossie-Ender Stan Readle of Ripley, a bra -"we weren't amused, it was empty", down onto Derby supporters standing on the Osmaston End terrace. Rams fans on the caged-in Ossie End, powerless to react, tried to climb over the high fences onto the pitch-side perimeter to escape the hail of missiles raining-down onto them from above. It was the worst trouble seen at the Baseball Ground since Chelsea's fans had rioted inside the stadium in November 1981.

There had been sporadic outbreaks of trouble throughout the game, and Derby received criticism from both Leeds and some of their own fans, that supporters were allowed too close a proximity. An official enquiry was announced by the Football League, and Derby decided to close the Ossie End terrace for the following game – the FA Cup 4th round tie against Chelsea – it had only been re-open as a terrace for one match, the Family Seating having only been removed a fortnight before.

In the aftermath of the game it was revealed that 512 seats had been destroyed, and the estimated cost of repairs was £20,000, an amount Derby County could simply not afford. Whilst the police acknowledged that Leeds United supporters were responsible for the major offences, they also stated that some of the trouble was caused by "baiting from a small section of so-called Derby fans". In addition to the cost of repairs, Derby County suffered again when the house-building company Bovis Homes, who had bought matchday sponsorship for the forthcoming FA Cup tie pulled out, saying that the mayhem at the Leeds match presented an image that their company did not want to be associated with – and withdrew their agreed £5,000 fee, plus an extra £2,000 should the Rams have won. Fortunately for the club, another sponsor was found at very short notice, and the same fee was negotiated with a local building contractor.

In the week following the Leeds United match, Peter Taylor signed the player he had been chasing for several weeks – Oldham Athletic central defender Paul Futcher, often touted as one of the best defenders outside the First Division. The Rams had agreed a fee of £120,000, beating offers by two First Division clubs, with the Latics for the player described by Taylor as "a touch of class by our standards...a cultured defender, the type to get us out of trouble. I've thrown first division visions at him, yet we could go down to the third...but I am selling a vision of the future, a future that players like Paul Futcher and his ilk can make even more certain to happen". Joe Royle, Oldham's manager, said of the player and the deal – "he really should be in division one, but apparently Derby convinced him that that is where they are going".

Futcher, 26-years-old, had won 11 England Under 21 international caps and appeared set for full honours whilst at Luton Town and then Manchester City, before falling out with new manager Malcolm Allison and leaving for Boundary Park. Oldham were higher in the league than Derby, but Futcher said – "I'm doing the right thing. I stepped down before because I was desperate to get away from City, but I am not stepping down here really. Derby are a big club despite their league placing, I was quickly convinced of that by Peter Taylor and Roy McFarland".

George Foster, the defender signed by John Newman in the summer of 1982, was the player whose position appeared most threatened by the arrival of Futcher. When asked about how he felt, Foster said – "I never funk a challenge on the field or off. I don't intend to be the one to go out permanently...I've never got any stick from this remarkable Derby crowd, they realised from the start that I was a ball-winning centre half, the type who gives 100%...I'm not a ball player and never will be...recently I have been told that each week is better than my last...the morale in the squad is tremendous". Foster was used to relegation battles, having featured in them six times in his ten seasons as a professional.

John Barton, the full back who had been dropped by, then quickly recalled to the side by Peter Taylor, was another who praised the Rams support – "we've had to follow some great international players, but that's in the past. We have to be judged on the present day and to be fair the crowd has been magnificent to us...I have witnessed Merseyside derbies, and the atmosphere here is equal". Barton was one of several Rams players who had been showered with spit and coins from Leeds supporters during and after the recent game at the Baseball Ground – "it came at you in bucketful whenever you were within reach of them...one or two of us were hit with coins...it was disgusting treatment".

The Rams reserves suffered a poor start to calendar year 1983, with three successive defeats – away at Bolton Wanderers and Oldham Athletic then, on 25th January, a 3-2 defeat at the Baseball Ground to Bradford City during which several travelling Bradford supporters took the opportunity to barrack Roy McFarland, their former manager, with obscene chants and gestures – McFarland, who had been sitting in the Directors Box, had to leave his seat and retire to the comfort of the Players' Lounge.

Steve Powell played 45 minutes of the reserves game against Bradford, as he attempted his latest comeback from injury – "we are delighted with his performance, if there is no reaction, he could be a contender for the side against Chelsea", said McFarland. Powell had partnered Paul Blades in the centre of defence for the first half and the score had remained goalless, but when Blades was sent off early in the second half, with Powell having already been withdrawn, the Rams capitulated and conceded three goals – Paul Emson and Tony Reid scoring Derby's consolations. Derby's reserve side against Bradford City: Banovic, Lovatt, Harbey, Powell, Blades, Skivington, Chapman, Reid, Hill, Shackleton, Emson and substitute Banks.

Youth team goalkeeper Robert Palmer was released by the club after it was decided not to offer him a full-time professional contract when he turned 18 in January 1983. Palmer had joined from schoolboy football in Hull with quite some fanfare and despite some good displays, had not shown the consistency required for the club to commit to a professional deal.

Damage caused by Leeds United supporters at the Baseball Ground was hastily repaired in time for the following week's FA Cup 4th round tie with Chelsea, on Saturday 29th January. The Rams were something of a bogey team for their visitors – who had not beaten Derby since 1972 and had been beaten already at the Baseball Ground earlier in the season. In a quirk of the fixture list, the sides would meet again at Stamford Bridge the following weekend in a Second Division encounter.

The two clubs had met twice previously in the FA Cup – first in January 1947 when the then cup holders Derby travelled to Stamford Bridge for a 4th round tie played in heavy snow and with poor visibility, in front of a crowd of 49,484. The game ended 2-2, the Rams having equalised 2 minutes from time through Raich Carter. Derby won the replay in front of 19,079 on a frozen Baseball Ground pitch, with Jack Stamps scoring an extra-time winner. The only other meeting in the FA Cup between the two sides was a third-round tie in 1953 at the Baseball Ground, where 24,867 struggled to see the game through clinging mist which made visibility very difficult, an exciting match ending in a 4-4 draw. Once again, the replay went to extra time, but this time Chelsea prevailed through a deflected shot by Parsons.

Peter Taylor was unable to field two of his new signings for the Cup Tie – both Bobby Davison and Paul Futcher were cup-tied. Wilson and Hill were again paired in attack, as they had been against Forest in the third round and Steve Powell came into the side to replace the injured Gemmill in midfield, his first game since November. Buckley's return from injury had lasted just one game, so Brian Attley returned to the side at left back. There was another big crowd at the Baseball Ground, this time 23,383, and Derby did not disappoint – easing to a 2-1 win against their fellow Second Division opponents, both goals coming from the resurgent Kevin Wilson, who's form was giving manager Taylor plenty to think about. The first, on 20 minutes, was a well-worked routine as Gary Mills's corner was headed back across goal by Swindlehurst, for Wilson, in space, to head into the Chelsea net at the Normanton End. Derby's winner came in the 89th minute, after goalkeeper Francis could not hold onto a fierce drive from Swindlehurst and Wilson was the first to react, slotting the rebound home to put the Rams into the Fifth Round, and spark a riot amongst Chelsea fans in the Osmaston Stand behind the goal.

The Chelsea game had been relatively peaceful off the pitch until the Rams' late winner, when it was unfortunately marred as visiting supporters followed the example set by Leeds United supporters the week before and ripped seats out of the Osmaston Stand, hurling them from the Upper Tier onto the pitch. It was a disaster for Derby, and dismayed chairman Mike Watterson, surveying the damage after the game said – "these people are not even fit to be called wild animals". Chelsea's chairman Ken Bates had left his seat in the director's box to walk over to the Osmaston End and try to restore order amongst his team's supporters – a well-meaning, albeit futile gesture. Derby looked sure to face trouble from the Football Association, after two successive weekends of mayhem at the Baseball Ground. Derby had taken steps to try and avert trouble and had taken a late decision to close the Osmaston End terrace for the Chelsea game, and to move season ticket holders out. Most were rehoused in C-Stand. In the event, with a second successive afternoon of seat-throwing and rioting, it proved a sensible decision.

A week after they had knocked Chelsea out of the FA Cup, the Rams did "the double" over them with a fine 3-1 win at Stamford Bridge in their Second Division encounter, with a penalty from Gemmill, plus a Bumstead own goal and one from Mills completing the Rams' scoring. It was resurgent Derby's fourth win in seven games, with two draws, since the turn of the year, and took them to 23 points from 26 games. New signing **Paul Futcher** made a classy and encouraging debut. Derby were still at the bottom of the Second Division table and had to keep picking up points to stay in touch with the clubs in the safe positions of 18th and 19th, currently Carlisle (30 points) and Middlesbrough (29 points). The Rams were now top of the divisional form table, based on the last six games – from which they had picked up 13 points, scoring 12 goals and conceding 8.

At Stamford Bridge, Peter Taylor was able to select his preferred team, without the burden of players being unavailable, and there were several changes – Barton and Attley continued at full back, although the injured Buckley was most likely the manager's preference at left back, if available. Both McAlle and Foster lost their places in the centre of defence, despite some recent improvements in that department – new signing Futcher was paired with the fit-again Powell in what appeared, on paper, a fair stronger pairing. Gemmill returned from injury, and was partnered with Swindlehurst in midfield, with Brolly and Mills either side of them. In attack, the in-form pair of Davison and Wilson provided excellent pace and movement, although both rather short in stature. For Kevin Wilson and Gary Mills in particular, there had been redemption – both players had found themselves out of favour and out of the team after Taylor's arrival, but with form, determination and ability they had forced the manager to revise his early opinions.

The Rams did not play well at Chelsea, and Roy McFarland conceded after the game – "we have played better and lost, we couldn't string three passes together". Fortunately for Derby, Chelsea were awful. Derby went ahead on three minutes, when home goalkeeper Francis diverted Mills's cross, which caught the wind and swerved and dipped late, into his own net – arguably an own-goal, although Mills claimed it. Derby's second really was an own-goal, as another Mills cross aimed at Davison and Brolly was lunged-at by Chelsea's Bumstead, diverting the ball past a stranded Francis. Gemmill's retaken penalty, awarded just after half time when Brolly was sent sprawling by Joey Jones, sealed the three points. After recent trouble with Chelsea supporters, it was perhaps not surprising that on 68 Derby fans occupied the visitors terracing at Stamford Bridge.

Paul Futcher was born in Chester in 1956, the twin brother of Ron, who was also a professional footballer, as was their older brother Graham. He made his debut for hometown club Chester City as a 16-year-old in March 1973 and was soon touted as one of the hottest prospects in lower league football. After just 20 league appearances at Sealand Road, Futcher was signed by Luton Town for £100,000 in the summer of 1974, a big fee at the time, especially for such an inexperienced player, and went on to play over 140 games for Luton, winning 10 England Under 21 caps in the process.

In June 1978, Manchester City made Futcher the most expensive defender in England when they paid £350,000, but he struggled at Maine Road and was not a favourite with the crowd. Just over a year later, City sold him to Second Division Oldham Athletic for a cut-price £150,000. He was unlucky not to receive full international caps – having been selected twice for the full England side, only to have to withdraw due to injury on both occasions. Peter Taylor considered Futcher to be a cultured defender who was playing at a level too low when he agreed a £120,000 fee with Oldham early in 1983. He proved a good signing for the Rams, but the relationship between player and manager broke down during Derby's troubled 1983-84 season and Futcher went to Barnsley, where he made 230 appearances before finishing his full-time playing career at Grimsby Town.

Futcher became a player-manager and had success at Gresley Rovers and then Southport, where, at 41 years-old, he became the oldest player to appear in a competitive Wembley Final (the 1998 FA Trophy final against Cheltenham Town). He died of cancer at aged 60, in November 2016 – there was a fitting tribute to a very fine player when Grimsby Town described him as "one of the greatest footballers ever to have graced Blundell Park". He was indeed a very good player and could have played a significant part in Derby's revival in the mid-late 1980's, had he have not fallen out with Peter Taylor.

Peter Taylor took his players to Majorca for a short break on Monday 7th February, following the two victories over Chelsea. The Rams by now one of the form-sides of the Second Division, having won 4 of their last 6 matches, scoring 12 and conceding 8 in the process. Derby's players paid for their own travel.

The Rams were scheduled to play Charlton Athletic at the Baseball Ground on Saturday February 12th, but the game was postponed due to bad weather and in the event, results elsewhere all went in Derby's favour as fellow strugglers Chelsea, Middlesbrough and Carlisle all lost, leaving the Rams still in touch, and with a game in hand on many of their nearest rivals. It would have been Derby's first home game since successive riots by first Leeds United, then Chelsea supporters had caused significant damage to the stadium, and the postponement gave the club an extra week in which to prepare for their next game, an FA Cup 5th Round tie against First Division Manchester United, on Saturday February 19th, 1983 – the draw once again being kind to the cash-strapped Rams.

Mike Watterson and his board were batting fines, costs and adverse publicity from several directions. The dispute with Bradford City over Roy McFarland rumbled on – although Derby had received something of a boost when a Football League Tribunal ordered that they should pay Bradford a sum of £55,000 as compensation for McFarland swapping Valley Parade for the Baseball Ground. Bradford had demanded £200,000 for their manager when Watterson had originally approached them in the Autumn of 1982, a figure which the Rams considered totally unrealistic for a man they had released on a free transfer just 16 months previously – and Watterson had at that point declined to proceed with a deal.

The controversy then came when McFarland quit his job at Bradford and became a free agent, and accepted Derby's offer to become team manager at the Baseball Ground, under his former boss and close friend Peter Taylor. Derby, and Watterson, strenuously denied Bradford's allegations that they had "tapped up" McFarland (at a cost of a £10,000 fine, £55,000 compensation and significant legal fees), whilst Bradford City lodged an appeal against the £55,000 award, claiming that their original figure of £200,000 was a true valuation of their loss. Most of the national press sided with the Yorkshire club – typical coverage included the Sunday Times's comment "Derby deserve no sympathy in the squalid affair of McFarland, who walked out on a club and a contract".

McFarland stayed quiet during the affair but did confirm that he had been unhappy at Valley Parade over the summer of 1982 regarding the issue of unpaid contractual bonuses due to him following Bradford's promotion in 1981-82. McFarland was missed at Valley Parade mostly for his performances on the field – he had played a lot more games than many had expected during his time in Yorkshire. He had wanted to quit playing, but his performances became invaluable to the club – despite which, he had warned Bob Martin, Bradford's chairman, that he wanted to sign a player to replace himself, but the club's financial situation had prevented that.

In addition to the McFarland affair, Derby were in trouble with the Football Association in relation to significant crowd disturbances at their home games against Leeds United on January 22nd and then against Chelsea a week later. The FA ordered the club to begin immediate rebuilding work in order to segregate rival fans at the Baseball Ground, at a cost of £25,000. Both Derby and the two visiting clubs were warned by an FA inquiry about the future behaviour of their supporters. The FA instructed that Derby must make structural alterations in either the Osmaston Stand or the Ley Stand which would lead to the complete segregation of visiting fans from home supporters, both in seated and standing areas. In addition, the club was ordered to make improvements to the entrance and exit of both stands. Plans were to be submitted within four weeks and the works to be completed to the FA's satisfaction before the start of the 1983-84 season. It was made clear to Derby County that any further trouble involving their supporters would result in severe consequences.

Derbyshire constabulary, in conjunction with the football club, began to use long-lens video and camera technology to scan the Baseball Ground for "the 150-or so Derby hooligans... the louts who have caused so much bad publicity for us all in recent weeks, aged from as young as 12, up to 24 or 25" - about whom they had compiled dossiers with a view to "weeding them out". Some national press reports also suggested that it had been Derby supporters who were responsible for crowd trouble at Barnet during their recent FA Trophy tie against Ilkeston Town. There was another warning that any further pitch invasions originating from the Paddock would result in the installation of fencing in front of the Main Stand – it was already in place around the other three sides of the Baseball Ground.

Despite the recent burdens on cash at Derby, Mike Watterson was not prepared to sell Dave Swindlehurst cheaply. Considered Derby's "prized asset" by both Peter Taylor and the board, and crucial to the club's battle against relegation, the club had placed a £400,000 valuation on Swindlehurst (slightly below what they had paid for him back in 1980, in the days before the transfer market had crashed). Aston Villa, the club who had shown considerable interest in him, considered that fee too high – especially considering Swindlehurst would be out of contract in the summer of 1983.

Football, especially at lower levels, was in the doldrums. In his 1983 report Sir Norman Chesters concluded that whilst First Division, and some Second Division clubs could cope with average player wage levels of £400-£500, those in the lower divisions were struggling to cope with wage levels of £150. Chesters suggested that the Third and Fourth divisions might be scrapped and replaced with two regional divisions, North and South, with the introduction of part-time professionalism at this level.

The Rams had met Manchester United four times previously in the FA Cup, and had not won any of the ties, although they had beaten the Manchester club twice in the days when they were still known by their original name – Newton Heath. Twice, United had beaten Derby at the semi final stage of the tournament, most recently a heart-breaking defeat at Hillsborough on 3rd April 1976, when the Rams were reigning League Champions and still in with a realistic chance of winning the League and Cup double – two goals from future Derby winger Gordon Hill won the tie for United. Although that game had been nearly 7 years before, the Rams had two survivors in their squad from their side that day – Archie Gemmill and Steve Powell, and United had one – Steve Coppell. Interestingly, Dave Swindlehurst played in the other semi-final that year, for Crystal Palace against eventual winners Southampton. Derby had not beaten Manchester United in any competitive match since September 1975.

Manager Peter Taylor was in fine form before the game, saying of Manchester United – "on paper, we don't compare with them in class, except in the managerial chair". Once again, he was unable to field his preferred team, and back into the side came George Foster and Andy Hill, to replace cup-tied Paul Futcher and Bobby Davison. Manchester United's team for the day included England Internationals Gary Bailey, Steve Coppell and Bryan Robson, Ireland Internationals Kevin Moran and Frank Stapleton, Scotland Internationals Gordon McQueen and Arthur Albiston, Dutch International Arnold Murhen, Northern Ireland International Norman Whiteside, plus Mike Duxbury and Remi Moses. England International Ray Wilkins was named as substitute – Taylor's point about not matching them on paper was perfectly valid. In a quirk of fate, the Ram Newspaper published its 300th issue for the FA Cup tie against Manchester United, the same opposition as there had been on the day on which it published issue number 1, in August 1971.

This time, the Baseball Ground was packed to the rafters and the official attendance of 33,022 far exceeded the maximum stated capacity of the time, 31,500. The entire Osmaston End was given over to Manchester United supporters and Ley Stand ticket holders were not permitted to enter the ground via turnstiles 56-59, situated at the Osmaston End – all admission to the Ley Stand for this match was via Vulcan Street, turnstiles 2-6. On the Popside, caged-in supporters were squeezed together so tightly that some struggled for breath and were unable to prevent themselves being carried around by the movement of the crowd. It was dangerously overcrowded, and the last time that the famous old ground would host numbers of that magnitude – considering the trouble that Derby County had been in with the Football Association regarding stadium infrastructure and crowd control, it was astonishing that such a huge number of people were permitted to enter the ground, perhaps an indication that profits mattered more than people in those days. Tragedy, caused by overcrowding on antiquated terracing at another stadium, was sadly just around the corner.

On the pitch, the spectators were treated to one of the most tense, exciting matches seen at the Baseball Ground for many years. United's intricate passing and patient build-up being held at bay by the aggressive, enthusiastic Derby midfield, and the Rams always threatening a break-away goal. United might have gone ahead in the first minute, but Steve Cherry athletically tipped away Stapleton's goal-bound header, and Derby remained in the game until the 84th minute, when Whiteside scored for an ultimately deserved United victory – although many supporters sat level with the play in B-Stand were adamant that the linesman should have flagged for offside. Once again, Archie Gemmill defied his age to urge the Rams on, and players whose spirit had previously been called into question responded with performances of astonishing determination and bravery. Derby had their chances, notably Andy Hill's drive which Bailey did well to cling on to, and George Foster's header which went narrowly wide.

In midfield, the cultured Robson and the fiery Moses were superb for United, but all 11 of the battling Rams emerged with credit, none more so that Foster, the central defender only in the side because Paul Futcher was cup-tied. John Barton and Steve Cherry, candidates for man of the match, both had their best games for the club. It was a remarkable occasion, and one in which Derby's team played their full part – the scoreline of 1-0 to United presented both sides with fair reward for their endeavour.

Peter Taylor, post-match, summed up the situation – "our players are beginning to apply themselves like professionals. They were amateurs when we came here. Our cup final is against Grimsby (next weekend) and that match will show us what we have learned...young Cherry's form has been a real bonus to the management". The Rams were yet to win two successive league games, a record which they hoped to crack when the Mariners visited the Baseball Ground the following Saturday.

Derby's 18-year-old central defender Paul Blades received his first international call-up when he was chosen for the England Youth squad which was due to travel to Israel to play two matches at the end of February. In the event, Blades played in both games against Israel's under-21 side, with England winning both matches. He was later called into Lilleshall for a 3-day England coaching course and had ambitions to be selected for England's squad for the forthcoming European Youth Championships, to be staged in England in the summer of 1983.

Derby's board took the decision to close the Osmaston End terrace following the Manchester United FA Cup tie. It was also decided that the present segregated seating area in the Osmaston Lower Tier, with its 400 seats for visiting supporters, would continue to be available for visiting clubs, as well as Rams season ticket holders for both the Lower and Upper Tiers, but there would be no further matchday admissions in that stand. The Colombo section of the Popside was given over for the exclusive use of visiting supporters, and in the event of demand from visitors exceeding space in that section, overspill would be housed on the Ossie End. The club made the decisions in the light of strict warnings they had received from the Football Association, in relation to segregation and crowd control.

Crowd segregation for the FA Cup tie against Manchester United had worked well for Derby, and behaviour was generally good, with only isolated incidents reported – a blessing, considering that it had cost the Rams £7,000 to police the fixture (compared to a usual figure for a home match of about £2,000). United's supporters had been housed in the Osmaston Stand – from where Derby's season-ticket holders had been relocated for the day "they appreciated that this was for their own safety", said Michael Dunford. Unfortunately, there had been one incident in which a coin was thrown from the Popside at United's winger Steve Coppell – thankfully for Derby, Coppell declined the opportunity to take the matter further.

It was likely, given the success of the segregation for this match, that the Osmaston Stand in its entirety would again have to be given over to visiting fans when clubs with big away followings visited the Baseball Ground and this could include Wolves, Sheffield Wednesday and Newcastle United, who were all scheduled to visit before the end of the season. This, according to Dunford, would inevitably mean that more terrace space would be needed for Derby supporters, and the Popside, including the Colombo section, would be given over to Rams fans.

By this stage in the season, Peter Taylor had managed the same number of Second Division games as his predecessor John Newman had, 13. Taylor's side had accrued 15 points from his 13 matches, compared to Newman's 8 from 15. It was a considerable improvement, but the Rams were still bottom the league and in desperate trouble, thanks to their awful start to the season - apart from one week, they had been 22nd and bottom since the beginning of November. The bottom of the Second Division at this stage read:

15th Chelsea, 32 points from 28 matches

16th Bolton Wanderers, 32 from 27

17th Carlisle United, 31 from 28

18th Crystal Palace, 31 from 26

19th Middlesbrough, 29 from 27

20th Cambridge United, 28 from 27

21st Burnley, 23 from 26

22nd Derby County, 23 from 26

The fourth member of Peter Taylor's managerial team was chief scout Ken Gutteridge. Derby-born Gutteridge was formerly assistant manager at Brighton & Hove Albion (where he had worked with Taylor) and Luton Town, and manager of Burton Albion – during which time he was credited with discovering Steve Buckley and Nottingham Forest's former Brighton striker Peter Ward. Working for him was a network of eight "proven scouts" covering the home nations, some of whom were new to Derby. Also working for the club was Brian Newton, a part-timer who also worked for British Rail and was described as "the ½ part of our 4 ½ man team...Brian has been with me since I was at Burton Albion, he is invaluable to me".

Gutteridge pronounced himself to find some young players at the Baseball Ground when he arrived who he instantly knew would not make the grade Derby County required, and he was in the process of removing those in question. Before joining Derby, he had most recently been chief scout at Wolverhampton Wanderers – "we are not working as a lower Second Division club, the management here is aiming at the day when Derby are back again at the top of the top flight...its not the number of scouts or players, its quality that matters", he said when interviewed in February 1983. Gutteridge also had cause to be unhappy with the attitude and application shown by Derby's reserve side, who, despite fielding 9 players with first team experience including John McAlle and Brian Attley, plus triallist goalkeeper Sparham, contrived to lose 2-1 at the Baseball Ground to a Notts County side consisting of mostly schoolboys and apprentices, on 20th February. Following the game, former first team player Tony Reid was released to join Scunthorpe United on a month's loan. Once considered the best prospect at the club, Reid had been unfortunate with injuries and had begun to fall out favour since Colin Addison's departure, and was not in the first team picture under Peter Taylor.

With the FA Cup run over, the Rams were free to concentrate on the battle to stay in the Second Division. They had 16 matches in which to achieve that, starting with a home game against fourth-placed Grimsby Town on Saturday 26th February. The attendance, 12,775, was perhaps disappointing given recent achievements, but was still far above anything the club could have hoped for earlier in the season, before Peter Taylor's appointment.

Paul Futcher and Bobby Davison returned to the side in place of Foster and Hill, and Derby ran out comfortable winners, 2-0, with Davison again on the scoresheet – scoring both goals at the Normanton End within two minutes early in the second half, the first after a blistering surge of pace left Grimsby's defence in his wake, and his snap shot deflected off Kevin Moore and into the net, and the second a fine header from a right-wing cross. Once again captain Archie Gemmill provided most of the class on display. Grimsby's goalkeeper was former Rams apprentice Nigel Batch, who had been released by Derby in 1976 when third in line behind Colin Boulton and Graham Moseley – Batch, who had not missed a game in four seasons, was a firm favourite with the Mariners' crowd. With three points taking them on to 27, from 28 matches, the Rams were now just 2 points behind Burnley and Cambridge United, and, crucially, just 5 behind Middlesbrough in the final safe place, 19th, but with 2 games in hand of the Teesiders.

Peter Taylor, who had needed only one look at Bobby Davison before signing him from Halifax Town, said of the new Baseball Ground favourite – "The lad will get us goals for a long time to come…he has the scent of goals, we mustn't rush him, but bring him slowly to the boil". In Davison, Gemmill and Futcher, Taylor had brought in players of First Division quality, to complement the better players who were already there when he arrived – Dave Swindlehurst, Steve Buckley, Steve Powell and Gary Mills. Powell's form, following his return from injury, had been a key factor in the Rams revival – and his partnership with the stylish Futcher was proving very successful.

By now, Taylor had the makings of the side he wanted – Cherry in goal, a back four of Barton, Futcher, Powell and Buckley, a midfield of Brolly, Swindlehurst, Gemmill and Mills, and Davison and either Wilson or Hill in attack. Of John Newman's signings, only attack-minded right back John Barton and hard-working midfielder Mike Brolly remained in favour – Brian Attley, John McAlle and George Foster not being part of the new manager's plans.

Following Tony Reid's departure, another of the Rams young players was allowed out on loan – Glen Skivington, previously a first team regular but who had not started a single game under Peter Taylor, was allowed to join Halifax Town for a month. Taylor's opinion of Derby's crop of young players was considerably different to that of his predecessors Newman and Addison – "some of them are Southern League standard", he said.

One player who had convinced the manager of his worth was Gary Mills. Taylor had not selected Mills when he first arrived as manager, but the midfield player had put in a series of impressive displays and was now considered a key member of the first team. Derby received a boost when, after talks with Mills's parent club Seattle Sounders, they were able to extend his stay at the Baseball Ground until after the scheduled Easter Monday (April 4th) match at home to Newcastle United – the original deal was due to expire in mid-March. Taylor said of Mills – "I have known him since he signed for Forest at 14-years old and he is now producing the goods as never before, and consistently so, which is what the game is all about. We are delighted to be able to get these extra games from him".

In the Boardroom, chairman Mike Watterson was busy negotiating with Derbyshire County Council, offering the authority a seat on the board - "as part of a plan to get the club actively involved with the community". Council leader David Bookbinder said – "I congratulate Derby County for taking the initiative in a move aimed to stamp out hooliganism and to encourage more people to become actively involved in the Baseball Ground". The Council would be spending money on the club, in return for a voice on the board – "any cash dispersed would be for the benefit of the community", said Bookbinder.

The Rams' finances were again the subject of national media attention early in March 1983 when it emerged that they had defaulted on the first down-payment of the £55,000 owed to Bradford City in relation to Roy McFarland. Derby explained their reasons – that when the payment date was agreed, they were anticipating an income of £16,000-£20,000 from the gate for their home game against Charlton Athletic a few weeks previously – the game was subsequently postponed due to bad weather. Derby expected to be able to fulfil their payment obligation after gate receipts from forthcoming home matches with Wolverhampton Wanderers and Sheffield Wednesday. Donations from local businesses, notably £1,000 from the owner of Derby's Carrington Club, John Blount, and an interest-free loan of £5,000 from stockbroker Colin McKerrow, a Vice-president of the Derby County, were received – "to help get the Bradford City debt off the club's back at this difficult time financially". Also, in the national press, there were more rumours regarding the possible outgoing transfers of Dave Swindlehurst (to Aston Villa), and Steve Buckley (to Nottingham Forest). When asked about the situation regarding his players, Peter Taylor said "neither club has been in touch with me".

On 5th March unchanged Derby played promotion-chasing Leicester City, who had beaten them easily earlier in the season, on a muddy and badly cut-up pitch at Filbert Street. In front of a crowd of well over 15,000, including 3,500 from Derby, a strong home side featuring Gary Lineker and Alan Smith in attack, plus future and former Rams Mark Wallington and Gerry Daly, found Derby a much trickier proposition this time around, and the result was 1-1, the Rams goal courtesy of full back John Barton.

In a very entertaining and high-quality game, the Rams matched Leicester stride for stride, and were excellent value for their point. Despite the attacking nature of the match, the score remained goalless until seven minutes from the end when Leicester took the lead – but the spirit in Derby's side drove them forward in search of an equaliser and got their deserved reward on 87 minutes with Barton's firmly-struck right foot shot, his first ever goal in League football – the full back had run 60 yards to be in position to finish off the move.

Peter Taylor, not a fan of Barton when he first arrived at the Baseball Ground, said of the former Everton reserve player – "he isn't the best right back in the World, yet he is reaching levels of performance I thought beyond him. He was one of those I thought I would have to write-off when I first came…he has soldiered on with character, guts and determination…he is playing out of his skin".

Taylor was delighted with his team's display at Leicester – "performances don't come much better than that, we need a few more exactly like it". Roy McFarland added – "that was the best performances since we arrived".

Gerald Mortimer, in the Derby Evening Telegraph – "it was hard to say which side was near the top and which at the bottom, such was the quality of Derby's football". Alan Boyes (News of the World) – "revamped Derby are showing no signs of the relegation blues…they showed far more grit and determination". Ken Burgess (Sunday People) – "the great escape is on for Derby. This battling display showed they have the guts to survive the drop"

Another who had managed to convince Taylor of his value was goalkeeper Steve Cherry – "I thought we'd need a new goalkeeper when I arrived, but I know now we don't need one. The boy has grown in confidence as the back four in front of him has improved…he is a dedicated professional and keeps getting better, the signs are highly encouraging…we are not looking for a replacement for him, in fact Steve Cherry is a real big plus point for me. Cherry, and Andy Hill, were both in discussions with the club about new contracts – "young players of this calibre and character give the future a rosy hue, no matter the immediate problems" said Taylor.

The Rams reserves picked up their standards with a 4-0 win over Oldham Athletic at the Baseball Ground on March 8th. The game was notable for John McAlle's goal – it was the first time he had scored in any competitive game since 1972, when he had scored for Wolves in a UEFA Cup tie. Kevin Wilson scored a hat-trick. The win followed a draw at Sunderland, 2-2, with goals from Ian Dalziel and Andy Hill. Rams Reserves team v Sunderland (2nd March): Banovic, Emery, Dalziel, Foster, Blades, Skivington, Attley, McAlle, Hill, Garner, Emson and substitute Ride.

Derby played promotion favourites and league leaders Wolverhampton Wanderers at the Baseball Ground on 12th March 1983 in front of an excellent attendance of 17,644, the fourth-highest in England on the day. Once again, the Rams presented a resilient and cohesive unit and the final score was 1-1. Wolves' manager Graham Hawkins acknowledging after the match that he could not understand why Derby were at the bottom of the table. In the first half particularly, it was the best the Rams had played for several years – at times, the league leaders appeared ready to sink without trace and only a shrewd tactical switch by Hawkins – dropping veteran Terry Hibbitt into a sweeper role behind his beleaguered back four, plus outstanding goalkeeping from future Ram John Burridge, prevented Derby from cruising to a comfortable win.

Dave Swindlehurst's header from Gary Mills's corner put the Rams a goal up, and they should have made it 2 just before half time when a great move featuring Archie Gemmill and Mike Brolly presented Swindlehurst with a straightforward chance, which he snatched at and sent just over the bar. Wolves' equaliser came from a corner, which Derby had opportunities to clear before the ball skidded through to debutant Kellock, whose mishit shot hit Swindlehurst, wrong-footing goalkeeper Steve Cherry. Derby still had chances to win the game, with Bobby Davison, who missed two decent opportunities, suffering a rare off-day.

Three days after drawing with Wolves, Derby travelled to the Abbey Stadium to play Cambridge United, where Archie Gemmill made his 350th competitive appearance for the club. For the first time in recent weeks, Peter Taylor was forced into a team change with George Foster deputising for Steve Powell, who went down with a stomach virus, at centre back. Andy Hill continued in attack, preferred to Kevin Wilson. The Rams started very strongly but a resolute and direct Cambridge side always posed problems, and the 0-0 draw was probably a fair reflection of a game of few chances. Gary Mills's fine last-ditch tackle on home skipper Spriggs prevented what appeared a certain goal 16 minutes from time, and Bobby Davison had the Rams' best chance on 84 minutes after outpacing two defenders, but his shot was straight at Webster in the United net.

The Rams remained bottom of the Second Division, but the gap was closing, and they had lost only once in the previous nine matches (although only three had been won). They had 29 points from 30 matches, with a goal difference of minus 11, just 4 points behind Carlisle United and Middlesbrough on 33 (in 18th and 19th respectively), and with a considerably better goal difference than the Teesiders' minus 25. Even 15th place Charlton Athletic were only 7 points ahead of Derby, and their goal difference of minus 18 effectively reduced that gap to 6 points. A confident Peter Taylor, speaking after the Cambridge match, said – "we are building a side of mid-twenties who can ride us up out of the trough back into the sunshine. From top to bottom, we mean business at this club. I have never been so convinced of ultimate success at any time in my career as I am now". Taylor also praised Derby's supporters – when it was pointed out that their 17,000-plus crowd for the Wolves game was some 3,000 higher than Nottingham Forest's, he said – "well Derbyshire is a football place isn't it. We'll always do better, given the team".

David Swindlehurst, who was approaching the end of his contract at Derby, appeared set to sign for Aston Villa – Peter Taylor confirmed that there had been an exchange offer on the table involving Swindlehurst and two Villa players when he had arrived at the club in November 1982 – "Villa do want him. He is still here and playing out of his skin for the club...one of the best half-dozen strikers in the country, he is doing a great job for us in midfield and is enjoying his football again…but Villa are one of the top clubs. The Board and I want Dave here, but his future is at stake and only he can decide". Mike Watterson said – "we don't need to sell David (to pay off Bradford)…Dave will go if and when both he and Peter Taylor are ready". In the event, it was not Villa's player-swap deal which won the day, but a cash bid from John Lyall at West Ham United just before the transfer deadline, which took Swindlehurst back to his native London, albeit at a fraction of what the Rams could have expected to receive, had his contract not been on the verge of expiry – the net result was a loss of a quarter of a million pounds to Derby County.

Peter Taylor decided to take a look at Oxford United's 20-year old goalscoring attacking midfielder Andy Thomas and signed the player, who had scored 18 goals in all competitions for Oxford during 1981-82, on a short-term exchange loan in time to play in Derby's reserve match at Valley Parade, Bradford on 15th March – Brian Attley, who was not in the first team picture at the Baseball Ground, went to the Manor Ground in exchange. Thomas, who scored the Rams' equalising goal, and another new player, Steve Devine, both played well in the centre of midfield in a 1-1 draw. Steve Emery, continuing his comeback from serious injury, also played at Bradford, as did another senior player not considered part of Taylor's first team plans, Paul Emson.

Steve Devine, an 18-years old former Northern Ireland Youth International, had been released after the end of his apprenticeship at Wolverhampton Wanderers, and joined the Rams on a permanent basis, with no fee being involved. Meanwhile the Liverpudlian Collins brothers, Jimmy and David, were released by Derby following Chief Scout Ken Gutteridge's assessment that they would not make the grade at the club.

On Saturday 19th March the Rams entertained FA Cup semi-finalists Sheffield Wednesday at the Baseball Ground in front of another bumper crowd, just under 17,000. The match marked Dave Swindlehurst's final appearance for Derby, and the one and only appearance of **Andy Thomas**, who had joined on loan from Oxford United – Thomas was named as substitute. The game ended goalless – "there was honesty in our performance. A fair amount of pace but no craft" said Peter Taylor. George Foster, who kept his place in the side alongside Paul Futcher, with Steve Powell returning to midfield, kept Wednesday's dangerous attack at bay in what was perhaps his best performance for Derby.

Andy Thomas, a forward or attacking midfield player born in 1962, played for his hometown club Oxford United between 1980 and 1986, making well over 100 appearances and scoring 32 goals, and was part of their 1986 League Cup winning side. He had loan spells at both Fulham and Derby County (for whom he made just one appearance), in 1982 and 1983 respectively, then signed permanently for Newcastle United in 1986. He later went to Bradford City, then finished his full-time professional career with Plymouth Argyle in the early 1990's. Later, he managed non-league sides Oxford City and Chesham.

After the Sheffield Wednesday game, the Rams accepted a bid of what was reported at the time as £200,000 for Dave Swindlehurst, from First Division West Ham United. Derby had no choice – the transfer deadline was approaching and Swindlehurst could have left for nothing at the end of the season. He finished with 125 appearances for Derby, in which he scored 29 goals. One of the more popular players of the era, Swindlehurst left with good wishes from both club and supporters – "one of the top half-dozen strikers in the Country", manager Peter Taylor had said of him – a player of his ability and attitude was entitled to prefer First Division football.

On 22nd March, with Swindlehurst having departed for West Ham United, Derby stepped back into the transfer market when they agreed to pay a fee of £50,000 for Notts County's 23-year old winger Paul Hooks. The following day, the Rams strengthened their defensive ranks with the loan signing of 29-year old Kenny Burns, from Leeds United. Derby also entered further talks with Seattle Sounders with a view to extending Gary Mills' loan contract until the end of the English season, the NASL objected, however, and Mills was forced to return to Seattle after Easter Monday's home game with Newcastle United – and as part of the same agreement, he had to return to his former English club Nottingham Forest in September 1983 – Roy McFarland said of the player, who appeared to have no future at Forest - "Derby will make a bid for the player if all the circumstances are right at that time". The Rams also tried to sign Bradford City's Northern Ireland international centre forward Bobby Campbell just before the transfer deadline, but the deal was blocked by the Yorkshire club, still unhappy with the terms of their settlement regarding Roy McFarland.

Below first team level, the Rams gave trials to midfield player Colin Meyer from Scottish Highland League club Fraserburgh, and Eastwood Town forward Mark Richardson. Meyer had been with Aberdeen as a professional and had also had short trial spells with Manchester City, Sunderland and Norwich City, all of whom had not taken him on due to his small stature and had been watched and recommended by Derby's chief scout Ken Gutteridge. Tall striker Richardson, who scored in Derby reserves' match against Barnsley, had been spotted by scout Jack Nesbit – "I went to watch another player by it was Mark who caught my eye with his all-round game". Derby were able to beat Arsenal and Notts County, amongst other clubs, for the signature of 15-year old Derby Boys skipper Brian McCord, on schoolboy forms. Meanwhile John Ackroyd, a 17-year old apprentice striker, was released by the Rams.

Leaving the Baseball Ground just before March 1983's transfer deadline were Steve Emery and Tony Reid, both of whom re-joined their former Derby manager Colin Addison at Newport County. The Rams' agreed to cancel both players' contracts to enable them to join the Welsh club. Emery, who's Derby career was ruined by a broken leg suffered in a game against Rotherham United, had made a total of 80 first team appearances for the Rams, two as substitute, and had scored four goals – and had followed Addison around, having also previously played under him at Hereford United (and he returned to Hereford in the summer of 1983, in a bid to prove his fitness to their new manager – former Rams boss John Newman). Reid, still not 20-years old, had made 30 first team appearances, with four as substitute, scoring one goal and had at one time been considered a great hope in Derby's Youth team.

Peter Taylor, Roy McFarland and Mick Jones all signed new three-year contracts with Derby at the end of March 1983. Reports of a rift between McFarland and Taylor appeared in the national press after the former said that had the Rams started the season with their current squad, they would be promotion contenders, a view which Taylor appeared to contradict when he said – "we are improving, but we can, and must, do better". These rumours, as well as a report that the manager "was set for a showdown" with chairman Mike Watterson, were dismissed as unfounded gossip.

Derby's reserves, with a side containing three triallists, beat Barnsley reserves 2-0 on 29th March, following up on 3-2 win over Chesterfield the previous week. In the Chesterfield game, defender John McAlle was forced to take over in goal after Yakka Banovic went off injured. Andy Hill also went off injured after breaking his nose, leaving Derby with nine men. The only goal McAlle conceded was a penalty, although he almost saved that, and 17-year old Andy Garner scored twice for the Rams, with Andy Thomas getting the other goal. The reserves, watched regularly by around 300 for home matches at the Baseball Ground, were now unbeaten in seven matches and in the hunt for promotion from Central League division two. Against Barnsley, triallist Mark Richardson and Paul Emson scored for the Rams. Also featuring, and perhaps the best player on the night, was 19-year old Fraserburgh midfielder Colin Meyer, and fellow Scottish player, goalkeeper John Sutter. Rams reserves team v Barnsley reserves: Sutter, Lovatt, Harbey, Foster, McAlle, Meyer, Emson, Garner, Richardson, Thomas, Devine and substitute Clifford.

At Burnden Park on 26th March 1983, Derby defeated Bolton Wanderers 2-0, with **Paul Hooks**, the winger signed from Notts County, making his debut in midfield, where he replaced the departed Dave Swindlehurst in the starting eleven. Another new signing, defender **Kenny Burns**, on loan from Leeds United, was named as substitute, but did not appear in the match. It was a comfortable win for the Rams, and the gulf in class between them and the home side was clear as they controlled the game, with Archie Gemmill once again the best player on the pitch. Hooks created the first goal, which was eventually finished by Mike Brolly just 17 seconds into the second half, then Kevin Wilson and Bobby Davison combined before Wilson, only in the side because Andy Hill had suffered a broken nose, hit a fine finish after controlling a pass on his chest to make the score 2-0 on 56 minutes.

Derby's win over Bolton took them off the bottom of the Second Division for the first time since the start of January, and on to 33 points. Survival was by now in sight and they were not losing games, but they were also not winning enough – 4 of the last 5 matches had been drawn, enough to keep them in touch with the other strugglers, but not enough to rise out of trouble.

Paul Hooks, born in Wallsend in 1959, joined Notts County as an apprentice and made his first team debut in 1977. A winger with not inconsiderable skill and trickery, but who could be inconsistent, he made well over 150 first team appearances for County, scoring 30 goals, before Derby County stepped in to sign him in March 1983, for a fee of £60,000. He was one of the few who stayed at the Baseball Ground through the transition from Peter Taylor to Arthur Cox over the summer of 1984 and was on Derby's books until the end of the 1984-85 season, when he was released on a free transfer and dropped out of full-time professional football having played over 50 games for the club, scoring 4 goals.

After leaving Derby, he signed for non-league Boston United following an unsuccessful trial at Mansfield Town. He later worked as a coal miner in Ollerton, Notts, playing occasional football for Cotgrave Miners' Welfare. A talented player, Hooks unfortunately never fulfilled his potential at the Baseball Ground and did not provide good value for the fee paid, especially when considered that he left the club on a free transfer.

Kenny Burns, a tough, uncompromising Glaswegian, was born in 1953 and started out as a centre forward, before making his name as a central defender. He joined Glasgow Rangers as a junior and then signed for Birmingham City in 1971, where he established a good reputation and had converted to defender by the time Brian Clough and Peter Taylor signed him for Nottingham Forest in the summer of 1977. In 1977-78, when Forest won the League Championship and League Cup, Burns was named Footballer of the Year. He also won two European Cups with Forest, partnering Larry Lloyd in the centre of defence, and was capped 20 times by Scotland.

He left the City Ground and signed for Leeds United for a £400,000 fee in 1981 (despite being named as Forest's player of the year in 1980-81), and was still a fine player by the time joined Derby County twice on loan, in March 1983 and February 1984, before signing on a permanent deal in March 1984 as Peter Taylor's reign came to an end. Burns stayed on at Derby until the end of the 1984-85 season, becoming one of the players who spanned the gap between Taylor's and Arthur Cox's teams in the summer of 1984.

After leaving Derby he joined Barnsley, staying at Oakwell for a year before taking up a management position at Sutton Town in August 1986, then moving on to Stafford Rangers. Later, he moved around non-league football and ended his career in 1983 at Ilkeston Town. Despite his aggressive demeanour and "wild-man" image, Burns was a high-class footballer and was always popular with his own team's supporters – and often the hate figure for opposition fans. In later life, Burns became a regular media correspondent with a notable bias towards the club where he was most successful, Nottingham Forest.

On Easter Saturday, 2nd April, Derby travelled to Gay Meadow to play Shrewsbury Town and drew the game 1-1, with recent signing Paul Hooks getting the Rams' goal. The Rams were just 90 seconds away from taking all three points, which would have moved them up to 17th in the table. They had led since the fifth minute when Hooks finished off a fine flowing move and could have already been ahead before then when Kevin Wilson clipped a shot wide of the post when clean through on goal just 15 seconds after kick-off.

The Rams' first half display left Shrewsbury chasing shadows, much to the delight of the travelling support numbering close to 3,000 (out of a total crowd of 7,194) including Derby Trader and future Derby County chairman Lionel Pickering, who chanted "we are staying up" throughout the second half. Steve Powell, shirt soaked in blood from an early head clash, and Archie Gemmill, epitomised Derby's spirit as they soaked up the inevitable counter attacks after half time and they deserved to hang on, but ultimately conceded a poor equaliser when a mistake on the Rams left forced goalkeeper Cherry to commit himself too early and allowed Colin Robinson to score at the far post. Derby remained 21st in the Second Division table, with 34 points, but now within just three points of 17th placed Cambridge United. Their nine-game unbeaten run was Derby's best since 1975-76.

With morale both on and off the pitch very high, it was announced that season tickets for 1983-84 were to go on sale a week earlier than previously, on Monday April 11th. The reason given was that "Peter Taylor is planning at least one big signing, of international stature, among a carefully-planned summer intake". Before the board were prepared to sanction Taylor's ambitious summer plans, they required an idea of the extent to which supporters would commit for the next season – "a big and early season ticket response would not only give the club a financial summer cushion, it could also mean even heavier investment by the directors into the club's future" said chairman Mike Watterson. Taylor added "if we get the players I'm after, then supporters will not only bay with delight, they will gasp in surprise". Season tickets for 1983-84 were to be increased by an average of £5 from current levels, the first increase in three years – the most expensive seats, in B-Stand, were to be priced at £85, and the cheapest seats, in the goal stands, £55. Terrace season tickets were priced at £40. Match day tickets ranged from £4 in B-Stand, to £2 on the terraces.

The club announced that from the start of season 1983-84, after consultations with the Football Association, the Osmaston Lower Tier seating and Osmaston terracing would be reserved for the exclusive use of visiting supporters. This would mean a greater area of the Popside, including the Colombo section, would be available for use by Derby supporters.

Easter Monday 1983 saw another bumper crowd at the Baseball Ground, this time 19,779 (with just under 3,000 visiting fans), for the Second Division match against Newcastle United. Loan signing Kenny Burns, named as substitute for the third successive game, finally made his debut when he came on to replace Steve Powell, who suffered a groin-strain, in the centre of defence, and Gary Mills played what was to be his final game for Derby – he returned to parent club Seattle Sounders after the match, having played a vital role in the

Rams' recovery and fight against relegation. Kevin Wilson and Paul Hooks (with his second in 3 days), scored for Derby in their 2-1 victory, against Arthur Cox's side which included Terry McDermott, Chris Waddle and Kevin Keegan. The match was played on a pitch with standing water and clinging mud, caused by incessant heavy rain.

The Rams were superb in the first half and were unfortunate to only lead by two goals at half time, but Cox's excellent Newcastle side fought back and dominated the second half, as Derby's key man, 37-year old Archie Gemmill began to tire following 2 tough matches in 48 hours. Keegan, operating in a deep-lying forward role, pulled the strings for the visitors and they grabbed a goal back via a deflected Waddle shot which looped over Steve Cherry and into the Rams net. Newcastle might have equalised late on but for Cherry's instinctive stop from an Imre Varadi effort.

The Rams travelled to Ayresome Park to play fellow relegation strugglers Middlesbrough on Saturday 9th April. Kenny Burns made his first start for the club alongside Paul Futcher in what looked a very strong back four, with Barton and Buckley the full backs. Archie Gemmill and Steve Powell were paired in central midfield with Mike Brolly and Paul Hooks on the flanks. Kevin Wilson and Bobby Davison formed a hard-working and pacey attack, and it was Davison who got two of the Rams goals in a 3-2 win, the other coming via a Gemmill penalty.

It was a fortunate victory in many ways. Derby's penalty, from which Gemmill sent the goalkeeper the wrong way, was hotly disputed and looked harsh. Davison's first goal came courtesy of two bad errors in the Middlesbrough defence. The home side fought back from 2 down, and Derby's poor defending cost them the penalty, conceded by Cherry, from which they equalised. Two minutes from time, Davison volleyed-home Buckley's cross for the winner, and the only real moment of quality in the game. The Rams' flow had been upset by an early injury to Paul Hooks, and they missed the quality and balance on the left of midfield provided by the now departed Gary Mills. From nowhere, Peter Taylor had put together a side which looked capable of a promotion run, rather than a relegation battle – it truly had been an astonishing turn-around, Derby were now 11 games unbeaten - but the battle was not yet quite won.

The win at Middlesbrough put Derby up to 40 points from 35 matches and lifted them five places to 16th in the Second Division. It was the highest they had been since early September 1982, but the table remained very tight – just 6 points separated Grimsby Town in 12th place on 44, with Bolton Wanderers in 21st on 38. Immediately below the Rams were Crystal Palace, Rotherham United, Middlesbrough and Charlton Athletic, all on 39 points.

Peter Taylor had spent money – Futcher, Davison and Hooks had all cost not inconsiderable fees, around a quarter of a million pounds combined (although he had recouped £160,000 from the sale of Swindlehurst, a player whom he had wanted to keep but who had rejected the Rams' offer of a new contract – for a net spend of £100,000), but the free signing of

Gemmill, perhaps the best midfield player in the Second Division, and later the loan signing of Burns, both players he was aware of from their previous achievements, were masterstrokes. He had also breathed new life into some players who had appeared to be on their way out of the Baseball Ground when he first arrived – most notably Barton and Mills, and showed faith and belief in youngsters Cherry, Wilson and Hill, faith for which the players had rewarded him with their improved performances. The fitness of Steve Powell was also a bonus – he had barely been available for selection by the unfortunate John Newman but had been mostly fit to turn out for Taylor. Mike Brolly, who had been perhaps Newman's best signing (and had cost no fee), had also performed admirably well for the whole season, and Steve Buckley remained a class-act at Second Division level.

Of the other Newman signings, who between them had cost £75,000, Brian Attley was completely out of the picture and Peter Taylor wanted nothing to do with him, John McAlle occasionally used as substitute thanks to his versatility – he could cover defensive and midfield positions, and George Foster, considered by Taylor to be a wholehearted trier but lacking in basic football ability, was far down the pecking order for the central defensive positions. Paul Emson, one of very few survivors of the Tommy Docherty era, was another former senior player in whom Taylor had no belief – he remained stranded in reserve team football. Youngsters Glen Skivington and Tony Reid, both of whom had featured prominently in the first team under previous management, were others who Taylor did not rate, and shipped-out – Skivington on loan, and Reid having had his contract cancelled before the transfer deadline, as had former first team regular Steve Emery.

The rearranged home game against fellow relegation strugglers Charlton Athletic took place at the Baseball Ground on Wednesday April 13th, in front of an attendance of just over 15,000. Featuring for the visitors was prolific goal scorer Derek Hales, the centre forward who had been with the Rams for a short spell earlier in his career. It was a game in which Derby struggled to find much rhythm, but they extended their unbeaten run to 12 matches, the club's best since 1971-72, with a 1-1 draw against their tough-tackling but limited visitors – it was undoubtedly Derby's worst performance in the whole of the unbeaten run.

Charlton went a goal ahead on 33 minutes when a misplaced pass was picked up by White, , who crossed to unmarked McAllister at the far post, with goalkeeper Cherry stranded. Derby equalised seven minutes later through Archie Gemmill's free-kick from the edge of the box, awarded for the latest of several very hard tackles by the visiting defenders – the Rams' midfielder reprising his very similar effort from the FA Cup win over Nottingham Forest. In the second half, Derby were dominant and had at least three good chances to win the game, but Charlton battled on – the Rams were not helped when Buckley was forced off injured after a shocking tackle. Kenny Burns almost won it in the last few minutes but his shot was cleared off the line.

As against Middlesbrough, Derby's midfield lacked balance without departed Gary Mills and injured Paul Hooks – Paul Emson, back in the side to provide width on the left in their absence, had a poor game. It was only the second time that Peter Taylor had selected Emson, and his presence in the side illustrated the lack of strength-in-depth that threatened to derail the Rams' fine recovery, should they suffer more injuries to First Team players. Roy McFarland said after the game – "we were pleased with the commitment and effort, which was maximum, but we have some work to do with the lack of balance in the line-up". Derby remained 16th in the Second Division, with 41 points from 36 matches. Paul Futcher, the cultured defender who had formed a fine partnership with Steve Powell, was yet to experience defeat in a Derby shirt – in his 11 games, they had won 5 and drawn 6, conceding 8 goals.

Increased interest in Derby County meant that the club moved its annual awards night, scheduled for May 9th, to the Assembly Rooms in the City. Last season's event attracted over 1,000 and the club expected more that double this time round. The club's Player of the Year award was likely to be hotly contested this season, with the main contenders being Archie Gemmill and Steve Cherry, with Bobby Davison and Kevin Wilson other possibilities. Gary Mills, had he stayed on, would also have been in the running, with Mike Brolly an outside chance. Had there been an award for most improved player, John Barton would have been the favourite. By mid-April, the club had sold more than 500 season tickets for 1983-84 and expected to pass 1,000 following the next home match.

On Saturday 16th April the Rams welcomed Norman Hunter's Barnsley side to the Baseball Ground. Peter Taylor was again forced into a change with Burns moving to left-back to replace the injured Buckley, Emson continuing on the left wing, and Hooks returning from injury. In an entertaining match, visiting goalkeeper Gary Pierce performed heroics to keep his side in the game as Derby dominated possession for long periods, especially during the first half. Kevin Wilson and Bobby Davison provided excellent pace and movement which kept Barnsley's defence on their toes, but the Rams' goal came courtesy of Kenny Burns, who netted from a rebound off the post after Pierce had saved Wilson's header from a Mike Brolly free-kick at the Normanton End. Derby should have scored more than one and paid the price when a moment of hesitation allowed Tony Cunningham time to lob the advancing Steve Cherry on 65 minutes, for the equalising goal. Late in the game, Wilson hit the bar after chipping the goalkeeper, and Barnsley were lucky that the rebound fell straight into Pierce's arms, then Cunningham missed a chance to win the game for Barnsley when he too hit the woodwork. The game ended 1-1 in front of a crowd of 14,861.

On Saturday 23rd April the Rams played their 38th league game of the season at Millmoor against Rotherham United. Peter Taylor had lost patience with Paul Emson, who's hapless display had been booed and jeered by Ram's supporters during the previous Saturday's game – Ian Dalziel came into the side for his first start since December 1982 and made what would be his final appearance for the club. Buckley remained out injured. The result was another 1-1 draw, the Rams' third such result in succession, watched by a huge contingent from Derby – around 3,000 in a crowd of 9,646.

Derby started the game on the front foot and opened the scoring in the fifth minute with a penalty from Archie Gemmill (his fifth goal from the spot in six attempts in the season so far). Inexplicably, however, the Rams retreated and allowed Rotherham to dominate the game from then-on, with Bobby Davison playing almost in midfield and Kevin Wilson ploughing on in attack on his own. Derby were fortunate to escape with a draw, Rotherham's goal also coming via a penalty after a very controversial award when the ball struck Steve Powell's arm. As well as Davison, other players were well below par – Hooks did not appear fully fit, and neither Brolly nor Dalziel made much contribution, leaving Gemmill to soldier-on without much support in midfield.

Despite Rotherham's dominance, the Rams might have snatched three points late on when home goalkeeper Steve Conroy made a remarkable save from Kenny Burns's deflected shot. Peter Taylor's assessment after the game – "the worst game since my arrival...some of the players were hiding". The Rams, though, had extended their unbeaten run to 14 matches and were now 15th in the Second Division, with 43 points and four games remaining. It was the longest unbeaten run since 1948-49. At the bottom of the league, things were incredibly tight – only 4 points separated 12th placed Cambridge United (44 points from 38 matches), with second-bottom Rotherham United (40 from 39). Even Burnley, 22nd and bottom, remained right in the survival mix – although they only had 36 points, they had played only 36 matches and had a better goal difference than 7 of the other teams in the bottom 11 of the table.

The Rams had drawn 19 matches so far in 1983-84, exactly half of their 38 games – ten at home and nine away. During the 14-match unbeaten run they had won 5 and drawn 9 and had picked up more points away from home (13) than they had at the Baseball Ground (11).

By 30th April, Derby County had sold a total of 1,683 season tickets for the following campaign, despite supporters having no idea whether they would be watching Second or Third Division football, including almost 500 newcomers – many of whom were former season ticket holders who had lapsed as the club went on a downhill slide. Peter Taylor said – "I have been lucky, everything has combined to gel for me – the fans, the board and the players...even in my Nottingham days I have been accepted here and I could walk through this town and feel at home, the Derby public was on my side from the off when I came back...then there is the board, it is the best I've ever worked under, my working conditions here are unbelievable, so I just cant go wrong in this place".

In two or three years, Taylor hoped he would be able to retire from full time management and "put my magnificent team (Roy McFarland, Mick Jones and Ken Gutteridge) on course to be a top managerial team...when the time comes, I will retire, I am a builder, that's what I'm about. When the building has been done, I will let the other three go on...and then I hope to become a board member somewhere because I don't want to end my involvement in football". Of McFarland, Taylor said "without doubt Roy was the finest player I've ever handled, I've worked with so many greats, but they don't compare...his contribution to the club, and our prosperity, was absolutely unparalleled...and now he is showing great qualities in the management art".

When asked about Bobby Davison in comparison to Kevin Hector, Taylor pointed out that Hector was "a manager's dream", and in that respect Davison had many similarities although the two were quite different players. "Davo is an exciting prospect, I believe he can go on to great things, he won't be another Hector, but I am certain he will be getting goals here for a long time". Steve Cherry "the most improved goalkeeper in the Country" was another on whom Taylor was backing his longer-term career at Derby – "if this progress continues, he will still be here in five years-time, I am over the moon about him". Taylor also reserved praise for defender George Foster, who had been out of the First Team due to the form and fitness of Steve Powell and Paul Futcher – "I rate all three of them in any pair, as First Division class and I hope we have all three available next August, although a lot can happen before then". One youngster was singled out – striker Andy Garner, who Taylor described as "an exciting prospect".

Structural changes at the Baseball Ground over the summer of 1983, in order to comply with the Football Association's instructions, would reduce the maximum capacity by 800 to 33,700 – and would mean that the 285 season ticket holders in the Osmaston Lower Tier seats would have to be moved, and most, it was expected, would prefer to relocate to the Upper Tier to join the present 493 season ticket holders there – the Upper Tier could accommodate 1,850. The FA also instructed that the Osmaston End season ticket holder's standing pen be completely closed for 1983-84, to avoid clashes with, and to provide a buffer between C-Stand and the Ossie End terrace (which had to be given over exclusively to visiting fans) – this meant that 117 season ticket holders would have to be moved. There would be new entrances built to the Osmaston Upper Tier over the summer, to completely isolate Derby supporters from visiting fans entrance and exit points – visitors would be marshalled by police when leaving the ground via Osmaston Road. The club were also considering an idea to remove seats from the Osmaston Lower Tier and replace them with nailed-down benches (as at Filbert Street, home of Leicester City) – which visiting supporters would not be able to tear out. "From now on, the Baseball Ground will be one of the safest, most segregated and best controlled football stadiums in the Country", said Michael Dunford.

In the Central League Second Division, Derby's reserves moved up to fifth place with 27 points from 25 matches (two points for a win), following victories over both Rotherham United and Burnley at the Baseball Ground. The 6-2 win over Burnley on 19th April was the reserves' best of the season and came despite falling behind in the 5th minute and the scores being level at half time. Derby's equaliser came via Brian Attley, recently returned from his loan spell, after good work from Andy Garner. In the second half George Foster's header put the Rams 2-1 ahead, then a brace in 2 minutes from Andy Hill settled nerves, putting Derby 4-1 up by 50 minutes. Paul Emson scored goals 5 and 6, to cap a good individual performance – his first, and Derby's 5th, was particularly excellent – a 60-yard run before cutting inside 2 defenders and finishing smartly.

Against Rotherham United reserves, 17-year old Derby Colts goalkeeper Liam Nason, a Nottingham-born Associated Schoolboy with the Rams, made his first appearance at reserve level. Brian Attley scored the only goal in a 1-0 win, after Andy Garner had dribbled through a packed penalty area to lay on a simple chance on 73 minutes. The reserves had taken 19 from a possible 22 points to give themselves a good chance of promotion to the First Division of the Central League. Roy McFarland said of 17-year old Garner – "his burst that produced the goal had class written all over it, he has a superb left foot, too, and we are building up his strength". Rams reserves v Rotherham United, 26th April 1983: Nason, Lovatt, Harbey, McAlle, Blades, Skivington, Attley, Garner, Hill, Dalziel, Emson and substitute Devine.

Derby County Colts won the Derbyshire County FA Junior League for the second successive season, and reached the Junior Cup Final, where they were due to play Alfreton club A.D.A.S.C. on 8th May at Belper Town's ground. The colts had scored 105 goals in 12 League matches and conceded just 8 – which suggested they were not playing at an appropriate level. The team comprised a mixture of associated schoolboys and apprentices, and the squad that season was Liam Nason, Darryl Beeston, Shaun Ride, Keith McCormack, Richard Butler, Andrew Roberts, Mark Clifford, Neil Bailey, Mark Aherne, Andy Garner, Mark Skinner and Robert Maskery.

Derby's 39th Second Division game of 1982-83 was their penultimate home fixture, against bottom of the table Burnley on Saturday April 30th in front of an attendance of 14,674. The Rams extended their unbeaten record to 15 matches with a fine 2-0 win, but there was bad news as first Steve Powell left the field with a broken jaw after 19 minutes, then Kenny Burns was injured, and later Archie Gemmill. After the game it was revealed that Paul Hooks was playing while carrying a stomach-muscle injury – it was a disaster for Derby, as four players who had all played key roles in their revival would now be out for the final, crucial matches. The Rams finished the game against Burnley with 8 fit men and 3 limping and struggling to defy the resolute visitors – "I cannot remember a more courageous performance" said Peter Taylor after the match. The Rams' goals, before the injury issues, came from Kevin Wilson, who steered the ball home after goalkeeper Stevenson appeared to have fouled him, and Bobby Davison, who scored after Wilson had beaten the keeper in the air to nod on to his strike-partner. The victory over Burnley moved the Rams up to a seasons'-high 14th place in the Second Division, with 46 points from 39 matches.

The Rams then faced two away matches with a squad decimated by injuries. Five senior players - Steve Buckley, Kenny Burns, Archie Gemmill, Steve Powell and Paul Hooks were out, in addition to key man Gary Mills, who had been forced back to the NASL (and suffered a double leg fracture in one of his first matches back in Seattle), and Peter Taylor was forced to call on players who had not been part of his first team plans. He still had goalkeeper

Steve Cherry, right back John Barton, central defender Paul Futcher, midfielder Mike Brolly and forwards Bobby Davison and Kevin Wilson available, but this constituted only just over half of his preferred side, and only one midfield player. Into the team came Brian Attley at right back, George Foster at centre back, John McAlle and Andy Hill in attack. Paul Emson was also in the side, on the left wing, but he was also not one of Taylor's preferred choices – he had missed the previous 31 matches until his recent recall.

Attley had been sent out on loan to Oxford United and had not started a first team game since early February. McAlle had regularly been substitute, thanks to his ability to cover several positions, but had not started a game since January. Foster was rated third best centre back at the club but had lost his place to Paul Futcher and had made only sporadic appearances in 1983, covering injuries. Hill had been usurped by Wilson as Davison's partner in attack and had been out of the first team picture since March.

At Ewood Park on 2nd May against Blackburn Rovers, the Rams suffered their first league defeat in almost four months. It was a depressing, dreadful display as the team appeared devoid of confidence and the replacements brought in showed little in the way of fight or ability and Blackburn won 2-0 at a canter, with Foster in particular, having a torrid time. Five days later at Selhurst Park against Crystal Palace things got even worse. Andy Hill, who had struggled as much as anyone at Ewood Park, was replaced by Glen Skivington, who made his first start since September 1982, and made what turned out to be his final appearance for the club. John McAlle missed an open goal from two yards before Palace went ahead, and from then on, the home side ran Derby ragged and won 4-1, severely damaging Derby's potentially crucial goal difference, which was now minus ten. The Rams' consolation goal came courtesy of an own-goal from Gilbert, who sliced Brolly's cross into his own net.

These two bad results contributed to leave Derby still in danger of being relegated from the Second Division, should they fail to beat Fulham in their final game, on Saturday 14th May and other results go against them – despite the Rams being 16th in the table. The Second Division table on the morning of Derby's final match read:

13th Carlisle United (47 points, 1 game remaining, goal difference -2)

14th Middlesbrough (47, 1, -21)

15th Chelsea (46, 1, -10)

16th Derby County (46, 1, -10)

17th Grimsby Town (46, 1, -25)

18th Crystal Palace (45, 2, -9)

19th Charlton Athletic (45, 1, -26)

20th Bolton Wanderers (44, 1, -16)

21st Rotherham United (44, 1, -23)

22nd Burnley (43, 2, -9)

Nobody was safe, and any combination of the teams from 13th to 22nd could go down, although Carlisle United's goal difference of minus 2 meant they were all but mathematically secure. Charlton would play Bolton in their final game, meaning that at least one of those teams had to finish below Derby, so the Rams could not finish bottom, but 20th and 21st places were still worryingly possible.

Peter Taylor was certain where the blame lay for the two miserable results at Blackburn and Palace – "the players brought into the side as replacements played a major part in ending the 15-game unbeaten run...we built a team that brought the club back from a nine point deficit at the bottom in January, that team put us into a safety spot before five injuries decimated us, it was achieved by courage and character...we put players in (to cover the injuries) that we inherited, whom we expected to pull us through, instead they played as poorly for us as they had for John Newman, they were among the ones who put the club in the cart in the first place".

Taylor's words were matched with actions. Seven players were transfer listed on Monday 9th May, 2 days after the debacle at Selhurst Park – George Foster, John McAlle, Brian Attley, Ian Dalziel, Glen Skivington, Paul Emson (all of whom had featured in the two rotten performances, apart from Dalziel, who had also barely featured under Taylor and had last appeared for the first team in the poor display at Rotherham on 23rd April) and Yakka Banovic, who hadn't, but who Taylor had made it clear he did not rate. Five of these players had contracts running beyond the end of the 1982-83 season. "The club is booming", said Taylor- "the fans are flocking back, the area is buzzing, sponsorships pour in, and my plans are made for the import of good, class players...and now, lack of character on the pitch has us staring relegation in the face". When asked if relegation would ruin his plans – "no, only the time table, but we won't go down, we'll have some of our class players there again (against Fulham), and they will battle...if we did go down, we'd have a side to get us back in 12 months".

Of the seven transfer-listed players, only George Foster drew any sympathy from Peter Taylor. "We couldn't by any stretch of the imagination offer George the certainty of much first team football, and he is too good to be pencilled-in as a stand in...with Paul Futcher and Steve Powell welding into a formidable pair and with our England Youth International Paul Blades gaining experience by the week, that's what George's future here looked likely to be...that would have been good for us but in fairness to him we had to give him the opportunity to keep what is a useful career going...he will do well for any club that needs a rugged, orthodox centre-half of strength, dedication and unbounded enthusiasm, a good club man".

The Rams placed a £50,000 price-tag on Foster (although he was eventually sold for £15,000 to Fourth Division Mansfield Town in August and went on to make nearly 400 appearances for the Stags, after a proposed move to Bournemouth broke down), but the other six listed players were all available on free transfers. Dalziel, who joined Hereford United and made 150 appearances over the next 5 years, and Emson, who joined Grimsby Town and played almost 100 games for them, would both be out of contract in the summer of 1983 so were to be released. McAlle, Attley, Banovic and Skivington all had contracts running until the summer of 1984, and only Skivington left, joining Southend United for whom he made just 2 appearances – the other three players, much to Peter Taylor's disappointment, and his open contempt, remained on the books at Derby until their contracts eventually expired. One player who did leave Derby in the summer of 1983 was Mike Brolly, who had done a solid job for the club in his one and only season at the Baseball Ground and had earned praise and respect from Peter Taylor, making 42 appearances (including 1 as substitute). Brolly left to join Third Division Scunthorpe United for a fee of £15,000, where he played almost 100 matches, as Taylor looked to improve the quality of his wide midfield players.

Apart from Foster, Taylor had nothing positive to say about any of the transfer-listed players. "if certain players are here for the start of next season it will be a slight against the management, especially me, and an insult to supporters". Derby were well aware that the five players still under contract beyond the coming summer would be perfectly entitled to see-out those contracts, should they be unable to find equal terms elsewhere. Some National newspapers reported that the Derby board and management would offer financial inducements to the five contracted players to encourage them to leave, but Taylor refused to either confirm or deny this.

In addition to the seven listed players, reserve full backs John Lovatt and Graham Harbey were offered non-contract terms – meaning they would be paid weekly by the club if they stayed but had no contractual security. By the summer of 1983, Taylor had already released ten players since his arrival, ranging from the £200,000 sale of Dave Swindlehurst down to apprentices and first-year professionals. "We have to create space for the new players we shall be bringing in over the summer, so why delay the retained list, let the fans see we mean business", said Taylor. The first three new arrivals, on the recommendation of chief scout Ken Gutteridge, were Andy Roberts, Richard Butler and Neil Bailey, who all signed apprentice terms in May 1983, and they were closely followed by the signature of 20-year old centre half Richard Pratley, from Banbury United (Kevin Wilson's former club). Teenager Paul Bancroft, who had been out on loan with Crewe Alexandra in the Fourth Division since January, would be returning to the Baseball Ground for season 1983-84, having made a good impression at Gresty Road. All three of the new apprentices featured in Derby Reserves' match at Vale Park against Port Vale on 7th May, and Roberts scored the only goal in a 1-0 victory. In the summer of 1983 two more youngsters joined the club, Andy Irvine and Mark Aherne.

22-year old goalkeeper Steve Cherry, who had been magnificent since Taylor's arrival, won the Player of the Year award for 1982-83. The manager was effervescent in his praise – "I would not swap the lad for Peter Shilton, even if he was available". Runner-up was Archie Gemmill, and third place went to John Barton. Of Barton, Taylor said – "mark this man for character and he gets 11 out of 10, his reaction to management instruction and advice is also unbelievable, this man is so genuine". Andy Garner, the teenage striker, won the Young Player of the Year award – "he has got a great chance to make it in the game if he remembers that this success is only a start", said Head Coach Mick Jones said of Garner.

Meanwhile, season ticket sales for 1983-84 were booming – with close to 3,000 sold even before the Rams' crucial match against Fulham. The club were confident that they would beat the total of around 6,500 sold for the current season – it was astonishing support in an era when football gates all over the Country were falling – 11 of Derby's rivals in the Second Division didn't sell 3,000 season tickets for the whole of the current season and only Newcastle United had more season ticket holders (and even then only by a couple of hundred).

The chairman, Mike Watterson, revealed that on the day he took over the club, October 23rd, 1982, it was not just the retention of Second Division status that looked remote – but that the finances were so bad, it seemed unlikely that the football club could survive. He described the appointment of Peter Taylor as "a masterstroke" and reminded fans of the not-too distant days such as 9th October 1982 – the occasion of his first visit to the Baseball Ground, when the attendance was 8,135. The average attendance now was over 15,000, and four times the number had exceeded 16,000 – it had truly been a remarkable turn-around. Watterson reserved praise for Dave Swindlehurst - "wonderful spirit on and off the field while transfer speculation surrounded him, a fine lad" and Kenny Burns – "for the way he gave us all his class and fire even though he was only here on loan, he proved he was prepared to die for Derby County on the field". Watterson also revealed that alongside the structural changes to the Baseball Ground already reported, new turnstiles would be installed to enable entry to the Popside from underneath the Ley Stand – "so ending the handicap of entrances and exits on only three sides of the Baseball Ground".

The Rams' opponents in their final game, Fulham, also had reason to need a victory. They were in with a chance of promotion to Division One, should they win at the Baseball Ground, and Leicester City fail to beat Burnley at Filbert Street. It was a different story to the final game of the previous season, when relegation-threatened Derby faced a Watford side with nothing to play for – Watford were already promoted to the First Division by the time they faced the Rams in their last game. Fulham, unlike Watford the season before, were badly out of form coming into the game and Malcolm Macdonald's team had lost four of their last five matches, whilst their rivals for the final promotion spot, Leicester, had put together a 15-match unbeaten run. They were an attacking, entertaining side containing excellent footballers like Ray Houghton, Ray Lewington, Tony Gale and Gordon Davies, and the uncompromising midfield player Sean O'Driscoll, and they were going for back-to-back promotions, having been promoted to the second division in 1981-82.

There was some good news on the fitness front for Derby's final match of the 1982-83 season. Kenny Burns, Archie Gemmill and Paul Hooks were all pronounced fit and available for the 14th May clash with Fulham, and they all came back into the side to replace transfer-listed John McAlle, Brian Attley and Glen Skivington. Three players made what was to be their final appearances for the club – Mike Brolly, who had done well for Taylor, plus Paul Emson, who had not, and the unfortunate George Foster, who had found himself down the pecking-order. Kenny Burns made the final appearance of his loan spell from Leeds United, but he was to return the following season.

As things turned out, Leicester City could not beat Burnley, their match ending 0-0, so victory at the Baseball Ground would have taken Fulham into the First Division. Dean Coney would have put the visitors into the lead in the first half but was denied by a great save by Steve Cherry, and the game remained goalless until the 71st minute, when a superb volley from Bobby Davison put the Rams ahead, edging them closer to safety and denting Fulham's promotion hopes. And then the problems began. Supporters began encroaching onto the pitch, to celebrate Davison's goal, and the floodgates opened as hundreds of excited Rams supporters, part of a crowd of 21,124, took their places on the narrow pitch-side perimeter. Fulham's midfielder Robert Wilson said later – "the fans simply kept coming off the terraces and it became very difficult to play, it was very intimidating".

The final 10 minutes were played out amid chaotic scenes as Derby fans stood on the touchline, often spilling over onto the pitch. After Cherry tipped a Houghton drive over the bar, fans ran on to congratulate him. There were appeals for calm over the PA System, but it had no effect. One fan kicked out at Wilson as he ran down Fulham's left wing – the player showed admirable restraint to avoid retaliating. On 89 minutes, referee Ray Chadwick blew his whistle and the ground erupted, as Derby's fans, believing the game to be over, flooded all over the pitch. Wilson said – "I have never been so frightened in my life, I wondered if I was going to make it". Fulham defender Jeff Hopkins was punched and kicked repeatedly and was left with a torn shirt.

The players ran for the safety of the tunnel but that was not the end of the matter. Chadwick told the teams that there was 78 seconds still to play, his whistle had been for an offside decision, but there was no hope of the teams being able to play on, and Fulham would now only have 10 fit players, as Hopkins had been assaulted and was on the treatment table. Malcolm Macdonald immediately called for the game to be replayed, and Derby's chairman Mike Watterson, increasingly disheartened by the behaviour of football fans, agreed that it would be the fairest outcome – "the rules state that the game should last for 90 minutes" said the frustrated Fulham manager. Fulham later lodged an appeal, but the Football League ruled against a replay – "it would be monstrously unfair to other clubs effected, most of all Leicester City" said Football League secretary Graham Kelly – "the circumstances cannot be recreated unless you replay the whole Second Division programme".

Mike Watterson was reaching the end of his involvement with football, at Derby County at least, and resigned the chair in the summer of 1983 – his eventful 10 months at the helm had included a change of manager, a successful fight against relegation, and, crucially for Watterson, scenes of crowd disturbances with which he was no longer prepared to associate himself. When it became clear that Peter Taylor wished to spend considerable sums of money on new players over the summer, and that other board members were prepared to back the manager's judgement against that of Watterson, it was the final straw and he decided to call it a day, handing the chairmanship to John Kirkland and resigning from the board altogether.

Macdonald cancelled his club's team holiday to Majorca to keep his players in full training, pending their appeal against the Football League's decision, but they could not get the result overturned and both teams remained in the Second Division for season 1983-84. The unfortunate Fulham manager never did get to manage a club in the top flight, and he resigned from his position at Craven Cottage in April 1984.

The next time Derby County took the field for a competitive match, on 27th August 1983, the only starters who had not been signed by Peter Taylor were Steve Cherry, John Barton, Steve Buckley and Steve Powell (plus Brian Attley, who was substitute). There were three new signings, wingers John Robertson and Calvin Plummer (who filled positions vacated by Mike Brolly and Gary Mills), and striker Bobby Campbell, who was preferred to both Kevin Wilson and Andy Hill. The other four starters were Paul Futcher, Archie Gemmill, Paul Hooks and Bobby Davison, all of whom were Taylor signings. All of this meant that only one player, John Barton, who had been signed by either of Taylor's predecessors Colin Addison and John Newman remained in the starting 11 – Cherry, Buckley and Powell having been at the club since before Addison's reign. Taylor had acted on his words from when he first arrived in the Autumn of 1983 – "most of them are not good enough...Southern League standard"

Thanks and Acknowledgments

The Ram Newspaper & The Ram Magazine, edited by Harry Brown

Derby County – A Complete Record 1884-1988 – Gerald Mortimer

There was some football too – 100 years of Derby County

Andy Ellis at The Derby County Collection, inspiration and advice

Harry Forsyth – over land and sea, through thick and thin

Derby County Football Club and everybody connected with it

Everyone who lives and loves Derby County

Printed in Great Britain
by Amazon